D0206309

# Critical Essays on
# John Updike

# *Critical Essays on John Updike*

## *William R. Macnaughton*

G. K. Hall and Co. • Boston, Massachusetts

Library of Congress Cataloging in Publication Data
Main entry under title:

Critical essays on John Updike.

(Critical essays on American literature)
Includes index.
1. Updike, John—Criticism and interpretation—Addresses,
essays, lectures.  I. Macnaughton, William R.  II. Series.
PS3571.P4Z62          813'.54          81-13482
ISBN 0-8161-8467-4                     AACR2

# CRITICAL ESSAYS ON AMERICAN LITERATURE

This series seeks to publish the most important reprinted criticism on writers and topics in American literature along with, in various volumes, original essays, interviews, bibliographies, letters, manuscript sections, and other materials brought to public attention for the first time. William R. Macnaughton's volume on John Updike is the most substantial collection of scholarship ever assembled on this important contemporary author. It reprints reviews by Granville Hicks, Anthony Burgess, Tony Tanner, Alfred Kazin, and Joyce Carol Oates, among others, and articles by Clinton S. Burhans, Jr., George W. Hunt, S.J., James M. Mellard, and other leading scholars. In addition, this collection contains five original essays by George J. Searles, Gordon E. Slethaug, Kathleen Verduin, Gary Waller, and Joyce Markle. We are confident that this book will make a permanent and significant contribution to American literary study.

JAMES NAGEL, GENERAL EDITOR

*Northeastern University*

# CONTENTS

# INTRODUCTION

## A Survey of John Updike Scholarship in English

### A. BIBLIOGRAPHIES

There are four volumes of Updike bibliographies. These are: C. Clarke Taylor, *John Updike: A Bibliography*; David E. Arnason and B. A. Sokoloff, *John Updike: A Comprehensive Bibliography*; Michael Olivas, *An Annotated Bibliography of John Updike Criticism 1967–1973, and a Checklist of his Works*; and Elizabeth A. Gearhart, *John Updike: A Comprehensive Bibliography with Selected Annotations*.[1] Taylor's work contains a useful history of Updike's own publications from 1949 (in such places as the Shillington *Chatterbox*) to 1967 (including Updike's *Harvard Lampoon* publications) as well as a good listing with brief annotations of early criticism (including reviews) of Updike's work. The annotated reviews are particularly useful. The bibliography of Arnason and Sokoloff to a very large extent duplicates Taylor's information about primary sources (but does not include pre-Harvard publications), although they extend this information to 1969. They also include titles of articles and reviews about Updike (without annotations) up to 1969 (including some information about foreign scholarship). Despite the title, their work is not "comprehensive" although, when first published, in some respects it was a useful supplement to Taylor. It has now been superseded, however, by the thorough bibliography and checklist prepared by Michael Olivas. His annotations of the reviews, scholarly articles, and dissertations about Updike's work are particularly useful (as is the list of and comments on interviews with the writer) even though they are descriptive, not evaluative. Gearhart's new bibliography is not "comprehensive" (although published in 1978, its listing of Updike's publications stops in 1975) and the "selected annotations" are almost non-existent. It does contain some helpful information, however, about foreign scholarship up to 1974 and translations of Updike's work up to 1971.

A thorough listing of critical material about Updike up to 1974 may also be found in the checklist prepared by Arlin Meyer and Michael Olivas for the special Updike number of the Spring, 1974 *Modern Fiction Studies*.[2] This checklist should be supplemented by the annual bib-

1

liography of short story criticism published by *Studies in Short Fiction*, by the annual bibliography of scholarship on modern literature published by the *Journal of Modern Literature*, and by the comments on Updike scholarship in the annual edition of *American Literary Scholarship* published by Duke University Press. Useful information about such items as special editions of Updike, recent publications by him, and interviews that he has granted may frequently be found in the *John Updike Newsletter* which has been published several times a year since 1977. In the fourteenth and fifteenth issues of the *Newsletter*, for example, reference is made to a forthcoming Updike bibliography to be published by *The American Book Collector*. The *Newsletter* will also, on occasion, reprint Updike material not easily accessible to most readers, although some of it is trivial, such as his report on the 1980 Boston Red Sox opening game for the *Boston Globe*. Readers who wish to keep abreast of some of his new poetry, short fiction, and book reviews should consult *The New Yorker*, where much of his new work continues to be published.

## B. BIOGRAPHICAL MATERIAL

There is, of course, no biography of Updike but information about his life may be obtained in most of the books on his work, as well as in the "First-Person Singular" section of *Assorted Prose* (1965) and in several interviews with him, in particular Jane Howard, "Can A Nice Novelist Finish First?" (*Life*, 4 November, 1966); "View from the Catacombs" (*Time* cover story, 26 April, 1968); and James Atlas, "John Updike Breaks Out of Suburbia" (*New York Times Magazine*, 10 December, 1978).[3] Despite his statement in *Picked-Up Pieces* that interviews "are a form to be loathed, a half-form like maggots,"[4] Updike has allowed himself to be nibbled on many occasions by reporters and T.V. personalities like Dick Cavett; readers wishing to be informed of the most recent interviews—many of which Updike edits himself before allowing publication—should consult the *Newsletter*.

## C. CRITICISM AND SCHOLARSHIP IN ENGLISH

"I cannot greatly care what critics say of my work; if it is good, it will come to the surface in a generation or two and float, and if not, it will sink, having in the meantime provided me with a living, the opportunities of leisure, and a craftsman's intimate satisfaction." (John Updike, *Picked-Up Pieces*, p. 503).

Primarily because of their own buoyancy, the products of John Updike's craft continue to float, even those like *The Poorhouse Fair* launched over twenty years ago. Another reason for this buoyancy, however, is because of the support provided over the years by admirers of Updike's craft. In a recent book on Updike, George Hunt asserts that *Of the Farm* "alone among Updike's fiction . . . has generated very fine academic criticism."[5] That this statement is patently false will, it is hoped, be shown through the following critical survey. Before beginning, however, two points must be made. The first is that this short discussion excludes foreign scholarship, despite the foreign interest evinced in Updike for many years (readers wishing to explore this criticism might start with the excellent bibliography in Edward Vargo's *Rainstorms and Fire: Ritual in the Novels of John Updike.*)[6] The second point that must be stressed is that Updike's comments about his own work are extremely insightful, particularly in his "One Big Interview" in *Picked-Up Pieces* (1975), of which he writes: "I have excerpted a few self-centered quotations from the six or so interviews I have saved, and closeted them in an appendix, where none but the morbidly curious, or academically compelled, need peek" (p. xix). The "excerpts" come from three previously unpublished interviews, from the *Life* interview referred to above, and from three other very important interviews worth listing here: Charles Samuels, "The Art of Fiction XLIII: John Updike"; Eric Rhode, "BBC Interview with John Updike"; and Frank Gado, "A Conversation with John Updike."[7] Among the many other interesting interviews with Updike, one more will be mentioned here: Richard Burgen's in issues 9 and 11 of the *New York Arts Journal*, reprinted in the spring and summer 1979 issues of the *John Updike Newsletter*.[8] The student of Updike will also wish to consult his essays about writing, e.g., "Why Write?" and his introductions, e.g., to the Czech edition of *Of the Farm* (both reprinted in *Picked-Up Pieces*). Updike's book reviews are also often indirectly revealing about his own work: his review of Kierkegaard's 1853–1855 *Journals*, for example ("The Fork," reprinted along with other reviews in *Picked-Up Pieces*); or of Denis de Rougemont's *Love Declared* and Karl Barth's *Anselm: Fides Quaerens Intellectum* ("More Love in the Western World," and "Faith in Search of Understanding," both reprinted along with other reviews in *Assorted Prose*, 1965). Updike also, of course, continues to review frequently for the *New Yorker*.

## 1. Criticism and Scholarship, 1958–1966

Almost all of the reviewers of John Updike's first three volumes—*The Carpentered Hen, and Other Tame Creatures: Poems* (1958), *The Poorhouse Fair* (1959), and *The Same Door: Short Stories* (1959)—greeted with enthusiam the skill and versatility of this young writer in his mid-20's who had published his first *New Yorker* story in 1954. Emphasized was the "great clarity and precision of language," the "almost Chekhovian musicality of pattern," and the commendably non-autobiographical subject matter of his first novel, *The Poorhouse Fair*. Critics spoke highly as well of *The Same Door*, T. E. Cassidy in *The Commonweal*, for example, praising, "the feeling of wonder in these people, wonder at the beauty in the simple strangeness of things." William Peden, writing in the *New York Times Book Review*, welcomed Updike's ability (reminiscent of both Chekhov and Joyce) to discern significance in the lives of ordinary people. Amidst this general praise, however, there were complaints of weakness which pre-figured attacks on Updike that would become commonplace. In a favorable review of *The Poorhouse Fair*, for example, Richard Gilman (one of Updike's most consistently sensitive admirers) wrote: "Occasionally, too, his book suffers from what Pascal described as the wearying effect of continuous eloquence. He would profit from knowing that it is in the spaces between images that their resonance is nurtured and maintained." And the anonymous *Time* reviewer concluded ominously, "Unfortunately, author Updike plays his talents cool; his passion for understatement seems to rule out all passion."[9]

The large majority of reviews of Updike's next novel (*Rabbit, Run,* 1960) were also favorable (although, anticipating a problem that continues to perplex many readers, some reviewers were puzzled about the writer's attitude toward his protagonist). Granville Hicks—who, as much as any early critic of Updike, influenced his reputation's leap upward—wrote, "From now on Updike has to be regarded as one of our important young novelists, a powerful writer with his own vision of the world" (Hicks's *Saturday Review* comments are reprinted in this volume).[10]

Despite their influence on the shape of Updike's reputation, almost all of the early reviews of his work are no longer worth reading. One exception, however, is Richard Lyons' 1961 "A High EQ" in *Minnesota Review*. Lyons' extremely sympathetic reading of the central character in *Rabbit, Run* suggests similarities between Rabbit and Salinger's Seymour Glass, but also points to one crucial difference: Seymour's intelligence allows him to understand himself, whereas Rabbit's relative inarticulateness causes suffering because he cannot verbalize feelings either to others or himself. Yet, "If nervous systems, like brains, could be measured for their appropriate quotients, Rabbit would have a high e.q. (emotion quotient)." Eccles, the minister, senses this quality, calling Rabbit a mystic (whose experiences, typically, are "all in the present tense"). Such experience is, unfortunately, not transferrable, although Rabbit attempts to share his joy "through the act of love or through a delicately balanced sense of successful physical experience." Lyons suggests that "What are in Rabbit selfish, physical indulgences become when translated into acceptable traditional vocabulary respectable and transcendent expressions of saints who have touched God in the night." The critic calls Rabbit's running "a tremendous positive action. . . . Its essence is not, as this book's is not, in external circumstances. It is the only thing that Rabbit in his alienation from everyone he knows can do. Love, joy, happiness are intense accumulations of energy, which demand release in some way."[11]

Updike's second volume of short stories, *Pigeon Feathers and Other*

*Stories*, was published in 1962, again to generally positive reviews. Arthur Mizener, who along with Granville Hicks probably had the most influence on Updike's early reputation, wrote of the short story collection that "it is a demonstration of how the most gifted writer of his generation is coming to maturity; it shows that Mr. Updike's fine verbal talent . . . is beginning to serve his deepest insight" (Mizener's excellent review is reprinted in this volume). A few other reviewers, however, were beginning to accuse him of "slickness" and triviality, with *Time* magazine beginning the beat of a drum which it did not silence until the publication of *Couples* in 1968: "This dedicated 29-year-old man of letters says very little, and says it very well. . . . The impressions left are of risks untaken, words too fondly tasted, and of a security of skill that approaches smugness."[12]

Among the very early more than review-length responses made to Updike, two articles contain discussions still of some relevance to an appreciation of his work. The first by Dean Doner, "Rabbit Angstrom's Unseen World," moves from a consideration of short stories such as "Ace in the Hole" and "Lifeguard," and Updike's novel, *The Poorhouse Fair*, to conclude, "Humanism and humanists have consistently been the villains of Updike's work." Seen in this light, Eccles in *Rabbit, Run* is a selfish meddler in a novel that "says clearly that no man understands enough to take it upon himself to repair the world, no man reads responsibility accurately enough to know where justice lies or how it is to be manipulated." For Doner, therefore, Rabbit becomes the hero victimized by the "net" of humanism, and, in the scene at the graveyard, "It is not because he is lascivious and irresponsible that Rabbit brutally accuses his wife and denies his guilt. It is because he alone, of all the characters gathered about the grave, believes in God."[13] The second article—John Ward's "John Updike's Fiction"—seems pedestrian from the perspective of 1980, but it was the first critical overview of Updike's work up to and including *Pigeon Feathers* published in a scholarly journal, and thus helped to call attention to scholars of his significance as a writer: "He is just thirty, and two of his works stand with the very few current American novels worth preserving." Moreover, individual comments made by Ward are occasionally provocative, such as his suggestion that many of the protagonists of *The Same Door* are "unconscious artists," trapped by self-deception, and that in Conner of *The Poorhouse Fair* (according to Ward, Updike's best novel), "all the fantasy-possessed young men of the short stories are combined and given a public forum, an official respectability."[14]

Although Updike's next novel, *The Centaur* (1963) won the National Book Award for fiction, its publication was not greeted with anything close to critical unanimity. The novel had many admirers (such as Renata Adler, whose review is reprinted here), but some reviewers objected to what Vereen Bell in *Shenandoah* called the "elaborate but largely arbitrary and irrelevant mythic parallels";[15] others were puzzled both by the identity of the novel's narrator or narrators and by the problem of the novel's ending: was George Caldwell's "death" literal or metaphorical? One of the most determined haters of Updike's work in general and *The Centaur* in particular was Norman Podhoretz who wrote in his "Dissent on Updike" about the Caldwell/Chiron parallel: "all it does is surround *The Centaur* with a fake aura of profundity while at the same time permitting Updike to plug up holes of motivation and to impose a spurious significance on characters and events which have failed to earn any significance in their own right." Podhoretz concludes his attack by asserting that, in general, Updike has nothing to say, and that his emotional range is very limited, confining itself primarily to "a rather timid nostalgia for the confusions of youth."[16] Even some critics generally sympathetic to Updike were beginning to worry about his supposed shallowness of thought and lack of emotional range. Guerin La Course, for example, in his "The Innocence of John Updike," after praising Updike for his "fresh perception of the appearing world," suggested that "He fears to foray into the night world of feeling for the significances. The polarity of genius has a double edge." Warning that "Updike cannot afford to sit on his hands," he concluded, "He relies, apparently, on language rather than thought, sense rather than sensibility, wit rather than wisdom—all of which afford only temporary harbor."[17]

One of the best explanations for the nostalgia in Updike's fiction appeared in a very fine essay by Arthur Mizener, "The American Hero as High School Boy: Peter Caldwell," in his *The Sense of Life in the Modern Novel*. Mizener observes a conflict throughout Updike's work between his desire to express his "cultivated humanistic self in complex forms and ingenious verbal patterns and his commitment to the everyday, homely life that is filled with inexpressible transcendent significance for him." According to Mizener, for a romantic like Updike, there is a glow of intensely felt experience which gathers around his memory of certain particulars from his past—childhood, home, parents—and which he is afraid of losing. Encounters with the past through memory, therefore, become the means of preserving his sense of some sublime quality in life, and of seeing how "the transcendent value of the people he loved as a child inheres in them, an intrinsic blessing."[18] What Mizener's article implies is that Updike's nostalgia is a kind of religious feeling, not a form of timidity or immaturity.

This sense of the religious in Updike is dealt with directly in another fine early essay, Michael Novak's "Updike's Search for Liturgy." For Novak, Updike has "already awakened themes dormant in American letters since Hawthorne and Melville." Most of the essay develops an excellent analysis of a story from *Pigeon Feathers*—"Packed Dirt, Churchgoing, A Dying Cat, A Traded Car"—and attempts to show how the narrator searches for images of "that deep, serene, perennial way of looking at life which the secular, active west has lost." Novak concludes that, in his fiction, Updike *is* attempting to impose meaning on flux, that he is dealing—at least by implication—with serious issues and that he is "beginning to make religion intelligible in America, and to fashion symbols whereby it can be understood." Quoting the final words of Updike's narrator in "Packed Dirt," Novak writes, " 'We in America need ceremonies', is, I suppose, the point of a great many of the words he has written."[19] The idea of Updike as a religious writer is also explored in Robert Detweiler's, "John Updike and the Indictment of Culture—Protestantism." Focusing on *Rabbit, Run*, Detweiler sees Updike fighting in the novel the same kinds of problems—false moralism, a belief in progress that ignores man's sinful nature, corrupt institutions—that the neo-orthodox theologian Reinhold Neibuhr had been fighting since the 1930's. Rabbit lacks inner resources, but with proper support he could have overcome his crisis. His tragedy as a man without grace is that his crisis does not lead to redemption; yet, "it is precisely the failure of the community and the institutions that comprise it which cause Rabbit to fail." In essence, therefore, the novel is an indictment of Protestant culture.[20]

Before moving away from these responses made to Updike's work in the important year of 1963, one should mention Norman Mailer's at times fascinating discussion, which appears in his "Norman Mailer versus Nine Writers." After complimenting the "Literary Establishment" for "improving its taste, Updike was not simply a general edition of James Gould Cozzens," Mailer attacks this "Establishment" for praising Updike's style and chiding his sexual explicitness. On the contrary, Updike must "go deeper into the literature of sex"; moreover, when the action in his novels lapses, he "cultivates his private vice, he *writes.* . . . In the run of Updike's pages are one thousand other imprecise, flatulent, wry-necked, precious, overpreened, self-indulgent, tortured sentences." Mailer praises in *Rabbit, Run* "the dread Updike manages to convey . . . of a young man who is beginning to lose nothing less than his good American soul, and yet it is not quite his fault." Although for Mailer the ending of the novel is a cop-out, there is a "real pain" and "touch of awe" in the book not unworthy of Hardy. Mailer concludes his essentially generous comments about Updike by observing "something too fatally calculated about his inspiration," and warning him to avoid the clutches of the Establishment: "Of course a man spends his life trying to get up his guts for such a caper."[21]

Between late 1963 and 1966 Updike's publications continued to illustrate his versatility and talent: one new volume of poetry, *Telephone Poles and Other Poems* (1963); a 1964 adaptation, for children, of Wagner, *(The Ring)*, illustrated by him and Warren Chapell (they had collaborated on *The Magic Flute* in 1962; the *Christian Science Monitor* referred to *The Ring* as "a well crafted set of program notes for, say, the precocious children of *New Yorker* subscribers"[22]); *Olinger Stories* (1964);

another children's book *(A Child's Calendar)*, *Assorted Prose* and *Of the Farm* in 1965; and the stories, *The Music School*, in 1966. In 1964 he also found time to visit several Soviet countries as part of a U.S.-U.S.S.R. cultural exchange program.

The reviews during these years began to harden into almost cliché responses to the work of this by now established writer (he was elected a member of the National Institute of Arts and Letters in 1964 and was picked as America's eighth most distinguished novelist in a 1965 *Book Week* poll of approximately 200 novelists, critics, and editors). *Time*, for example, in reviewing *Of the Farm*, wrote, "So far, Updike's performance has been mostly footwork displaying the virtuosity of a writer who can say very little very well."[23] And some of the responses were extremely nasty, most notoriously John Aldridge's "The Private Vice of John Updike" in his *Time to Murder and Create*. In a tone almost slimy with condescension, Aldridge speaks of Updike's "charming but limited gift"; of how, when on the verge of profundity "he does not, after all, know quite what he means to say and is hoping that sheer style will carry him over the difficulty"; of the classical parallels in *The Centaur* as being chosen because of "intellectual chic or status value"; of the "easiness" of Updike's fiction as a reason for its popularity, and so on. The closest that Aldridge comes to praise of Updike is when he says about *Of the Farm* that "There's also a very good description of a tractor mowing a hay field."[24] Like many examples of this kind of cruel, obtuse hatchet job, Aldridge's is at times very funny; the value of statements such as this is in their ability to encourage intelligent replies.

Updike, of course, did not lack champions. In his review of *Assorted Prose*, for example, Granville Hicks asserted, "It might be a good thing for critics to contemplate what Updike has accomplished in a decade— two excellent novels and many first-rate stories—and not to spend so much time worrying about the books he hasn't yet even attempted."[25] Moreover, although, writing in the 1964 *American Literary Scholarship*, William Stafford had lamented that "John Updike, more talented than Styron (in my opinion) has received far less attention,"[26] during the next few years Updike began to receive considerable scholarly analysis.

In his quick overview of Updike's career entitled "John Updike and William Styron: The Burden of Talent," for example, William Van O'Connor predicted that either Styron or Updike "could turn out to be the foremost novelist of his generation": "If the gods continue to favor him [Updike] he should have a magnificent future." And William Peden's first edition of *The American Short Story* contained a brief but appreciative discussion of Updike's short fiction. Paul Doyle's "Updike's Fiction: Motifs and Techniques" praises the writer's subtlety and generosity. Speaking of Eccles in *Poorhouse Fair*, Doyle says, "Again, Updike extends considerable sympathy toward a viewpoint one feels he does not share. . . . They are not straw men, and Updike neither sermonizes nor moralizes."

Doyle also discusses some of Updike's experiments in his short fiction, and suggests that "Much of Updike's fiction might be subtitled 'The Problem of Goodness and the Search for the Good Man.' " Thaddeus Muradian, in "The World of John Updike," points to the writer's major themes as being childhood memories of the past, pain and loneliness, death, and "the Hope," and asserts "In this light, Updike is a Fundamentalist or perhaps a Medievalist in showing us the need to 'escape from life' with death a necessary end but the beginning of something better." Norris Yates also speaks of religious matters in "The Doubt and Faith of John Updike"; Sister Judith Tate in "Of Rabbits and Centaurs" contrasts Rabbit's inability to love himself, others, or God with George Caldwell's success in these areas; for Sister Tate, *Rabbit, Run* shatters the myth "that happiness and freedom are synonomous with concupiscence and irresponsibility"; Hazel Gayol points out comic elements in *The Centaur*, c.f. "The Lord Loves a Cheerful Corpse."[27]

Of the discussions mentioned in the previous paragraph, only Paul Doyle's is of more than historical interest. Four other commentaries published around this time, however, still may be consulted with profit by readers interested in Updike's work. David Galloway's existential interpretation of *Rabbit, Run,* for example, still possesses a certain plausibility, particularly if one cannot tolerate the plethora of Christian interpretations of the novel. In *The Poorhouse Fair,* Galloway sees Updike attacking the "life-denying impulses of the age" but creating a hero (Hook) who "remains too much a part of the system to be a true rebel." Rabbit Angstrom, on the other hand, is a "picaresque saint" (R. W. B. Lewis' phrase) with a vision of the absurd and the need "to find that world in which he can again experience the sacredness of achievement." Rabbit wants to "comfort and heal" and is selfish only in the manner of the searcher after truth. Updike's own faith is capricious, and he continues to explore "rituals which sustain men in a godless universe." In *The Centaur* (in which the "objective chapters [are] told by Caldwell himself and the retrospective chapters narrated by Peter"), Updike describes a "world apparently devoid of meaning." George is not a true existentialistic hero because he lacks a vision of absurdity; Peter, however, provides this awareness.[28] (A second existential interpretation of Updike published around this time is in Sidney Finkelstein's *Existentialism and American Literature.* Finkelstein's discussion is very simplistic, however; at times, in fact, it seems as if he does not know Updike's plots very well.)[29] A second worthwhile discussion of Updike may be found in Charles Walcutt's *Man's Changing Mask.* Opposing Galloway, Walcutt argues that "The perspective that sees them [Rabbit and Caldwell] as saintly must ignore the action in which they are enmeshed and treat them as essences who really live somewhere else." Rabbit, for example, "is not strong; he is rich and complex and full of potential but *weak*"—the "centripetally diminished man." Speaking about the action in *The Centaur,* the critic observes that—unlike naturalistic fiction—it is not linear, but in reality a series of confrontations—action as "a field of force"—that reveals George's personality and the quality of his will; such confrontations also establish tensions that create energy, which "vibrates with its contained force and so gives a powerful sense of life."[30]

A third fine article that remains interesting is by a Russian critic—Inna Levidova—writing in English in her "John Updike's *The Centaur* in Russia." She suggests that, at first, the classical material in *The Centaur* may seem "superfluous" because of the "overwhelming authenticity" of the rest of the novel; yet, the myth is organic: "If George Caldwell were just a school-teacher, we would be faced with a novel of an extremely different spirit, different inner rhythm and, naturally, different philosophical overtones." Levidova goes on to comment on the "Chekhovian suggestiveness" of Updike's setting and its "details selected in Chekhov's manner." She observes as well a dimension of social criticism in the novel—the high school, for example, "depicted by Updike with truly savage and Hogarthian strokes"; and George, "a true son of the 1930's with his instinctive democratic spirit and bitter contempt for the local Jupiters, and with his unbounded sympathy for all the disinherited and hopeless."[31]

A fourth article by Gerry Brenner is isolated in this paragraph (although it will not be discussed here, since it is reprinted in this volume) because it remains the most sensitive interpretation of *Rabbit, Run.* The article is called, "*Rabbit, Run:* John Updike's Criticism of the 'Return to Nature' " and was first published in *Twentieth Century Literature* 12 (1966), 3–14.

Perhaps the most useful publication about Updike to appear during this period is the article in *Life* magazine by Jane Howard, "Can a Nice Novelist Finish First?" The interview contains not only valuable biographical information—about his childhood, for example, where he learned to laugh a lot and "examine everything for God's footprints"—but also revealing comments made by Updike about his own attitudes: "I believe that all problems are basically insoluble and that faith is a leap out of total despair"; "It is in middles that extremes clash, where ambiguity restlessly rules. Something quite intricate and fierce occurs in homes, and it seems to me without doubt worthwhile to examine what it is"; "My novels are all about the search for useful work." One final example will suffice—a statement implicitly directed at many of his own critics: "It seems to me that critics get increasingly querulous and impatient for madder music and stronger wine, when what we need is greater respect for reality, its secrecy, its music. Too many people are studying maps and not enough are visiting places."[32] It could be argued that this review—edited by Updike himself—points to 1966 as the plausible end of this first stage of Updike's career. In the review he seems to be consciously attempting to explain elements in his fiction that had been increasingly under attack, and perhaps thus to help stop the attacks. Moreover, appearing as it does in this large circulation national magazine—the article in a sense symbolizes the popular reputation that Updike had achieved by 1966. A further reason for seeing this year as an appropriate end date for this first stage of Updike's career is that, by this point, he had left the childhood Olinger world in his fiction, and had increasingly begun to describe the adult world of "pilgrims faltering toward divorce" as the narrator remarked in the title story for *The Music School*, published in 1966.

## 2. Criticism and Scholarship in English, 1967–1974

The period 1967–1974 was an important one not only because of Updike's own publications, but also because of what was published about him by a number of good critics and scholars. In addition to a children's book (*Bottom's Dream*, 1969—another adaptation of a classic with Warren Chapell: *Midsummer Night's Dream*), an important volume of poetry (*Midpoint*, 1969), a comic short story cycle (*Bech: A Book*, 1970) and another excellent volume of short stories (*Museums and Women*, 1972), Updike also published two large and controversial novels—*Couples* (1968) and *Rabbit Redux* (1971)—and a peculiar, almost totally ignored closet drama, *Buchanan Dying* (1974, which has been performed at least once successfully: in March, 1977 at San Diego State University, directed by Professor Robert McCoy). Thus, during this period Updike again demonstrated his versatility and willingness to upset reader expectation.

Only a few reviews provoked by Updike's work will be mentioned here. *Time* rewarded the publication of *Couples*, the big book they had been asking him to write (although for Granville Hicks it was "not the major novel many of us have been hoping for"), with a magazine cover and a useful article, "View from the Catacombs."[33] Many reviews were creatively hostile (William Gass in the April 11, 1968 issue of the *New York Review of Books* called *Couples* the "suburbanite entry in the porno pageant," for example).[34] Many were also very favorable, such as Michael Novak's eloquent defense reprinted in this volume. Among the essay reviews still worth reading are those by John Ditsky, "Roth, Updike, and the High Expense of Spirit"; and John Peter, "The Self-Effacement of the Novelist."[35] *Rabbit Redux* was also greeted with mixed responses, but many of the reviews were good. Among the most interesting of both types are Richard Locke's "Rabbit Redux"; Robert Alter, "Updike, Malamud, and the Fire This Time"; Christopher Ricks, "Flopsy Bunny"; and the two reviews by Charles Samuels and William Stafford reprinted in this volume.[36] *Bech*, because it seemed to many reviewers to be something delightfully new in the Updike canon, was very favorably received, although some were puzzled by the "oddly moving" quality of its comedy, while *Buchanan Dying*, because it seemed so dull, was virtually ignored. So also was *Midpoint* (although Anne Gates writing in the August 15,

1969 *Christian Science Monitor* gave to it some thoughtful technical analysis) and *Museums and Women,* perhaps because reviewers felt there was not really very much to say (Tony Tanner's review reprinted in this volume is, of course, an exception). Writing in the August 1972 *Library Journal,* for example, Matthew Hartman referred to "the unique Updike blend of irony and pathos that critics either love or despise."[37]

*a) Books and Pamphlets about Updike, 1967–1974*

Although the vast majority of the reviews written during this period need no longer be read, such is not the case with the scholarly books and articles. In fact, if it does not seem fatuous to speak of a golden age of Updike criticism, then this "golden age" came into existence around the beginning of 1970 and continued for several years, during which a number of good books and articles about Updike were published.

Two studies of pamphlet length were published in 1967 (by Alice and Kenneth Hamilton) and 1969 (by Charles Samuels). The Hamiltons' *John Updike: A Critical Essay* appeared as part of the William Eerdmans *Contemporary Writers in Christian Perspective* series and serves as a modest, quiet introduction to their more stridently Christian interpretation of Updike published in 1970. According to the Hamiltons, "Updike thinks of [his characters] as musical instruments which, even though untuned, can reverberate with the sounds of eternity." On occasions, they oversimplify Updike in stressing his Christian vision (the mother in *Of the Farm* thus becoming a pristine representative of a generation close to God while the narrator's new wife Peggy "in her vulgar way embodies the negative side of sexuality").[38] In general, however, their pamphlet provides a useful, unassuming introduction to a legitimate way of viewing Updike's work. The second study is Charles Samuels' taut, perspicuous University of Minnesota Pamphlet on Updike (1969); this is very much a "critical" study of Updike which draws its inspiration in part from Samuels' excellent 1968 *Paris Review* interview mentioned earlier. Samuels has no real thesis about the writer, other than that his work is important and worthwhile, and that it does not "develop" in the sense of improving; both his earliest and most recent fiction, according to Samuels, contain examples of good and bad writing. The discussion proceeds thematically, therefore, rather than chronologically and in the process makes some useful comment about most of Updike's work including *Couples.* Of *Rabbit, Run,* for example, he writes shrewdly, "Wanting us to admire Rabbit's authentic energy, Updike does not forget its terrible cost"; or of Joey's problem in *Of the Farm,* "Definition requires that we keep faith with our past; freedom demands that we move beyond it"; or finally, of the sex in *Couples,* "so much suckling so lovingly described also makes one suspect advocacy— despite all the conceptual disclaimers."[39]

After the publication of these two short studies, six books appeared rapidly between 1970 and 1973: the Hamiltons' *The Elements of John Up-*

*dike*, Rachael Burchard's *John Updike: Yea Sayings*, Larry Taylor's *Pastoral and Anti-Pastoral Patterns in John Updike's Fiction*, Robert Detweiler's *John Updike*, Edward Vargo's *Rainstorms and Fire: Ritual in the Novels of John Updike*, and Joyce Markle's *Fighters and Lovers: Themes in the Novels of John Updike*.

The learned, humorless study by the Hamiltons is both illuminating and irritating. Consciously setting out to prove beyond doubt that Updike has "something to say," they emphasize their Christian quasi-allegorist theory until one sometimes forgets that Updike is a maker of fiction. They write, for example: "every choice is actively a decision between desolating idolatry and faith in the true God who gives the gift of peace"; or "Whether or not the Maples have eyes to see it, the messengers of God ride without fail down 13th street to enforce the eternal law of Things as They Are"; or "Snow from heaven, bringing to a halt earthly busyness, allows man to know that he is in the care of a Providence ordering all things in a fashion beyond his comprehension." It would be grossly unfair, however, to imply that the book is always this reductive, because it is extremely good at times. The Hamiltons are very sensitive to Updike's allusiveness, for example, and not simply his allusions to the Bible or Karl Barth or Kierkegaard but also to sources as varied as Robert Herrick (about whom Updike wrote his Harvard thesis) or Pliny's *Natural History*. One is frequently compelled to object to the way in which they interpret the functions of the allusions, or to the significance that they sometimes attach to them, but the reader must be grateful to the Hamiltons for suggesting dimensions in Updike's work (and they discuss almost all of it through *Couples*, including the poetry) which well may exist.[40]

Rachael Burchard's study also traces his career up to and including *Couples* and also attempts to prove that he has "something to say," in this instance a serious, honest and—despite ambiguity—"yea saying to the goodness of life." Her book is on occasion poorly written and sentimental (about David Kern in "Pigeon Feathers," for example, she writes, "he listens to life and from its sobs and its songs composes a poignant melody"; and, "Updike, it seems, would have man accept life's little rewards and press on toward understanding his relation to his Creator"). Yet, one side of the book's unevenness is insight, as when she observes that the Mouseketeer scene in *Rabbit, Run* is "perfectly geared to his [Rabbit's] level of maturity"; or when she discusses the symbolic importance of Caldwell's car in *The Centaur;* or when she writes of Mrs. Robinson in *Of the Farm*: "Wily and subtle, she can manipulate a conversation as if it were a searchlight to bluntly reveal the weakness of the others but can turn off the switch before exposing herself." Even her overly long, repetitious, sometimes contradictory defense of *Couples* contains good material. Burchard's book is the weakest of the early long studies of Updike, but it still has "something to say."[41]

Larry Taylor's 1971 analysis of Updike's "central theme—pastoral and anti-pastoral in our time," is sometimes confusing and sometimes annoyingly thesis-ridden. In general, however, this is a good, tightly written short book. His first two chapters focus primarily on pastoral and anti-pastoral conventions and traditions in world and American literature, mentioning that for the pastoral to exist, the sophisticated author's (and audience's) positive attitude toward the rural setting and unsophisticated characters is crucial. The rest of the study proceeds chronologically through Updike's fiction (concluding with *Bech*), arguing that early in his career he tends to view pastoralism positively, whereas later he becomes progressively more satiric and ironic in his treatment of pastoral assumptions about life. Taylor is very good on *Rabbit, Run*, which he calls "a type of fable, with satiric overtones" ("The irony is that his [the protagonist's] attitude toward sex is more a rabbit's attitude than a sensitive human being's"; Taylor also points out that Rabbit never gets close to a real farm, but in Mrs. Smith's garden raises only exotic rhododendrons). His discussion of *The Centaur* is also good (he sees it as pastoral elegy on the analogy of "Lycidas"), as is his discussion of *Of the Farm* (reprinted in this collection). Many of his other comments are also suggestive, as when he sees *Couples* as an indictment of pastoralism, for example; or when he compares Updike with the Hawthorne of "The Maypole of Merry Mount"—the anti-pastoralist who longs to be a pastoralist.[42]

Robert Detweiler's book on Updike in the Twayne series is a brilliant performance, clearly the most continually illuminating study of the author up to and including *Museums and Women*. Compelled by the Twayne format to proceed chronologically and to say something pithy about practically everything in the Updike canon, Detweiler does this without seeming mechanical or exhausted. In speaking of "Snowing in Greenwich Village," for example, he concludes, "A fine line may exist between lust and love, but the libido need not always incite to sexual consummation; it can produce other kinds of knowledge as well. Lust can teach." Detweiler is not only sensitive to the complexities of theme, but also to the manner in which technique may inform theme and help to create it. He comments, for example, on what he calls the "non-protagonist strategy" in *The Poorhouse Fair* (with the reader becoming the protagonist), and writes, "The weak old man and the state's flunky are accented enough to project negatively the ironic theme but not enough emphasized to dominate the novel." He is helpful in his explanation of the "cumulative epiphany" technique in *Pigeon Feathers*, and in his analysis of surrealistic (the expansion of reality through distortion) and cubistic (the simultaneous perception of many facets of personality and action) techniques in *The Centaur*, and the varieties of tone in the same novel. His observations are also acute about the links with Wallace Stevens in *The Music School* ("In loving, one overcomes self-consciousness; but, in the poetic shaping of the experience, one gains a means of esthetic distance without dissolving the experience itself"); perceptive too is his analysis of *Rabbit Redux*, in which, he suggests, the action "is based on the imagery and is reinforced by the history and not vice versa." And so on. Detweiler views Updike as an experimenter in fiction (although not an "experimentalist"), as a man who continually takes risks while writing "secular baroques," which he defines as "elaborate, texture-conscious, structurally balanced, highly controlled, mythologically resonant fiction, yet a kind that does not celebrate such a rich and ordered world but instead ironically marks its passing." Detweiler's thesis is flexible enough to enable him to respond to Updike's versatility, but sufficiently firm to provide structure for his discussions. To sum up: his is a very fine book and very much worth reading.[43]

Edward Vargo's *Rainstorms and Fire* is also worth reading, but it is another quite uneven book, much influenced by the Hamiltons' Christian reading of Updike ("He is a primitive God, a fierce, terrible God, . . . , the God of rainstorms and fire in *Couples* and *Rabbit Redux*"). According to Vargo, Updike tries in his fiction to "visualize the transcendent" through his own (and sometimes his characters') sophisticated use of ritual—the various components of which are pattern, myth and celebration. At times, Vargo pushes too hard his vision of Updike as prophet, but in general his book is useful because of the thorough bibliography (which includes references to reviews and to foreign critics), the good summaries of criticism with which he usually begins his major discussions of Updike, his consistent and thoughtful attempts to parallel Updike with other writers, and the occasional insights into the Updike texts themselves. About *The Centaur*, for example, he writes, "The entire narrative is a patterned ceremony of word and action in which Peter celebrates his former experience with his father." His description of the clashing mythologues of Joey in *Of the Farm* is also good, although one may object to the conclusion that Joey "refuses to accept any responsibility for his past or for his family and the refusal kills any ceremonial connection between himself and tradition." And Vargo's generalization about *Couples*—"The condom and the candy wrapper are the discarded wrappings of the society's futile sacraments"—although overstated, has a certain epigrammatic verve.[44]

The last book written during this period, Joyce Markle's *Fighters and Lovers*, is, except for Robert Detweiler's study, the most intelligent analysis of Updike's early work. Moreover, despite her sub-title "Theme in the Novels of John Updike," Markle is not a theme-monger, but a critic sensitive to the way in which form complements meaning in Updike's work, particularly in her analyses of his "continuously operative and highly complex systems of imagery." Her title points to her thesis that in almost all of Updike's novels there exists a protagonist with a "vivid sense of human specialness" who fights against the pressure towards two types of death—physical and metaphorical (the death of dehumanization). Opposed to this protagonist is often a person like Conner in *The Poorhouse Fair*, "the well-intentioned but essentially sterile man who fails to recognize or augment people's sense of their own specialness." In light of this thesis, *Couples* is seen as the novel in which "The struggle against death and insignificance is . . . hyperbolized to its greatest possible degree" and Piet's final "tragedy is the *loss* of tragedy"; *Bech's* comedy suggests "A self-deprecating sense of humor [which] replaces hope and ambition"; and *Rabbit Redux* represents a new search for status and energy with "a renewed belief in human causality." The validity of Markle's developmental approach to Updike's fiction is very much open to debate; operating, however, within a seemingly restrictive thesis, she almost always manages to say something provocative about Updike's novels: about the four symbolic moments in *The Poorhouse Fair*, for example, which cast doubt on the value of Hook's theological point of view; about *The Centaur* as George's narrative, not Peter's; about the ways in which the oedipal conflicts limit Joey's freedom in *Of the Farm*; about the influence of Denis de Rougemont's theories on *Couples*. Moreover, her explanations are helpful concerning the ways in which Updike establishes value systems in his novels (his use of children, for example). For Markle, the "yes-but" quality of his fiction increases with each book and the force of the moral framework decreases until *Bech*. According to her, Updike sees Christianity as contributing to one's sense of worth, but the author's reservations about Chritianity "become increasingly obvious" after *The Poorhouse Fair*.[45] *Fighters and Lovers* is another book that should be read by anyone wishing to understand and appreciate Updike's fiction.

### b) General Articles and Comments about Updike, 1967–1974

In addition to the several good books about Updike, there were a number of fine articles published, a few of which appear in the Spring, 1974 special Updike issue of *Modern Fiction Studies*, an issue whose publication provides a convenient stopping place for a survey of this next stage of Updike's critical reputation.

Of the general articles on Updike whose value is not always high, but which offer occasional insight into his work, five should be mentioned: Richard Rupp, "John Updike: Style in Search of a Centre" (despite the promising title, Rupp's article is primarily an impressionistic tour through Updike's fiction, and a prediction that Updike will not endure unless his style finds a moral centre to act as ballast); Bryant Wyatt, "John Updike: The Psychological Novel in Search of a Structure" (according to Wyatt, it is an informing structure for which Updike searches; Wyatt also refers to the "blatant eroticism" in the fiction, "frequently in perverse, or, at least, unsavory manifestations"); John Hill, "Quest for Belief: Theme in the Novels of John Updike" (another quite simplistic study); and Joseph Waldmeir's "Only an Occasional Rutabaga: American Fiction Since 1945." Waldmeir's comments on Updike are—given his large topic—

necessarily brief, but they are interesting. For the critic, Updike resembles most of the best novelists since 1945 because he is a quest novelist, focusing on characters who search for value; unlike most of his contemporaries, however, Updike does not give up his belief that there is something to find of "essential, or even transcendent—value." This assumption "obstructs any tendency to turn his naturalistic or existentialist frame of reference into doctrine." Sex, in the quest, becomes the substitute for God and Law; sin becomes "the failure to love strongly enough to accept responsibility." A fifth, minor article (the weakest piece in the *Modern Fiction Studies* 1974 special issue), is by Robert Gingher and entitled "Has John Updike Anything to Say?" Yes, says the critic; Updike, like Faulkner, wishes to dramatize the " 'problem of the human heart in conflict with itself.' " Updike's focus, however, is not on "individual psychodramatics"; his is primarily "an aggregate portrayal of the human condition."[46] Among the other short general comments on Updike worthy of note are those contained in Granville Hicks's *Literary Horizons*, James Ginden's *Harvest of a Quiet Eye: The Novel of Compassion*, and Alfred Kazin's *Bright Book of Life: American Novelists and Storytellers from Hemingway to Mailer.*[47]

There are five general essays on Updike that should be singled out because of their excellence: Howard Harper's "John Updike and the Intrinsic Problem of Human Existence" in his *Desperate Faith: A Study of Bellow, Salinger, Mailer, Baldwin, and Updike*, H. Petter's "John Updike's Metaphoric Novels," (reprinted in this volume), Tony Tanner's "A Compromised Environment" in his *City of Words: American Fiction, 1950–70*, S. A. Zylstra's "John Updike and the Parabolic Nature of the World," and Robert Regan's "Updike's Symbol of the Centre."[48] Tanner's is the most thoughtful article, Regan's the most idiosyncratic and provocative.

Harper (like David Galloway) reads Updike as an existential novelist and around this premise builds a series of useful readings of the novels up to *Of the Farm*. He writes, "In Updike's first novel the belief in God is shown to be a spiritual necessity stronger than humanitarian illusions of the welfare state. But in the later work, God becomes increasingly vestigial, a ceremonial ideal to be invoked against the world. . . . The memory of heaven and earth is entirely human, and the feeling that this memory is transitory gives Updike's work its most moving quality." For Harper, Chiron becomes the perfect symbol for existential man, at home in neither material nor spiritual realm. Many of Harper's comments are sensible. About the ending of *Of the Farm*, for example, he writes that, although the problems between the characters are not resolved, "they are at least brought out into the open during the weekend, and all three characters achieve—or perhaps, are given by the others—much of the freedom they need." Tony Tanner's very perceptive essay centers on his observation of Updike's fear of entropy, and the writer's fascination with means of staying this force: the environment sometimes provides this stay and sometimes does not, but Updike's love of language itself becomes "a way of holding on to the fact of growth, holding out against entropy." Given his fear of this force, Updike's sense of "cosmic vertigo" is sometimes pervasive in his fiction. A few of Tanner's comments on particular works are noteworthy: that Conner in *Poorhouse Fair*, for example, is not totally unsympathetic, yet, "in him a dislike of mess and dirt has been taken to the point of antipathy to life itself"; that the effect of Updike's dense prose in *Rabbit, Run* is to help the reader feel the crush that almost overwhelms Rabbit, and that "His particular dismay is to realize how the entropic process also affects him, turning him into an object of junk where once vitality flowered." Commenting on the allusiveness of Updike's fiction, Tanner observes, "Paradoxically, the effect of much of his work is to leave us feeling that there is only one world, and that the wall of detail with which he confronts us looms all too authentically large." Tanner's most significant generalization is about the conflict which tears at many of Updike's characters: between the fear of losing their selfhood by becoming submerged in their environment ("a deeply American feeling"), and their intuition that life in that environment "is the best antidote to that great cosmic dread and sense of universal waste which besets [them]. . . . Because this fear can be so intense Updike sometimes seems to write in support of this compromised environment."

S. A. Zylstra's "John Updike and the Parabolic Nature of the World" is a plea against overly allegorical readings of Updike's work and in favor of a respect for the writer's openness. Working from Auden's definition of parables ("secular stories with no overt religious overtones"), Zylstra suggests that Updike's fiction is parabolic in that "He does not impose a closed interpretation of 'phenomena' ": Updike's "imagination . . . retains a character open to all readers whatever they believe" (although, Zylstra implies, Updike hopes that his readers will respond to the spiritual implications of his parables). In discussing *Rabbit, Run,* and the writer's sympathy with Rabbit's sense of mystery combined with his recognition of Rabbit's childishness, Zylstra notes that, "the *possible* significance of 'the late sunshine in the little jungle of plants' and 'the almost wordless supper' is there for the reader's imagination to act upon." Writing of sex in Updike, the critic suggests, "Eros *per se* leads to disenchantment but retains, as parable, hope in 'unsearchability'." And commenting on *Bech*, whose central character laments the individual's diminishing ability to read and feel, Zylstra observes a possible parallel with Updike himself—perhaps a growing fear "That all the windows of the spirit are being nailed shut." The value of Zylstra's study is that it respects both Updike's interest in religion and his tact in expressing it.

Robert Regan's ("Updike's Symbol of the Centre") at times obfuscatory prose helps make a difficult concept seem even more difficult, but the concept, nonetheless, is worth considering. Noting the numerous circle images in Updike's work, Regan asserts that they are related to the writer's interest in the Jungian "mandala"—the symbol of psychic integration—and Updike's Christian belief that mandala figures are gifts from God. Focusing primarily on *Midpoint*, "First-Person Singular" (in *Assorted Prose*), and "Pigeon Feathers," Regan observes how "The centres in . . . Updike's [work] faithfully exemplify mysterious centres of life." Updike agrees with Karl Barth that there is no way for the individual to reach God, but there is "a way from God to us": His chosen form of communication is "through mandala imagery." Updike's purpose as a writer is to make his reader *see*, if not necessarily to understand, the principle of unity that exists in the universe. David Kern in "Pigeon Feathers" is transported into mystery through circles; Rabbit Angstrom sees only a "minor sun" and is not saved. According to Regan, the hypothesis of Updike's art is that "The 'controlled rapture' of the first Creator should be emulated by all creators"; thus, his completed, circular stories "make oblations of order and harmony to a human psyche distraught with chaos and confusion." It is difficult to decide, in reading Regan's argument, whether he is simply dressing up the Hamiltons' theories about Updike in trendy new clothes and pretentious language, or whether he is pointing to a dimension in Updike's work that should be observed. Readers of his article will, of course, have to decide for themselves.

### c) Articles about Updike's Specific Works, 1967–1974

During this period there were many articles focusing upon Updike's specific works, the most impressive being devoted to explicating and appreciating *Couples*.

*Apprentice Work and Poetry*. Robert McCoy, in his "John Updike's Literary Apprenticeship in the *Harvard Lampoon*," discusses not only the *Lampoon* material but also Updike's writing and drawing before he reached Harvard. Through this analysis McCoy helps to explain the astonishing quickness with which Updike became a successful professional, in that the apprentice work, "clearly sharpened his wit, his artist's descriptive eye, and his sense of the essential ambiguity of life." Two good articles on Updike's poetry also were published during these years: Elizabeth Matson's "A Chinese Paradox, But Not Much of One: John Updike and His Poetry," and the Hamiltons' "Theme and Technique in John Updike's *Midpoint*." The latter's article is particularly good in suggesting links between the ideas in the title poem and Updike's general values, and in demonstrating the influence of various models for his poetry: Dante, Pound, Whitman, Pope, and Spenser. Matson, on the other hand, comments briefly on many of his poems, shows links between them and a plethora of poets—e.g., Ogden Nash, Robert Frost, W. C. Williams, and in particular, the English metaphysicals—and suggests to the reader the sometimes serious wittiness of this neglected area of Updike's art.[49]

*Short Fiction (Excluding Bech)*. Elmer Suderman in his "Art as a Way of Knowing" moves from a discussion of Suzanne Langer's theories about the way in which art can chart the inner life through forms not possible in discursive language, to illustrate her theory by analyzing Updike's "Unstuck," a story about a man who needs his wife's help to free his car. To Suderman, the story helps us to see "the logic of consciousness itself—its rhythms and connections, crises and breaks—incarnated in a single experience." He also says, pertinently, "Those critics who complain that Updike has little to say often forget that the primary function of art, even of the short story, is not to make profound observations about the meaning of life but to present the forms of feeling for our examination." Ellen Baldeshwiler in her "The Lyric Short Story: The Sketch of a History" charts two streams of the story—the "epical" and the "lyrical" (in which the structure is shaped by feeling), concluding with an interesting analysis of Updike's "Leaves," which she sees as "a sophisticated quest story in the modern manner," which is at the same time "a probing of moral guilt" and "man's movement in and out of purely natural processes."[50]

Two brief articles in *Studies in Short Fiction* quarrelled about the question of William Young's maturity at the end of "A Sense of Shelter" (R. W. Reising, "Updike's 'A Sense of Shelter' "; and A. S. G. Edwards, "Updike's 'A Sense of Shelter' "). Another short, insightful article in *SSF* suggests the depth of an ostensibly insignificant story ("The Astronomer"), which is about the narrator's subtle recognition and revelation of the shallowness of his hitherto admired friend, Bela. Gilbert Porter also suggests the significant dimension (in an Emersonian act of self-reliance) in an ostensibly trivial action and story ("John Updike's 'A & P': The Establishment and an Emersonian Cashier"). Two articles in the special Updike issue of *MFS* also point to unsuspected subtleties in Updike stories. Albert Griffith suggests plausible parallels between the frame of "Should Wizard Hit Mommy?" (in which the father refuses to follow his usual practice of providing a happy ending to the story he tells his daughter) and the actionless story itself (the husband and wife discuss household chores), in which the man's frustration with his dead four year marriage is revealed. Less plausible is Griffith's suggestion of an allegorical implication: should "the artist defend himself against the prosaic responsibility that circumscribes his creative impulses?" Alfred Rosa in his "The Psycholinguistics of Updike's 'Museums and Women' " focuses on the narrator's infatuation with two letters (M's and W's) in the story's opening paragraph, his talk of the "humming" of the letters, and the sense of something mystical and providential in letters. Rosa concludes, "There is, as one can see from the letters themselves, a divine hand at work here."[51] All of the articles possess not only intrinsic interest, but also suggest how other of Updike's short stories may be appreciated in and for themselves, rather than simply as intimations or echoes of his longer, more "important" fiction.

*The Poorhouse Fair* and *Rabbit, Run*. The significant discussions of *The Poorhouse Fair* appeared in either the books or the general articles on Updike. The one brief article on this novel is W. W. de Grummond's "Classical Influence in *The Poorhouse Fair*," in which the author points out how the classical influences that are so obvious in *The Centaur* are also present in the earlier novel in some of the names and in the source of Conner's argument about the origin of the universe.[52]

Three good articles were published on *Rabbit, Run:* J. C. Stubbs's fairly conventional but solid "Search for Perfection in *Rabbit, Run*," in which it is argued that "Updike's purpose is to show the dilemma of the man who faces the fundamental human anxiety and tried to combat it"; Clinton Burhans Jr.'s 1973 article reprinted in this volume; and Joseph Waldmeir's excellent "It's the Going That's Important, Not the Getting There: Rabbit's Questing Non-Quest" (*MFS* special issue). Waldmeir concludes that Updike's "real concern is a critical examination of the temptations, the problems, the questions, and the answers as they conflict both inside and outside the protagonist, alternatingly promising and denying solutions to the quest. It is a question of emphasis: perception and examination rather than revelation are in fact the theme; the quest functions primarily as a structural motif." Waldmeir is very good at delineating the stages in Rabbit's quest and in showing how Updike controls the reader's involvement at each stage.[53] Among the other articles written about *Rabbit, Run* are the following: Fred Standley, "*Rabbit, Run:* An Image of Life," *Midwest Quarterly* 8 (1967), 371–86; Alvin Alley and Hugh Agee, "Existential Heroes: Frank Alpine and Rabbit Angstrom," *Ball State University Forum* 9 (1968), 3–5; Elmer Suderman, "The Right Way and the Good Way in *Rabbit, Run*," *University Review* 36 (1969), 13–21; Barbara Rotundo, "*Rabbit, Run* and *A Tale of Peter Rabbit*," *Notes on Contemporary Literature* 1 (1971), 2–3; and Lewis Lawson, "Rabbit Angstrom as a Religious Sufferer," *Journal of the American Academy of Religion* 42 (1974), 232–46.

*The Centaur*. Alvin Alley's "*The Centaur:* Transcendental Imagination and Metaphoric Death" is good about the way in which the real and mythical converge at the novel's end: Chiron moves toward a chariot that will carry him to his literal death, George to a car and metaphorical death as a teacher. David Myers' article is sometimes helpful (although hyperbolic) in its explanation of the Christian dimensions in the novel, and in his theories about the "two" narrators ("The Questing Fear: Christian Allegory in John Updike's *The Centaur*"). Wesley Kort's chapter, "*The Centaur* and the Problem of Vocation," in his *Shriven Selves: Religious*

*Problems in Recent American Fiction,* considers this novel at some length and other works briefly (and not very helpfully) in the context of Luther's ideas about vocation. Kort focuses on the problem which Updike's characters have in dealing with unfulfilling work, and their need to be affected by "the law and grace of vocation." Edward Vargo, in his "The Necessity of Myth in Updike's *The Centaur,*" argues that through a fusion of dreams, reveries, and narrative, Peter celebrates his former experiences with his father; in his retelling, Peter searches for a pattern that will help bring renewed hope to his present life. Vargo suggests that the reader himself must believe in the value of the mythic consciousness if he is to be affected by this aspect of the novel. The most complex, interesting article on *The Centaur* during this period was also the last published: John B. Vickery's "*The Centaur:* Myth, History, and Narrative." For Vickery, "the mythic and historical elements are not antagonistic forces vying for supremacy and ultimate authenticity but coordinating aspects of a narrative that unflinchingly encompasses the spectrum of conceivability." Commenting on the author's desire to make the reader conscious of the "fictiveness of the narrative," Vickery argues that the novel is not so much about George Caldwell as it is "about the modern writer's efforts, and need, 'to keep an organized mass of images moving forward' " (this last phrase is from the *Paris Review* interview, which had an important influence on Vickery's study.)[54]

*Couples.* The novel that benefitted most from the academic journal criticism was undoubtedly *Couples,* because a number of articles were written about the novel, several of which are very illuminating. Joyce Flint's "John Updike and *Couples:* The Wasp's Dilemma" points to Updike's "quiet courage in the decision to examine the unpopular WASP in an age when most novelists are writing from the perspective of minority group traumas." She observes, of the book's tone: "That they [the characters] react as rational and relativistic human beings is the key to both the blandness of the work and the horror it inspires." In David Lodge's "Post-Pill Paradise: John Updike's *Couples,*" the author explains how, in *Couples,* Updike tries to create a "clandestine, erotic utopia" employing "extensively the matter and diction traditionally reserved for pornography." Lodge further suggests how in the "note of celebration checked by irony," Updike reveals his links with the Hawthorne of *The Blithedale Romance.* One critical comment from Lodge about the novel is noteworthy: "Updike's incorrigible greed for stylistic effect makes nonsense of his attempt to portray his hero as a kind of primitive, a rough diamond, who doesn't really belong among the college educated couples." Robert Detweiler's 1971 article, "Updike's *Couples:* Eros Demythologized," the best single study of the novel, is reprinted in this volume.[55]

Gary Waller's "Updike's *Couples:* A Barthian Parable" is also an excellent article, which employs an unsurprising thesis (that it is Karl

Barth's "stance of compassionate neo-orthodoxy that provides the distinctive moral backbone for *Couples*") as the basis for a series of sensitive observations about the novel. Waller argues, for example, that the relationship of Piet and Foxy is not merely an adventure, "but a genuine and growing relationship between . . . individuals who may fight for mastery, yet fulfil each other richly and strangely." Waller points to the odd lightness of tone of the novel's end, suggestive to him of the justness (if not the happiness) of the characters' fates; the critic asserts, "accepting men as they are, Barth's God wills everything to be ultimately well in the apparently worst of all possible worlds." Roger Sharrock's "Singles and Couples: Hemingway's *A Farewell to Arms* and Updike's *Couples*" first points out that, despite their superficial similarities, significant differences exist between the couples in Updike's novel. Sharrock then goes on to sketch interesting parallels between the two novels: the couples in both novels seem caught in the toils of impersonal forces; "they attempt to settle for the terms of a peace that is more like war"; and only Piet and Foxy try to "get off the rail of history." Two articles in the *MFS* special issue also focus on *Couples*: Paula and Nick Backscheider's clear but pedestrian attempt to show that *Couples* is not Updike's *Airport* and Alan McKenzie's more effective close analysis of the scenes centering around the games of "Impressions" and "Wonderful." Through the analysis McKenzie shows how these scenes—like the parlor games in Austen's *Emma*—help to reinforce the implications of other passages in the novel.[56]

*Bech: A Book* and *Rabbit Redux*.  Outside of the comments on *Bech* in the general studies on Updike, and a few good reviews, little of substance was written about the novel except for the Hamiltons' essay review, "Metamorphosis through Art: Updike's *Bech: A Book*," which is reprinted in this volume.[57] Most of the best criticism on *Rabbit Redux* also appears in the books. Five articles are, however, worthy of note.

The first, by John Gordon ("Updike Redux"), is really a review, but is such a thoughtful review that it is mentioned here. Gordon is good, for example, in his comments about the links between the Rabbit books and in his feel for *Rabbit Redux*'s ambiguity ("He [Updike] doesn't believe anymore . . . that people really know what to do or how to change things"); he is also perceptive in his references to Updike's "Platonic eroticism" (which reminds Gordon of Donne), his appreciation of the book's "strong, metaphor-laden narrative line," and his references to the " 'novel of ideas' " tendency in *Rabbit Redux* "where it threatens to become one of those novels . . . like *The Shoes of the Fisherman*." Gordon concludes by suggesting that, if Updike ever finds a solution to the problems that trouble him, "it will not be just a book, it will be a national event." Kermit Turner argues, in "Rabbit Brought Nowhere: John Updike's *Rabbit Redux*," that during the novel Rabbit does not change, remaining at the end the person he was at the beginning—someone who does things primarily because they are easy. Eugene Lyons, in his highly critical "John Updike: The Beginning and the End," asserts that "to read the novel is to be taken on a guided tour of virtually every negative cliché that can be applied to America today"; and that, "One sometimes has the feeling that Updike has a certain number of set pieces in his notebooks and is determined that they be delivered, regardless of who delivers them or how much characterization has to be wrenched in order to do it." Wayne Falke in a meandering but useful article ("*Rabbit Redux*: Time/Order/ God") focuses on the novel's sociological dimension, and suggests, "it is as if Updike is writing a spiritual and sociological history of the nation as it approaches its third century." Sharply in contrast with those critics who stress Updike's Christian beliefs, Falke says that "Updike's fiction is calling for humanism that has little justification in theology. Its elements are rather simple: joy, love, warm family ties, beauty in our lives; social justice." Finally, in his interesting "Ken Kesey, John Updike and the Lone Ranger," Andrew Horton points out how the "Lone Ranger" motif in *Rabbit Redux*, particularly Updike's subtle references to the silver bullet, is used to reinforce his criticism of American values and also to suggest a kind of positive ending—a future in which the Lone Ranger (Harry Angstrom) will finally become a man.[58]

### 3. Criticism and Scholarship in English, 1975–1980

During the years 1975–80, Updike has continued to demonstrate his skill, versatility, and productivity by publishing a large volume of miscellaneous prose (*Picked Up Pieces*, 1975), a volume of poetry (*Tossing and Turning*, 1977; in this year he was also elected to the fifty-member American Academy of Arts and Letters), two volumes of short fiction (*Too Far to Go*—a short story cycle of Maples stories, and *Problems and Other Stories*, both in 1979), and three novels (*A Month of Sundays*, 1975; *Marry Me*, 1976; and *The Coup*, 1978). Although his "African" novel, *The Coup*, was greeted with surprise (at Updike's ostensible large change in direction), and generally very positive reviews, the responses to both *A Month of Sundays* and *Marry Me* were decidedly mixed (Peter Prescott in *Newsweek* called the latter "quite simply Updike's best novel yet," while Brigid Brophy in a savage review in *Harpers* wrote: "Although John Updike is awful, he just isn't virtuoso enough to be excruciatingly awful")[59]. Readers wishing to taste the mixed flavor of the responses to Updike's most recent long fiction should read the reviews in this volume, those in the *Twentieth Century Views* volume edited by Thorburn and Eiland, and a few of the following: George Stade's "The Resurrection of Reverend Marshfield" in *N.Y. Times Book Review*, Rosemary Dinnage's review of *Sundays* in *TLS*, David Thorburn's comments on *Marry Me* in *Yale Review*, Brigid Brophy's diatribe mentioned above, Daphne Merkin's

"Updike in Africa" in *New Leader*, and Douglas Hill's "Rabbit Angstrom, I presume?" in *Books in Canada*.[60] The reviews of the two volumes of short stories reveal more about the tastes of the reviewers than the books themselves: by this point in Updike's career, there are those who will almost always like whatever he writes and those who will not.

### a)  Books about Updike

During this period, three new books were published about Updike, one of which—the 1979 *Twentieth Century Views* volume edited by Thorburn and Eiland—has already been mentioned in passing. It is generally a helpful introduction to those readers modestly interested in the writer, but it is relatively short, and does not contain much academic criticism—as opposed to reviews—on Updike; the annotated bibliography is also skimpy. More will be said later about several of the essays in the volume. The two other books are Suzanne Henning Uphaus' *John Updike* in the Frederick Ungar Series called *Modern Literature Monographs* and George Hunt's difficult and ambitious, *John Updike and the three great secret things: Sex, Religion, and Art*.[61] Uphaus has shown herself to be a perspicuous commentator on Updike in two journal articles that she has published (one of which—on *The Centaur*—appears in this volume). In her book, however, she seems severely limited by the popular purpose of the Series (the dust jacket says that the book is "a lively introduction for the new Updike reader and brings his longtime fans up to date"); as a result, much of this quite short study of all of the novels (with some discussion of his "most popular short stories") is very superficial (despite good analyses of the Rabbit novels)—at times not going much beyond plot summary (as in her comments on *Marry Me* and *The Coup*, for example). The bibliography of "Works about John Updike and Interviews," is reasonably thorough and useful, however, (although the book has almost no footnotes), and her introduction contains some helpful comments, particularly about what she calls "the lyric intensity of the comic style": the "steadily accelerating, extraordinary long sentences, in which detail is piled on detail, leading the reader, breathless, to a delightfully comic denouement."

The thesis of George Hunt's book is that "three great secret things [the phrase comes from Updike's "The Dogwood Tree: a Boyhood") . . . characterize the predominant subject matter, thematic concerns, and central questions found throughout his adult fiction." The focus in the early fiction is on the first "secret thing," religion; beginning with *The Music School* (1966) it is on the second—sex; and "with *A Month of Sundays* (1975) Art and the problems relating to fictional creation come to the fore." Working loosely with this thesis, Hunt discusses Updike's career beginning with *The Poorhouse Fair*, with chapters on all of the novels (including *Bech*) up to and including *The Coup*. Hunt's is a complex, at times confusing but in general rewarding study, valuable not only because of his familiarity with all of Updike's work and almost all of the criticism on it, but also because of his ability to show how the ideas of such figures as Karl Barth, Søren Kierkegaard, and Carl Jung can increase one's understanding of Updike's world. Given all of the work that has already been done on the influence of Barth and Kierkegaard, it would seem initially that any further statement might be redundant. Hunt's book proves, however, that this need not be so through his treatment of aspects of the theological influence not explored in detail before: Barth's attitude toward evil, for example, and the relevance of this attitude to Updike's treatment of Rabbit Angstrom; Kierkegaard's ideas about dread, guilt, and sin—particularly as they relate to sexuality, which in Updike's fiction according to Hunt, "is not only psychologically complex but also morally and religiously ambivalent" (thus Joey in *Marry Me* becomes a Kierkegaardian "exhibit-specimen of ambivalent dread personified"). Hunt also suggests the possible influence on Updike of the "compellingly dramatic voices" of these theologians, as well as of their distinctive dialectical and ambiguous modes of argumentation.

In addition, Hunt seizes upon his own knowledge of Carl Jung's theories about the anima and individuation to illuminate Updike's fiction, in particular *Of the Farm* and *A Month of Sundays*: "Marshfield's 'month' records a man's psychic movement from his concern with his *Ego*, that dwelling of his conscious life, to his encounter with the unconscious symbol of his self." In essence, however, Hunt is eclectic and creative in his use of sources and parallels, at times employing Barth, Kierkegaard, or John Bunyan, at others Jung, Freud, de Rougement, Frye, Joseph Campbell, or R. W. B. Lewis (Bech becomes a new American Adam with a vision of abundance "which a century ago sparked exhileration, [but] now generates nightmare"). In sum, he seizes upon whatever "source" is needed to explain the resonances of Updike's fiction. Thus, in discussing *The Coup*, Hunt suggests that we see Ellelou as a kind of Adam, or a Jungian man trying to confront various anima figures, or finally and most persuasively—a Humbert Humbert figure: "Kush is Ellelou's Lolita"; "Kush resides within his skull, not so much an orange as an image of one"; "Ellelou's account is that of a man who cannot possibly separate what seems from what is, whether the subject be his own sexual relationships, his own recollections, his own self." Although on occasions Hunt's prose is convoluted, and at times it is difficult to accept the parallels he stresses, in general he has written a useful, provocative book.

### b) General Articles about Updike

Two excellent general articles on Updike focusing on the religious implications of his work are reprinted in this volume: Bernard Schopen, "Faith, Morality, and the Novels of John Updike"; and Victor Strandberg, "John Updike and the Changing of the Gods."[62] In addition to these essays, the following religiously oriented studies should be mentioned:

Alice and Kenneth Hamilton, "The Validation of Religious Faith in the Writings of John Updike" (in which they trace the consistent opposition in Updike's work—which they call an "apologetic"—up to *Buchanan Dying* between Christian faith and "a culturally dominant humanism"); Sue Mitchell Crowley, "John Updike: The Rubble of Footnotes Bound into Kierkegaard"; George Hunt, "Updike's Pilgrims in a World of Nothingness"; and Terence Doody, "Updike's Idea of Reification." Doody's unusual approach is particularly worthy of note. Arguing against "the kind of allegorical readings that are the least interesting interpretations of Updike's work," Doody posits the "idea of reification . . . based upon the idea of God's existence" that Updike has been developing since *The Poorhouse Fair*. The writer, Doody argues, believes that things are not "nullity," but are suggestive of God, and that there is an "immanence" in things; a related proposition is that "human nature is best thought of as a state of matter; that people are really things." The belief has implications for Updike's style: "because of its tactile intimacy and great patience with the surface of things, [the style] is an act of reverence toward those things in which God is imminent." There are, moreover, implications for Updike's treatment of ethical questions. "Morality is a relative matter compared to the absolutes of life, which are death and the physical relations of bodies to each other." Love is seen as a twin of gravity and implies fatality: "Updike is arguing that sex is beyond conventional moral categories." Seen from this perspective, the narrator of *A Month of Sundays* (Doody's analysis of this novel is very interesting) is not writing a confession, nor is he interested in refurbishing his marriage or his vocation. He "wants something deeper: an ontological confirmation, a substantiation that is literal." The novel ends "with the intimation that identity, morality, and community are less important than the gravitation of human bodies."[63]

Four other general statements about Updike should also be mentioned here: Mary Allen's "John Updike's Love of 'Dull Bovine Beauty'," in her *The Necessary Blankness: Women in Major American Fiction of the 1960's*; Josephine Hendin's "The Victim Is a Hero," in her *Vulnerable People: A View of American Fiction Since 1945*; David Thorburn's introduction to the *Twentieth Century Views* collection of criticism; and Joyce Carol Oates's superb "Updike's American Comedies." Allen argues for Updike's dependence in his fiction on the idea of the "undeniably stupid woman," observing about *Rabbit Redux*, for example: "something sinister occurs in Updike's writing: he allows his bias on behalf of the stupid-sexual woman to intrude to the point of forcing a violent death . . . upon the intelligent girl [Jill] whom he dislikes and cannot deal with"! Josephine Hendin's analysis of Updike's treatment of sexual relationships is much more intelligent than Allen's. Observing that "What Updike bares in his beleagured male chauvinists are the forces that keep men rivitted on women as the solitary source of meaning in life," Hendin focuses on one force—the oedipal conflict—using her analysis of it as the impetus for comments like the following: "Joey's [*Of the Farm*] self-hatred turns to hatred for his wife who is the living sign of his bad taste"; "What Updike embeds in the story [*The Centaur*] is how primal and engulfing male hatred of women can be." Much of what Hendin says in her unscholarly study (there are no footnotes) is overstated; usually, however, there is enough truth in her hyperbole (and her analysis of *Marry Me* is very good) to compel the reader to reconsider his response to Updike's fiction. David Thorburn's introduction to the *Twentieth Century Views* collection on Updike is a brief, well written overview, with acute comments on *Marry Me*. Thorburn suggests, for example, that this novel is *Couples* stripped and re-visited, with Updike's plain names for his characters signaling his "reluctance to impose any abstract religious symbolism on their fiercely ambiguous behavior." In the story, all is "exposed as projection of his [Jerry's] ego, as unconscious strategems for eliciting sympathy and mothering care from his wife and mistress."[64]

Joyce Carol Oates's "Updike's American Comedies" is a beautifully written, continually suggestive appreciation of her fellow novelist. According to Oates, Updike's "genius is best exited by the lyric possibilities of tragic events that, failing to justify themselves as tragedy, turn unaccountably into comedies." Updike's preference is "to glance without judgement on all sides of a melodramatic situation." His work exhibits a quality seldom recognized by critics—"a basic clownishness . . . which gives it its energy, its high worth." Yet, "when the comic vision is weak in Updike's writing, a terrifying nihilism beckons," as in the "middle-aged weariness of *Rabbit Redux*." Often, Oates speculates about Updike's characters as possible projections of himself: Chiron/Caldwell, for example, who "accepts the comic ironies and inadequacies of ordinary life"; Bech, who "gives voice to suspicions Updike may play with but cannot take seriously"; Rabbit, "Updike's conception of Updike without talent, Updike trapped in quantity"; Piet, one of the few recent characters "who can somehow synthesize the knowledge of human 'valuing' with a religious faith that sustains it while reducing it to scale."[65] Oates has written an extremely generous tribute to a writer very different from herself.

*c). Articles about Updike's Specific Works*

Among the articles which should be mentioned, but which do not contribute a great deal to one's knowledge or appreciation of the work discussed, are the following: William Peden's "Metropolis, Village, and Suburbia: The Short Fiction of Manners" ("At their best and taken singly, these stories are a triumph of the art of the usual. . . . At their least successful, or taken in large, sustained doses, however, they seem trivial rather than significant"); several studies of *Rabbit, Run* (that of Wiley Lee Umphlett in his *The Sporting Myth and the American Experience*; Albert Wilhelm's "The Clothing Motif in Updike's *Rabbit, Run*"; Paul

Borgman's "The Tragic Hero of Updike's *Rabbit, Run*"—"Rabbit's quest is tragic because it is simultaneously so much better than the seeking and accepting of those around him, while so much worse for everyone, including Rabbit, because the quest is forced inward"; Ralph Lundrén's "*Dark Laughter* and *Rabbit, Run*: Studies in Instinctive Behavior"—"*Rabbit, Run* could well have been written as a counter-statement to *Dark Laughter*"; and Wayne McGinnes' "Salvation by Death in *Rabbit, Run*"); one essay touching on *The Centaur*—Thomas LeClair's "Death and Black Humor" (after a lengthy discussion of the pessimistic treatment of death in black humor, LeClair contrasts this with *The Centaur*: "In its proud elegiac tone, the novel implicitly honors Caldwell senior's religious acceptance of immortality and devalues Peter's responses to death, love and art."); and two studies of *Couples* (William Wahl's long, vapid chapter in *Essays in Honor of Professor Tyrus Hillway*, and Linda Plagman's reasonable, "Eros and Agape: The Opposition in Updike's *Couples*)."[66]

Three good articles on Updike's short stories appeared during this period: George Hunt's on "Leaves" (reprinted in this volume); William Shurr's "The Lutheran Experience in John Updike's 'Pigeon Feathers' " (Updike traces parallels between Luther's moment of conversion as described in Norman Brown's *Life Against Death* and David Kern's experience: "David seems typologically another Luther, fleeing the same enemies again in his own experience"); and Robert Waxman's "Invitation to Dread: John Updike's Metaphysical Quest." For Waxman, two short "fragment" stories—"Packed Dirt, . . ." and "My Grandmother's Thimble . . . "—illustrate clearly, "the struggle between Barth's insistence on God's totally transcendent nature, hence man's complete dependence on His acts of grace, and Pascal's approach to God through anxiety, disillusionment and despair." Waxman observes that, although it is true that we "need ceremonies" (as David Kern says at the end of "My Grandmother's Thimble . . ."), "even more directly do we hunger for a new revelation, a bursting of the spirit's sleep which will make a ceremony a joyous and organic part of our lives."[67]

There were no individual articles on *The Poorhouse Fair*, although the novel was mentioned, usually only in passing, in several of the books and general studies discussed above. The most illuminating comments on *Rabbit, Run* appear in an article whose primary focus is on *Rabbit Redux*: Yves Le Pellec's "Rabbit Underground." In this dense, very interesting study, Le Pellec reveals how "the author plays on the intentional shuttle which modifies the separate meaning of each book." He suggests, for example, that Skeeter in the second book has replaced Rabbit "as a flagbearer of saintliness" and is meant to signal the "absurdity inherent in the mystical enterprise"; that the inside/outside polarity of the first book has been reversed in the second (in which Rabbit's home gradually becomes an underground fortress); that Bech's *Travel Light* is "the picaresque novel *Rabbit, Run* would have been" if Updike had allowed Rabbit to roam. Le Pellec predicts—since he observes no essential change in the passivity of the second Rabbit throughout the book—that "Updike probably will not wake him up again, for a third Rabbit might be a Rabbit Redundant."[68]

Two excellent articles on *The Centaur* are reprinted in this volume (by James Mellard and Suzanne Henning Uphaus). Another thoughtful article is R. W. Hoag's "A Second Controlling Myth in John Updike's *The Centaur*." The myth referred to in the title is Camus' version of Sisyphus, whose relevance to the novel Hoag convincingly demonstrates, concluding that, after George "transcends his long-cherished martyrdom" and his "compulsive good deeds" by providing genuine aid to his son (during the storm), "George and Peter become each other's rock."[69]

An intelligent reading of *Couples* is contained in Howard Eiland's "Play in *Couples*." Eiland clearly reveals the Jamesian subtlety in the novel through his analysis of the complex ways in which play and metaphors for it (including adultery, which combines "sport and theatre") are made to function. After the many articles exploring the religious meanings in the novel, it is refreshing to read a sensitive study about *Couples* as a kind of novel of manners.[70]

Two good articles were published during this period on *A Month of Sundays*. The argument in one—George Hunt's "Updike's Omega-Shaped Shelter: Structure and Psyche in *A Month of Sundays*"—in essence appears in Hunt's book on Updike, which has been discussed above. The other article is Suzanne Henning Uphaus' "The Unified Vision of *A Month of Sundays*" (a truncated version of this article appears in her book on Updike). Her argument is that, in the process of moving from woman to woman and ending with Ms. Prynne, Marshfield comes finally to a point where he can unite body and soul, faith and good works, and move from his subjectivity out into the world. For Uphaus, Marshfield's increasing awareness of others is suggested by the progress of his sermons and involvement with the disturbed preachers, and mirrored in his increasingly close relationship with the reader. Uphaus mars her analysis with a silly allegorical suggestion about "Marshfield's progression among various ladies . . . epitomizing the large movements of American religious history."[71] Most of the article, however, is plausible and interesting. Readers interested in Updike's other work should consult the books and general articles discussed above.

## D. CONCLUSION

Because they appear at the end of an already lengthy introduction, the comments here will be brief about the reviews and essays in this text; the assumption is that they will speak well for themselves. The reviews have been chosen not only because they are, in a sense, representative, but also because they are unusual, continuing as they do to comment clearly on the works whose newness they originally confronted. The reprinted essays appear because they are among the best examples of academic criticism on John Updike. Five articles are published here for the first time. George Searles attempts to remind readers of something they may have forgotten—the importance and excellence of John Updike's first novel, *The Poorhouse Fair*. Gordon Slethaug, in his detailed analysis of the treatment of freedom in *Rabbit Redux*, clearly implies the worth of Updike's most critically neglected and undervalued major novel. Kathleen Verduin, in her discussion of "fatherly presences" in Updike, adds to the large body of perceptive critical literature that has traced the links between his fiction and theology. Gary Waller observes a conflict in *A Month of Sundays* between Updike the religious writer and Updike the would-be metafictionist. Finally, Joyce Markle ponders the possible influence of that supreme metafictionist—Vladimir Nabokov—on the confusing world of *The Coup*. It is hoped that readers of these new essays will find them to be genuine contributions to John Updike scholarship.

## Notes

1. C. Clarke Taylor, *John Updike: A Bibliography* (Kent, Ohio: Kent State University Press, 1968); David Arnason and B. A. Sokoloff, *John Updike: A Comprehensive Bibliography* (Darby, Pa.: Darby Press, 1970; Folcroft, Pa.: Folcroft Press, 1971; Norwood, Pa.: Norwood Press, 1973. Limited editions); Michael Olivas, *An Annotated Bibliography of John Updike Criticism 1967–73, and a Checklist of his Works* (New York: Garland Publishing Co., 1975); and Elizabeth A. Gearhart, *John Updike: A Comprehensive Bibliography with Selected Annotations* (Norwood, Pa.: Norwood Press, 1978).

2. Arlin Meyer and Michael Olivas, "Criticism of John Updike: A Selected Checklist," *Modern Fiction Studies*, 20(1974), 121–33.

3. John Updike, *Assorted Prose* (New York: Alfred A. Knopf, 1965). Henceforth, specific references to this collection will be made in the body of the text; Jane Howard, "Can a Nice Novelist Finish First?" *Life*, 4 Nov. 1966, pp. 74–82; "View from the Catacombs," *Time*, 26 April 1968, pp. 66–68 ff; and James Atlas, "John Updike Breaks out of Suburbia," *The New York Times Magazine*, 10 Dec. 1978, pp. 60–64, 68–76.

4. John Updike, *Picked-Up Pieces* (New York: Alfred A. Knopf, 1975), p. xix. Henceforth, references to this collection will be made in the body of the text.

5. George Hunt S.J., *John Updike and the three great secret things: Sex, Religion, and Art* (Grand Rapids, Mich.: Wm. B. Eerdmans, 1980), p. 84.

6. Edward Vargo, *Rainstorms and Fire: Ritual in the Novels of John Updike* (Port Washington, N.Y.: Kennikat Press, 1973).

7. Charles Samuels, "The Art of Fiction XLIII: John Updike," *Paris Review*, 12(Winter 1968), 84–117; Eric Rhode, "BBC Interview with John Updike," *The Listener*, 81(1969), 862–64; and Frank Gado, "A Conversation with John Updike;" *The Idol*, 47(Spring 1971), 3–32. Reprinted in *First Person* (Syracuse, N.Y.: Syracuse University Press, 1973), pp. 80–109.

8. Richard Burgen, "A Conversation with John Updike," *New York Arts Journal*, Nos. 9 and 11 (1978). Reprinted in *John Updike Newsletter*, Nos. 10 and 11 (Spring and Summer 1979), n. pag.

9. Thomas E. Cassidy, "The Enchantment of the Ordinary," *Commonweal*, 11 Sept. 1959, p. 499; William Peden, "Minor Ills that Plague the Human Heart," *The New York Times Book Review*, 16 Aug. 1959, p. 5; Richard Gilman, "A Last Assertion of Personal Being," *Commonweal*, 6 Feb. 1959, pp. 499–500; and "Cool, Cool World," *Time*, 17 Aug. 1959, p. 98.

10. Granville Hicks, "A Little Good in Evil," *Saturday Review*, 5 Nov. 1960, p. 28. Reprinted in his *Literary Horizons* (New York: New York University Press, 1970), pp. 110–13.

11. Richard Lyons, "A High E.Q.," *Minnesota Review*, 1(1961), 385–89.

12. Arthur Mizener, "Behind the Dazzle Is a Knowing Eye," *New York Times Book Review*, 18 March 1962, pp. 1, 29; and "Put and Take," *Time*, 16 March 1962, p. 86.

13. Dean Doner, "Rabbit Angstrom's Unseen World," in *New World Writing 20*, ed. Steward Richardson and Corlies M. Smith (Philadelphia: J. B. Lippincott, 1962), pp. 63–75. Reprinted in Howard Eiland and David Thorburn, ed., *John Updike: A Collection of Critical Essays* (Englewood Cliffs, N.J.: Prentice-Hall, 1979). Henceforth, referred to as Eiland and Thorburn.

14. John Ward, "John Updike's Fiction," *Critique*, 5(Spring–Summer 1962), 27–40.

15. Vereen Bell, "A Study in Frustration," *Shenandoah*, 14(Summer 1963), 69–72.

16. Norman Podhoretz, "A Dissent on Updike," *Show*, 3(April 1963), 49–52. Reprinted in Norman Podhoretz, *Doings and Undoings: The Fifties and After in American Writing* (New York: Farrar Straus, 1964), pp. 251–57.

17. Guerin La Course, "The Innocence of John Updike," *Commonweal*, 8 Feb. 1963, pp. 512–14.

18. Arthur Mizener, "The American Hero as High School Boy: Peter Caldwell," in his *The Sense of Life in the Modern Novel* (Boston: Houghton Mifflin, 1964), pp. 247–66.

19. Michael Novak, "Updike's Search for Liturgy," *Commonweal*, 10 May 1963, pp. 192–95. Reprinted in Thorburn and Eiland (op. cit., note 13), pp. 183–91.

20. Robert Detweiler, "John Updike and the Indictment of Culture—Protestantism," in his *Four Spiritual Crises in Mid-Century American Fiction*, University of Florida Monographs, No. 14 (Gainesville, Florida: University of Florida Press, 1963), pp. 14–24.

21. Norman Mailer, "Norman Mailer versus Nine Writers," *Esquire*, July 1963, pp. 63–69, 105. Reprinted in his *Cannibals and Christians* (New York: Dial Press, 1966), pp. 120–22.

22. M.M., "The Ring," *Christian Science Monitor*, 5 Nov. 1964, p. 8.

23. "Narrowing Compass," *Time*, 12 Nov. 1965, p. 118.

24. John Aldridge, "The Private Vice of John Updike," in his *Time to Murder and Create: The Contemporary Novel in Crisis* (New York: David McKay, 1966), pp. 164–70.

25. Granville Hicks, "They Also Serve Who Write Well," *Saturday Review*, 15 May 1965, pp. 25–26. Reprinted in his *Literary Horizons*, pp. 120–23.

26. William Stafford, "Fiction: 1930 to the Present," in *American Literary Scholarship: An Annual/1964*, ed. James Woodress (Durham, N.C.: Duke University Press, 1966), p. 166.

27. William Van O'Connor, "John Updike and William Styron: The Burden of Talent," in *Contemporary American Novelists*, ed. Harry T. Moore (Carbondale, Ill.: Southern Illinois University Press, 1964), pp. 205–21; William Peden, *The American Short Story: Front Line in the National Defense of Literature*, 1st ed. (Boston: Houghton Mifflin, 1964), pp. 68–72; Paul Doyle, "Updike's Fiction: Motifs and Techniques," *Catholic World*, Sept. 1964, pp. 356–62; Thaddeus Muradian, "The World of John Updike," *English Journal*, 54(1965), 577–84: Norris Yates "The Doubt and Faith of John Updike," *College English*, 26(1965), 469–74; Sister Judith Tate, "Of Rabbits and Centaurs," *Critic*, Feb./March 1964, pp. 44–51; and Hazel Guyol, "The Lord Loves a Cheerful Corpse," *English Journal*, 55(1966), 863–66.

28. David Galloway, "The Absurd Man as Saint: The Novels of John Updike," *Modern*

*Fiction Studies*, 11(1964), 111–27. Reprinted in his *The Absurd Hero in American Fiction*, (Austin: University of Texas Press, 1966. Rev. ed., 1970), pp. 21–50.

29. Sidney Finklestein, "Acceptance of Alienation: John Updike and James Purdy," in his *Existentialism and Alienation in American Literature* (New York: International Publishers, 1965), pp. 243–52.

30. Charles Walcutt, "The Centripetal Action: John Updike's *The Centaur* and *Rabbit, Run* and Wright Morris' *One Day*" in *Man's Changing Mask: Modes and Methods of Characterization in Fiction* (Minneapolis: University of Minnesota Press, 1966), pp. 326–32.

31. Inna Levidova, "John Updike's *The Centaur* in Russia," *Soviet Literature*, 10(1965), 188–94.

32. Jane Howard, op. cit., note 3.

33. Granville Hicks, "God Has Gone, Sin Is Left," *Saturday Review*, 6 April 1968, pp. 21–22; reprinted in his *Literary Horizons*, pp. 128–32; "A View from the Catacombs," op. cit., note 3.

34. The review by Gass is reprinted in the chapter entitled "Cock-a-doodle-do" in his *Fiction and the Figures of Life* (New York: Alfred Knopf, 1970), pp. 206–11.

35. Michael Novak, "Son of the Group," *Critic*, June/July 1968, pp. 72–74; John Ditsky, "Roth, Updike, and the High Expense of Spirit," *University of Windsor Review*, 5(Fall 1969), pp. 111–20; and John Peter, "The Self-Effacement of the Novelist," *The Malahat Review*, 8(Oct. 1968), 119–28.

36. Richard Locke, "Rabbit Redux," *The New York Times Book Review*, 7 Nov. 1971, pp. 1, 2 ff (reprinted as "Rabbit's Progress" in Thorburn and Eiland, pp. 35–38); Robert Alter, "Updike, Malamud, and the Fire This Time," *Commentary*, October 1972, pp. 68–74 (reprinted in Thorburn and Eiland, pp. 39–49); Christopher Ricks, "Flopsy Bunny," *The New York Review of Books*, 26 Dec. 1971, pp. 7–9; Charles Samuels, "Updike on the Present," *New Republic*, 20 Nov. 1970, pp. 29–30; and William Stafford, " 'The Curious Greased Grace' of John Updike: Some of his Critics and the American Tradition," *Journal of Modern Literature*, 2(1972), 569–75.

37. Anne Gates, "John Updike—Wearing his Poet's Hat," *Christian Science Monitor*, 15 Aug. 1969, p. 9; Tony Tanner, "Museums and Women," *The New York Times Book Review*, 22 Oct. 1972, pp. 5, 24; and Matthew Hartman, "Museums and Women and Other Stories," *Library Journal*, 97(1972), 2649.

38. Alice and Kenneth Hamilton, *John Updike: A Critical Essay* (Grand Rapids, Mich.: William B. Eerdmans, 1967).

39. Charles Samuels, *John Updike* (Minneapolis: University of Minnesota Press, 1965).

40. Alice and Kenneth Hamilton, *The Elements of John Updike* (Grand Rapids, Mich.: William B. Eerdmans, 1970).

41. Rachael Burchard, *John Updike: Yea Sayings* (Carbondale: Southern Illinois University Press, 1971).

42. Larry Taylor, *Pastoral and Anti-Pastoral Patterns in John Updike's Fiction* (Carbondale: Southern Illinois University Press, 1971).

43. Robert Detweiler, *John Updike* (New York: Twayne, 1972).

44. *Rainstorms and Fire*, op. cit., note 6.

45. Joyce Markle, *Fighters and Lovers: Theme in the Novels of John Updike* (New York: New York University Press, 1973).

46. Richard Rupp, "John Updike: Style in Search of a Centre," *Sewanee Review*, 75(1967), 693–709; reprinted in his *Celebration in Postwar American Fiction, 1945–1967* with a "Postscript" on *Couples* (Coral Gables, Florida: University of Miami Press, 1970), pp. 41–57, 210–18; Bryant Wyatt, "John Updike: The Psychological Novel in Search of a Structure," *Twentieth Century Literature*, 13(1967), 88–96; John Hill, "Quest for Belief: Theme in

the Novels of John Updike," *Southern Humanities Review*, 3(1969), 166–178; Joseph Waldmeir, "Only an Occasional Rutabaga: American Fiction since 1945," *Modern Fiction Studies*, 15(1969/70), 467–81; and Robert Gingher, "Has John Updike Anything to Say?" *Modern Fiction Studies*, 20(1974), 97–105.

47. Granville Hicks, "John Updike" in his *Literary Horizons* (op. cit., note 10), pp. 107–33; James Gindin, *Harvest of a Quiet Eye: The Novel of Compassion* (Bloomington: Indiana University Press, 1971), pp. 343–46; and Alfred Kazin, "Professional Observers: Cozzens to Updike," in his *Bright Book of Life: American Novelists and Storytellers from Hemingway to Mailer* (Boston and Toronto: Little, Brown and Company, 1973), pp. 95–124.

48. Howard Harper, "John Updike and the Intrinsic Problem of Human Existence" in his *Desperate Faith: A Study of Bellow, Salinger, Mailer, Baldwin, and Updike* (Chapel Hill: The University of North Carolina Press, 1967), pp. 162–90; H. Petter, "John Updike's Metaphoric Novels," *English Studies*, 50(1969), 197–206; Tony Tanner, "A Compromised Environment," in his *City of Words: American Fiction 1950–70* (New York: Harper and Row, 1971), pp. 273–94; first published as "The American Novelist as Entropologist," *London Magazine*, October 1970, pp. 5–18; S. A. Zylstra, "John Updike and the Parabolic Nature of the World," *Soundings*, 56(1973), 323–37; and Robert Regan, "Updike's Symbol of the Centre," *Modern Fiction Studies*, 20(1974), 77–96.

49. Robert McCoy, "John Updike's Literary Apprenticeship in the *Harvard Lampoon*," *Modern Fiction Studies*, 20(1974), 3–12; Elizabeth Matson, "A Chinese Paradox, But Not Much of One: John Updike in his Poetry," *Minnesota Review*, 8(1967), 157–67; and Alice and Kenneth Hamilton, "Theme and Technique in John Updike's *Midpoint*," *Mosaic*, 4(1970), 79–106.

50. Elmer Suderman, "Art as a Way of Knowing," *Discourse*, 12(1968), 3–14; and Ellen Baldeshwiler, "The Lyric Short Story: The Sketch of a History," *Studies in Short Fiction*, 6(1969), 443–53.

51. R. W. Reising; "Updike's 'A Sense of Shelter,' " *Studies in Short Fiction*, 7(1970), 651–52; A. S. G. Edwards, "Updike's 'A Sense of Shelter'," *Studies in Short Fiction*, 8(1971), 467–68; Robert Sykes, "A Commentary on Updike's 'Astronomer'," *Studies in Short Fiction*, 8(1971), 575–79, Gilbert Porter, "John Updike's 'A and P': The Establishment and an Emersonian Cashier," *English Journal*, 61(1972), 1175–78; Albert Griffith, 'Updike's Artist's Dilemma: 'Should Wizard Hit Mommy?'," *Modern Fiction Studies*, 20(1974), 111–15; and Alfred Rosa, "The Psycholinguistics of Updike's 'Museums and Women'," *Modern Fiction Studies*, 20(1974), 107–11.

52. W. W. de Grummond, "Classical Influence in *The Poorhouse Fair*," *American Notes and Queries*, 13(1974), 21–23.

53. J. C. Stubbs, "Search for Perfection in *Rabbit, Run*," *Critique*, 10, No. 2 (1968), 94–101; Clinton Burhans Jr., "Things Falling Apart: Structure and Theme in *Rabbit, Run*," *Studies in the Novel*, 5(1973), 336–51; and Joseph Waldmeir, "It's the Going That's Important, Not the Getting There: Rabbit's Questing Non-Quest," *Modern Fiction Studies*, 20(1974), 13–27.

54. Alvin Alley, "*The Centaur*:Transcendental Imagination and Metaphoric Death," *English Journal*, 56(1967), 982–85; Wesley Kort, "*The Centaur* and the Problem of Vocation," in his *Shriven Selves: Religious Problems in Recent American Fiction* (Philadelphia: Fortress Press, 1972), pp. 64–89; Edward Vargo, "The Necessity of Myth in Updike's *The Centaur*," *PLMA*, 88(1973), 452–60 (reprinted in his *Rainstorms and Fire*, op. cit., note 6); and John B. Vickery, "*The Centaur*: Myth, History, and Narrative," *Modern Fiction Studies*, 20(1974), 29–43.

55. Joyce Flint, "John Updike and *Couples*: The Wasp's Dilemma," *Research Studies*, 36(1968), 340–47; David Lodge, "Post-Pill Paradise: John Updike's *Couples*," *New Blackfriars*, Nov. 1970, pp. 511–18; reprinted in his *The Novelist at the Crossroads* (Ithaca, N.Y.: Cornell University Press, 1972) and in Eiland and Thorburn, pp. 84–92; and Robert

Detweiler, "Updike's *Couples*: Eros Demythologized," *Twentieth Century Literature*, 17(1971), 235–46 (reprinted in his *John Updike*, op. cit., note 43).

56. Gary Waller, "Updike's *Couples*: A Barthian Parable," *Research Studies*, 40(1972), 10–21; Roger Sharrock, "Singles and Couples: Hemingway's *Farewell to Arms* and Updike's *Couples*," *Ariel*, 4(1973), 21–43; Paula and Nick Backscheider, "Updike's *Couples*: A Squeak in the Night," *Modern Fiction Studies*, 20(1974), 45–52; and Alan McKenzie, " 'A Craftsman's Intimate Satisfactions': The Parlor Games in *Couples*," *Modern Fiction Studies*, 20(1974), 53–58.

57. Alice and Kenneth Hamilton, "Metamorphosis Through Art: Updike's *Bech: A Book*," *Queens Quarterly*, 77(1970), 624–36.

58. John Gordon, "Updike Redux," *Ramparts*, April 1972, pp. 56–59; Kermit Turner, "Rabbit Brought Nowhere: John Updike's *Rabbit Redux*," *South Carolina Review*, 8(1972), 35–42; Eugene Lyons, "John Updike: The Beginning and the End," *Critique*, 14, No. 2(1972), 44–59; Wayne Falke, "*Rabbit Redux*: Time/Order/God," *Modern Fiction Studies*, 20(1974), 59–75; and Andrew Horton, "Ken Kesey, John Updike and the Lone Ranger," *Journal of Popular Culture*, 8(1974), 570–78.

59. Peter Prescott, "To Have and to Hold," *Newsweek*, 8 Nov. 1976, p. 103; and Brigid Brophy, "Love in the Garden State," *Harper's Magazine*, Dec. 1976, pp. 80–82.

60. George Stade, "The Resurrection of Reverend Marshfield," *New York Times Book Review*, 23 Feb. 1975, p. 4; Rosemary Dinnage, review of *Month of Sundays*, *TLS*, July 4 1975, p. 713; David Thorburn, "Recent Novels: Realism Redux," *Yale Review*, 66(1977), 584–85; Brigid Brophy; Daphne Markins, "Updike in Africa," *New Leader*, Dec. 4 1978, pp. 21–22; and Douglas Hill, "Rabbit Angstrom, I presume?" *Books in Canada*, March 1979, pp. 12–13.

61. Suzanne Henning Uphaus, *John Updike* (New York: Frederick Ungar, 1980); and George Hunt, op. cit., Note 5.

62. Bernard Schopen, "Faith, Morality, and the Novels of John Updike," *Twentieth Century Literature*, 24(1978), 523–35; and Victor Strandberg, "John Updike and the Changing of the Gods," *Mosaic*, 12(1978), 157–75.

63. Alice and Kenneth Hamilton, "The Validation of Religious Faith in the Writings of John Updike," *Studies in Religion*, 5(1976), 275–85; Sue Mitchell Crowley, "John Updike: The Rubble of Footnotes Bound into Kierkegaard," *Journal of American Academy of Religion*, 45(1976), 1011–35; George Hunt, "Updike's Pilgrims in a World of Nothingness," *Thought*, 53(1977), 384–400; and Terence Doody, "Updike's Idea of Reification," *Contemporary Literature*, 20(1979), 204–20.

64. Mary Allen, "John Updike's Love of 'Dull Bovine Beauty,' " in her *The Necessary Blankness: Women in Major American Fiction of the 1960's* (Urbana: University of Illinois Press, 1976), pp. 97–132; Josephine Hendin, "The Victim Is a Hero," in her *Vulnerable People: A View of American Fiction Since 1945* (New York: Oxford University Press, 1978), pp. 88–99; and David Thorburn, "Introduction: 'Alive in a Place and Time'," in Eiland and Thorburn, pp. 1–9.

65. Joyce Carol Oates, "Updike's American Comedies," *Modern Fiction Studies*, 21(1975), 459–72; reprinted in Eiland and Thorburn, pp. 53–68.

66. William Peden, "Metropolis, Village, and Suburbia: The Short Fiction of Manners," in his *The American Short Story*, 2nd ed. (Boston: Houghton Mifflin, 1975), pp. 30–68; Wiley Lee Umphlett, *The Sporting Myth and the American Experience* (Lewisburg, N.Y.: Bucknell University Press, 1975); Albert Wilhelm, "The Clothing Motif in Updike's *Rabbit, Run*," *South Atlantic Bulletin*, 40(1975), 87–89; Paul Borgman, "The Tragic Hero of Updike's *Rabbit, Run*," *Renascence*, 29(1977), 106–12; Ralph Lundren, "*Dark Laughter* and *Rabbit, Run*: Studies in Instinctive Behavior," *Studia Neophilologica*, 49(1977), 59–68; Wayne McGinnes, "Salvation by Death in *Rabbit, Run*," *Notes on Contemporary Literature*, 8(1978), 7–8;

Thomas Le Clair, "Death and Black Humor," *Critique*, 17, No. 1(1975), 5–40; William Wahl, "Updike's World and *Couples*," in *Essays in Honour of Professor Tyrus Hillway*, ed. Erwin Stütz (Salzburg: Salzburg Universität, 1977), pp. 256–95; and Linda Plagman, "Eros and Agape: The Opposition in Updike's *Couples*," *Renascence*, 28(1976), 83–93.

67. George Hunt, "Reality, Imagination, and Art: The Significance of Updike's 'Best' Story," *Studies in Short Fiction*, 16(1979), 219–29; William Shurr, "The Lutheran Experience in John Updike's 'Pigeon Feathers'," *Studies in Short Fiction*, 14(1977), 329–35; and Robert Waxman, "Invitation to Dread: John Updike's Metaphysical Quest," *Renascence*, 29(1977), 201–10.

68. Yves Le Pellec, "Rabbit Underground," in *Les Américanistes: New French Criticism on Modern American Fiction*, Ira D. and Christiane Johnson, ed. (Port Washington, N.Y., and London: Kennikat Press, 1978), pp. 94–109.

69. James Mellard, "The Novel as Lyric Elegy: The Mode of Updike's *The Centaur*," *Texas Studies in Literature and Language*, 21(1979), 112–27; Suzanne Henning Uphaus, "*The Centaur*: Updike's Mock Epic," *Journal of Narrative Technique*, 7(1977), 24–36; and R. W. Hoag, "A Second Controlling Myth in John Updike's *The Centaur*," *Studies in the Novel*, 11(1979), 446–53.

70. Howard Eiland, "*Play in Couples*," Eiland and Thorburn, 69–83.

71. George Hunt, "Updike's Omega-Shaped Shelter: Structure and Psyche in *A Month of Sundays*," *Critique* 19, no. 3(1978), 47–60; and Suzanne Henning Uphaus, "The Unified Vision of *A Month of Sundays*," *University of Windsor Review*, 12(Spring/Summer 1977), 5–16.

# REVIEWS

# Writer's Writer

**Whitney Balliett***

Since the successful poetic novel—for lack of a more precise term—has long been the most rarefied form of prose fiction, John Updike, the poet and short-story writer, has done a startling thing in his first novel, "The Poorhouse Fair" (Knopf), by producing, with almost academic precision, a classic, if not flawless, example of one. A liqueur distilled and aged alongside the great, whale-size fiction chronicles of Tolstoy, Balzac, Dickens, and Proust by such as Mark Twain, Forster, Hemingway, Faulkner, T. F. Powys, Richard Hughes, St. Exupery, Ivy Compton-Burnett, and—to bring the list right down to the tape—Malcolm Lowry, Eudora Welty, Vladimir Nabokov, Penelope Mortimer, and Mr. Updike, the poetic novel is characterized mainly by (1) a prose that, falling in the queer land just this side of pure poetry, is tight but never brittle, that is breaded with simile and metaphor, and that continually suggests, but never apes, the beat and flow of poetry, and by (2) a semi-philosophical moralistic vision (of a better world, of a declining world, of tradition preserved, or the like), which rises like an intangible mountain at the end of the book, forming, in a sense, a second and endless ending. A third and less apparent element is the form's overall reliance on the sort of tough, hounding selectivity of materials that, again, reaches its greatest intensity in poetry. It is this selectivity that is at the back of most of Hemingway's dialogue in his earlier work—dialogue, certainly, that was never spoken in life but that, because of its foreshortened imitation of life, effected through poetic ellipses and rhythms, has so often perversely tricked its admirers into thinking of it as archetypically realistic.

Mr. Updike has adhered to these rules with such knowing and steadfast intentness that what he has written is not so much a novel as a kind of poetic vision, tied loosely to earth only by its outward form of narrative prose. (The price for such exertion has, unfortunately, been dear; whatever emotional content first propelled the author has been exhausted, or perhaps only disguised—a peculiarity that deserves to be taken up only after the book's virtues.) A more obvious but equally untoward aspect of

*Review of *The Poorhouse Fair*. From *The New Yorker*, 34 (February 7, 1959), 138–42. Reprinted by permission; © 1959 The New Yorker Magazine, Inc.

"The Poorhouse Fair" is that it couldn't be farther from the thinly veiled, self-purgative catalogue of an author's adolescence that constitutes the usual first novel. Indeed, it seeks to enter into the minds of people ranging from their seventies well into their nineties, and, within the book's purposes, succeeds—no mean feat for a novelist born in 1932. As if to unshakably reinforce this switch, Mr. Updike has also set his novel in the America of the early nineteen-seventies. It is a horrible place he envisions, and this adds one more unusual dimension to the book; it is also a work of the macabre, far more littered with decay and disorder than any of the brooding mountains or melancholy Venice of Thomas Mann. The story takes place on the annual Fair Day at the Diamond County Home for the Aged, in New Jersey, and is concerned with the ideological struggle between a handful of the inmates—John Hook, their leader and a ninety-four-year-old ex-schoolteacher; Billy Gregg, a retired electrician; George Lucas, a former farmer and real-estate man—and the head of the institution, a young man named Conner. Hook is a frail, stately, ethereal creature, whose universe rests squarely on God, and Conner is a plump, neat, morbidly oversensitive idealist and atheist, who, in his three years at the home, has revealed himself as a kind of inhuman humanist. Hook represents the old In-God-We-Trust America of unfettered nature, ornate political debate, and things made by hand of wood, while Conner is the new America, in which medicine has become free, the Republic Party has disappeared, homosexuality flourishes, teen-agers no longer neck but instead strip off their clothes and merely ogle one another, no one remembers how to read a sundial, old people live on and on in more and more homes for old people, and peace lies on the land like a layer of fat. (Seldom has symbolism been more adroitly and subtly used; Hook and Conner seem to waft invisibly and at no exact time into their separate roles.) Most important, it is a place where old-fashioned virtue, according to Hook, has vanished. He defines it as

> An austerity of the hunt, a manliness from which comes all life, so that it can be written that the woman takes her life from the man. As the Indian once served the elusive deer he hunted men once served invisible goals, and grew hard in such service and pursuit, and lent their society an indispensable temper. Impotent to provide this tempering salt, men would sink lower than women, as indeed they had. Women are the heroes of dead lands.

But this strange hand-me-down nostalgia for times unknown to the author himself never spreads into sentimentality, for it is continually ringed by a feeling of dread that is never allowed out of the reader's mind. During the day, an ominous storm breaks, temporarily postponing the fair and realizing Conner's fear that "the weather of this one day would be . . . a judgment on his work;" a grizzly one-eyed cat, festering with disease, appears on the grounds; Gregg, a horribly exaggerated Lear's

Fool, ceaselessly fills the air with insane curses; a teen-ager, delivering soda pop in a truck, knocks over part of the old stone wall surrounding the grounds, his head blocked with the memory of his girl's bare stomach, viewed, but not touched, the night before; Conner, on a freakish impulse, is harmlessly stoned by the inmates. At the same time, the surface reality of the book is thickly infused with a dark, feverish surrealism. Lucas visits the infirmary for an ailing ear that, in accord with the climate he moves in, he deliberately inflames with a matchstick:

> The figures beneath some of the sheets made faint movements; a skeletal form lifted to gain attention, a pink scrubbed head turned list-lessly to take in the new entrant. The sheets did not seem to have beneath them persons but a few cones, from the points of which the folds sloped apparently to the mattress, and Lucas thought of parts of bodies—feet, the pelvis, shoulders without arms—joined by tubes of pliable glass, transparent so the bubbling flow of blood and yellow body juices could be studied.

A short time later, he blunders into a patient's room while chasing his parakeet, and, without warning, we are plummeted inside the sick person's mind and see not a man and a bird but a bear and a flower. It is a stunning passage:

> The green flower had sprouted unsurprisingly; the appearance of a bear seemed to follow from that. Now the bear growled. It seemed sorry for something, but then he was sorry too, and though there was no need to say so he smiled. The bear pointed; the flower leaped; the flower skimmed over the ceiling, and at a command from the bear the door closed sharply, saying "Idiot." The bear lifted its black arms and sank from view, and the flower bloomed on the bed, its bright eye frightening. He was glad when the bear came again. A chair fell lazily, and the bear was of course sorry about that, and ashamed. Then the bear grew very clever and plucked the green flower from a picture on the wall. He was so proud, he tried to show it, but of course if he opened his hands too wide the flower would leap again. It occurred to him that it all had been arranged to amuse him, and he laughed obligingly, so they would not feel sorry, and continued laughing when they had gone through the door, for them to hear, though curiously he was not sorry when they had left him alone again.

In these hot, teeming fancies, which occur repeatedly, the book reaches its greatest intensity and Mr. Updike comes closest to a display of emotion. It is almost as if, like a child suddenly shy before adults, he were slipping into crazy dances or shouting mumbo-jumbo rather than give himself away. Dickens and Faulkner are hypnotized by similar grotes-queries, which they see as part of the machinery that drives men; Mr. Up-dike, one suspects, uses them only as briliantly colored smoke screens.

One may come away from the book untouched (curiously, one never thinks of *liking* or *disliking* it), but one also realizes from the first sentence that Mr. Updike is a writer's writer. The poet's care and sensitivity lie lightly on every word, on each hand-turned sentence, in each surprising and exact metaphor and simile:

> The doctor was a middle-aged Italian, highly handsome, though his head was a bit too big for his body, and his eyes for his head. It was as if the years of service and fatigue that had subdued his Latin mannerliness to mere staring, indeed dazed, gentleness had also been a drag on his lower lids; his green irises rode a boat of milk, under a white sky. Thus his eyes were targets.

> Hook relit his cigar, now short. His eyes crossed in a look of savagery behind their magnifying lenses, and the gasps of his sucking lips assumed, in the enveloping hush, high importance. Moisture walked out from his mouth along the skin of the cigar; the nipple burned; smoke writhed across Hook's face and was borne upward.

> The air turned white; a fork of lightning hung above the distant orchards, shocking each spherical tree into relief. Seconds later the sound arrived. The clouds above formed a second continent, with its own horizon, a bar of old silver stretched behind the nearly tangent profiles of the farthest hills and clouds. Again lightning raced down a fault in the sky, the thunder following less tardily.

If, in his next book, Mr. Updike can somehow let loose the impelling emotion locked so tightly behind these sentences, it will be an invaluable event.

# A Little Good in Evil

Granville Hicks*

John Updike, in "Rabbit, Run" (Knopf, $4.00), has told the story of an irresponsible and troubled young man, Harry Angstrom, commonly called Rabbit. In high school he was a basketball player, famous in his own country. Now, at twenty-six, he works in a department store and has a wife and a child, with another child on the way.

The novel is a record of his flights. One day, on the most sudden of impulses, he sets off in his car, heading vaguely south. As suddenly he comes back, but not to his wife. Instead he takes up with a part-time prostitute, but he abandons her when he learns that his wife is in labor. He and Janice are not re-united for long, however, and when he leaves this time, she gets drunk and allows the baby to drown in the bathtub. He runs away again after the baby's funeral, seeks refuge with Ruth, the semi-prostitute, then runs once more.

Updike shows us Rabbit in all his weakness. He can be abysmally

*Review of Rabbit, Run. From Saturday Review, 43 (November 5, 1960), 28. Copyright © 1960 by Saturday Review. All rights reserved. Reprinted by permission.

selfish, not only with his women but with all those who try to help him. In his sexual activities, about which Updike is uncommonly explicit even for these times, he shows little consideration for his partners. To the consequences of his deeds he gives no thought. The only solution he can discover for any of his problems is flight.

On the other hand, Rabbit has qualities that are not contemptible. For one thing, he has an idea of excellence, associated in his mind with his erstwhile prowess in basketball. He tells Ruth: "I *was* great. It's the fact. I mean, I'm not good for anything now but I really was good at that." To Jack Eccles, a clergyman who is trying to patch up the marriage, he says: "I once played a game real well. I really did. And after you're first-rate at something, no matter what, it kind of takes the kick out of being second-rate. And that little thing Janice and I had going, boy, it was really second-rate."

He has an inner life of considerable intensity. After his fashion he is religious; Mr. Eccles calls him a mystic. At any rate he has a feeling for what he believes to be "rightness" in a situation, and he is convinced that his impulses are somehow inspired. "He is a good man," Eccles says to Rabbit's mother-in-law, who is by no means ready to accept this evaluation. When Rabbit asks Ruth why she likes him, she replies, " 'Cause you haven't given up. 'Cause in your stupid way you're still fighting." "I'm lovable," he tells her later on, and some persons find him so.

As epigraph Updike uses a quotation from Pascal: "The motions of Grace, the hardness of the heart, external circumstances." It is a summary of the novel. The hardness of the heart is what one sees first and sees again and again. But then there are the external circumstances, particularly the fact that society has no use for Rabbit's one talent, his way with a basketball. Finally, and most important, there are the motions of Grace. Updike does not make too much of them; they are, he lets us see, uncertain and questionable; but Rabbit is not merely a selfish wretch nor is he merely a victim of circumstances. One may say that he is deluded: when, for instance, at the end of the book, he feels that he is entering upon a new life, the reader has every right to be skeptical. The fact, however, that he can still think of a new life, after what he has been through, may be evidence of Grace.

Although Updike is only twenty-eight, "Rabbit, Run" is his fourth book, for he has published a volume of verse and a collection of short stories, some of them very fine, before the appearance last year of "The Poorhouse Fair." The novel was highly, even extravagantly, praised by many critics. The quality of the writing and the characterization deserved praise, but I felt that Updike had been mistaken in trying to make the book a kind of political parable. There is no such extraneous element in "Rabbit, Run."

"The Poorhouse Fair" was admirably written, but the style of the present novel, while just as controlled, is more flexible. Updike can be perfectly straightforward, particularly in dialogue, but he lets himself go whenever occasion demands. Here, for example, is a piece of description that is conventional in conception but distinctive in execution:

> Sun and moon, sun and moon, time goes. In Mrs. Smith's acres, crocuses break the crust. Daffodils and narcissi unpack their trumpets. The reviving grass harbors violets, and the lawn is suddenly coarse with dandelions and broadleaved weeds. Invisible rivulets running brokenly make the low land of the estate sing. The flowerbeds, bordered with bricks buried diagonally, are pierced by dull red spikes that will be peonies, and the earth itself, scumbled, stone-flecked, horny, raggedly patched with damp and dry, looks like the oldest and smells like the newest thing under Heaven.

Here is the drunken Janice with her baby: "She lifts the living thing into the air and hugs it against her sopping chest. Water pours off them onto the bathroom tiles. The little weightless body flops against her neck and a quick look of relief at the baby's face gives a fantastic clotted impression. A contorted memory of how they give artificial respiration pumps Janice's cold wet arms in frantic rhythmic hugs; under her clenched lids great scarlet prayers arise, wordless, monotonous, and she seems to be clasping the knees of a vast third person whose name, Father, Father, beats against her head like physical blows. Though her wild heart bathes the universe in red, no spark kindles in the space between her arms; for all of her pouring prayers she doesn't feel the faintest tremor of answer in the darkness against her. Her sense of the third person with them widens enormously, and she knows, knows, while knocks sound at the door, that the worst thing that has ever happened to any woman in the world has happened to her."

In recent months I have discussed a number of novels about irresponsible young men, and sometimes I have complained that the author has failed to convince me that I should take an interest in the character he has created. I make no such complaint about "Rabbit, Run." Updike seizes upon qualities in Harry Angstrom that are of large significance, and with his stylistic resources, he makes them real to us. There is something in this man—call it "the motions of Grace" if you choose—that demands our respect. Although compassion is one of his gifts, Updike is not merely compassionate; he has a deep sense of human fallibility but he treasures the goodness, slight as it is, that he finds in Rabbit.

From now on Updike has to be regarded as one of our important young novelists, a powerful writer with his own vision of the world. In "The Poorhouse Fair" that vision sometimes seemed blurred, but here it is clear and compelling. It is a vision of good struggling in a morass of evil, and Updike has as sure a hold on one quality as on the other.

# Behind the Dazzle
# Is a Knowing Eye

Arthur Mizener*

John Updike is the most talented writer of his age in America (he is 30 today) and perhaps the most serious. His natural talent is so great that for some time it has been a positive handicap to him—in a small way by exposing him from an early age to a great deal of head-turning praise, in a large way by continually getting out of hand. He has already written five books—two novels ("The Poorhouse Fair" and "Rabbit, Run"), a volume of verse ("The Carpentered Hen"), and two books of stories ("The Same Door" and this book). Read in chronological order, they show clearly the battle that has gone on between his power to dazzle and his serious insight.

His love of words and ideas for their own sake is almost Joycean, and he has often imitated Joyce in the almost mechanical way of someone doing an exercise in a creative-writing class: How his virtuosity must have charmed his writing teachers! His evident school-brightness and the first class education it brought him provided every opportunity for the over-development of his onomastic tendencies. They are most obvious in his verse ("Conceptually a blob,/ the knob/ is a smallish object which,/ hitched/ to a larger,/ acts as verger"), but they are present also in his fiction, a constant pleasure to anyone who enjoys watching an artist at work.

Verbal brilliance of this kind, however, can be a danger for a writer of fiction. The young man who, under various names, is the hero of the stories in "Pigeon Feathers" says of one of his unknown rivals, "he would wear eyebrow-style glasses, be a griper, have some not quite negotiable talent, like playing the clarinet or drawing political cartoons," thus nicely illustrating his author's highly negotiable talent for adorning his stories with a cosmatesque surface of very great and radically irrelevant decorative charm. This lovingly executed, verbally elegant surface makes people describe Mr. Updike as a "poetic" writer, as indeed he is in a book like "The Poorhouse Fair." But charming as the poetry of "The Poorhouse Fair" is, Mr. Updike's preoccupation with it made him lose track of something he started to express in the book—that is, his sense of life itself—that is far more important than elegance.

This conflict between wit and insight stands out strongly in his early work because his insight, though it will stand romantic irony, cannot survive merely intellectual wit. It requires sincerity, even earnestness. Mr. Updike is a romantic; for him the instinctive, unselfconscious sense of "what feels right" is the source of life and the means to salvation. Rabbit Angstrom, the hero of "Rabbit, Run," may often inadvertently do harm,

*Review of *Pigeon Feathers and Other Stories*. From *The New York Times Book Review*. 18 March 1962, pp. 1, 29. © 1962, The New York Times Company. Reprinted by permission.

cause pain; but he is never evil or dead. "I don't know," he says to Ruth. "I don't know any of these answers. All I know is what feels right. You feel right to me. Sometimes Janice [his wife] used to. Sometimes nothing does."

Rabbit is touchingly inexperienced and naive, but he has, as an old lady tells him, "Life. It's a strange gift and I don't know how we're supposed to use it but I know it's the only gift we get and it's a good one." When Rabbit, at the end of the book, runs away for the second time, it is a desperate and perhaps futile act, but it is at least a continuation of the fight for life. Rabbit, run, is the author's imperative cry from the heart.

Mr. Updike is a romantic in a second sense which goes far to explain what has always been a curious source of strength in his work, his inclination to write almost exclusively about the life of a young man from the small Pennsylvania town he usually calls Olinger that seems very like the Shillington, Pa., that John Updike remembers from his own boyhood. Like all American romantics, that is, he has an irresistible impulse to go in memory home again in order to find himself. The epigraphs of his first book, which is dedicated to his parents, have to do with the importance of memory to desire and of family love, "within the light of which/All else is seen." The precise recollection of his own family-love, parental and marital, is vital to him; it is the matter in which the saving truth is incarnate.

Thus, in "The Persistence of Desire," Clyde Behn goes home to see an eye doctor and entangles himself with his childhood sweetheart, though they are both now married, with the result that "the maples, macadam, shadows, houses, cement, were to his violated eyes as brilliant as a scene remembered; he became a child again in this town, where life was a distant adventure, a rumor, an always imminent joy." Thus Allen Down in "Flight," remembering what looks like this same girl and his mother's jealousy of her, reconstructs a glowing world of details about his grandfather and grandmother (who turns up in several other stories), of school and classmates, of dances and debates. It is a meticulous, loving and beautiful re-creation, and Mr. Updike's mind probes it with the delicacy of a surgeon, seeking what makes it in memory seem "an always imminent joy."

Even the knowledge that it was not the shelter from nothingness that it now seems comes to him as a memory of how he got up his nerve to tell Mary Landis, the most mature and mysterious of his classmates, that he loved her, only to discover that she was having a bitterly unhappy love affair with an older man. "You never loved anybody," she said. "You don't know what it is." It is true. Now, he can remember what he thought then with a schoolboy's uncertain insight—"after all, it was just a disposition of his heart, nothing permanent or expensive; perhaps it was just his mother's idea anyway"—as true in a way he had not then been able to imagine.

It always seems to Mr. Updike, as he says of his grandmother, "necessary and holy to tell how once there had been a woman who now was no more," to tell everything, "all set down with the bald simplicity of intrinsic blessing, thousands upon thousands of pages; ecstatically uneventful; divinely and defiantly dull." This conviction of the "unceasing and effortless blessing" of life when it is rightly apprehended makes Mr. Updike the kind of religious writer that every serious romantic must be.

The intensity with which he perceives this intrinsic blessing of life, however, seems to him incommunicable. Writers, he believes, "walk through volumes of the unexpressed and like snails leave behind a faint thread excreted out of [themselves]." These observations all come from "The Blessed Man of Boston, My Grandmother's Thimble, and Fanning Island," one of two experimental stories at the end of "Pigeon Feathers," in which Mr. Updike puts together three wholly unrelated episodes that seem to him images of life blessed, images that would be, if he could wholly invoke them, full of joy, "Just as a piece of turf torn from a meadow becomes a *gloria* when drawn by Duerer." But he despairs of realizing life that fully. "As it is," he tells the reader, "you, like me, must take it on faith."

This is not, of course, faith in the conventional sense; one should not be misled by Mr. Updike's frequent references to clergymen and church services: these are the accidents of his subject-matter, of the Olinger that he remembers. But a religious sense of the sacredness of life itself, with its accompanying sense of the absolute horror of death, is at the very center of his perception.

As he says in the almost too brilliant story, "Lifeguard," "Young as I am, I can hear in myself the protein acids ticking; I wake at odd hours and in the shuddering darkness and silence feel my death rushing toward me like an express train." The lifeguard of this story is concerned with the life of the spirit, and what he knows is that "every seduction is a conversion." "Someday," he believes, "my alertness will bear fruit; from near the horizon there will arise, delicious, translucent, like a green bell above the water, the call for help, the call, a call, it saddens me to confess, that I have yet to hear." To have that vocation is to be saved by saving, by experiencing a love that is intensely and specifically physical, because "our chivalric impulses go clanking in encumbering biological armor."

This is the special significance of the second large group of stories in "Pigeon Feathers," the recollections of married love. Like the episodes of married love in "Rabbit, Run," they are unqualifiedly candid because they are dealing with the supreme moment, the moment at which the blessedness of life realizes itself, in the vivifying context of family life, with maximum intensity—or seems, in memory, to have done so.

"Pigeon Feathers" is not just a book of very brilliant short stories; it is a demonstration of how the most gifted writer of his generation is coming to maturity; it shows us that Mr. Updike's fine verbal talent is no longer pirouetting, however gracefully, out of a simple delight in motion, but is beginning to serve his deepest insight, that his "Love's Labor's Lost" and even his "Romeo and Juliet" (that is "Rabbit, Run") are now behind him.

# Arcadia, Pa.

Renata Adler*

The conscious use of myth in the novel presents a unique problem—it inverts the normal process of artistic endeavor. The author normally strives to *create*—out of topical material—a new myth, an archetypal personality or situation. Don Quixote, Falstaff, Swann, Raskolnikov, Joseph K., and Captain Ahab all entered the literary imagination as new themes of almost mythical proportions, upon which authors of lesser stature than their creators could play minor, unconscious variations. Thomas Mann, however, working deliberately within the legend of Joseph and his brothers, managed to infuse an old myth, in its own time and form, with new poetic life; Joyce, working within the legend of Ulysses, managed not only to adapt an old myth to a contemporary situation but to forge a new myth—the trials of Bloom—within the structure of the old. When John Updike, in "The Centaur" (Knopf), tells the story of a Pennsylvania high-school teacher and his adolescent son in terms of the ancient legend of Chiron and Prometheus, he manages to achieve a few of Joyce's effects and some of Mann's: the Greek legend acquires at his hands new poetry, and the American father and son can stand, as modest contemporary archetypes, on their own. Chiron, the most learned and innocent of centaurs, was wounded in his cave by a poisoned arrow intended for another centaur, who had disrupted the boar hunt of Heracles. The undeserved wound would have tortured Chiron through eternity had he not sacrificed his immortality to expiate the sin of Prometheus, who had stolen fire from the gods and given it to men. Zeus rewarded Chiron for his sacrifice by placing him among the stars, as the constellation Sagittarius.

In Mr. Updike's Pennsylvania town, Zeus becomes the omniscient, lecherous principal of Olinger High School. Chiron is George Caldwell, an unlucky, well-meaning general-science teacher and the father of Prometheus—Peter Caldwell, whose affliction is a skin disease, psoriasis. By making Prometheus the son of Chiron (in the legend, the fire-stealer is a Titan, son of Iapetus), the author takes his first liberty with the myth, and he takes many others: with time (the novel covers four consecutive days, in the course of which a week somehow elapses), with the seasons (the story takes place in January, but one scene in mid-novel occurs on a spring day), with the laws of narrative (sometimes we are in Olinger, sometimes in Arcadia), and natural probability (an otherwise ordinary French class, under the direction of a fine teacher, is made to chant an outrageous grammatical error in uncorrected unison).

But the inconsistencies are deliberate. The author sheds his self-imposed mythical form whenever it impedes rather than heightens his

*Review of *The Centaur*. From *The New Yorker*, 39 (April 13, 1963), 182–88. Reprinted by permission; © 1963 The New Yorker Magazine, Inc.

narrative, and the narrative becomes surrealistic whenever it deviates widely from the myth. What is remarkable is the ease with which Mr. Updike modulates from the key of myth to the key of fact. The novel consists, after all, of stories framed within stories: the outermost frame is a reminiscence of boyhood told by the adult Peter Caldwell to his Negro mistress, who lies in bed beside him; this tale in turn contains a sociological document within the obituary of a citizen, George Caldwell, of a rural Pennsylvania community; the document encompasses an allegorical poem that recounts the sufferings of a devoted pedagogue who finds himself a man above the waist, an animal below. The fiery gift that the boy Prometheus has stolen from the gods is Peter Caldwell's artistic talent. His punishment is twofold: he is chained by his inhibitions to the rock of his adolescence, and he is racked by a sensitivity so acute that it takes the form of allergy—the skin disease. His experiences are also twofold: his high-school girl friend Penny opens for him the Pandora's box of his own sexuality, and his father's sacrifice precipitates him from youth into adulthood. The arrow George Caldwell receives from one of his students is poisoned with hatred and disillusionment; his suffering is an inability to cope with the pragmatic problems of daily living. His redemption occurs through a sexual encounter with Aphrodite as Vera Hummel, gym teacher. And his metaphoric "death" lies in the complete sacrifice of himself to the profession of teaching.

This outline makes the story appear complicated enough, but Mr. Updike imbues it with such richness of observation and detail and constructs it with such skill that it requires an elaborate parallelism; novels about teachers are usually remarkable for their reticence on the subject of teaching (it is presumably too trivial and boring an element of the teacher's life to deserve treatment), but Mr. Updike manages to play no less than five distinct variations on the theme of pedagogy (the first lesson concerns the theory of evolution, the second the myth of creation; the third consists entirely of mathematical drill, the fourth of the tutoring of a dull girl for a quiz in geology, the fifth of commentary on a bright boy's faltering translation of Vergil), and each rings so fresh and true that the reader wears a continual smile of assent and revived memory. Of the longest and most ambitious scene one can give only a superficial inventory. Within the lecture itself: five billion condensed years of the earth's history. Throughout the classroom: the rape of Io by Zeus, and of a flirt by a centaur; the blowing of a bubble by a gum chewer in the first row, and the flight of a paper airplane from the hand of a prankster in the last; the eliciting, by the teacher's sheer will, of a correct answer from a reluctant student, and the teacher's restraint, by another effort of will, of the flow of wrong answers from an overeager one. The whole scene is so symmetrical and its sense of reality so strong (Mr. Updike summarizes the standard American classroom situation in one short aside: "Mute faces marvelled and mocked") that the author can permit himself any number of extravagantly daring touches—as the lecture approaches its climax, "all of the boys in the room began to hum . . . the air was filled with a hovering honey of insolence," and five minutes before the end of the class, a boy releases a bagful of live trilobites upon the floor and "one of the girls, a huge purple parrot . . . plucked a small one up . . . crunched it in her painted beak and methodically chewed." The scene degenerates into madness, but it is the genuine madness that descends, at the end of the hour, upon the classroom of the imperfect disciplinarian, and it is the controlled madness of the stylist who is in perfect command of his effects.

The reader's credulity is repeatedly stretched until he is sure that he has been drawn irrevocably into the realm of myth, only to have Mr. Updike, with a particularly astute observation on life as it is, restore him to the realm of the real—the domain of Poseidon becomes, with the words "In the great tiled chamber . . . a barking resonance broke everything into fragments," a Y.M.C.A. swimming pool; the world of Pan reverts, with the precision of the author's ear for the small-town adolescents' idiom, to a high-school gymnasium during a basketball game; Venus speaks of Diana ("tittering around the woods with a pack of Vassar freshmen whose so-called virginity not a doctor in Arcadia—") and becomes only a rather catty Olinger beauty. The author modulates as easily from fact to myth—Dr. Appleton lays his stethoscope on his desk, "where it writhed and then subsided like a slain rubber serpent," and we are instantly in the world of Python and Asclepius; Chiron spits into the dentist's little whirlpool and evokes Charybdis; the schoolboy Johnny Dedman displays his skill at the pinball machine in Minor Kretz's luncheonette and becomes Daedalus, the genius of the labyrinth in Minos's Crete; a reference to the bulls on Johnny Dedman's pornographic playing cards arouses Minor's anger, and it has clearly reawakened memories of the Minotaur. Chiron thinks, in the presence of the garagist Hephaestus, "These Olinger aristocrats . . . they forced a favor on you and that made them gods," and we are left in midtransition between the mythical and the actual, between Olinger and Olympus.

All through the novel there is a delicate symmetry and balance, and the story seems a fragile and colorful mobile suspended in slow rotation. In his farmhouse Chiron has two clocks—one antique, metallic, measured, given to him by his wife's father, Kronos; the other electric, plastic, hurrying, bought at a discount by himself. Chiron supervises two athletic events—one a swimming meet that his team loses, the other a basketball game that Olinger wins. His car is twice stalled—once by a failure of its internal mechanism, once by the external operation of nature in a snowstorm. Both Chiron and his son have one imagined sexual encounter (Prometheus dreams of Pandora, Chiron remembers a meeting with Aphrodite in Arcadia) and one actual seduction (Prometheus's is explicit but incomplete, Chiron's is complete but only implied). Father and son spend two nights in country households—one their own, which is affectionate, discordant, impractical; the other the household of Aphrodite and Hephaestus, which is smooth, practical, loveless. They encounter two homosexuals—one, Hermes, in their car; the other, Dionysos, in the street. Each scene or event of the narrative is set off by another, until the balance appears almost forced; what saves the symmetry from becoming monotonous is the accuracy of Mr. Updike's observation and the richness of his prose. A dissolute tramp's voice "scribbled; maybe it was a laugh;" a stalled car's reviving engine, "like a slapped baby, coughed;" from the basement of the Y.M.C.A. "drifted the patient *ga-glokka, ga-glokka* of a pingpong game;" a boy touched a dog and "the texture of her throat was feathery, the top of her head waxen;" a sip of overheated coffee in the morning "seared my sense of taste away;" and on a winter's day "in the far distance the wooded hills still showed as blue and brown, but the tints were weak, as in the prints of an etching taken to clean the plate."

Mr. Updike's facility is not limited to the communication of sights, sounds, and textures; his psychological observations are acute almost to the point of aphorism. "The first impulse after a humiliation," he wrote in one of his early stories, "is to look into a mirror," and in "The Centaur" he says, of homosexuality and adolescence:

> I felt, as long as my love of girls remained unconsummated, open on that side—a three-walled room any burglar could enter.

The scene in which Prometheus self-consciously reveals his skin disorder to Pandora (she has already noticed it) is psychologically sound and truly moving. Prometheus has all the adolescent shame and pride in being different, and the shyness and insistence of one who confides; Pandora displays the mixture of forgiveness and contempt in the loving receiver of repellent confidences. The dialogue, trite and poetic, rings absolutely true.

It is not surprising that Mr. Updike should have chosen in this novel to reconcile a naturalistic story with a myth; even in his earliest stories it was clear that the author's greatest literary gift was his command of metaphor:

> He smiled at this foible and carried his smile like an egg on a spoon into the living room.

> As the months passed harmlessly, James's suspicion increased that the city itself was poised to strike.

> Behind him the bus doors closed: pterodactyl wings.

Most of these metaphors were ornamental—decorations of the author's prose style rather than elements of his point. A few, however, were functional, pivotal, and sustained. In the story entitled "Dentistry and Doubt," for example, the characteristic postures of two men in the face of their uncertainty (the patient reacts to doubt by quoting from a seemingly reliable source of faith, the dentist reacts by filling a tooth, which is the very real source of pain) were summed up in a single image:

> Outside the window, two wrens, one by pretending to locate a crumb and the other by unobtrusively flicking a real crumb away, out-maneuvered a black bird.

The reader could accept this passage as the key to the story, or he could reject the metaphor and appreciate the story all the same. A later piece, "Lifeguard," left the reader no choice. Mr. Updike had discovered or fancied a similarity between the guardian of physical life on the beach and the pastor of physical life in the world, and if the metaphor failed to take hold in the reader's imagination as it had in the author's, the whole story was meaningless. The narrative turned upon an image, and succeeded or failed with it. So does "The Centaur," with the additional complication that the novel's theme, the myth itself, is already—almost by definition—metaphoric. The novelist is not so much creating an image as adapting one.

The novel has its faults. (So, on a scale commensurate with the grandeur of its scope, has "Ulysses.") Mr. Updike is occasionally carried away by his joy in naming and enumerating objects, cataloguing flowers in a garden, or inspecting the sweepings of corridors, with a minuteness that serves to display his stylistic virtuosity rather than to accelerate his narrative. He insists too firmly on the saintliness of Chiron; the centaur's ineffectual righteousness is carried to a degree just short of tedium. There are characters in whom even the author appears to lose interest: Ocyrhoe, Chiron's daughter, is merely mentioned, near the beginning and the end of the novel. And sometimes the shifts of scene within the narrative are jarring; the reader perceives a grinding of formal gears. Mr. Updike has, moreover, appended an index of characters that is superfluous (the reader can identify the major mythical figures without benefit of an index) when it is not pointless (the characters are listed only under their Olympian names) or utterly artificial (Mr. Updike has gone to bizarre lengths to establish mythical heroes in minor characters that simply cannot support them). And, finally, the figurative-literal structure of the novel is, after all, a tour de force, with all the sense of strain that such an ambitious venture implies. But novelty in the arts is often heralded by tours de force, and the patterns of the English novel appear to be undergoing a change. "Pale Fire" was fully as drastic a formal innovation as "The Centaur," with the difference that Mr. Nabokov was able to cover, in his ironical fashion, the sense of strain—slyly to erase, as it were, his serious literary footsteps behind him. Mr. Updike does not take cover in irony, and his novel is delivered to the critics in all the vulnerability of its seriousness. "The Centaur" is a fine, rich work ("resonant," in Mr. Updike's phrase, "with metaphor"), and its faults are minor in the light of its achievements.

# Off-Centaur

**Jonathan Miller***

This is a poor novel irritatingly marred by good features. The title, grindingly reinforced by the tasteful Hellenic fragment on the cover, sounds the warning note of "significance" and the severe intention is further signalled by a dark quotation from Karl Barth on the title page: something about man being "a creature on the boundary between heaven and earth." As if one were not tuned by this time to the "universal" wave length, there follows on the next page, before our story really begins, a precis of the myth of Chiron, the weary centaur who sacrifices his immortality as an atonement for Prometheus. Then, lest we forget, the author has appended, at the suggestion of his wife, an index of the mythical references which crop up throughout the text. Nearly three pages are devoted to this catalogue, which instead of being explanatory is more in the nature of a score card. The nymphs and deities are simply listed, in alphabetical order, along with their page references. Achilles scores three appearances, Adonis five, Argus runs neck and neck with Daedalus with four references, while up in the big league, Aphrodite, Zeus, and Pandora get ten or eleven mentions each. The novel itself ends with an untranslated, five-line quotation in Greek. The work collapses finally under this freight of classical reference.

Human affairs, of course, cast allegorical shadows. Gods and nymphs are vivid ciphers which do dramatize some of the more permanent themes of mortal business. We all of us, at one time or another, approximate in our behavior and in our predicaments, to one or other of these mythical stereotypes. Suggestions of this dualism can sometimes intensify fiction by projecting it into an immortal perspective, letting the reader in on a dramatic irony where the characters, unknown to themselves, are worked, like marionettes, by the ideal forms of which they themselves are simply the flawed and provisional replicas. So far so good; the trick calls for tact and finesse, though. If the allegorical theme is announced too clearly the irony becomes monotonous and the art gives way to pedantry. Exactly what has happened in *The Centaur*. It is interesting in this respect to contrast the work with two successful novels with which its shares certain issues.

*The Centaur* is a portrait, not just of Chiron, the schoolteacher, wearied by domestic and professional struggles, but also of his son, an artist, who recalls three ice-bound days of his Pennsylvania childhood. In this sense it is another *Portrait of the Artist as a Young Man* and Updike's didactic allegory suffers by contrast with the delicacy with which Joyce

---

*Review of *The Centaur*. From *The New York Review of Books* (1 Nov, 1963), 28. Reprinted with permission from *The New York Review of Books*. Copyright © 1963 New York Review, Inc.

uses the myth of Daedalus. Stephen's mythical role is deftly introduced by
Joyce in the final paragraph of the book, with an image of the winged
craftsman, phantasmal almost, which lingers in the mind, subtly and
retroactively illuminating all that has gone before. Updike's quotations,
his pretentious index, and interpolated episodes of mythical narrative
simply provide an irritating distraction.

The other book with which his suffers by illustrative comparison is
Saul Bellow's *Seize the Day*, which also treats the theme of the reciprocity
of psychic energy between father and son. Bellow's novel is resonant with
intimations of immortality, but in firm subordination to the dense bulk of
the two main characters around whom Bellow merely puffs a hint of eternity. A gleam of sunlight, refracted through a glass of water, casts an
image which seems, in passing, to be the imprint of an angel's mouth.
Such fleeting innuendoes, confidently occasional, are quite enough to indicate the larger scale against which the human events are set.

The fact is that Updike does himself a great disservice by enamelling
his tale with elaborate reference. At the center of all that wearisome
pedantry he has a neglected germ of literary imagination. The father is
carefully and sympathetically observed with a shambling heroism,
fatigued and gullible, which is nicely set off against the irritable fondness
of his son. He has chosen however to inflate this compact moral set-up,
blowing it up into a volume which is out of proportion to its weight. It
finally becomes flounderingly portentous and pompously intoned, like
Hemingway's *Old Man and the Sea*.

The book is still further damaged by the necessity which Updike
makes out of his own virtue. His sly adjectival prose creates an extraordinary surface effect. This is what I think is called sensitive writing. It
certainly shows nimble, almost feline, accuracy of physical perception,
capturing in a few supple lines the essence of certain observations.

I say that he has made a necessity out of his own virtue, but perhaps I
should say virtuosity, since it is his enslavement to his own bravura skill
which finally disqualifies this novel from genuine literary consideration.
He is hung up on his own sensitivity and unable to drive his story on with
the narrative urgency of genuine literary work. There is a term, used in
physiological optics, which perfectly illustrates this defect. The "critical
flicker fusion frequency" is the rate at which a sequence of still pictures
must pass before the eye before they eventually fuse into a moving progress. There is, I believe, a counterpart in literature: call it a "literary fusion frequency," a critical tempo without which we, as readers, merely
receive a show of beautiful still frames, And this is where Updike has
failed. The first half of his book is so heavily cargoed with physical effects
that it can never get up the necessary speed. Then, quite suddenly,
towards the middle, the projector becomes synchronized and the figures
begin to move with convincing fluency and a genuine sense of motive.
This middle sequence, taken up with the father and son snow-bound in a

small Pennsylvania town abruptly jerks into motion and the characters seem to move against a landscape of physical detail which is in relieving proportion to the human figures in the foreground. This passage is startling in its quality standing out from the smooth pretentiousness of everything with which it is surrounded. Without this relief the novel is just a counterpart of *Sundays and Cybele*, a tidbit for Bosley Crowther.

# Language, Myth and Mr. Updike

Anthony Burgess*

We in Europe still, when it comes to comparing the distinctive contributions of America and our own continent (with its offshore islands) to Western culture, tend to think in terms of the old Henry James dichotomy—that America is all energy and Europe is all style, and that any marriage between the two is impossible. Now the fact is that some of the most remarkable contributions to prose style of recent years have been made by Americans, and these not always émigrés like Nabokov.

Nabokov, indeed, has been turned by America into the sort of European that Europe no longer produces—autocratic, defiantly intellectual, seemingly avant-garde but actually closing in to a little lost world of brilliant pedantry. Pedantry is often the real adopted country of the intellectual exile (think of *Pale Fire*, *Finnegans Wake* and *Doctor Faustus*). Pedantry is also frequently the clown's outfit endued by the homegrown misfit: it is seen in the mockery of Art Buchwald and the self-mockery of Peter de Vries. The homegrown writer who is not a misfit tends, so we think in Europe, to the prosethickets that call for editorial pruning, or to the typewriterese which looks avant-garde when it is merely illiterate: the impression is of clumsy muscularity, not careful art.

Young Mr. John Updike is an exception. The "young" is not meant to be patronizing: the youthfulness of his exuberance is matched by a youthful, even sophomoric, devotion to style; one is aware, too, that, despite a considerable corpus of achievement already known and admired on both sides of the Atlantic, he is only now approaching a maturity of aim and craft. He is a young American writer, and Europe likes its American writers to be young. We are a two-faced lot over here in these cold lands of corruption: youth can excuse the sprawling vital ill-composed epic, but it can also excuse qualities which Europeans still think they monopolize—fastidiousness, Flaubertian martyrdom, an innocent belief in the power of exact language.

Updike became very well-known in England for his novel *Rabbit, Run*. The title probably has false connotations for us: there was a popular

*Review of *Of the Farm*. From *Commonweal*, 83 (February 11, 1966), 557–9. Copyright © 1966. Reprinted by permission of *Commonweal*.

song in 1939 called "Run, rabbit, run," later—when war broke out— parodied to "Run, Adolf, run." God knows what English people thought they were buying when they picked up this novel from railway bookstalls. They could hardly have been prepared for the meticulous notations of male weakness that make up the book. When I read and reviewed it I made a judgment that I have since had no cause to revise—that Updike was guilty of a sort of democratic heresy in pouring the riches of language on characters and situations so trivial.

The exactness of the writing was at the opposite pole to the exactness of the writing of Hemingway: where Hemingway strips language of its literary connotations, Updike makes us aware of the whole history of language—not so much in vocabulary, perhaps, as in rhythm and sentence-organization. Now the use of a whole complex palimpsest of literary associations, brought to the delineation of drab lives and weak wills, can be ironic: it can imply social criticism. There didn't seem to be any social criticism, any real irony, in *Rabbit, Run*; there seemed rather to be a very piquant parallelism of content and style. This made one want to read his next novel, in the hope that a fusion of these two elements might have taken place, the richness of the fictional material matching the richness of the writing. We expected, many of us, a book with a mythical framework, and this is precisely what we got.

## THE LINK

*The Centaur* was a noble attempt at adding fresh dimensions to a contemporary story by calling on ancient myth. James Joyce, when writing *Ulysses*, saw that the use of a Homeric parallel to thicken, ennoble and (in art's paradox) to light up with irony the details of ordinary Dublin lives, would not only justify great length but would also be the best pretext for throwing at the reader great hunks of learning and linguistic experiment. Joyce was dogged in planting his Odyssean allusions in low-life street-scenes; sometimes the pedantry was humorous and mocking, sometimes (as in the lying-in hospital chapter, where a procession of prosestyles from *Beowulf* to Carlyle symbolizes the growth of the embryo in the womb) it was self-defeating.

In *The Centaur*, Updike's own pedantry leads him to an explicit list of parallels and (his modern centaur defecates in the corridor) to a confusion of actuality and symbol. But the brillance of the language seemed no longer to be functioning in a void, unrelated to the subject-matter of the book: it was appropriate to the complexity of the over-all image; it was the true link between the story and the myth.

His latest novel, *Of the Farm* (Knopf, $3.95), is very brief and unpretentious, but it is still a book by a deliberate stylist, and the style sometimes subsists on its own, unrelated to the simple events it is intended to serve. The story seems to a European reader to be very American. Joey

Robinson is a New York advertising consultant who brings his new wife and his stepson to the family farm in southeastern Pennsylvania. His mother lives there alone, and the farm itself is no longer under cultivation.

On the first level we meet the nostalgia of an overurbanized American for his country roots, and the sense that a highly industrialized monster feeding on stereotypes must, sooner rather than later, open its claws to crush this rural pocket of tranquillity and sane values. On the second level there is the interaction of past and present time—memories of Joey's first wife (strongly reinforced by Joey's mother) battling with the actuality of his second, the sense of the break-up of families, the need to adjust to new loyalties and yet somehow remain faithful to the old. There is nothing so gross as a plot-structure, only the interplay of living voices with each other and with the voices of ghosts.

## ANTHROPOMORPHIC SPELLS

I am concerned here with the how rather than the what, and I take at random a typical brief paragraph:

> To close the window I left the bed. The small thump of the sash seemed to trigger the night; lightning flashed behind Schoelkopf's hill and thunder, like a violent guest grown too much at home, clapped. I got back into bed facing Peggy. Her warmth altered my flesh. She put her oval hand upon me.

Here we see faults inseparable from certain virtues. The need to relate the impersonal world of nature to the personal world in the bedroom produces a purely fanciful kind of anthropomorphism, whose possible effect of sentimentality the author attempts to mitigate with the language of mass-communication—"trigger the night," indeed. Nor is it easy to reconcile the two elements contained in "clapped." A thunderclap is violent; a guest claps his host's imitation of Sinatra, but the violence of the action is no indication that he himself is violent, nor that he has "grown too much at home." By the time we have tried to sort out the incompatibles the power of the description is much diminished. After the attempt at sharp particularities comes the apology of the vague "Her warmth altered my flesh." Finally, Peggy's hand may be oval, but its shape is not relevant to the situation, and the small surprise we may feel at the revelation of its shape may drag us away from that situation.

Updike's willingness to let language draw our attention from his narrative is, nevertheless, a healthy sign that language means something to him. Now look at this:

> It had been June, hot. The windows were old-fashionedly flung open and the sounds of the East River lifted into the room. The judicial sanctum was capacious along obsolete lines of office space, and the furniture, which included a wooden bench where my mother sat, looked sparse and

> stray, as if these inanimate survivors of a vanished courthouse era had
> been humanly subjected to the bewildered thinning of mortality.

Here is the ghost of Henry James, invoked with the generalizing language.
Once admit "judicial sanctum" and you are bound to be led along
familiar paths of imprecision to a kind of post-Dickensian anthropomorphism of domestic objects. My failure to see why the throwing open of
windows should be old-fashioned may have something to do with not living in an air-conditioned country.

I quote these two examples to show Updike's awareness of linguistic
effects, but also to show how the effects tend to get out of hand. Sometimes, however, the self-consciousness triumphs:

> My wife is wide, wide-hipped and long-waisted, and, surveyed from
> above, gives an impression of terrain, of a wealth whose ownership im-
> poses upon my own body a sweet strain of extension; entered, she yields a
> variety of landscapes, seeming now a snowy rolling perspective of
> bursting cotton bolls seen through the Negro arabesques of a fancywork
> wrought-iron balcony; now a taut vista of mesas dreaming in the midst of
> sere and painterly ochre; now a gray French castle completely fitted to a
> steep green hill whose terraces imitate turrets; now something like Antarc-
> tica; and then a receding valleyland of blacks and purples where an unrip-
> pled river flows unseen between shadowy banks of grapes that are never
> eaten.

There is more of this, evoking the sexual landscape in the penultimate
chapter of *Finnegans Wake*, but totally wideawake, a cunning rococo
cadenza or perhaps something earlier and baroque—the fantasy-making
extravagance of the metaphysical poets. Sometimes the preciosity is
unbearable—"sere and painterly ochre," for example—but on the whole
the thing works. It is the sort of thing that brings poetry back to the
novel—not the poetry of action or casual close description but the poetry
of digression, the only kind really admissible.

Touches like this give *Of the Farm* an intensity, as well as a relaxed
quality of genuine "pastoral," very rare in contemporary letters. It does
not dare as much as *The Centaur* but, in the sense that it knows almost
perfectly how to encompass a foreknown and limited success, it is far
more mature. What we expect from John Updike now is a book which
essays margins of the consciousness which will justify linguistic extravagance and a further exploitation of myth. He is one of America's
most exciting talents, but much of the excitement is still to come.

# Son of the Group

Michael Novak*

More than any other American writer, John Updike celebrates the middle-class, mildly religious culture most of us are familiar with: our supermarkets and their parking lots, our ranch houses and the sloshing scotch and ice of neighborhood parties, our churches and the pressure of death beneath our skins. It is startling to recognize how seldom *our* lives have been made the stuff of literature. So often voyagers to Africa, soldiers on foreign shores, nihilists, Hollywood queens, detectives, and despairing, lost non-heroes populate our fictional imagination that we begin to think novelists dwell in underworlds as unlike as possible our sub-rurban habitats.

With a fundamental honesty and an even more remarkable courage Updike has refused to be intimidated into escaping to other hells than ours. His critics wish him to dare bolder things, to visit travel agencies and head for elsewhere; to write us *significant* lessons. A writer, one is led to suppose, cannot be middle class. Social and political criticism is desired: tell us about the poor, the desperate, the guerillas. Above all, tell us—again—that the world is falling in upon us, that ancient values no longer grip known sides of a familiar universe, that we wander alone, alienated, piteous in an endlessly open, shifting universe.

John Updike, therefore, took a very long risk when he settled down in Ipswich, Massachusetts, several years ago, with wife and (now) four children, in a rambling thirteen-room wooden house, with an office for three solid hours of work every day in a loft over a downtown store. Many have watched the experiment closely: would his experience close in upon him? Would he write himself into a narrower and narrower corner of imagination? Could Ipswich, Massachusetts, bear meaning enough to support his art?

No American writer, with the possible exception of Norman Mailer, has greater gifts: a more exquisite and poignant poetic sense, an almost absolute command of descriptive language, an inner voice that sings through resistant sentences as genius sings. No one esteems the little beauties of our life as Updike does: to delight in the rose-white shell of a hardboiled egg upon a blue saucer in the breakfast sun, in the scores of colors in our ever-changing skies, in the many different pressures, intensities, and scents of our breezes. I do not believe that any American writer's senses have been more alive.

Updike's sensibility, moreover, is specifically Christian— an alert, open, human, sensual Calvinism; a tension of the spirit stung by the pressure of death, uncommonly driven by passions of sensual and sexual

*Review of *Couples*. From *The Critic*, 26 (June/July, 1968), 72–74. Copyright © 1968. Reprinted by permission of Michael Novak.

nostalgia. Updike's inner world is not Catholic. It is almost wholly Platonic: his art is ever bitten by the pain of memory. His vision forces itself to press through the hard, defined realities of toothpaste tubes, wooden shingles, sea coral, and exquisitely described female nakedness to a world more real. So deep is Updike's confidence in that distant world that the hard, glorious shapes of this one are no danger to him; his exquisite control of sensual detail springs from a consciousness whose source is elsewhere. His radical dualism makes myth and symbol his necessary tools, familiar, warm and restful in his hand.

It is difficult for the Jewish sensibility, and for the hard, pragmatic, secular sensibility, of our critical establishment, to enter this delicately hung, delicately balanced cave where flame-tinted shadows dance and reel and the really real intermingle. So thoroughly does Updike dwell upon the complex of detail—of a single martini, or a rock, of the shape and color of a woman's pubic hair—that we are led, through the very act of concentration, beyond the immediate object of sight or touch. Each thing, dwelt on, gains a tongue to speak an elemental poignancy. Things *are* and *are not*, and the very sharpness of their being defines more clearly the nothingness on which they momentarily rest.

Hence the peculiar preciousness of Updike's prose. It springs, not from self-indulgence, but from superb self-discipline; it proves his fidelity to the sources of his passion. I do not know exactly how it is, but I am certain that the young Jew in our society (certainly in our literature) enters into the sexual life with sensibility of different timbre than the Calvinist. It is no accident that the philosopher of *Playboy* springs from Methodism, or that Updike's exquisite explicitness about a score of acts of intercourse in *Couples* should ring with surprise, delight, and almost boyish fantasy. How wonderful, he seems to feel, that the merely real should be so beautiful; how much more so the yearned for, unseen really real! The flesh is bound to disappoint: a truth whose learning requires the breaking of bounds.

*Couples* is set in the year of John F. Kennedy's assassination. It is the story of affluent couples—contractors, professors, stock-brokers, bankers, engineers—whose lives reduce to such routine that the most plausible form of interpersonal development for them to explore is adultery. The reason for suburban life is isolation from the poverty, misery, and noisomeness of the human race; its aim is security, placidity, likemindedness. The end is flatness.

Updike creates the couples of the story, the couples of Tarbox, Massachusetts, affectionately and respectfully. Each is treated with dignity, the struggles of each call forth our sympathy. Ben Whitman, for example, the ambitious young scientist forced to face the fact that his work is second-rate, forced to face as well his own human coldness and inhumanity, is granted a last moment of freedom and joy. It is not Updike's failure but his achievement that the couples are flat, and yet even in their flatness human beings.

Similarly, the lovemaking scenes are among the most beautiful and compassionate in our literature. The color and touch of the skin, the bone-contour, the hair, the manner and emotive quality, the scent of each man, each woman, is recreated. Inadequately, fleetingly, the couples become one with each other, helping one another to escape the quiet despair of segregated living. Yet they must do so by a code which says, publicly, that their conduct is destructive. And, quite clearly, it is destructive, for their children especially, abandoned to their own devices, lonely, pampered on the one hand and on the other quite clearly mere nuisances. Children do not weigh heavily in the scales of adult life in Tarbox. And, finally, the mobility of the monstrous, growing American way of life shoves the couples aside like trees in front of a bulldozer; they are cleared away for a new wave of suburbanites with newer ideas, and the adulteries of those who remain give way to quiet evenings of bridge.

The structure of *Couples* is not that realism [sic]. The plot is Victorian, full of symmetries and reversals and ironic parallels. The bounce of basketballs, the smell of boxes of hot pizza, and the interiors of suburban stationwagons are so richly observed, however, that one might comfortably forget the contrivances of plot and accept the genre as realistic.

Failures occur. The conversations surrounding the death of Kennedy—and some others—are awkward and self-conscious. (Historical fact seems to inhibit Updike's imagination; the world of his mind does not coincide with the contours of real events. He most accurately reveals our truth when faithful to his own world.) Often, too, Updike's stream of consciousness becomes boring; for, though he has mastered sprung rhythm (a reading of Hopkins' "The Wreck of the Deutschland" prepares one to predict the fall of the syllables in many Updike sequences), he has not yet discovered how to vary it.

In *Couples*, Updike proves himself as a storyteller; he fulfills the promise reposed in him. Piet Hanema and Foxy Whitman and Angela Hanema take on warm, strong, although America-flattened life. (Americans are more homogenized than "underdeveloped" peoples, more carefully trained, more thoroughly repressed.) The discovery of a new form of paganism is the first order of business in America; we have got to regain unity with our bodies, our sexuality, our passions. And yet Tarbox is not the model: poor, sad, self-destroying circle, children of Mary McCarthy's *Group*, and parents of a disdaining, disowning generation yet to come.

# Talking Head

**Jonathan Raban***

Updike's style—or ironic hyperbole, glittering, exact, yet thrown away with a casual, disarming grin—is as winning and as polished as the people from whose voice it derives. It evokes those clever, furry, peripatetic Americans who slip from theatre foyers in London to the great libraries and museums of Europe; Guggenheim fellowship holders, liberal democrats, occasional contributors to late-night chat programmes on TV, mild anglophiles with an etiolated passion for seafood. It is the neo-augustan style of the calculatedly down-at-heel suburb—a style of discreet disengagement, in which the witty periphrasis of the wry raconteur is seen, in effect, as the last resort of the cultivated writer confronted by the contemporary abstractions and extremities of America.

*Bech* is a lucid, deliciously (indeed, maliciously) readable exploration of this style; a book which deliberately fails to become a novel about a famous, blocked, Jewish-American novelist. Henry Bech is a subsidised cultural tourist; touting [sic] a document-case of lecture notes, he treks across eastern Europe, through a Mayfair party, down the King's Road, into a Southern college full of belles blooming and popping with warm, pink sex. He is a tourist even in his own backyard; he tries pot with an ex-student just as his vacationing countrymen might try squid, fortified with stomach pacifiers; in bed with his mistresses, he makes love like a man pointing a Kodak at the Parthenon. But Updike's special achievement lies in the way that he makes us aware that such tourism is far more than an attitude of mind; it is an—one might almost say *the*—American style. For, through Bech, Updike carries his own witty, circumlocutory delivery to the point of self-parody, exposing its most celebrated and well-reviewed virtues as the lonely charade of a man on the run.

The characters in *Bech* are reduced to brilliant, comic, illustrative figures of anecdote. We know them by their accessories—granny glasses, a flesh-coloured hearing aid—or through images which turn them into birds, plants or gaudy knick-knacks off an assembly line. Deadly, dehumanising metaphors race through Updike's prose like a facetious, nervous tic. Bech's block is not really a block at all; his writing of fiction has simply been transformed into his whole style of social behaviour. Society has become social detail; people have turned into characters; conversations into dialogues. In fact, the dialogue in *Bech* reads like a marathon competition; a nightmare extension of those promotional quizzes which end up asking you to think up 'the most amusing, witty or apt' continuation to a given sentence in 'not more than 15 words'. The tone of Bech's interiorised narration is wry, self-ironising; an elaborate

*Review of *Bech: A Book*. From *New Stateman*, 80 (October 16, 1970), 494. Copyright © 1970. Reprinted with permission of The Statesman and Nation Publishing Company Ltd.

pastiche of the Hasidic soul-searching of that soulful double-act, Mallow and Belamud. It is as if Moses Herzog, Yakov Bok and Alex Portnoy had become so engrossed in their own spiritual development that they had succeeded in turning the entire external world into a series of bizarre shadows on a screen. At one point, Updike calls this assortment of *contes* 'Bech's pilgrimage', but the word is inflected with self-mockery. Pilgrimages, and novels too, grow out of more stable and continuous environments than this scrapbook tour of the nodal points of the Sixties and their associated styles in American fiction.

Yet if *Bech* is primarily an affectionate rejection of one kind of recent American novel, it signals Updike's own earnest apprenticeship to another. The book is studded with small acts of homage to Nabokov, and comes rigged out with spoof appendices, a bibliography and a commendatory introduction by Bech himself. We are in the vertiginous territory of the fiction of fiction; the looking-glass world of Borgés, where the universe is described as a library, the library as a universe. In the Borgésian maze, everything is inverted. What looks at first sight like brilliantly observed social detail turns out to be a facetious exposé of the literariness, the strict conventionality of observation itself. 'Russia', 'Rumania', 'London', 'Massachusetts' all go into implicit quotation marks; stylistic figments in the mind of the archetypal writer, of Henry Bech.

What is most disturbing about this book is the degree to which one questions Updike's control over these mind-bending devices. It turns from a confident, swashbuckling exercise in pastiche into an extraordinarily cold and echoing novel about loneliness; not the loneliness of Henry Bech, exactly, so much as the loneliness of a style—the loneliness of the talking head filling a bright screen in the centre of an empty room. The places and the characters in the book slip away, like so many gaily-painted cartoons, leaving that clever, ironic, cultivated voice chattering in well-turned antitheses. *Bech* is a book of desolate wit; but Updike never finally manages to reveal whose desolation we are witnessing.

# Updike on the Present

## Charles Samuels*

Last year, in *Mr. Sammler's Planet*, Saul Bellow attempted to analyze the chaos of the present. His novel is distinguished by intellectual cogency, but the narrative from which he draws his inferences is lamentably inadequate to the energy of his denunciation. Also a study of con-

*Review of *Rabbit Redux*. From *The New Republic*, 165 (November 20, 1971), 29–30.
Copyright © 1971. Reprinted with permission of *The New Republic*.

temporary problems, John Updike's new book, *Rabbit Redux,* offers far more compelling a plot and characters, but it disappoints precisely where Bellow is strong: in fathoming causes and asserting judgments.

Both novels focus on heroes who have survived an age that puts them out of step with its successor. Both see the new period as one of unbridled permissiveness. But whereas Mr. Sammler clearly expresses his author's own strictures, Updike's hero exhibits the problem as much as he is repelled by it.

At the beginning of the novel, Rabbit is a diminution of his former self. Starting, in *Rabbit, Run,* as a man in conflict with his culture, he has become in the sequel, a perfect example of its repressiveness. Ten years older now, he has lost the nickname—emblem of his former vitality; he has become Harry, "pale and sour." Gone are the hopes of truth to self and God, that, baleful in their effects, were nonetheless inspiring in their fervor. Harry has settled into a mediocre job, a sterile marriage, a tired acceptance of all the second-rateness he once tried to flee. Through guilt at his youthful rebelliousness, he has become meanly conservative ('I once took the inner light trip and all I did was bruise my surroundings. Revolution, or whatever, is just a way of saying a mess is fun."). Because his attempted flight produced his daughter's death, he no longer hopes to fly. Personally exhausted, he can only summon enthusiasm now for the power of the State. To him the Vietnam War is a flaccid society's last sign of commitment. Self-contempt and boredom have, through a kind of reaction formation, turned him into a chauvinist.

By a deliberate reversal of his original plot, Updike hurls this burnt-out case into contemporaneity. The earlier book began with Rabbit's escape from marriage; this novel begins with his wife's. Janice has now found a lover who holds out the same promise of sensual fulfillment that Rabbit once pursued. But whereas possessiveness and fear of scandal had caused Janice and her family to fight Rabbit's decision, Harry is now too passive to repay the compliment. So Janice bolts, leaving him, as he had earlier left her, to tend their house and son.

In the earlier book, after he leaves Janice, Rabbit is taken by his coach to a restaurant where he meets the loose-living Ruth. The two then set up house and fall in love. Rabbit infuses the cynical Ruth with some of his own hopefulness, but the affair ends badly. In *Rabbit Redux* a black co-worker takes the hero to a bar, where he meets a loose-living hippie from Suburbia. Jill and Harry also set up house, this time in Harry's home. The affair ends even more tragically, and Harry never helps the girl. Now it is the female rather than the male who tries to rouse the loved one from lethargy. Though Harry can feel a renewal of sexuality that had been quelled in his marriage, he can neither embrace Jill's hippie ethos nor her love.

The third part of *Rabbit, Run* is essentially a debate between Rabbit and Reverend Eccles, a false apostle of the pharisaical humanism. But

Rabbit's authenticity proves too vital for the pale cleric, whose dialectical net the hero breaks through. In *Rabbit Redux* the interlocutor is a black revolutionary friend of Jill's, in flight from police pursuing him on a drug charge. This section of the novel is both more powerful than anything Updike has written and more terrifying a picture of social tension than Bellow shows in his collection of caricature vices and farcical pecadillos.

Watched by the girl and Harry's son, the black man, Skeeter, and the white enter a love-hate relationship that ends in tragedy. Skeeter holds Harry in thrall to his own rage and hatred for America through long evenings in which Harry begins to take on the marks of hippie and black. The flamboyant Skeeter sees Vietnam as an apocalyptic result of America's evil, which will be succeeded by a "great *calm*," and then by black hegemony. To all this, Harry listens attentively, finally reading Skeeter tracts on black triumph and producing literally orgiastic pleasure in his guest.

Along with this intellectual seduction goes the sexual brutalization of Jill by Skeeter, which Harry watches. The girl had fled her suburban home with the help of a lover who hooked her on drugs so that she could, in her hallucinations, help him to see God. Realizing itself first in acts of perverse sexuality in which he demands Jill's participation, Skeeter's racial rage finally brings her back to the drugged stupor she had originally tried to escape. Yet Harry does not try to prevent Skeeter from hooking Jill, much less admit to himself that this is the terrible drama transpiring in his home. Nor does he prevent the black from flaunting his power over Jill before the neighbors, though that eventually ignites the fiery hatred which claims both Jill's life and Harry's dwelling. Instead, Harry drives Skeeter to safety when the fire is being investigated, thus keeping the man from falling victim to the same racist fury that cost Jill her life.

The last section of the novel introduces Harry's sister, Mim, formerly the embodiment of innocence but here a sage of cynicism. Mim sleeps with Janice's lover, thus helping to break up the affair; but Janice, who had always predicted that it could not end in marriage, decides, on her own, to return to Harry. The novel ends with husband and wife wanly reconciled, in connubial sleep, Skeeter and Jill consigned to oblivion, and a tentative "OK?" addressed by Updike to the reader.

This "OK?" suggests that Updike knows how great a risk he has taken in this book by telling a dreadful story and yet refusing to express rage or dread at its conclusion. He has documented the crisis of the present more movingly than Bellow; it is arguable that were he to join Bellow in expressing judgment and a more positive prescription, the very power of his story would render the attempt unconvincing. When all this has been acknowledged, however, Updike remains too mute about questions of motivation to keep *Rabbit Redux* from having the dispiriting effect of a sordid story that is told to no clear purpose.

The questions arise in Part II, after Updike has established his hero, cut him loose from his past and faced him with the possibility of coming back to life. We understand that sexual desire impels Harry to take Jill home with him, just as we understand that spiritual exhaustion can only allow him to toy with the idea of loving her. But as his failure with Jill escalates into active collusion in destroying her, his motivation becomes less clear. Why, for example, does he allow Skeeter to stay? When the man appears, Harry is drawn into a brawl with him. Then, on an impulse that even surprises Jill, he reverses his attitude. More importantly, what are we to think of Skeeter and, consequently, of Harry's domination by him?

If we judge by the plot, Skeeter is an even more dangerous teacher than Reverend Eccles, whom Rabbit, to his credit, resisted. Considering Skeeter's apparent motives, isn't Harry to be condemned for his greater susceptibility in this case? Skeeter seems less interested in changing the world than in playing out a psychodrama in which Harry is forced to atone for white racism by voluntarily witnessing the humiliation and destruction of a white woman by a black man. Why does Harry watch this so willingly? Why doesn't he eject Skeeter, since not only Jill but his son fears the man? Unacknowledged national guilt may predispose him to hear Skeeter out, but what dark bond draws him into nearly sexual identification with his sinister guest? Emotional exhaustion both accounts for and partially excuses his acceptance of an atmosphere of polymorphous perversity, but does Jill really seem to want this as much as Harry thinks she does or is he shamefully trying to escape that minimum of responsibility we feel for another human being, even without love? And what explains his failure to recognize that Skeeter is hooking Jill, despite the many hints that she and the child provide? Perhaps he hates Jill, who is upper-class, out of a resentment parallel to Skeeter's resentment of whites (one scene suggests this); perhaps he sacrifices her to his own yearning to recontact God (there are also clues to this); perhaps, like America itself, he is merely an exhausted being who can only be quickened by cruelty? We can never quite sort these possibilities out. When Harry protects Skeeter after Jill's death, even Skeeter expresses bewilderment about the hero's motive.

This obscurity makes Updike's final refusal to pass judgment particularly disturbing. In the last scene of *Rabbit, Run*, after his behavior has also brought disastrous results, Rabbit disclaims responsibility for the death of his child. This we accept not only because, as in *Rabbit Redux*, he did not literally perform the crime, but because the characters and the motives ranged against him justify his denial. They are inspired by vindictiveness and egotism rather than ethics; even in his selfish destructiveness, Rabbit is more moral than they in their moralistic conformity. But in *Rabbit Redux* Harry has no connection with anything that might be called a value, and his victim is more nearly his responsibility than the baby he barely saw in the earlier book.

Hence, the refusal to determine the moral significance of the terrible events is Updike's and not his hero's. Indeed, Harry himself feels guilty for Jill's death, but the fourth part of the novel seems to resist his impulse to shame. Its primary functions are resolution of the plot and expression, through Mim and even Janice, of a bleak desolating imperturbability. Janice tells Harry that "Not everything is [his] fault," but we are not sure exactly what was. After having had his life transformed by the highlights of contemporary discard (Vietnam, racism, drugs, hippies), Harry can only assert that "utter confusion" is "Just a local view of things working out in general." When the Angstroms are reconciled, they refer to Skeeter and Jill as items that settle a moral score (the baby's death paid by the girl's), but surely Jill and Skeeter mean more than fortuitous renovation of the crumbling household.

Though we know from life that these figures are portentous, in the novel they merely illustrate a general malaise, the causes of which are barely explored. In *Rabbit Redux* Updike absorbs into his fiction some of the chief sources of our discontent and distills them into characters realistically impelled by conflicting motives. However, refusing to sort out the motives or to explain the discontent, he leaves us as baffled and dispirited as the age itself.

This is to pay no small compliment. But, can we settle for analysis in excess of narrative power, as in Bellow, or the reverse, as in Updike? Since both men have had their greatest successes in fathoming more intimate relations, shorn of the largest historical dimension, they suggest that warnings against realism in so chaotic a period may be well taken. So one puts down a book like *Rabbit Redux* moved, respectful of the writer's bravery, but still waiting for the perhaps impossible novel that will not only show us how we live now but also why we live in this awful way.

# From "The Curious Greased Grace" of John Updike

## William Stafford*

John Updike . . . appears already to have established a clearly-discernible fictional world, one uniquely his, with an impressive array of characters, a variety of settings that reflect the world outside even as they establish his world within. It is a world with its own language, a style, that is, Updike talk, as recognizably *his* as Yoknapatawpha is Faulkner's or the vast post-Victorian internationalized America and Europe are Henry James's. That Updike's fictional world also discernibly relates to

*Review of *Rabbit Redux*. From *Journal of Modern Literature*, 2 (1972), 569–75. Copyright ©
1972. Reprinted with permission of *Journal of Modern Literature*.

his literal world is no more a fault than similar ties between Melville and his sea adventures, James and the world's metropolitan capitals, or Faulkner and northern Mississippi. And none of these great writers—is even Faulkner an exception?—laid the outlines of his fictional world (in, say, his five novels) with more sureness, imagination, or style (in all senses of that last word) than has John Hoyer Updike.

This was never clearer than with the publication of *Rabbit Redux,* his sixth novel, his audaciously bold sequel to *Rabbit, Run.* The impishly interrogative "O.K.?" . . . with which Updike ends his latest chronicle of Rabbit has provoked widely differing critical responses. And it might be instructive to look briefly here at two disparate ways that last book has been reviewed, . . . . One is a resounding "Nay" to Updike's question; the other, a clear-cut "Yea."

The Nay-sayer, Christopher Ricks, in the *New York Review* (December 14, 1971), begins with this account of the novel's actions:

> *Rabbit Redux* brings back after ten years—and brings back to health (Webster's Dictionary, quoted on the blurb)—Rabbit Angstrom, now thirty-six. He's with his wife Janice, but cold and stale. What then happens is that she commits adultery; Rabbit lets her go, and takes up with a classy addicted hippie, Jill, and her black messianic angel, Skeeter. Neighborhood arsonists burn down the house, and Jill is killed. Rabbit and Janice come back together. The book is mildly optimistic—is indeed more warmly optimistic than it thinks prudent to make patent.

This is succinct and fair enough. And the cute disclaimer in his final sentence, " . . . more warmly optimistic than it thinks prudent to make patent," is precisely his objection to the novel.

For Ricks, Updike here is merely clever, an old charge—"There is more activity than purposefulness." The 1969 moon shot, which frames the action of the novel, doesn't really work. The novel's "rich . . . sense of possible parallels between oral sex and verbalism or certain verbal habits" is "funked or slighted," as is "a sense of parallels between the job of linotyping and the job of writing." Next to being merely clever, the novel is seen as being merely observant. But "noticing," we are told, "is not enough." And following several examples of the mere cleverness of the moon-shot frame and of the word-play via Rabbit's job as type-setter, we are told that "it isn't that one refuses to behave in ways that suit his book; it's that the book itself isn't clear what would suit itself." In a word (or two), it is too coy, too cute, too ultimately empty. The novel for Ricks has no aesthetic rationale. And returning to the Angstroms rather than beginning anew is "likely to do retrospective damage to that better book *Rabbit, Run."* It ends with manipulation, "plotting" instead of "plot." There are innuendos about the sales appeal of nostalgia, charges of soft-headedness ("kind at heart, and at head"), and the assertion that Updike is incapable of any aesthetic distance from Rabbit which, "as his first great success," is "always in danger of becoming to his, Updike's career, what Rabbit's early success [his basketball?] was to Rabbit['s]." Updike's rendered retribution there was a little too easy—and here much too easy. Ricks makes no reference to any of Updike's other books, or, indeed, to other American writing. "Flopsy Bunny" is the review's title.

The Yea-sayer, Richard Locke, in *The New York Times Book Review* (November 14, 1971), not only surveys the canon; he places Updike among his immediate American contemporaries (Bellow, Mailer, Malamud, and Roth, among others), declares *Rabbit Redux* "the best of the lot" among recent offerings by these other writers, and was no doubt instrumental, as an editor of the *Times Book Review*, in getting Updike, under the guise of his fictional Henry Bech, facetiously to interview himself about the novel in this same issue. (Updike's prediction there that 1981 may well see still another sequel, "Rural Rabbit," and in 1991 still another. "Rabbit is Rich," is perhaps less facetious than it at first appears. Poverty of subject-matter, repetitiveness of theme, will apparently never be a problem for Updike, as it never was for Faulkner, in contrast, say, to Hemingway and Fitzgerald.)

Locke's praise for the novel is often precisely over the points about which Ricks demurs. His view of the resolution is that "a more complex health and order *is* [my italics] achieved." The moon-shot frame is highly praised, " . . . elements are subtly brought together in the controlling image of space exploration, a journey out into a void and then back to earth." Updike is seen as dealing "in a large way with public subjects" for the first time: "violence, the Vietnam war, black revolution, drug addiction, middle American anger and frustration, hippie life-styles, the moon shot." Arguments about the war, for example, are seen as beautifully integrated into their "psychological, novelistic base. Rabbit gets wild about Vietnam when he feels personally and sexually threatened; he overcomes his fear and dislike of blacks when he himself is an outcast and a cuckold." And the blacks in Bellows' *Mr. Sammler's Planet* and in Malamud's *The Tenants* are described as coming "nowhere near the depth and accuracy of Updike's black characters." Finally, the sequel doesn't weaken *Rabbit, Run*; it augments it. Rabbit is driven inward by a static social situation in the first novel; in the latter, "a dynamic social situation" plunges him outward, "beyond his family, his class, his race and his normal earthbound feelings and behavior." One is a book of the 1950's; the other of the 1960's. And only Mailer, he concludes, approaches Updike here in helping "us come to some unsteady and evolving understanding of our human and cultural predicament as we slide into the seventies." His final praise for the book "as by far the most . . . successful . . . Updike has written" rests on its coming closer than any other to Updike's most ambitious statements about his artistic creed, his attempts to come to grips with that eloquent truth that " 'everything is infinitely fine and any opinion is somehow coarser than the texture of the real thing . . .' " and his consequent belief that " 'everything unambiguously expressed seems somehow crass. . . .' "

That "somehow crass" is my key—for Locke's high praise no less than Ricks's Funny Bunny-isms, . . . . Updike's writing, you see, for me, is itself "the real thing" and perhaps nowhere more "infinitely fine" than here in *Rabbit Redux*. Yet, how somehow more than coarse it is to say that this is so. How crass the comment, however, admiring or damning, when set up against the achieved fact of the fiction.

The black-white relations in the novel, for a single example, go way beyond the Bellow-Malamud parallels Locke refers to. They go back to Melville of "Benito Cereno" and of course to *Huckleberry Finn*. They go back to Updike's own fiction too, to Peter Caldwell's black mistress in *The Centaur* and to some of Updike's complex attitudes toward blacks in such early stories as "Toward Evening" in *The Same Door*. Yet, that complex is so intricately developed in *Rabbit Redux* (with sex, the war, and drugs) that justice to its achievement by literary analogue is suggested, for me, only through some wild imaginary literary offspring of conglomerate attitudes toward blacks that would result, say, from a metaphorical marriage of William Faulkner and James Baldwin. But pose even that against the fiction itself:

> Physically, Skeeter fascinates Rabbit. The lustrous pallor of the tongue and palms and the soles of the feet, left out of the sun. Or a different kind of skin? White palms never tan either. The peculiar glinting lustre of his skin. The something so very finely turned and finished in the face, reflecting at a dozen polished points: in comparison white faces are blobs: putty still drying. The curious greased grace of his gestures, rapid and watchful as a lizard's motions, free of mammalian fat. Skeeter in his house feels like a finely made electric toy; Harry wants to touch him but is afraid he will get a shock.

"The curious greased grace of his gestures" is vintage Updike, thematically and stylistically, "a sentence that is 100-proof Anchovy," as E. B. White once said about one of Thoreau's. And the critic touches it at his own peril. It is Updike's own. No one else could have written it; and the complex of its context, the Rabbit-Skeeter relationship, their relationship in turn to Rabbit's marvelously-rendered son, Nelson, and to his hippy-mistress-"daughter," Jill, all radiate outward to his wife, her lover, Rabbit's parents, the town, space—before turning back inward to the curious greased grace of Updike's own reflectively familiar world.

Other elements of the novel are also both reminiscent of America's literary past and uniquely Updike's own. His women, for example, are almost without parallel in American fiction. Yet, when Harry observes, near the end of the novel, that "all this fucking . . . makes . . . [him] too sad. It's what makes everything so hard to run," it is the now returned wife, Janice, who replies, "You don't think it's what *makes* things run?

Human things?" And when Harry retorts, "There must be something else," it could have been, we think (except of course for the language) a discussion between Hawthorne's Dimmesdale and Hester Prynne near the end of *The Scarlet Letter*. The young hippie, Jill, is equally good, almost a mixture, one is tempted to say, of Maisie Farange and Lolita. And Harry's returned sister, Mim, now a Las Vegas call girl who had also been a Disneyland guide, is simply good fun, as she seduces, for Harry's sake, his wife's lover. (It is also good fun if she is also the little Gloria Angstrom of that very early story, "Tomorrow and Tomorrow and So Forth" [*The Same Door*], who cons her high school teachers with mash notes!)

The play with American literary history (*and* John Updike's own) is rampant in the novel. (Even the typographical play with the linotype has the precedent of *As I Lay Dying*, not to mention *Midpoint*.) But that "fact" is a crass fact too, as "coarse" as any other. Updike somehow deserves more. Uncritical adulation is not the answer. But neither is smart-assed aphorisms. Pretentious and tendentious pedantry is as bad as approaches to fiction as social history. Literary antecedants and parallels establish similarities, but what of the differences? Literary history is fun, but where, ultimately, does it take one? Great finished fictional worlds are marvels to behold. We can learn their languages and plot their perimeters, stamp and staple and standardize their inhabitants, relate part to part and each to the whole. We can define their gods and come to know their devils. But when still a-building, they are gluey "things" indeed. What appears as heavenly edifices today can rapidly melt to hovels tomorrow. And prophecy *can* be fatal.

Even so, Updike's still-embryonic fictional world, for me, is already more finely tuned (to the ambiguous thens *and* nows) of modern life than that of any American novelist since Faulkner's. And if literary criticism, including my own, doesn't quite know what to do with that fact, it probably doesn't really matter. For not until Updike is dead, I predict, will his "world" have come fully alive. But come alive, it will.

# The Sorrow of Some Central Hollowness

**Tony Tanner***

There is a character in Gogol's "Dead Souls" call Plyushkin, all of whose life energy goes into accumulating and hoarding things, down to the smallest pieces of sealing wax, scraps of paper and feathers. With a

*Review of *Museums and Women and Other Stories*. From *New York Times Book Review*, 22 October 1972, pp. 5, 24. Copyright © 1972 The New York Times Company. Reprinted by permission.

brilliantly appropriate metaphor, Gogol tells us that "in the end he himself became a kind of gaping hole in humankind." The crucial human emotions have been crowded out by the amassed litter of his life. There is something about a lot of John Updike's characters that reminds me of the terrible inner hollowness of that man emotionally deadened by his submission to things. Not that Updike presents us with an American suburbia tenanted by untidy misers (though some of his characters are deep in clutter). On the contrary, he is astute enough to detect that a distaste for litter is one of the fostering emotions in much American suburban life. I am referring to the feeling I have of reading about people in whom the capacity for a key emotional response or experience has been omitted or eradicated, leaving a small central void that diminishes or undermines the authenticity of their other emotional experiences.

We know by now what Updike can convey to us of familial experience in suburban America, and in many of these stories once again he does it incomparably well—the abrasiveness of children quarreling; the insecurities and anxieties involved in moving house or changing district; the trivial tumescences of the cocktail party; the irresolvable misery of participating in an affair that lacks the stability of marriage and in a marriage that cannot recapture the passion of an affair; the modest pleasures of the kitchen, the garden, a picnic, a day out with the children; the exhaustions of middle age; the drifting apart of friends; the tensions between different generations; the sudden waves of dread in which the reassuring forms of suburbia dissolve in cosmic panic. And perhaps above all—a growing fear at the inexorable approach of death and the ungraspable notion of personal annihilation.

What I seldom if ever feel is that these inhabitants of Tarbox or wherever have experienced the capacity to love—as distinct from the inclination to copulate and the compulsion to propagate. And without that, their furtive embraces and tired loyalties, their households and their hangovers—all seem miserably meaningless, as though the sorrow of some central hollowness has seeped into every corner of their lives.

It may be, of course, that this is part of Updike's vision of American life. This could be supported by considering one of the best stories in this book, "I am Dying, Egypt, Dying," which is Updike's version of the beautiful Ugly American. The blurb, which is sufficiently direct and unpretentious to make one think that perhaps the author wrote it, calls this story an allegory of American foreign policy. Given the international juxtapositions and confrontations among the characters taking a voyage down the Nile to the Aswan Dam, such a reading is possible. Thus the Russian couple are surly, graceless, keep to themselves, while the American, Clem, is tirelessly extrovert, charming, always trying to please. But whereas Clem can hear the Russians making love in a fairly direct functional way, he has a pillow for a bed partner, and when a girl offers herself to him, he proves impotent.

As an allegory it doesn't go very deep; but as a portrait of a certain kind of American it seems to me very penetrating. Thus Clem, rich and drifting, feels himself to be "merely visiting the world." He cannot ever be said to be in his element because he doesn't have one. His treasure, and his curse, is his "lightness"—he can move on, he can be blown away. He is aware of an "untouched emptiness" inside him and experiences the sensation of "hollowness, of being in parentheses." He is a mirror but not a lamp; he can reflect love but not originate it. "The world was his but slid through him."

His relationships, or non-relationships, with the other people on the ship are deftly sketched in, the evocation of his shifting moods and changing inner weather is convincing, and Updike's undeniable gift for establishing terrain and setting is as operative in Egypt as it is in America (though, as usual, his gift for the unusual simile is sometimes a little obtrusive, as when bats move on the walls "like intelligent black gloves.") Perhaps it was partly the enjoyment of seeing Updike allow himself to spread his imagination beyond the rather wearisome boundaries of Tarbox, etc., but I responded as positively to this story as to anything else in the book.

The title story is clever (Updike must be tired of being told how clever he is, but there it is—he really is very clever), but less satisfactory. It reads like an essay, a reminiscence, but we discover that the narrator is not Updike and the piece devolves into a scrap of fiction which is gratuitous and unresolved—and, frankly, sentimental. The clever part is the unforced interplay and connection between the ways in which men enter women and museums with different needs, in search of different things. In both, man must always reach "the limits of unsearchability." And the narrator is not really referring only to museums when he describes his apprehension that "each new entrance" will bring less exaltation and a more rapid disenchantment.

Updike's narrator writes with sympathy and insight about women. But despite his sensitivity, he fails to persuade me of the genuineness of his experience of love. Clem, the American, is utterly convincing in his inner emptiness. I find it hard to think of any character in Updike's work who is convincing in his, or her, inner plenitude. Whereas Clem is obviously intended as a study in emotional aridity, it is less clear in the other stories whether the hint of inner vacuity is a defect in the characters, or a flaw in the author's vision.

Having made that observation, it is only fair to add that most of the stories are extremely readable, not one of them without some moments of dazzling minute observation, some sudden glide of psychological percipience, some abrupt accuracy about the harassments and consolations of day-to-day living. The narrator of one story refers to the "fragmentary illuminations" he experiences and recalls. The thought occurred to me that in some ways Updike may well be a better short-story writer than he is a novelist, for in his way he is quite phenomenally alert to "fragmentary illuminations" and can find them anywhere—thus one story is simply about a street corner, another focuses on an abandoned swimming pool, and so on.

On the other hand, I have to admit that his last novel, "Rabbit Redux," struck me as a deplorable performance by a writer of Updike's abilities, revealing an embarrassing straining from contemporaneity, and a sad capitulation to the stereotypical thinking of Middle America. It was a pleasure to read this collection of stories after that, and perhaps the shorter mode reveals Updike at his best. Summary of each plot or situation would be pointless. For the record, the book offers 14 varied stories dealing with aspects of contemporary America, 10 short pieces collectively called "Other Modes," and five more stories about the Maples, another of those couples in Updike's fictional world.

If Updike is not convincing, to me, about love, he is convincing about the continual presence of fear—that fear engendered by the realization that everything decays, erodes, deteriorates and dies, which has been in his work from the start. One story is simply about "Plumbing," the commonplace need for some expensive new pipes. But Updike's plumber is a "poet . . . musing upon the eternal presences of corrosion and flow." Updike, too, is just such a poet, carefully inspecting the strained and faulty substructures that maintain family suburban life, admiring the machinery that holds and works, but noting the gathering rust, the spreading cracks. And, like the narrator of this particular story, he comes up to the surface and looks up into the sky and, with a shiver of mortality, recognizes our ephemerality—"All around us, we are outlasted."

# Doughy Middleness

## D. Keith Mano*

John Updike is a slummer. In his fiction. Extradited from the real world to imaginary Brewer or Tarbox, I doubt if he could sustain ten minutes' conversation with Rabbit Angstrom, with any of the many singles in *Couples*. Updike's characters don't deserve a form letter obituary, let alone a novel. They are pathetic folk; even the pathos is undistinguished. Great issues aren't at issue in Updike's fiction. When ignorant armies clash by night, his people are somewhere else on the beach, skinny dipping perhaps.

Updike is our genteel Gentile: the sweet, lonesome singer of Protestant mediocrity. For his first historical venture Updike has chosen America's rabbit, run President: James the Worst. In another novelist it

*Review of *Buchanan Dying*. From *National Review*, 26 (August 30, 1974), 987. Copyright © 1974. Reprinted by permission of National Review Inc.

would seem affectation. In Updike it's merely shyness, modesty, and—despite all the bestsellers—underconfidence. Apparently his romance with middleness has a geographic sanction. In the guileless, delightful "Apologia pro Opere Suo" afterword to *Buchanan Dying*, he writes, "Here is Buchanan, I am rid of him, and this book, a mosaic with more tesserae than matrix, constitutes, I trust, my final volume of homage to my native state [Pennsylvania], whose mild misty doughy middleness, between immoderate norths and souths, remains for me, being my first taste of life, the authentic taste."

Pennsylvania, my God. Only a magnificent eccentric could run up debts to Pennsylvania. Updike has pulled it off somehow. He started *Buchanan Dying* "in 1968 as an act of penance for a commercially successful novel set in New England." This bizarre assertion of guilt can be credited. For some time Updike and I shared publishers. A mutual editor told me that Updike had been mortified by *Couples'* success, felt he had committed a gross abuse of the artistic will. He wouldn't look at the royalty statements. They accused him.

Eccentric, sure: Updike belongs in a Cheever novel. And, like most eccentrics, he is not a funny man. You may laugh at the aptness of his characterizations or, for joy, at the nifty metaphors, but there is no slapstick in his heart. Updike people don't astonish you; they don't do preposterous things. That, after all, would be another gross abuse. Updike, the gentleman, never asks you to suspend disbelief. He takes Rabbit and Pennsylvania and, yes, James Buchanan dead seriously. This is a nice trick. The title itself appears crammed with bathos, *Buchanan Dying*. Might as well be *The Dialogues of Calvin Coolidge* or *Archie Bunker Agonistes*. But Updike has been fair to Buchanan. This fairness is certainly a strength: his first ground rule. It's also a severe limitation. Updike takes none of those liberties which are the novelist's only pleasure. He's a middle class realist. By all standards Updike should be unread. He is read a lot. It's the best tribute yet to frankness and deft style.

Yet, one or two stage directions aside, that style is absent with leave in *Buchanan Dying, A Play*. Updike, of course, has perfect pitch: his mimic ear fixes the several accents of nineteenth century America. But these are mostly public accents: ornamentation and rhetorical periods grind gears in the sentence, so many 40-foot trailers on an upgrade. I read plays aloud: 70 percent of *Buchanan Dying* induced thumps from the floor above or barks from a neighbor dog. At 180 pages this top of the voice dialogue feels about four score and ten too long. *Buchanan Dying* is the great man's hobby horse: equivalent to a ride on Walt Disney's backyard steam engine. Updike plays the historian: his 80-page afterword is deadpan, footnoted, scholarly, and more entertaining by far than the play. In effect *Buchanan Dying* is a versatile penance: not only about Pennsylvanians, but also built to repel vulgar royalties, as silicone waterproofing sheds rain. Updike, I think, meant it as a rebuke to those who relished the sexual mix and match of *Couples.* Don't, says he who crafted *The Centaur,* enjoy me too easily.

Fairness disabled Updike. His Buchanan research was the matrix of a novel. But consecutive narrative would have required presumptions, ahistorical bridges. Unfair. "An actual man, Buchanan, had done this and this, exactly so, once and no other way. There was no air." Also few associations for the quick-fingered metaphorist to reshape. Updike is a realist; he approaches the real through his five senses. "But researched details failed to act like remembered ones, they had no palpable medium of the half remembered in which to swim." He compromised with a play. The play is trite in form; a pastiche of letters, speeches, reported confrontations. Blackouts over the death bed provide bridges. Updike handles it well enough; still this dramatic mechanism is hackneyed as the flashback montage in film.

Buchanan is Updike's kind of people. The well-intentioned, middling man, hung up in a rundown between North and South, abolitionist and slaveholder. Despite presidential prerogatives, he's hardly more decisive than Rabbit Angstrom, vegetating between moonwalkers and militant blacks. Buchanan is also Updike's kind of Christian: that's to say, he'd make agnosticism look zealous. Updike knows a whole lot about being Protestant: the carpentry of churches, the half remembered smell of old hymnals. His Tarbox-Brewer folk consider this half-memory a middle class prerequisite, like dancing lessons. Take, for instance, Buchanan's passionate vision on the road to Damascus: "My mind is now made up. I hope that I am a Christian. I think I have much of the experience which you describe, and, as soon as I retire from office as President, I will unite with the Presbyterian church." A statement made, certainly, by the light of burning martyrs. He's not much more emphatic on the slavery question.

Yet Updike is fair to Buchanan. "All in all, I did not find in these general histories confirmation that Buchanan was 'the worst President in the history of the country.' " Updike is fair to just about everyone; he must be a superb father and husband. There are neither villains nor saints in his fiction. He plumps for no ideology: that would be an abuse of the artist's position. In fact, John Updike, out of kindness or acedia, has very little to say. And no one writing in America says it better.

# Never on Sunday

**Gilbert Sorrentino***

The surface of Mr. Updike's writing twitches and quivers incessantly, never more so than in this new novel about a faintly hedonist minister "with doubts." By some process of intellection that is foreign to me this prose tic has been critically taken to be a sublime style; the disparaging word, as it were, is rare to come by apropos Mr. Updike's work. When it is discovered it manifests itself as no more than a slight reservation. I don't know why this should be so. Mr. Updike has all the grievous faults of an Oscar Wilde updated to include contemporary paraphernalia, speech, etc., but none of these things can disguise the purple blush that suffuses the work. It is, if I may use such a word, unachieved, i.e., its fancy images are not in touch with the world but emblazon it. The writing is what is in some quarters known as "vivid."

We played in each other like children in puddles.

Mr. Updike writes. Why not "mud" instead of puddles? Or "dogs" instead of children? Or anything at all for that matter? When the aim is "vivid" writing, it seems that anything goes as long as the surface dances.

The work buckles and falls apart time after time under the weight of this concatenation of images, often linked together by comparisons that work to conceal the reality they are supposedly revealing.

. . . newsletters and quarterlies that pour through a minister's letter slot like urine from a cow's vulva.

Mr. Updike has many more tricks in his book, one of them the disfiguring and falsifying one of anthropomorphizing anything that threatens to escape the net of his ego.

The moon peered crookedly over his shoulder, curious enough to tilt its head.

The blue night barked as I opened the door.

It might however be argued, fairly enough, that this is not Mr. Updike's voice, since the novel purports to be a diary/journal kept by the Reverend Thomas Marshfield, the narrator. In fact, the flap copy, taking note of this, bubbles that the minister's confessions are rendered in a "wonderfully overwrought style." This might legitimize the flaws of the novel except for the fact that Marshfield's style as given in *A Month of Sundays* is the author's in other books. The only one I have to hand is *Pigeon Feathers*, but haphazard rummaging through it turns up—in the third person—the same "wonderfully overwrought style."

*Review of *A Month of Sundays*. From *Partisan Review*, 43 (1976), 119–21. Copyright © 1976. Reprinted by permission of *Partisan Review* and Gilbert Sorrentino.

> The walls of the college buildings, crusty and impregnable, swept past like an armada of great gray sails.

Which, in its way, is almost as shiny and meaningless as this fragment of Wilde's:

> It seemed to me that all my life had been narrowed to one perfect point of rose-coloured joy. She trembled all over, and shook like a white narcissus.

Both specimens work to remove us from the matter under observation; the comparisons muddy the things compared; the adjectives function so as to give us the appearance of specificity, lest we see the rabbit being put into the hat. These are triumphs of that sensibility that cannot leave off worrying the world into its own design. I cannot accept the Reverend Marshfield's style as being his own—Mr. Updike's other works of fiction display the same style with endemic consistency.

There are a couple of other things to say about this novel. While it is not "about" sex, sex is the engine that drives it. However, it is neither pornographic nor filled with the grim and humorless details of the post-Sadean technologist. It does not stand in breathless awe of sex-as-mystery as invented and patented by Lawrence. It is—what can I say?—amused. It is witty and bored and knowing. There is nothing of the comic in the novel—Mr. Updike cannot make anyone laugh. The comic writer accepts reality as intelligible in itself, not as a poor drab thing that awaits his gilding. Comic things are inherently comic and we laugh when the comic intelligence reveals their essential essence, when it recognizes them. Wittiness does not recognize, it explains. It gives us an "insight" into its subject whereas it seems to me that the comic grasps the entire outside of its subject. I go on about this because I don't understand why a writer would choose to use this kind of wryly amused and sophisticated cleverness to deal with a subject that does not respond to it—that, in fact, resists it tenaciously except on the level of bedroom farce—which is rarely farcical and never sexual. I suspect that this mode allows Mr. Updike's romantic sensibility full play. With it, he can most certainly eat his world. But he can't have it too.

Then we have the characters. Mr. Updike is of that school that holds that characters are the sum of their parts, i.e., add layer upon layer of description touching upon modes of dress, manners, speech, habitations, possessions, mores, etc., and presto! we know who the character is and how he will act in a given circumstance, we know, that is, his reality. Conversely, if we know what he says and thinks, we know what he will wear, his tastes, and so on. The author partakes, in other words, of the tried and true novelistic signals in ordering his characters' activities and lives. An odd sophistry of causality inheres in such constructions. Jane, Marshfield's wife, is prim, proper, intelligent, educated, athletic. It routinely follows that she is sexually unsatisfying to Marshfield; she is civilized when she is confronted by his lover, and so on. His lover is slight-ly shabby, a trifle vulgar, rather embarrassingly emotional, and divorced. She, of course, lives in a raw, new housing development; she is crass when she meets Jane, etc. The reader almost expects Mr. Updike to make her chew gum and subscribe to the *Reader's Digest.* Marshfield's assistant is young, soupy-minded, liberal, "against the war." His attitude toward, for instance, young people with drug problems? You guessed it. And on and on. The signals flash, the attitudes stiffen, the characters "walk off the pages." This is the kind of characterization one expects from Neil Simon, an effortless sliding into the path of least resistance. It has little to do with the making of serious fiction.

Yet all these things that I touch upon are reckoned by Mr. Updike's admirers—and they are many—as strengths, not weaknesses, as wonders of truth, style, audacity, vision, even as indications of greatness. But each page of this book throws up a wall behind which it is well-nigh impossible to discover the manifold realities of the world that the author chooses to deal with. We are given this world as seen by Mr. Updike, as interpreted by him. We are given wit and talent and we are given invention. But we are not given literature.

Oddly (and sadly) enough, this kind of fiction is often thought to be poetic, though it has nothing to do with poetry unless one conceives of the poem as a bauble. On the other hand, Hugh Kenner has termed this sort of writing "a surface scummed by iridescent prose." That strikes me as both just and exact.

# From *Alfred Kazin on Fiction*

## Alfred Kazin*

John Updike's *Marry Me: A Romance* (Knopf; $7.95) is an elaborate and ingenious working out to the last decimal of a strictly American situa-tion. Jerry passionately makes love to another man's wife and is still in love with his own. The other man, Richard, has something of the same problem. But despite Updike's many cunning variations on the American husband tied round and round by knots of his own "moral" devising, Jerry is the usual Updike husband, and his plight is the same. How to love oneself, the other woman, one's wife and "God" all at the same time.

Updike is by now a positive virtuoso at drawing every facet of per-sonal style out of himself and every fantasy out of his characters. *I dwell in possibility,* sang the great maiden poet in Amherst. Too much possibil-ity is trouble, especially when there is this American contradiction of love, sex and marriage conceived as separate elements. From the headline love

*Review of *Marry Me.* From *The New Republic,* 175 (November 27, 1976), 22–23. Copyright © 1976. Reprinted with permission of Alfred Kazin.

scene on the lovers' favorite beach with which the novel begins to the brilliantly alternating scenes of fantasy and reality with which Updike winds up poor Jerry's tortured yet plausible circumambience of himself and everyone else, Updike writes all this out at the top of his powers, his knowledge of American byways, and his tenderness for Jerry.

In its own way *Marry Me* is as original in its development as it is familiar in its situation. There is a felt insistence on the truthfulness of Jerry's confusion as well as on its pathos and humor. We are down to the bare bones of "personality" and "relationships." These are our fixtures, our themes, our American grammar. I wonder if people so overburdened with the world's goods ever felt so naked and exposed before. To show the burden of the nakedness itself is a great accomplishment.

Yet Updike subtitles his book "a romance." It *is*, at the end of many false turnings for Jerry, a love story finally. But in the course of carrying some immensely complicated suburban freight to a necessarily difficult conclusion, Updike again superimposes his own concern with God, death and Karl Barth on a cartoonist just not real enough to carry it. Even his much-mentioned "fear" is not real. The particular weakness of Updike's fiction is that he uses the same man over and over. Despite his playful intelligence and faith in his novelist's power of fantasy, he is unable to disguise this. Indeed, even women roughly of his own generation and professional circle are equally quite dim. It is the older men, like the father in *The Centaur* and the father in *Rabbit Redux*, who are in no danger of melting into Updike's one big situation: the marital tangle.

Where characters are indistinct, blur into each other, become essentially anonymous, we get an excess of style, of meditative fluency. Updike is always at his best in handling the social matter: cars, children, parties, the drinks, the kitchen talk late at night, the bitter sympathy between women rivals for the same man who equally mistrust him. There is all that American role playing, very real indeed when we are all in suburbia and find our only models in each other. But the *people* in this book are just not interesting.

So the contradicton between the momentum of the book (very brilliant indeed) and the characters being pushed along by it *is* a complication.

# *The Coup* by John Updike

## Joyce Carol Oates*

At a table in an open-air café in Nice there sits a small, prim, unprepossessing black man, the former president of the impoverished

*From *The New Republic*, 180 (January 6, 1979), 32–35. Copyright © 1979. Reprinted by permission of *The New Republic*.

mythical state of Kush (formerly the mythical Noire), ex-Colonel Hakim "Happy" Felix Ellelloû. Having narrowly escaped death at the hands of Kush's new, pragmatic young president, Ellelloû (whose name means "freedom" in Berber) has been pensioned off, along with one of his four wives and a motley gang of children, so long as he remains "anonymous" and "silent." But Ellelloû sits at the café scribbling his memoirs, an account of his experience as dictator of Kush. What he has to say is mordant, outrageous, and bitterly self-mocking, a lengthy monologue that really *is* a coup of sorts, constituting Updike's most experimental novel to date. Kush is Ellelloû's fiction just the *The Coup* is Updike's fastidiously circumscribed fiction, a country set in an "Africa" of words. And what a virtuoso display Updike gives us! Not even *Pale Fire*, another inspired work by another displaced "ruler," is more darkly comic, more abrasively surreal, than Updike's Ellelloû's testimony.

Africa's most majestic feature, Ellelloû tells us, is the relative absence of Man. But where Man exists there is either pitiless suffering (northern Kush has suffered a five-year drought), or buffoonery (literally everyone Ellelloû encounters, from his four incompatible wives to his comic Russian "advisors" and the slangy, hearty, PR-minded Americans who call their exploitation of oil-rich Kush "philanthropy," are buffoons, locked into the most stereotyped of languages). Where Márquez's Faulknerian *The Autumn of the Patriarch* presented a bizarre dictator seen from without, filtered through the voices of a number of close observers, Updike's Nabokovian *The Coup* gives us the dictator in his own voice, as he sardonically and brokenly recounts the comic-opera events that led to his spiritual assassination. Nabokov's presence is felt throughout, but lightly and ingeniously, for Updike, unlike the self-indulgent Nabokov of *Ada*, that most relentlessly private of novels, has linked personal and authorial obsessions so gracefully with the outer chaos of Kush and the drama of the "superparanoids" America and Russia that Ellelloû's story works quite satisfactorily as a story, without self-referential props. Updike's homage to Nabokov is clear enough, and rather touching: it is Ellelloû's "opposite number," the Soviet Colonel Sirin, who saves his life at a characterically absurd moment—and Sirin, as we know, was Nabokov's early pseudonym.

Ellelloû is, or was, a devout Muslim and a jargon-ridden Marxist whose hatred for all things American—"America, that fountainhead of obscenity and glut"—is explained partly by the fact that he attended a small college in Franchise, Wisconsin where he received an unfair grade of B– in African history from a trendy professor who was jealous of his relationship with a white girl named Candy, and partly by the fact that he married this girl and brought her back to his kingdom, where their marriage quickly deteriorated. (Candy, called "Pinktoes" by the blacks she compulsively pursues, is coarse-mouthed, nagging, stereotyped as any cartoon suburban wife; even her most ostensibly idealistic actions—like marrying a ragamuffin Negro who seemed so lonely at college are motivated by clichéd notions of "liberalism." And of course she marries Ellelloû to enrage her bigoted father.)

Updike acknowledges numerous sources for his African information—books by contemporary historians and scholars, *National Geographic, Beau Geste,* children's books, *The Koran*—but his Africa, like his Kush, is a surrealist creation; and so, in part, is his increasingly debased and contemptible America. Ellelloû, composing his hallucinatory memoirs, pursues himself quixotically through a bewildering variety of masks. He views himself as a child, as a college boy in an alien country, as an ambitious though idealistic young soldier, as "dictator" of an ungovernable, indeed incomprehensible country, and finally as the hapless husband of four wives, chronically impotent, the passive butt of cruel jokes. Ellelloû experiences himself in stylish Cartesian terms, as two separate selves: "the one who acts, and the 'I' who experiences. This latter is passive even in a whirlwind of the former's making, passive and guiltless and astonished." He has sent many people to their deaths, and in person decapitates the former king, an elderly, blind, decadent fellow who was "like a father to him," but the reader hasn't the sense, any more than Ellelloû does, that he *is* a murderer: his elaborate syntax convinces us otherwise.

Difficult as Kush's mountainous terrain is to navigate, by camel or Mercedes (an air-conditioned Mercedes follows the dictator as he travels disguised through his troubled country), the prose Updike has fashioned for him is even more difficult, and resembles nothing so much as an arabesque superimposed upon another arabesque. Motifs, phrases, "imagery," coarsely comic details from the "external world," Ellelloû's various and conflicting pasts, are rigorously interwoven into complex designs. The outer world, filling up slowly with American and Soviet junk, is a nightmare of vulgarity, and depressingly simple-minded; the inner world, the world of Ellelloû's ceaseless brooding, is correspondingly rich, elusive, teasing, ingenious. Updike has been accused in earlier, far more straightforward narratives like *Couples* and *The Centaur* (the novel that *The Coup* most resembles in its audacity and inspiration, if not in its tenderness) of writing self-indulgent, tortuous prose. That Updike has a painter's eye for detail, that he glories in what Joyce would call the suchness of a thing, and sees no reason, since it exists, *not* to describe it in detail, seems to me quite evident; but surely this is one of his strengths, one of the great virtues of his writing. By assigning the prose voice of *The Coup* to the defeated dictator Updike allows himself more freedom (or license) than he might ordinarily allow himself, and Ellelloû, plunging onward in his memoirs, as in his murky grotesque situation-comedy adventures, does the difficult work of characterizing himself. He remarks at one point that he knows his sentences are "maddeningly distended by seemingly imperative refinements and elaborations"; at another point— as he is about to execute the old king with a giant scimitar taken from its case in the People's Museum of Imperialist Atrocities—he thinks, "My mind in its exalted, distended condition had time to entertain many irrelevant images." Updike echoes or parodies earlier Updike, the earlier Updike (in the story "Wife-Wooing") paying homage to James Joyce of *The Sirens*: "Wide wadis remember ancient water, weird mesas have been shipped into shape by wicked, unwitnessed winds." When Ellelloû burns alive, on a pyramid of American gifts to the drought-stricken Kushians of the north, one Donald Gibbs, who assures him that his people really *want* this "manna" (Kix Trix Chex Pops, cream of celery soup, sorghum meant for cattle, and shipped in transparent sacks along with wood chips and dead mice) he thinks with characteristic scrupulousness:

> I could smell on the victim, under the sweat of his long stale wait and the bland, oysterish odor of his earnestness, the house of his childhood, the musty halls, the cozy bathroom soaps, the glue of his adolescent hobbies, the aura of his alcoholic and sexually innocent parents, the ashtray scent of dissatisfaction. What dim wish to do right, hatched by the wavery blue light of the television set with its curious international shadows, had led him to the fatal edge of a safety that he had thought had no limits?

This is Ellelloû's voice; and in sharp contrast to his indefatigable syntactical acrobatics the other voices of the novel are either flat and silly or a parody of US advertising rhythm and jargon. The wife who joins him in exile, the openly promiscuous Sittina, complains of lack of money "since you blew the dictatorship"; Candy greets his infrequent visits with "Holy Christ, look who it isn't," refuses to listen to his formal Islamic pronouncements which are, to her, "Kismet crap," and says of his strategic execution of the old king: "Well, chief, how's top-level tricks? Chopping old Edumu's noggin off didn't seem to raise the humidity any." Updike does this all very skillfully, and one guesses that *The Coup* was immensely enjoyable to write, once the ankle-thongs of African "history" were disposed of. For instance, Ellelloû discovers that office supplies stolen from the capital city of Kush are being smuggled by camel caravan to Iran, and this embarrassment is explained cheerfully by the caravan's leader:

> "The Shahansha has much wish to modernize. In his hurry he buy typewriters from West Germany and paper from Swedes and then discover only one type spool fit typewriter, only one type eraser not smudge paper. American know-how meanwhile achieve absolescence such that only fitting spool stockpiled in Accra as aid-in-goods when cocoa market collapse. Formula of typewriter eraser held secret and cunning capitalists double, redouble price when Shah push up oil price to finance purchase of jet fighters, computer software, and moon rocks. French however operating through puppet corporations in Dahomey have secured formula as part of multibillion-franc deferred-interest somatic-collateral package and erect eraser factory near gum arabic plantations. Much borax also in deal, smuggled by way of Quagadougou. Now Sadat has agreed to let goods across Nile if Shahanshah agrees to make anti-

Israeli statement and buy ten thousand tickets to son-et-lumière show at Sphinx."

Everything, every human act or gesture or vision, is explained away glibly in language taken from popular magazines or television shows: American women are "unbridled Amazons who drive our men outward from the home to perform those feats of engineering and merchandizing that dumfound the world"; Ellelloû's mistress, formerly a native wench whose grandmother was a leopard, soon acquires Western clothes, shoes, wristwatches, even contact lenses (which make her brown eyes blue), and assures Ellelloû that her response to his love-making is genuine: "Only my President can lead me so utterly to forget myself, I am led to the brink of another world, and grow terrified lest I fall in and be annihilated. It's neat."

Beneath, behind, informing every scene of this inspired novel, which a superficial reading might judge as almost *too* inspired (*a tour de force* against readers' expectations, like Updike's very first novel *The Poorhouse Fair*, which was anything but a "young man's novel"), is a passionate and despairing cynicism which I take to be, for all its wit, Updike's considered view of where we are and where we are going. No moral uplift here; no gestures, like Bellow's, toward the essential "health" of the commonplace. If American know-how is only another word for exploitation, if American statesmen (like the unctuous Klipspringer) and advisers are asinine jargon-filled fools, the Soviets are, if possible, even more ridiculous. "Islamic socialism" is "pure" of corrupting capitalistic investments, but it has the disadvantage of not working—so long as Ellelloû's anti-American policy holds, his people are doomed to die of thirst and starvation. Ellelloû is devoutly religious, and everyone who surrounds him is atheistic and materialistic, but what does faith in Allah matter when the sky is pitilessly blank, and all Ellelloû can think of in defense of his faith is the feeble observation, "The drought is a form of the Manifest Radiance, and our unhappiness within it is blasphemy. The book accuses: *Your hearts are taken up with worldly gain from the cradle to the grave.*"

America, Updike hypothesizes, reached in the 1960s and early 1970s (and *The Coup* takes place during the Watergate hearings) "that dangerous condition when a religion, to contradict its own sensation that it is dying, lashes out against others. Thus the Victorians flung their Christianity against the heathen of the world after Voltaire and Darwin had made its tenets ridiculous; thus the impoverished sultan of Morocco in 1591 hurled troops across the Sahara . . . a conquest that profited him nothing and destroyed the Songhai empire forever." And: "It may be . . . that in the attenuation, dessication, and death of religions the world over, a new religion is being formed in the indistinct hearts of men, a religion without a God, without prohibitions and compensatory assurances, a religion whose antipodes are motion and stasis, whose one rite is the exercise of energy, and in which exhausted forms like the quest, the vow, the expiation, and the attainment through suffering of wisdom are, emptied of content, put in the service of a pervasive expenditure whose ultimate purpose in entropy. . . . Millions now enact the trials of this religion, without giving it a name, or attributing to themselves any virtue."

("The Fifties were when all the fun was," Candy says bitterly, "though nobody knew it at the time.")

Judging from the stories in "another mode" in *Museums and Women*, and the highly self-conscious voice of *A Month of Sundays*, it might have seemed that Updike's genius was for fiction and not metafiction. (For why parody art if you can create it, why devise clever paste pearls if you own genuine pearls?) But *The Coup*, which makes only the most perfunctory gestures toward old-fashioned realism, let alone naturalism, is an immensely inspired and energetic work, striking, on page after page, the comic brilliancy that leaps from Joyce's *Ulysses*, in such chapters as *The Cyclops*, for instance, in which ferocious exaggeration becomes an art that is self-consuming; in its possibly more immediate relationship to Navokov and Márquez, the novel sets down the improbable beside the probable, creating a "fictional" nation that is altogether convincing, and yet populating it with fools and knaves and tough-talking, nagging wives who have the depth, if not the distinctiveness, of playing cards. *The Coup*'s coup is style. If entropy is capitalism's goal, just as it is socialism's goal, if life in our time has become so sterile that even Ellelloû's traitorous minister Ezana can say, casually, "Life is like an overlong drama through which we sit being nagged by vague memories of having read the reviews," there is the more need for style, for art, for that unique, quirky, troubling vision that our finest artists force upon us.

Updike has grown amazingly cynical with the passage of time: how odd that the author of *Pigeon Feathers* should be evolving, before our eyes, into the Mark Twain of *The Mysterious Stranger*, or the Swift of Gulliver's final voyage, or the Samuel Beckett who says laconically that failure, not success, interests him. One would not have guessed that direction his novels might take, considering even the bitterly ironic ending of *Rabbit, Run* (which, if set beside *Rabbit Redux* of a decade later, is nevertheless characterized by an odd "Fifties" optimism despite the current of its remorseless plot—the sense of a world of promise, a world awaiting exploration, even exploitation, to which the dissatisfied Candy alludes in her banal fashion, calling it "fun"), and the understated, unheroic conclusion of *Couples*, in which the hero and heroine, about whose emotions we know so very much, in such exhaustive detail, become, merely, in the end, just "another couple" in suburban America. Admirers of Updike's sardonic Bech stories, however, have sensed quite clearly the drift of Updike's mind, which finds its sharpest, least muffled, and least sentimental expression through the *persona* of Henry Bech, Updike's daimonic opposite (bachelor, Jew, perpetually blocked novelist who, at the conclusion of a recent story, finds that he cannot even sign his own name); Bech's view of the universe and of man's striving within it is as droll as Céline's, and he would, adroitly, with an allegorical instinct as habitual as Updike's, sketch in quick analogues between the drying-up of creative powers and the drying-up of fertile lands.

The world in which "Kush" is located is, after all, a "global village" in which individuals no longer exist, and tribes are relocated in a matter of days, to make way for multi-level parking garages, shopping malls, and McDonald's hamburger restaurants. Ellelloû's prophetic zeal is commendable, but who among his people cares?—if "You will be Xed out by Exxon, ungulfed by Gulf, crushed by the US, disenfranchised by France, not only you but your entire loving nation of succulent wives, loyal brothers, righteous fathers, and aged but still amusing mothers. All inked out, absolutely. . . . In the vocabulary of profit there is no word for 'pity.' "

Is such cynicism soluble in art? Indeed yes.

# A Marriage of Mixed Blessings

Paul Theroux*

So many of John Updike's characters seem to inhabit the suburbs of Splitsville and to toy with infidelity as soon as the shower presents are unwrapped that one thinks of them as naturally polygamous, like the over-educated tribesman who was the hero of his more recent novel, "The Coup." Updike described Felix Ellelloû's various wives and mistresses with great fluency and was not thrown by the marital algebra of it into quintuple confusion. It seems odd, too, that the grace-note of Updike's fiction should be optimism—a radiant box of corn flakes in the kitchen mess, a cascade of Calgonite offering an epiphany in the dishwasher, and so forth—because his people are not so much learning marriage as pondering a way out of it. A hundred years ago, a novelist's reputation was based on how many wedding bells he could get ringing in the last chapter (Trollope's final chapters are the best example); but lately most marriages in fiction end, rather than begin with, "a quickie"—even our cutest word for chummy sexuality has come to mean a divorce.

The first story in this group of 17 has a hint of betrayal in it, and Richard Maple has been married only a little over a year. It is not until the last story that he says "I do" (he is answering the question "Do you believe that your marriage has suffered an irretrievable breakdown?"). Leaving aside the banality of this collection's title (is it the "so long, so far" line of Donne's "The Extasie" hammered into Americanese?), there

*Review of Too Far to Go. From The New York Times Book Review, 8 April 1979, p. 7. Copyright © 1979. The New York Times Company. Reprinted by permission.

are several implausibilities in the stories. I am used to Updike's married men not having jobs, just as I am used to having him send his characters into the den to watch television so that he can make "Charlie's Angels" into a theology lesson, but Richard Maple looks so damnably unemployed that one begins to think this may be the cause of all the domestic uproar. "Domestic uproar" is a wild overstatement; indeed, that is my second suspicion of implausibility. Why is it that a full dozen of these stories have come and gone before Richard Maple thinks of punching his wife Joan in the face, and even then only *thinks* of it ("He wondered if he could punch her in the face and at the same time grab the glass in her hand so it wouldn't break. It was from a honeymoon set. . . .")? It strains one's credibility to read divorce stories in which none of the partners say "I could kill you!" or "You'll be sorry!"

But perhaps this is the very feature that distinguished them from the common run of howling, wound-licking, look-what-you-did-to-me fictions of recent years. They are the most civilized stories imaginable, and because of this the most tender. Updike, I thought when I read his novel "Marry Me," is the poet of the woe that is in marriage. It is rather to his credit that he conceives of marriage as something other than a Jabberwock; and because he avoids the pique and self-pity in that trap, his stories are celebrations rather than warnings.

"Twin Beds in Rome" begins: "The Maples had talked and thought about separation so long it seemed it would never come." So, by story four the issue is in the air, and successive stories show how the Maples' loyalties are further subdivided. The titles say a great deal: "Marching Through Boston" (it is Joan, not Richard, who is the under-dogger); "A Taste of Metal" (a car crash that flings Richard into the arms of Eleanor); "Your Lover Just Called" (by now both have lovers, but a stolen kiss in this story is beautifully done); and so through "Waiting Up," "Eros Rampant," "Sublimating," "Separating," "Gesturing" and "Divorcing." The titles are more explicit than the stories themselves and imply a modesty of ambition; the surprises come when, as in a story like "Plumbing," the reverie of a householder moves from pondering the pipe-joint and the plumber's bill (itemized like human anatomy) to memories in empty rooms and the temporality of passions and vows.

If there is something seriously missing here, it is Joan's point of view. I think any married woman could quite justifiably accuse Updike of weighting his argument in favor of Richard; worse, he seems to want us to sympathize with and understand Richard, while at the same time pitying Joan. If the Maples were not being whirled apart—without a divorce they would hardly be worth writing about—this probably wouldn't matter; but it strikes me as special pleading to omit the other side of the story. We know too little about Joan and her analyst and her lovers and her panic.

"The moral of these stories is that all blessings are mixed," Updike writes in his foreward. "Also, that people are incorrigibly themselves." He might say as well that no one really belongs to anyone else and that marriage is an institution in which the exits are clearly marked. Updike is one of the few people around who has given subtle expression to what others have dismissed and cheapened by assuming it is a nightmare. The Maples are never closer than when they are performing their ceremony of divorce.

# ESSAYS

# *Rabbit, Run:* John Updike's Criticism of the "Return to Nature"

Gerry Brenner*

Although *Rabbit, Run* aligns itself with the 20th century lament for the loss of traditional values, John Updike examines the loss from a refresheningly muted perspective. Much of the freshness comes from his use of a limited focus for probing the conflicts in his narrowed hero, Harry (Rabbit) Angstrom. By adopting a sensitive but not-too-bright, middle-class hero, Updike avoids hectoring his readers with the heavy machinery of earlier tradition-lamenting authors: ponderous quest, archetypal figure, resounding symbol. Updike colloquializes the lament without losing any of its seriousness. His colloquialization derives from naturalizing the scene, a naturalization that tones down potential lugubriousness by placing the situation in the hum-drum world of insignificant jobs, marital spats, brazen whores, and ineffectual authority figures: father, coach, minister, and in-laws.

And more than simply examining and describing the problems of the traditionless hero, Updike predicts effects. Rabbit is belabored by a permissive society. Without prescribed values, he not only lacks guidelines for action, but also, Updike more importantly suggests, he reverts to animalistic responses both in crises and in normal situations. Deprived of the relief of shared responsibility provided by prescriptive values, Rabbit is compelled to evaluate his entanglements alone. His resultant actions partially resemble those of his namesake—when in danger he runs. But Updike equates his hero with the animal through more than just their escapism. The novel is unified around Rabbit's impulse for the natural and the consequences of this impulse. Since abstracted values promulgated by sublimating prescriptions have eroded, Rabbit must root his values out of the tangible, natural world. Hence, his sensual hedonism. And his sense of duty is aroused only by natural events: his return to his abandoned wife, Janice, when she labors in childbirth, is prompted only by his natural impulse to protect the mother of his child, not by any social dictum. Thus Updike suggests that modern man's impulse for the natural, his instinct, is urged upon him by the breakdown of the prescriptive world.

*From *Twentieth Century Literature*, 12 (1966), 3–14, by permission of the Journal.

An outgrowth of this breakdown is seen in the ineffectuality of expected figures of authority. (And in this defection from traditional stalwarts of authority, as with other traditional values, Updike refrains from the invidious comparison with the days of yore. The contrast with the looming shadow of the past is merely one of the givens.) Rabbit's father is dealt with abbreviatedly. In one of Rabbit's self-centered but aimless reminiscences that recalls his father secretly cutting a much-disputed strip of grass that the neighbor was obligated to cut, the father, with a wink that shocked Rabbit, lied to Rabbit's mother and denied cutting it, a denial of responsibility and male authority. Rabbit's debilitated Chiron, Marty Tothero, is more savagely dismissed an an authority figure. When Rabbit returns home to Mt. Judge after his all-night escape to nowhere-and-back and stakes out Tothero, he expects guidance from his old basketball coach, now a castoff from society living in the attic of the Sunshine Athletic Association (a euphemism for the old men's bar and card-playing den: just one of Updike's versions of degenerated present-day athletics). But Tothero fails to give him good counsel. Instead, Rabbit gets sententious platitudes, " 'Do only what the heart commands' "; pompous oratory, " 'It makes me happy, happy and humble, to have, as I do, this very tenuous association . . . ' "; a date with a whore; a view of Tothero slapped by a tart; and he gets left with the bill for dinner, which indicates the shift in responsibility. Late in the novel Tothero's commiseration over the death of Rabbit's daughter exudes a senile sagacity when he assures Rabbit that he had warned him earlier to go back to Janice. Tothero only accepts the responsible authority of all second-guessers.

Jack Eccles, the Episcopal minister, demonstrates the extreme example of ineffectual authority. He differs, however, from Rabbit's father and Tothero in that he attempts to provide Rabbit with guidance. Part of his ineffectuality stems from his family's background of religious division, the grandfather a "Darwinian Deist," the father an orthodox Anglican, himself a skeptical Episcopalian. As a spiritual authority, Eccles' background lays out an inversion of Rabbit's problem: Eccles is swamped by a surplus of traditions which leaves him in the same predicament as having none. The surfeit of choices forces him to handle Rabbit as he himself sees fit, independent of stricture. Eccles' failure as authority is also partly caused by this attempt to treat Rabbit as an individual needing special consideration. By piecemealing his authority in advice to individuals, he loses his larger authoritativeness and becomes an amateur psychologist, a "meddler" according to his wife, to Rabbit, and to Kruppenbach, the Lutheran minister. His concern with Rabbit as an individual proceeds from his permissiveness, which Rabbit resents soon after he meets Eccles: "He is getting slightly annoyed at the way the minister isn't bawling him out or something; he doesn't seem to know his job."[1] And Rabbit is sensitive to Eccles' minor infractions. When Eccles first drives up to him, parking his car askew on the wrong side of the street, Rabbit registers, "Funny how ministers ignore small laws" (86). Rabbit undoubtedly questions Eccles' authority when he sees his inability to control his nagging daughter and when he notes his subordinate position to a domineering wife. And Eccles' own skepticism hampers his control over Rabbit. He is incapable of responding positively to Rabbit's childish faith. Rabbit confides to him, " 'Well I don't know all this about theology, but I'll tell you. I *do* feel, I guess, that somewhere behind all this . . . there's something that wants me to find it!' " (107). (Rabbit's egotism inverts the heroic quest; the absolute is searching for him!) Eccles can only respond acidly, " 'Of course all vagrants think they're on a quest.' " His jibe also reflects the intimacy of his method. The method abandons the austerity and aloofness necessary in a heeded authority figure, such a figure as the Lutheran minister Kruppenbach imposes.

In contrast with the ineffective normal male authority figures, Updike hints at a matriarchal group. Yet the women only wield a Lawrentian suggestion of power, imposing only fear, not control. Rabbit's mother-in-law, Mrs. Springer, exerts constant reproof upon him, a reproof that he is wary of. But the fear she insinuates into him arises from normal resentment at a worthless son-in-law, reflecting her poor education of her daughter. Mrs. Angstrom, Rabbit's mother, a white, enduring-Dilsey, represents the sole character whom Rabbit fears. This is attributable to his associating her with the childhood world of nearly absolute rights and wrongs. Yet even she refuses to mete out the punishment he fears he deserves and even desires. Ruth, Rabbit's brazen, Reubens-goddess whore, provides the only resistance to Rabbit's marital leave of absence. Although she capitulates to his natural charm, she is antagonistic to his disregard of consequences, resents his smug egotism, and at the climax lays out clearly the alternatives he has available: divorce Janice and marry herself, or "get out"—a crystalization of absolutes that fails to appear throughout the rest of the novel. But to Rabbit, these absolutes, like all his choices, are muddled in another of the many web images in the novel, this one in the web of divorce litigation.

Rabbit's relationship with Ruth tests and finds unattainable D. H. Lawrence's cure of domestic bliss by placing it in the workaday world of characters with limited intelligence. Earlier commitments and the social world intrude upon them. And the domestic bliss turns matriarchal, not only with Ruth and Rabbit. Both Mr. Angstrom and Mr. Springer squirm under relatively domineering wives. Tothero is slapped by his whore, Margaret, and coldly nursemaided by his wife after his strokes. The only reason that Janice fails as a matriarch is that she lacks the intelligence. She tries, however, but her power exists only over "fetching and hauling." The loss of traditional figures of authority makes an authority out of everyone with sufficient intelligence to carry it off. When the gods go, the half-gods arrive, to twist Emerson.

Since Rabbit is unable to find authority in traditional figures, he is at a loss to discriminate between good and bad advice. (Rabbit's job re-emphasizes this loss in an Empsonian ambiguity: his MagiPeel gimmick mirthfully suggests a spilling—Rabbit's son "peels" a spoon of food—of the clear distinction between good and bad that the Magi had.) He rejects the advice of the aging, whiskey-breathed hardware and gas station operator who urges him, " 'The only way to get somewhere, you know, is to figure out where you're going before you go there' " (27). Rabbit dismisses this advice because it suggests that he is lost if he lacks the knowledge of where he is going. And although Rabbit considers himself as identifiably self-sufficient, Updike artistically objectifies the contrary, in a way fitting to the naturalistic setting. On Rabbit's escape to West Virginia as well as on minor excursions from place to place, for example, Updike maps out with scrutinizing detail the objects along Rabbit's path:

> He crossed the Running Horse Bridge and is among streets he knows. He takes Warren Avenue through the south side of town and comes out on 422 near City Park. He drives around the mountain in company with a few hissing trailer trucks. As he turns left from Central into Jackson he nearly sideswipes a milk truck idling yards out from the curb. He con-tinues up Jackson, past his parent's house, and turns into Kegerise Alley, and in the clear dawn light he glides past the old chicken house, past the silent body shop, and parks the car in front of the Sunshine-Athletic Association . . . (36)

This map-like detail implies a sense of directed identity. By accounting for the objects and places along a given route, Rabbit gains a false sense of identity by being able to place himself geographically. If he knows where he is in space, he can attribute a spatial identity to himself, a comforting sense of identifiable existence to Rabbit. And to list the path of objects assures himself, figuratively, of a sense of direction. His identity is not dependent upon himself, but upon the external objects he measures himself against. And, like the shift of traditional values, the geography shifts, presenting new objects with his necessary movement. Similarly, while on the trip his sense of loss becomes rendered in time as well as space, indicated in a long paragraph that tabulates the radio songs and ads over an hour and a half period.

The conclusion of the recorded radio song and ad paragraph repeats one piece of news that had been noted earlier: "Where is the Dalai Lama?" (30). That Rabbit should observe this indicates his search, however unsustained, for authority. And later, unable to find authority, he tells himself that "*He* is the Dalai Lama" (40). This decision wells up again from his inability to discriminate between good and bad advice. The assurance that he is the Dalai Lama grows out of his acceptance of advice from a parody of authority, Jimmy the Mouseketeer, moderator of a children's television program. Rabbit accepts Jimmy's misconstrued interpretation of "Know Thyself" when Jimmy informs his audience that it means "be yourself." Hence, Rabbit's egotistic anarchy. The voice of authority that he obeys tells him that his own will is the only guide to right action that he needs. Rabbit heeds this authority throughout the novel. At one point when Ruth warns him that he will have to pay the price for his holiday from responsibility, he tells her of his having learned that " 'If you have the guts to be yourself, . . . other people'll pay your price.' " (125).

More than just loosing anarchy upon Rabbit's values, Jimmy's advice gives added impetus to Rabbit's impulse for the natural. This impulse is seen most obviously in his sexual obsession. He revels in his relationship with Ruth because she "feels right" to him, as long as she doesn't use a "flying saucer," that is. Subjectivity alone determines his morality. So ingrained is his sexual involvement that he rewards and punishes sexually, the latter exhibited when he compels Ruth to "blow" him. His sexual impulse develops from the prowess of his earlier basketball days. The intensity of physical action found then is missing from the workaday world, and Rabbit replaces it with an intensity of sex. His sexual prowess also supplies him with the sense of identity that his basketball playing had given him.

Updike's use of athletics simultaneously shows Rabbit's physical impulse and quite cleverly comments further upon the loss of eschatological values as a result of a paradoxical surfeit of values. Like basketball, the game of golf which Eccles supposedly uses as moral therapy becomes a naturalistic symbol of the plethora of goals that Rabbit has to choose from, eighteen instead of one. Eccles thinks to himself, "Harry gives the game a desperate gaiety, as if they are together engaged in an impossible, startling, bottomless quest set by a benevolent but absurd lord, a quest whose humiliations sting them almost to tears but one that is renewed at each tee, in a fresh flood of green" (141). And whereas Rabbit is a natural at basketball, as the opening scene of the novel dramatizes, when he loses direct physical contact with the ball as in golf, he blunders, just as he does in a world which refuses to permit continual natural action without codified restraint. When Rabbit selects his own athletic activities, other than sexual, he prefers to walk up Mt. Judge, his walk up with Ruth intimating his vaguely defined search for some single absolute. And his other sport, running, identifies with his undirected desire to find an answer to his problems. But unlike golf and basketball, Rabbit's mountain climbing and running are without rules. Without them the achieved goal becomes valueless since it is recognized only by the participant; that is, the individuality of the sports represents another chaotic value. And as the novel proceeds, Rabbit's escapes become increasingly aimless, panicky, valueless. What starts out as a willing dislike (" '. . . that little thing Janice and I had going, boy, it was really second-rate' " [90]) ends up as instinctual fear (his flight from Ruth's ultimatum).

Updike extends Rabbit's impulse for the natural even into the world of occupation. Not only does Rabbit sell a gimmick that peels fruits and vegetables. He also works as a gardener. In the solid American tradition of the anti-intellectual hero, Rabbit becomes another Adamic figure who ignores prescribed laws. He interestingly lacks even the mental ability to rebel against prescription. He is hardly aware of it. In the natural world of the garden Rabbit's supposed innocence requires no laws, an occupation suitable to his character.

Besides this obvious symbolic objectification of portraying Rabbit's impulse for nature, by having him be a gardener, Updike sets the scene to establish Rabbit's natural charm. Rabbit's relationship with widow Smith exhibits him at his best. He brings out her pleasant effusion just as he nurtures the flowers. When he quits the job, having returned to Janice, she compliments him:

> "I won't be here next year to see Harry's rhodies come in again. You kept me alive, [Rabbit]; it's the truth; you did. All winter I was fighting the grave and then in April I looked out the window and here was this tall young man burning my old stalks, and I knew life hadn't left me. That's what you have, [Rabbit]: life. It's a strange gift and I don't know how we're supposed to use it but I know it's the only gift we get and it's a good one." (187)

Updike restrains the sentiment from sentimentality since Rabbit's hand is incongrously full of the oozing chocolate-covered cherry that his son has just spit into it.

A considerable part of Rabbit's life-giving ability sprouts from his boyishness. Updike tags Rabbit as a "boy" in the second paragraph of the novel. While Rabbit watches some boys playing basketball, Updike comments, "His standing there makes the real boys feel strange." This sympathetic boyishness shows through in his disarming enthusiasm which overpowers Ruth's tough-hearted attitude and wins her over; in his childlike begging to Ruth: " 'Let me undress you. Please. . . . Please. Please.' " (66); in his mildness that she acknowledges; in his simple faith; in his exciteable egotism that draws him on to boast winsomely of his past basketball success; in his kinesthetic sensitivity to nature: "He walks downhill. The day is gathering itself in. He now and then touches with his hand the rough bark of a tree or the dry twigs of a hedge, to give himself the small answer of a texture" (17). Yet Rabbit lacks the intelligence to retain the natural grace that these boyish attributes afford him. Unlike the natural grace of Augie March, for example, Rabbit's is missing the suppleness to respond to the demands of the external world. He resembles a boy too closely in his intolerance and self-centeredness. And in concord with the tonal structure of the novel, he becomes increasingly more boyish, in the poorer senses of the word. Like the allegorical car trip to West Virginia, the novel progresses tonally through a sense of easy irresponsibility, mounting egotistic tension, and panicky ensnarement, suggested in the Pascal epigraph to the novel: "The motions of Grace, the hardness of the heart; external circumstances." In the second part of the novel Rabbit's enthusiasm becomes a melancholy lament for his lost childhood; his begging and mildness transform into childish despotism when he punishes Ruth, roughs up his sister's boyfriend, and abandons Janice; his simple faith yields up to doubt—"His life seems a sequence of grotesque poses assumed to no purpose, a magic dance empty of belief" (165); his winning egotism repels, as caught in Ruth's judgment: "That was the thing about him, he just lived in his skin and didn't give a thought to the consequences of anything" (125). But though he is insensitive to Ruth's pregnancy, his sensitivity to nature remains. In part three his boyish traits coalesce into fear. His simple faith, since rooted in no intelligible understanding, readily succumbs to despair, even before his bolting at the cemetery: "Coldness spreads through his body and he feels detached, as if he is, what he's always dreaded, walking on air" (235)—a lucid statement criticizing the results of detachment from traditions. Rabbit's egotism causes his indignation at his muddled life. He feels "that somewhere there was something better for him" (225), the indignation of all unarrived inheritors of natural grace. He becomes hypersensitive to artificiality, thinking they should bury his dead daughter like a bird in the yard, and criticizing the "unnatural" carpet, colors, music, hothouse flowers, and face of the undertaker's man at the funeral parlor. But now even the forest he flees into strikes him as "unnatural." His enthusiasm to forgive Janice and to clarify the situation backfires into a tactless blunder. And as a boy's would, Rabbit's egotism interprets others' responses to his daughter's funeral as judgment upon his waywardness. His sensitive egotism here needs tempering with mature intelligence. But he has repudiated maturity earlier. He has told Eccles, " 'If you're telling me I'm not mature, that's one thing I don't cry over since as far as I can make out it's the same thing as being dead.' " (90). Although Rabbit regresses increasingly as the novel progresses, he is never totally unsympathetic. Our response is much like Ruth's: though he wrongs us by his stupidity, his amiableness makes us willing to give him another try.

The point of this analysis of Rabbit's regressing boyishness is to see Updike evaluating an American ideal of getting by on natural charm. But Updike sets the "natural" hero in a society without the quick means for rising above the original background. Rabbit is the "natural" hero without luck. His life-giving ability can do some good, as to Mrs. Smith, but probably more harm, as to Ruth and Janice. Updike's cold-eyed view dispels a myth by creating a more likely hero, one with only a smattering of intelligence, with an adolescent sensitivity, with a talent for doing "nothing."

Part of Ruth's appeal to Rabbit is that her occupation consists of "doing nothing." She does what comes easiest to her, making her living by her natural endowments, her body. She, like Rabbit, is a natural. She has merely channeled her inherited natural function into providing herself with the means to live. Her job is full-time, her vocation and avocation, so that acting according to nature engulfs her life. Rabbit also finds her rudeness appealing. This way of ignoring artificial social graces by merely acting natural sets well with him. Moreover, Rabbit thinks "she's good-natured," and to him "In all the green world nothing feels as good as a woman's good nature" (79). Janice differs from her only in that she has become a domesticated, desensitized "natural." Like Ruth, she too does "nothing," but does it all too literally. Janice represents a later, surly view of Ruth, a natural animal become vegetable.

The troubles of Ruth and Janice are brought about by an excess of naturalness. Ruth's trouble, her pregnancy, derives from loving Rabbit too naturally, failing to take the necessary precaution—an infraction of occupational code. Janice's trouble, drowning the baby, results from her drunkenness which uninhibits her to such a degree that she loses total physical control. Her drunkenness—a total rejection of both external restraints and values, since oblivious to both—and the result of her drunkenness, naturalistically symbolize the destructive chaos of excess naturalness unfettered by stricture. However, in keeping with the setting of the novel, the destructive chaos is limited. But its small-scaled representativeness moves out into larger spheres of symbolic meaning.

The destructive chaos of following the impulse for the natural takes its fullest form in Rabbit. By responding naturally to every situation, he compounds his problems without making any progress. In his initial flight from Janice he drives to West Virginia only to return on the same night. The circularity of this escape, leading nowhere, establishes his pattern of action. Yet, unlike his animal counterpart, his escapes are not total. The social world rebounds with a mesh of relationships that snares him when he attempts to act like an animal. So instead of escaping free, even though he is free of externally imposed punishment, Rabbit's natural impulses only lead him into greater difficulties. But Updike breaks away from a heavy American tradition; he doesn't insist upon cataclysmic difficulties to a dynamic hero. The very domesticity of the difficulties is fetching in its reluctance to plead urgently for correction. Though Updike is predicting, his tone of voice is dryly descriptive.

But the dry descriptiveness is only in the tone he directs at Rabbit's situation. Updike's literal descriptiveness is quite wet—to keep with the "natural" of the novel. In varying ways he lyrically objectifies the thematic conflict between tradition and nature. He images the loss of traditional values and the encroachment of destroying nature in Rabbit's initial walk to get his car and son at the opening of the novel:

> He turns down Kegerise Street, a narrow gravel alley curving past . . . a truly old stone farmhouse, now boarded up, one of the oldest buildings in town, thick crude masonry of Indianskin sandstone. This building, which

once commanded half of the acreage the town is now built on, still retains, behind a shattered and vandalized fence, its yard, a junkheap of brown stalks and eroded timber that will in the summer bloom with an unwanted wealth of weeds, waxy green wands and milky pods of silk seeds and airy yellow heads almost liquid with pollen. (17–18)

The alliterative luxuriance of the last lines sympathetically feels out Rabbit's impulse for the natural as opposed to the artificial world of man-made buildings as representations of abstract past traditions. So predominating is Rabbit's impulse that the artificial world is even transformed into images of nature:

> Outdoors it is growing dark and cool. The Norwegian maples exhale the smell of their sticky new buds and the broad livingroom windows along Wilbur Street show beyond the silver patch of a television set the warm bulbs burning in kitchens, *like fires at the backs of caves.* . . . At the corner, where Wilbur Street meets Potter Avenue, a mailbox stands leaning in twilight on its concrete post. *Tall two-petaled street sign,* the cleat-gouged trunk of the telephone pole holding its insulators against the sky, *fire hydrant like a golden bush: a grove.* . . . *The insulators giant blue eggs in a windy nest.* (17; my italics)

Yet these lyrical passages wane as the novel progresses, appropriate to both the tonal progression of the novel and Updike's ultimate comment upon the natural. He sets down almost too clearly the disparity between the past and the present just after Ruth's ultimatum at the end of the novel by contrasting the unity of a past symbol of light to the multiple splintering of present symbols of light:

> Afraid, really afraid, he remembers what once consoled him by seeming to make a hole where he looked through into underlying brightness, and lifts his eyes to the church window. It is, because of church poverty or the late summer nights or just carelessness, unlit, a dark circle in a stone facade.
>
> There is light, though, in the streetlights; muffled by trees their mingling cones retreat to the unseen end of Summer Street. Nearby, to his left, directly under one, the rough asphalt looks like dimpled snow. (254)

As the last sentence further indicates, even the modern symbols of light lead to nature, however bleak and illusory it may be: snow.

The vigor of Updike's style also lends itself to the novel's treatment of nature. Just as Rabbit's golf clubs hallucinatingly metamorphose into Janice and Ruth, and the ball becomes himself, so too does Updike's style give a pulse to everything that passes through its focus. The pulsation is due partly to his unflagging use of the present tense, an active voice, and justifiably used pathetic fallacy as seen in the way Updike can make even a normal situation throb:

> [Rabbit and Ruth] approach the mountain through the city park. The trash baskets and movable metal benches have not been set out yet. On

the concrete-and-plank benches fluffy old men sun like greater pigeons, dressed in patches of gray multiple as feathers. The trees in small leaf dust the half-bare ground with shadow. Sticks and strings protect the newly seeded margins of the unraked gravel walks. The breeze, flowing steadily down the slope from the empty bandshell, is cool out of the sun. Pigeons with mechanical heads flee on pink legs from their shoetips and resettle, chuffling, near their heels. A derelict stretches an arm along the back of a bench to dry, and out of a gouged face sneezes petitely, cat-like. A few toughs, fourteen or younger, smoke and jab near the locked equipment shed of a play pavilion on whose yellow boards someone has painted with red paint Tex & Josie, Rita & Jay. Where would they get red paint? Threads of green poke up through matted brown. He takes her hand. The ornamental pool in front of the bandshell is drained and scum-stained; they move along a path parallel to the curve of its cold lip, which echoes back the bandshell's silence. A World War II tank, made a monument, points its guns at far-off tennis courts. The nets are not up, the lines unlimed.

Trees darken; pavilions slide downhill. (93–94)

In contrast with the flashy vigor of this narrative style, his dramatic dialogue and internal monologue pale, but again, justifiably so. The naturalistic setting and the lack of exuding glamour in all of the characters require Ruth's stream-of-consciousness coarseness, Harrison's vulgar jokes, Tothero and Eccles' banal platitudes, and Rabbit's adolescent "Gees," "Screw yous," and colloquially rendered reminiscences and day-dreams:

A barefoot Du Pont. Brown legs probably, bitty birdy breasts. Beside a swimming pool in France. Something like money in a naked woman, deep, millions. You think of millions as being white. Sink all the way in softly still lots left. Rich girls frigid? Nymphomaniacs? Must vary. Just women after all, descended from some old Indian-cheater luckier than the rest, inherit the same stuff if they lived in a slum. Glow all the whiter there, on drab mattresses. That wonderful softness they have when they want it. Otherwise just fat weight. That wonderful softness, but they want you up and hard on their little ledge. The thing is play them until just a touch. You can tell: their skin under the fur gets all loose like a puppy's neck. (25–26)

Rabbit's penchant for reminiscing and day-dreaming also demonstrates part of his failure to get out of his animal-like self-absorption. By always reminiscing, which differs markedly from actively thinking about the past with an intent to understand both it and the self, Rabbit unconsciously forces himself to obliterate the present. And he gives no thought to the future, to the end consequences of his impulsive actions, telling Eccles that he has no plans for action, that he will just "play it by ear." His reminiscing becomes an egotistic indulgence, thinking often of past or wished-for love affairs, an escape from the real world. Although his real dreams forbode difficulties, they vanish with daylight. Rabbit's memory and anticipations continually reflect the caged egotism that surrounds all of his actions. Drawing upon his past basketball days transfers past glory and identity into his jumbled present. He makes no effort to understand his own pattern of action, sensitive enough only to be aware of his own feelings.

This awareness of only his own feelings, as an outgrowth of his animal-like egotism, accounts also for another result that emanates from the break with older traditions: alienation. The initial scene of the book dramatizes this alienation. Watching some boys playing basketball in an alley, Rabbit invites himself to play with them. His skill makes them surly, and he realizes their rejection of him. But he should have realized before he started to play that he was unwanted because he was an adult, even though his attempt to join them makes him somewhat sympathetic. Throughout the novel he repeats this pattern. He expects others to accept him as he is without trying to accommodate himself to the situation he enters. Though he later discovers that if he has the nerve to be himself then others will pay his price, this opening scene indicates that his discovery has been part of his customary action. And the scene also denies his supposed discovery. Just as he is rejected here by the boys, not willing to pay his price, he is also rejected later. Ruth refuses to pay the price for his being himself when she hands him her ultimatum at the end of the novel. And others refuse him time and time again, since his egotism alienates him from everyone. His self-liberation transforms him into a stranger to everyone else, his alienation becoming a social cage. This is nicely prefigured in the escape to West Virginia when he enters a roadside cafe:

> Somehow, though he can't put his finger on the difference, he is unlike the other customers. They sense it too, and look at him with hard eyes, eyes like little metal studs pinned into the white faces of young men. . . . In the hush his entrance induces, the excessive courtesy the weary woman behind the counter shows him amplifies his strangeness. . . . He had thought, he had read, that from shore to shore all America was the same. He wonders, Is it just these people I'm outside, or is it all America. (31)

Rabbit resembles a stranger not only to other strangers, but also to his own family and friends. And it is interesting to note the highly restricted social scene which Updike presents as a reflection upon alienation. That is, Rabbit has no chums. His alienation is quite total. His very mobility that disregards the basically alien situations he enters leaves him absolutely homeless; by the end of the novel he has nowhere to turn. Unconscious of the demands that require him to accept a social group similar to his background, he is bereft of any home. His intellectual failings make him unfit for the mobility he desires. For him there is no larger world to enter. The absence of a larger social scene symbolizes the rabbit-hutch world available to him. And the most interesting facet of his social isolation is that he doesn't care, at least not enough to take active steps to remedy the alienation. That his father rejects him fails to scar him. And although he is indignant over his sister's arrival at an unrespectable tavern, his concern, like all his concerns, is only fragmentary, unsustained.

Updike's treatment of the isolation finds the fragmentation of the family unit a result of the disregard for older traditions. Yet Updike restrains from clamoring about the fragmentation. The severely narrowed focus implies a separation from the rest of the world, Rabbit's problems covering only a small scene. This separation from the larger world is also indicated in the proximity of the Springers to the Angstroms to Rabbit's apartment. The geographical compression implies isolation from the larger social world. And the three families reside on the hillside of Mt. Judge, Rabbit living only blocks away from the wilderness of the mountain itself, his contiguity to nature expressed topographically: ". . . above them all there was the primitive ridge, the dark slum of forest . . ." (183). Hence, in spite of an external, modern-world drive toward centralization, it goes unrecognized by a growing return to nature, indicated in the novel's silent comments upon the results of twentieth century iconoclasm. The social fabric unravels into a return to more primitive, fragmented group antagonisms, witnessed by the lack of communication between the Angstroms and Springers, their hostilities to daughter- and son-in-law, Eccles and Kruppenbach's differences, and the strife smouldering in all the families.

The framentation of unity is echoed in the novel's point of view. The first section of the novel proceeds through a limited third person narrative, following Rabbit's actions. But as Rabbit's actions encroach upon others, the point of view includes several of them; the second part of the novel proffers events through the eyes of Eccles, Ruth, Lucy Eccles, Janice, as well as Rabbit. As a larger web metaphor, Rabbit's self-indulging actions enmesh others without regarding the trouble inflicted upon them. For example, he tells Eccles he is sorry that Eccles was awakened in the middle of the night that Rabbit had left Janice, but Rabbit considers this as the only inconvenience. The expanding point of view corresponds to the unmanageable sequence of events as they naturally pursue their irrevocably irrational course: the spark of love that Lucy incites in Rabbit and that Janice repulses leads eventually to the drowning of the baby. The uncontrol over the emotional progressions leading up to this final event, like Rabbit's earlier impulsive departure, like Ruth's impregnation, occur quite without rationale. The inconsistency and irrationality of these events justify the multiple points of view—also technically re-emphasizing the lack of single authority. But unlike the virtuosity of the technique Updike uses in the end of *The Poorhouse Fair* in which the dialogue of the middle-class town folk crowds out the precedingly predominant dialogue of the old people, dramatizing how the present crowds out the past, Updike returns to the limited third person point of view in the last section of the novel. But the return to this point of view is essential both to his focus upon the individual hero and to his treatment of Rabbit's self-absorbing concern. This point of view is able to register upon Rabbit the impact of the consequences of his earlier blithe actions.

Updike sets Rabbit's blithe actions to work during a controlled time span: spring. As added reinforcement to the picture of the "natural," un-circumcized hero, the spring season finds him paradoxically at his most creative and destructive. The untended seeds of his actions gestate in minor destruction within the unobtrusively noted period from "a day before the vernal equinox" (19) to "a day before the summer solstice" (195), the days of his two departures from Janice, the latter departure culminating in his daughter's drowning. In accord with the complex of nature imagery in the novel, the season becomes the appropriate time to look at the natural hero who is defecting from the restraints of both the past and the past winter. His blithe actions flower all too well.

Contrary to Ward's interpretation that the novel is "marred . . . by its sympathetic view of irresponsibility and retreat . . . ,"[2] Updike's focus upon the consequences of Rabbit's unconsidered blithe actions criticizes with calm insistence the omnipresent desire to "return to nature" by showing the logical extension of that desire. More, he shows that instead of just a vague romantic ideal, it has become an integrated part of reality. Like all the values whose worth has depreciated in the 20th century, the value of returning to nature, for example, has been immersed in the world of daily action, a colloquialization of the ideal. And made accessible, it is adulterated and abused until it is converted into a distorted way of life. The ideas of the past, which have value precisely because they spur effort for unattainable goals, have become misinterpreted (like the "be yourself" interpretation of "Know Thyself"), debased (like the anarchy of author-ity), and pursued unconsciously without understanding. Now that the ideal has been lost, Updike suggests that a practiced return to nature, car-ried to its logical conclusion, ends in destruction. As an opiate, the ideal is both contenting and inspiring; as reality, it is destructive, especially when it is set within the framework of the workaday world of a middle-class, unintelligent society that is sensitive enough only to get itself into diffi-culty. The return to nature, like all impoverished ideas, is wrenched out of its original context and thrust into an alien situation. In the original context, the return was only to geographical nature. In the present-day context, the return has been to a psychological nature of physical impulse, lacking external, prescriptive refinements. The shadow of neanderthal man clearly hangs over modern man who, like Rabbit, possesses more id (in his impulse for nature) than ego, and possesses only wisps of a superego.

Updike's philosophical conservatism conceives of the romantic dream of returning to nature, in its worst sense, as the ultimate extension of the loss of traditional values, ideals, laws. Set into a society that persists in adhering to some prescriptive mores, Rabbit, as a "noble" urban savage, images modern man's traditionless character and portends his concommitant problems. And the effectiveness of the novel resides in Updike's projection of this statement through the use of the tacky social setting and a line-up of only moderately sympathetic characters.

Notes

1. Quotes in my text are taken from the Crest Paperback reprint, Jan., 1963.
2. J. A. Ward, "John Updike's Fiction," *Critique* V, i, 35.

# John Updike's Metaphoric Novels

H. Petter*

Gifted and prolific, within a few years John Updike has acquired a considerable reputation.[1] Yet this reputation has not gone unchallenged, and the style and earnestness praised by his admirers have also been sharply criticized. Norman Podhoretz, reviewing *The Centaur*, recollected his clash with Mary McCarthy five years earlier: 'She insisted that Updike was an extraordinary stylist; I replied that his prose was overly lyrical, bloated like a child who had eaten too much candy. She thought that he had an interesting mind; I said that he had no mind at all.'[2] Quite a few readers and critics of Updike seem to have been put off by the care which he obviously brings to his writing. Elaborate verbal effects may, indeed, serve to conceal an author's lack of substance; but they should in fairness first be considered as an index to his seriousness. This essay assumes that Updike is a good and important writer. It defines some of the main issues of his five novels and gives an account of his style and the function of his concern with formal aspects of the novelist's art.

## I

Communication is the major issue with which Updike's characters grapple. Even before this problem can be further defined, it strikes one as essential to the discussion of a writer as visibly concerned as Updike with the resources of a literary language. Three forms of preoccupation with communication are thrust upon the protagonists of his novels, arising out of these characters' confrontations (i) with the creation, (ii) with society, and (iii) with themselves.

Man's spiritual dimension becomes a source of anxiety and anguish to Updike's characters when they find themselves unable to articulate it or lose touch with its aims; this is caused by interfering institutionalized concepts and materialistic interests. Updike's first novel, *The Poorhouse Fair*, is about the misunderstandings between three groups of people, misunderstandings eventually deriving from a spiritual consciousness ac-

*From *English Studies*, 50 (1969), 197–206, with permission of the author.

cepted or rejected. The poorhouse has become the last home of old people who more or less consciously expect to find a certain amount of spiritual comfort as they move towards death together. Their administrator or prefect, a man named Conner, believes in material comforts: there is no after-life, according to him, and easing the old people's last years is mainly a matter of organization, of keeping them as healthy and busy, and thus happy, as possible. The episode with the injured cat which Conner orders to be killed need not mean that he might be correspondingly ruthless with his human charges; such an interpretation may be dismissed as growing out of the image-making world of Conner's admirer Buddy, 'soaked in thrillers' (*PF*, 13), or Ted, with his youthful absolutes (*PF*, 40–41). Ted represents the outside world which takes notice of the poorhouse once a year. To the townspeople who come to the August fair, however, the old people do not really exist; they may stand behind their tables and be approached about their wares, but they seem to belong to a remote past or to a future better ignored. Meanwhile, the fair provides a meeting-ground where arrangements, for fun or business, can be made.

During the afternoon Conner provokes a discussion in which a former schoolteacher, 94-year old Hook, stands up for religion. The church plainly needs defenders. Not only is it generally ignored but it seems to be betrayed by its very officers. Eccles and Kruppenback in *Rabbit, Run*, March in *The Centaur*, the young minister in *Of the Farm*, Pedrick in *Couples*: these clergymen appear to fail their charges and to betray essentials of their faith. They have plenty of good will but sound petty and dogmatic, hampered by words and confined by interpretations. Eccles, who must cope with Rabbit, has the reader's understanding, but he can hardly be believed ever to win the sympathy of his flock. He is more human than Conner, yet he is no Mendelssohn, either: no one is likely to glorify him as do Mendelssohn's old friends three years after he has died. The church of Tarbox burns down, its ruins are dismantled, and there remains 'The sky above [ . . . ] empty but for two parallel jet trails' (*Co*, 457).

The breakdown of a workable faith leaves Updike's characters with no shining purpose and yet with fears and yearnings to which they react variously. Rabbit's ideas of what feels right and natural sound suspiciously like hedonistic rationalizations. Caldwell, and especially Piet Hanema, are intense about details of doctrine but otherwise consciously indifferent, while Joey responds intellectually to the minister's 'quaintly learned' sermon (*OF*, 110). Yet man's awareness of death, complicated, as the case of Hanema shows most clearly, by his moral responses, is sensed throughout Updike's world of fiction. Death is naturally what is uppermost in the minds of Hook and the others at the poorhouse. It haunts Rabbit independently of Tothero's stroke and little Rebecca's drowning; it hovers over Caldwell, and threatens Joey's mother. The thought of death lingers with the Tarbox set while John Ong is dying of cancer; kept alive by his youngest daughter's fears, it is constantly with Hanema, who for all his nightmares first suggests that Foxy should have an abortion. What Rabbit dumbly senses, the need for a powerful remedy to cure man's spiritual helplessness, is felt by Hanema with existential urgency. He, like Caldwell, is denied a substitute to which others resort eagerly: the consoling terminology of modern psychology and psychoanalysis. Lucy Eccles and, even more glibly, many of the characters of *Couples* use it to explain away the mysteries of their own conduct and their friends'. For Peter Caldwell to reach an understanding of what happened to his father and himself fourteen years earlier, it takes something more penetrating. Peter is helped by a current of mythology which first translates Chiron's abandonment of immortality into an acceptance of mortality. On this level of common humanity, the notion of (Christian) sacrifice is rendered intelligible, translatable in turn into acts of love and social behaviour.

## II

Communications also prove inadequate within the social organism. The term of alienation here suggests itself but must be rejected, since it usually applies to individuals unable to fit into the normal patterns of their social environment. In the world of Updike's novels groups tend to crystallize round some few ideas, thus isolating themselves from other groups and individuals: the refusal to speak a common language, to come to terms with the full meaning of some of its concepts, keeps groups and individuals apart.

The meaning of 'success', for instance, is enormously flexible, even though success can be measured or counted. Conner's poorhouse has 'one of the five highest ratings in the north-eastern sector' (*PF*, 15), Rabbit's basketball scores establish memorable, 'first-rate' (*PR*, 87) standards, and the Tarbox couples enjoy a pleasing affluence that can doubtless be expressed in sizable taxes. Yet these forms of success, after all, cannot compete with Caldwell's, in the retrospective judgment of his son, regardless of Caldwell's protestations of failure, the chaotic scenes in his classroom, and the Olinger swimming-team's defeat. In Rabbit's surroundings, in particular, ideas of success vary considerably and characteristically. Mrs. Springer thinks of success in terms of her daughter's material security and well-being, her husband's notion of success is associated with the second-hand-car business, Angstrom deplores his son's irregular ways (which Springer perhaps sneakingly envies) and his unwillingness to devote himself to a neat craft, while Rabbit's mother apparently compounds a meaning of success out of Rabbit's non-conformism, his ability to despise Janice, and maybe his continued dependence on her own 'force' (*RR*, 16). Rabbit wants to succeed, like anyone else, yet he finds no better alternative to the choices which he is offered than his combined memories of basketball and making love to Mary Ann, who used to act 'As if she wasn't sure but he was much bigger, a winner. He came to her as a winner and that was the feeling he missed since' (*RR*, 160).

If his unwillingness to conform seems a sign of independence, defiant like the jolly indifference to usage and national concerns cultivated by the young set of Tarbox, yet he can hardly be granted the status which is Caldwell's: the status of a 'saint' in a corrupt environment;[3] for his non-conformism develops all too opportunely just when he must shoulder the responsibilities that come with his privileges. Similarly, the Tarbox young set very much enjoy the gilded present but let their children, symbols of the future, take care of themselves, as Freddy Thorne, that shrewd fool, observes (*Co*, 8). Rabbit, who like Hanema hates being hated, realizes his and his fellow-beings' need for love and understanding vaguely, at a level below articulateness in thought and speech. Others have a clearer conception of this need; they are the more articulate characters. Caldwell and Peter, Joey Robinson and his family, some of the Tarbox people, especially Foxy and Piet Hanema.

Piet's success, measured in conquests and orgasms, is spectacular, and he is duly envied and copied. Yet his potency goes hand in hand with a troubled sense of man's loneliness. If sexual frustration is one motive for his wanderings, this is not enough to explain his affair with Foxy. Perhaps there *is* rather more hope for these two, finally, than for the rest of Tarbox (and there is precious little hope for any of them) because they have been brought together by their individual responses and not just by the accidents of trade and conviviality and the ways of their set. They have this to fall back upon after being sent packing by 'self-centered' Angela (*Co*, 210) and Ken Whitman, who 'wants sex to stay in a compartment' (*Co*, 203). The ritualized non-conformism of the Tarbox set seems to free them for a mutual trust, whereas those they leave behind fearfully return to normality.

## III

Freddy Thorne contributes to one of the set's party-games the idea that man's capacity for self-deception is the most wonderful thing in the world (*Co*, 240). Updike's characters demonstrate again and again that self-deception is universal, and thus show up another area of deficient communication: the individual fails to understand or believe himself. Rabbit is perhaps incapable of realizing that his confidence in what he feels to be right should also serve those who depend upon him. He evidently sees himself as a victim, blamed for all of Janice's ineptitude, which in reality her parents first conditioned (yet they refuse to admit this to themselves); *he* did not kill Rebecca, but people seem to be holding him responsible all the same (*RR*, 238)! Because of his desire to be loved, Rabbit habitually imagines in others a favourable response to him or to his sex-appeal; this makes the apparent injustice of their judgment all the more cruel. Joey, too, indulges in self-pity as he pictures his mother and Peggy fighting over him; the fact that he is the narrator of *Of the Farm* delays the reader's understanding of how subtly Joey distorts what he remembers and registers. While he dramatizes, as presumably his father did before him (and the related figure of Caldwell, too), the battle of the sexes and the rival preferences for town or country, he intimates that he must agree to possession by either of the women. The Tarbox adulterers contrive a code sanctioning their private irresponsibilities, though they cannot simply live them down. Piet, in bed with Georgene while his wife pays off his debt to Georgene's husband, tells himself that fate can be appeased (*Co*, 372), but he really fools himself as little as does Caldwell. It is one of the ironies of *The Centaur* that Caldwell should not be taken seriously by his family and colleagues when, obsessed with his duties, he is acutely conscious of, and honest about, his weak points; his level of honesty is high at any time.

## IV

The individual's consistency, human relations, man's attempts at grasping the meaning of existence, mind and spirit: these are Updike's themes. With all of them alike, sympathy yields to detachment, and synthesis is pushed back by continual analysis. The fragmentation of experience pin-points dazzling individual moments for Updike's various characters, but a saner view suggests how precarious man's existence remains in spite of such climaxes. Yet there is in Conner, Rabbit, Peter, Joey, Piet, Foxy, a surviving susceptibility to a comprehensive view of things, a sense of what is durable. Rabbit's need for neatness and order seems insignificant in the mess for which he, too, is responsible; it has also another dimension, however: Rabbit is yearning, like Angela, for an order such as the one underlying the stars, untouchably aloof and thus permanent (*RR*, 22; *Co*, 241).

Reliability, solidity: the qualities which Updike's characters seek for are found in the novelist's own language; the frightening disruption which they experience as participants and onlookers is set off by the purposeful coherence of Updike's exposition. His resourceful language is the effective tool of a painstaking craftsman; his dialogue is made possible by his ear for the right words, idioms, proverbial phrases, as well as for intonation and rhythm.

In *The Poorhouse Fair* he controls the cadences of brief exchanges or of an intellectual argument (*PF*, 5–12, 76–81). The kaleidoscopic montage of snatches of conversation as the people stroll among the tables of the fair preserves the individual pressures exerted by the speakers' preoccupations: the businessman's insistence, the boys' curiosity and desire, the gossip-monger's pleasurable report (*PF*, 117–126). Conner's reflections have a discouraged lilt to them (*PF*, 123), the invalid's thoughts as Lucas enters in pursuit of the parakeet the speed of fantasy (*PF*, 63). Updike doubtless made a very clever use of words in his first novel. Yet it took more than cleverness to manage some of the descriptions of the book, especially those reflecting Hook's concentrated use of the perceptive faculties left him (*PF*, 28–30, 34–35). The descriptions of later books have a comprehensive, sensuous appeal making for immediacy rather than detachment (*C*, 59–61; *OF*, 72–74; *Co*, 428–9). Behind such a difference in technique and effect there is the work of a careful observer whose empathy is a gift well used. Again, in *The Centaur*, subtlety rather than cleverness was required to achieve the transition from the nervous Olinger climate to the temper of the Olympian scenes (*C*, 21, 73).

The mythological background of *The Centaur* is a large simile constantly echoing through the everyday turmoil of Caldwell's and Peter's endeavours and frustrations. This is the large-scale correspondence to one of Updike's characteristic stylistic features, metaphoric richness. A wealth of similes, images, associations (things animated, actions personified, synaesthesia) renders his prose immensely suggestive.[4] No doubt this does not make for easy reading but then good novelists (as opposed to good story-tellers) rarely provide easy reading; even Hemingway's uncluttered narrative forces the reader to read slowly, so as to take in the things not spelled out. When necessary Updike can be completely factual, as in the information about the poorhouse (*PF*, 29) or Piet's hamster-cage materials (*Co*, 80). In addition to abundant imagery, sensuousness, and precision, Updike employs a trick which more deliberately, and more objectionably, aims at stopping his reader: the use of difficult words, unexpected juxtapositions.[5]

## V

Updike's manner may have distracted or exasperated some readers, but it achieves other effects as well. The verisimilitude of his descriptions, of his reconstructions of a simultaneity or sequence of events, is an impressive virtuoso realism. Beyond this, the very density of the visualizations granted his characters suggests the existence of something below the surface so accurately observed and rendered: the class implications of a house like the Hanemas' (*Co*, 5) or, much more importantly, the kind of people that may be expected to live in a room like the Saltzes' (*Co*, 179). The erratic movements of a dinner-table conversation, skilfully caught, reflect the participation of the diners, the relative importance of the thing said and the things implied, to each of them individually (*Co*, 25–36). Foreground and background balance and become a mutual comment as we take in both the talk of some spectators and the rush of the basketball game or the swimming contest, in *The Centaur*.

The presentation of objects, scenes, people, talk, demands a firm outline, for only clear shapes can intelligibly translate the intellectual, emotional, and spiritual potential of things, events, people. Updike's sense of form also finds expression in a feature of his novels that is less striking than his style: their patterning. Concentrating the events of *The Poorhouse Fair*, *The Centaur* and *Of the Farm* to a very brief lapse of time he emphasizes their close connection, meanwhile buttressing what seems an accidental flow with a structure of parallels, echoes, contrasts.[6] In *The Poorhouse Fair* there is the interplay of close-range and long-range observation; the *leit-motiv* of the letter to Conner, the mention of Harry Petree whom Hook finally can no longer keep out of his thoughts; the repeated scenes: the tables before and after the storm, the music indoors and outdoors; the fantasies of Gregg and Buddy, the sex-ritual of Ted and the anonymous young visitors to the fair. To convey the subtle adjusting of relationships in *Of the Farm* much depends on the use of absent characters; meanderings bring truth and saga close together or dislocate them. The symmetries of *Rabbit, Run* are embodied in the Springers and the Angstroms, the Eccleses and the Totheros, those of *Couples* in the Applesmiths, the Saltines, the Hanema-Thornes. Rabbit's alternating impatience and intimate contentment with Janice, his two evenings out with Ruth, his reaction to Janice's pregnancy and to the announcement of Ruth's; his encounters with Lucy; the circles he runs, with their narrowing compass: these structural stresses shape the story of Rabbit's adventures, helped by lighter touches (the wood on Mount Judge, the ice-plant water, the flowerpot red of Brewer, Peggy Fosnacht's dark glasses). Parties punctuate one strand of the narrative of *Couples*, where things just happen; to another level, where things hang together, belong Piet's thought-ridden bouts of insomnia, his reflections on death, Foxy's early and late letters, Piet's inspections of Indian Hill; their calls on Thorne at his office: Foxy's innocent, Piet's guilty and defiant; the church service and the church fire; and above all the two weekends at the ski-lodge. The two levels occasionally coalesce, then part again; meanwhile some words and images return, accumulating meaning: Piet's dusty car, his apricot windbreaker, Bea's warnings, Piet's fears of Freddy Thorne.

## VI

The created order of Updike's novels is a metaphor for the order which his characters come to discover as a need. It is also a metaphor for a need to which any young country grows up, and of which it is especially conscious when its further development appears uncertain. The sense of America as a new country is everywhere in Updike's novels. It is still being settled, with the landscapes of Alton and Galilee altering (from *The Centaur* to *Of the Farm*), expansion reaching Indian Hill, names still indicating national origins (Angstrom, Hanema) and a fusion of disparate elements (the Musquenomenee Luncheonette). Rabbit driving out into the country and running into the wood; Caldwell and Peter, Joey and his father, unwilling pioneers on farms far away from town; Piet on Indian Hill and Foxy looking across the marshes: they all experience what Europeans face with a shock in the United States, the still uncivilized state of the country. Even the megalopolis of the Northeast and the mass agglomerations of California are yet oases. Hardly out of a city, wilderness and waste land close in on either side of a highway or turnpike. The snug aspect of New England villages is the reverse of a sense of insecurity: the red devils may have been exterminated or exorcised, but it is only a thin veneer of civilization that covers the land which they used to infest. There have been spectacular achievements, to be sure: profitable business ventures pioneered by 'some old Indian-cheater luckier than the rest' (*RR*, 23), technological and scientific discoveries that keep busy whole tribes of Ongs and Saltzes and Whitmans. Such exploits and projects do little to diminish the people's awareness of the size of their country, the gaps between their towns, this separateness perhaps increased by their different concerns, an inadequate comprehension of their role in the huge country and beyond.

In the face of immensities, contact becomes a substitute, eagerly welcomed, for communication; sex a substitute for love; busy-ness kills the spirit; the sound of words (clichés, slogans, jargon) is dissociated from their meanings. This is what Updike's novels are about. Yet Updike has been accused of retreating into his boyhood memories while neglecting the present experience of his country. He has also been charged with cultivating an antiquated tradition of style. Or as Norman Mailer has said: 'He could become the best of our literary novelists if he could forget about style and go deeper into the literature of sex.'[7] Underlying these objections there seems to be a common denominator not uncharacteristic of a young country: impatience with slow time, indifference to the transitory nature of the moment, a distrust of permanence and tradition. The country moves quickly, the writer must keep pace with it. Updike himself has commented upon this specific connotation of the comparative rawness of America. According to him, whereas the English writer assumes 'that society has a place (however modest) for him', the American writer must still assert his social validity. In America, therefore, 'the strenuous task of *being* a writer always threatens the task of writing', a statement elaborated with a characterization that would fit Mailer's work rather well, 'a succession of self-aggrandizing protests'.[8]

Updike's stopping in order to shape a past experience in terms of its present significance is deliberate: Peter Caldwell reconsiders his present life in the light of his father's, which he was unable to understand fourteen years earlier. The understanding, and the response to it, must be put into words. Here Updike relies both upon his Americanness as a sense of place and native speech, and his familiarity with a living tradition, more particularly that of the English novel derived from Henry James. It is hardly surprising to find him paying his respects to Muriel Spark and Iris

Murdoch, and only at first sight perhaps more unexpected to read how much he appreciates Henry Green. Like Nabokov, another of his masters, they are writers with a shrewd eye for human limitations, and a great respect for the resources and beauties of their language as a vehicle and a comment on such frailties. To this Updike has added his own kind of vivid texture, and a more insistent seriousness with perhaps, in spite of his Pennsylvania background, a New England flavour to it.

## Notes

1. Updike, born in 1932, has published five novels (*The Poorhouse Fair*, 1958; *Rabbit, Run*, 1960; *The Centaur*, 1963; *Of the Farm*, 1965; *Couples*, 1968) and three collections of short stories (*The Same Door*, 1959; *Pigeon Feathers*, 1962; *The Music School*, 1966). He has also published two collections of poems and a volume entitled *Assorted Prose*, 1965, which contains among other things some revealing autobiographical sketches and book reviews. My references are to the (Fawcett) Crest reprints of *The Poorhouse Fair* (*PF*), 1964, *The Centaur* (*C*), 1964, and *Of the Farm* (*OF*), 1967; to the Penguin revised ed. of *Rabbit, Run* (*RR*), 1964; and to *Couples* (*Co*), London; André Deutsch, 1968.

2. Norman Podhoretz, *Doings and Undoings: the fifties and after in American writing* (1964), London: Rupert Hart-Davis, 1965, p. 251.

3. David D. Galloway, *The Absurd Hero in American Fiction*, Austin and London: University of Texas Press, 1966. This study has chapters on Updike, Styron, Bellow and Salinger; the Updike chapter bears the title, 'The Absurd Man as Saint' (pp. 21–50).

4. Some examples: *RR*, 126, line 17 to the end of the paragraph (Eccles watching Nelson, young Fosnacht, and their dog); *The Centaur*, 165–166 (the five paragraphs about Heller); *Co*, 271–272, line 13 (Piet looking at the stars).

5. E.G. 'the lenient wall of Hook's eyes' (*PF*, 5); 'His talk was unreeling wider and wider' (*C*, 91); 'the scintillating dregs of my corruption' (*OF*, 17); 'a treasurable dreadfulness' (*Co*, 110); a few lines from *RR*: 'As he climbs the stairs, the steps seem to calibrate, to restrain by notches, a helpless tendency in his fear-puffed body to rise' (80). Cf. also the paragraphs on Ken's field of special competence.

6. Structural patterns of *C* have been glanced at in the *New Yorker* review of the novel (by Renata Adler, April 13, 1963, pp. 182–188). They emerge as one of the results of an excellent essay by Rudolf Haas, 'Griechischer Mythos in modernen Roman: John Updike's *The Centaur, Lebende Antike: Symposion fur Rudolf Suhnel*, hrsg. Horst Meller und Hans-Joachim Zimmermann, Berlin: Erich Schmidt Verlag, 1967, pp. 513–527. (See review in *E.S.*, Dec. 1968.)

7. Norman Mailer, 'Some Children of the Goddess', an *Esquire* article (July, 1963) repr. in Harry T. Moore, ed., *Contemporary American Novelists*, Carbondale: Southern Illinois UP (1964), Arcturus Book Ed., 1966, pp. 3–31, esp. p. 17. The same volume contains William Van O'Connor's 'John Updike and William Styron: The Burden of Talent' (pp. 205–221).

8. *TLS*, June 4, 1964, p. 473. Updike's brief 'Comment' also contains the remarks about English authors referred to in the concluding paragraph of my essay.

There are chapters about Updike in Pierre Brodin, *Presences Contemporaines: Ecrivains americains d'aujourd'hui*, Paris: Debresse, 1964, pp. 194–201; Howard M. Harper, Jr., *Desperate Faith: a study of Bellow, Salinger, Mailer, Baldwin and Updike*, Chapel Hill: Univ. of North Carolina Press, 1967, pp. 162–190 ('John Updike—the intrinsic problem of human existence'); Arthur Mizener, *The Sense of Life in the Modern Novel* (1963), London: Heinemann, 1965, pp. 266–274 ('The American Hero as High-School Boy: Peter Caldwell').

Charles Child Walcutt, *Man's Changing Mask: Modes and methods of characterization in fiction*, Minneapolis: Univ. of Minnesota Press, 1966, also has a few pages and some good remarks concerning *Rabbit, Run* and *The Centaur* (pp. 326–332). Some information may also be obtained from Judith Serebnick, 'New Creative Writers', *Library Journal*, 84: 499 (February 1, 1959: references to the composition of *The Poorhouse Fair*); and from *Time* (Atlantic Ed.,) April 26, 1968, pp. 50–55. David D. Galloway (see above, note 3) has a very useful 'John Updike Checklist' (pp. 183–200).

# Metamorphosis Through Art: John Updike's "Bech: A Book"

Alice and Kenneth Hamilton*

In 1965 John Updike's short story, "The Bulgarian Poetess," came out in the *New Yorker*. It was about a Jewish novelist in his forties, Henry Bech, whose "reputation had grown while his powers declined." A second story, "Bech in Rumania," followed in 1966. Three more Bech stories were later printed, also in the *New Yorker*. Now these five, with two more added, have been published within hard covers under the title of *Bech: A Book*.

Reviewers have welcomed *Bech: A Book* as an amusing report of the literary world and an ironically sympathetic study of an individual caught up in the machinery of the modern industry that has grown up to exploit (and feed off) writers. There is, indeed, a good deal of obvious humour in the way the book has been constructed. It has a Preface purporting to have been written by Bech and complimenting Updike on "this little *jeu* of a book." It is furnished with two Appendices: the first an "unpublished" journal of Bech's Russian travels, together with an "unmailed" letter (copyrighted) to his mistress; and the second a bibliography of Bech's works and a Selected List of Critical Articles.

Updike has embellished these trimmings with his characteristic wit. The Preface mimics the wordy self-display and affected modesty common to such productions. Though less than three pages in length, it is dated Dec. 4th–12th, 1969. It originally included, so the "Editor" informs us, a "list of suggested deletions, falsifications, suppressions, and rewordings" that have been scrupulously incorporated.

*Appendix A* carries a wealth of pedantic annotations. *Appendix B*, the bibliography, is a *tour-de-force* of parody. Its six pages of thoroughly authentic-seeming entries (complete with critical "apparatus") features the names of the most esteemed contemporary critics and the most prestigious literary journals. Among these are hidden one or two wildly improbable items: for example, an article by Bech entitled "The Landscape of Orgasm" in *House and Garden*. A German critic is credited with having written on "Bechkritic und Bechwissenschaft."

Although Updike gives the appearance of approaching his subject

*From *Queen's Quarterly*, 77 (1970), 624–36, by permission of the authors.

tongue-in-cheek, we would be ill-advised to conclude from this that we know just what to expect. He is a writer who has shown himself in the past consistent in his ability to do what is *not* expected. In fact, the seven stories in *Bech: A Book* are no more than incidentally humorous or satirical.

Satire of a mild kind can be found in the first story, "Rich in Russia," where the narrative takes the form of an address to a university class in mid-century literature. Here Updike takes the opportunity to make fun of the attitudes current in the groves of academe. This story and the pair following, "Bech in Rumania" and "The Bulgarian Poetess," show Bech on a cultural mission to Eastern Europe. The humorous possibilities of the American Abroad, exposed to the dangers of the cultural *faux pas* and to the vagaries of translation-English, are exploited to some extent in these three stories. Yet the humour is gentle, never reaching beyond quiet irony. More academically-slanted satire returns as a secondary motif in "Bech Takes Pot Luck," where Bech meets a former pupil of his from a creative-writing class at Columbia. "Bech Panics," the fifth story, is a chilling one, even—or more especially—when it emphasizes the ludicrous. The final two stories, "Bech Swings?" and "Bech Enters Heaven," are savagely ironic. They are not in the least humorous.

In the end, *Bech: A Book* is more than the comic commentary upon the artificial world of letters that is suggested by its posturing Preface and jesting Appendices. The focus is upon Bech himself, who is a serious, if unfulfilled, writer. He is no mere figure of fun. Bech's failure to bring his early promise to fruition is a subject nearer to tragedy than to comedy, and Updike's treatment of this subject is a searching one. Going beyond the surface picture of the modern writer's enslavement by a philistine society, Updike raises some basic questions concerning the artistic consciousness and the nature of art itself. This "little *jeu* of a book" turns out to contain unlikely depths and surprising revelations.

Possibly Updike's reflections upon the social predicament of the writer today gave the initial reason for bringing Henry Bech into being. At any rate, already in 1962 Updike was speaking of the existence of "a very sick literary situation." His concern was voiced in a review of the *Letters of James Agee to Father Flye* appearing in the *New Republic* (13 August) of that year. Updike explained:

> A fever of self-importance is upon American writing. Popular expectations of what literature should provide have risen so high that failure is the only possible success, and pained incapacity the only acceptable proof of sincerity. When ever in prose has slovenliness been so esteemed, ineptitude so cherished? In the present apocalyptic atmosphere, the loudest sinner is most likely to be saved: Fitzgerald's crack-up is his ticket to heaven, Salinger's silence his claim on our devotion. The study of literature threatens to become a kind of paleontology of failure, and criticism a supercilious psychoanalysis of authors. I resist Agee's canoniza-

tion by these unearthly standards. Authors *should* be honored only for their works.[1]

Three years later this sickness in American literature appeared as the theme of "The Bulgarian Poetess." In Updike's short story, Henry Bech finds himself honoured in proportion to the decline of his literary production.

Because he is speaking about a social phenomenon, Updike has been careful in choosing the social setting for his fictional author. Some critics have claimed that Henry Bech is quite like John Updike—an incredible judgement in view of the fact that the Pennsylvanian-born, Protestant writer, who is highly critical of liberalism and very much a family man, has made Bech a New York Jew, a liberal, a determined bachelor, and nine years his senior. Updike has prepared himself for this type of misunderstanding. In "Bech Swings?" an interviewer asks Bech whether he feels any affinity with Ronald Firbank. Bech answers, "Only the affinity I feel with all Roman Catholic homosexuals." But the interviewer's written report brackets Bech with Firbank just the same.

Updike has drawn upon his own experience of being on a cultural mission behind the Iron Curtain in order to portray Bech in a similar situation. He has also brought Bech to Swinging London, where he himself was during 1968–69. He has given him something of his own estimate of the seriousness of the writer's task. But there the resemblance ends. Every author, of course, finds that something of himself is reflected in each of his characters. "Bech's" Foreword refers to "something Waspish, theological, scared, and insultingly ironical that derives, my wild surmise is, from you." Age, temperament, racial and personal memories, attitudes towards religion and politics and human relationships: all these mark off sharply the character from his creator. The subjects they write about seem to be completely diverse, as well.

One reason for trying to link the two together may be found in the event that Updike, somewhat like Bech, met warmer critical acclaim for his early works than for his later ones. But the comparison breaks down because their literary careers are so utterly diverse. In the essential point which Updike makes about Bech's authorship, moreover, they are polar opposites. Updike, refusing to be distracted by what he has called "hallucinatory critical voices," continues to produce in quantity novels, short stories, poems, articles, and reviews. He has drawn in Bech a writer who gave up writing when the popularity of his work waned after his third novel appeared, and who did so in order to retain the prestige which he now possessed as an "honourable" failure. So Bech has died as a writer. He lives only to "pose as himself" and "scribble" little, inconsequential pieces of journalism.

Such is the character that Updike presents to us: a man not strong enough to refuse the shoddy rewards of "idiot" publicity, yet resenting and despising the role he plays. The loss of his author's integrity weighs upon Bech, for he has never laid aside his inner vision of his calling; and he still expects the "block" in his creativity to give way, and his power over words to come flooding back again. He expects this deliverance almost to the last moment of the final story, "Bech Enters Heaven." He thinks he has seen "something hopeful . . ."—but it proves to have been a mirage. *Bech: A Book* is the record of how hope deferred makes the heart sick, until at last all hope is abandoned. However much incidental humour it may contain, this book is tragic rather than comic. It ends in a heaven which is very similar to hell.

Nevertheless, it is not a depressing or dismal book. The vitality of the central character guarantees that. In this connection, Updike stresses one essential fact about Bech: his Jewishness. "Bech's" Preface, taking Updike to task for not presenting him entirely as himself, mentions various Jewish writers whom his fictional image seems to resemble: Mailer, Bellow, Malamud, H. Roth, Fuchs, and Salinger. The point is not that Bech has been modelled on any of these authors, or is a composite of them all. It is that Updike finds the pre-eminence of the Jewish writer in post-1945 America a notable social phenomenon. He makes Bech supply an explanation. The American Jew has known, and kept for a generation longer than the Gentiles, the secret of laughter—"the specifically Jewish, embattled, religious, sufficiently desperate, not quite belly laughter." (p. 143) This is a sustaining memory from the past.

Updike's specific "placing" of Bech in the generation just preceding his own is not casual. He depicts him as one of those who, coming out of service in the Second World War, looked for a literary renaissance in the fifties. Bech remembers the Jewish immigrants to America who became the great names in Hollywood responsible for making America conscious of itself as a nation. Now, after the war, he may be involved in a comparable achievement as part of the new writing in America that may rival—may even surpass—the surge of writing in Europe during the twenties.

In 1955 this dream brought forth Bech's first novel, *Travel Light*. But the dream's fulfillment tarried, while Bech fleshed out and his hair silvered. When he wrote *Travel Light* (a story of motorcycling across the country, written entirely out of second-hand knowledge while he was living like a recluse in Manhattan), he had been free and busy. When he became famous, each day was an empty space to be crossed somehow. Travel and a succession of actresses were always available, and always unavailing to fill the void.

The renaissance Bech hoped for would surpass that of the twenties. "But it was there, with the gaunt Titans of modernism, with Joyce and Eliot and Valéry and Rilke, that one must begin." (p. 108)

Updike's work is always rich in detailed literary reference and allusion. In the Bech stories the four Titans he has singled out for mention are brooding presences. Valéry and Rilke play an especially important part.

In "The Bulgarian Poetess" Rilke is quoted, and Valéry is prominent in "Bech Panics." Between them, these two stories give us considerable insight into Updike's method of communicating to us the inner tragedy of Henry Bech. Since Bech is no posturer, but a true artist trapped and almost destroyed, his creator allows us to glimpse the soul of the man who still lives within the world-travelling, fornicating public image that has come to call itself Henry Bech, the well-known American novelist. Updike does so, not directly, but through the verbal imagery that consitutes the life blood of the writer's imagination. First in Sofia and again in London Bech explains how his writing is based upon "interlocking images." That Bech here is echoing Updike's own convictions can be seen from Updike's statement in a fairly recent interview.[2]

"The Bulgarian Poetess" tells how Bech has agreed to join a cultural mission to "the other half of the world," chiefly with the faint hope of escaping from himself. At a Writer's Union meeting in Sofia he is nauseated by the artificiality and futility of the proceedings. Then a blonde woman in a blonde coat enters the room. Vera Glavanakova is a poetess, unmarried and dedicated to her art. Bech feels that she is his "golden woman," the love that he has been waiting for all his life. Official functions—visits to the Rila Monastery and the Sofia ballet, and a cocktail party at the American legation—allow for only a few brief, and public, conversations. Before Bech's plane leaves they exchange books. Bech writes in his gift to her: "It is a matter of earnest regret for me that you and I must live on opposite sides of the world." (p. 50)

Updike's story sets Bech's total love for Vera in the context of other romantic attractions he has felt on his travels. One of these was for "an entire roomful of girls" at the Moscow Ballet School. Watching them turn their heads to look at themselves on the mirror-lined wall of the practice room, he recalls these lines of Rilke: *did not the drawing remain/that the dark stroke of your eyebrow/swiftly wrote on the wall of its own turning.* The lines come from Rilke's *Sonnets to Orpheus*, Sonnet XVIII (Second Part), which is addressed to a dancer. The central image of this particular sonnet is of the metamorphosis of the dancer's moving body into a symbolic tree of life and rapture. This image explains an incident recorded earlier in "The Bulgarian Poetess." Bech takes a walk and sees a tree so full of birds that it seems to move and talk.

The *Sonnets to Orpheus* were dedicated to the memory of Wera Knoop, a young girl whose brilliant promise as a ballet dancer was cut short by illness and who died in her late teens. Rilke saw himself as an Orpheus who was able through his art to descend to the Underworld which had claimed Wera. His songs would give her immortality. Bech's own unconscious identification with Orpheus is shown in his desire to "rescue" all the women he falls in love with—as Orpheus had desired to rescue Eurydice. Hence the *Sonnets to Orpheus* stir in his mind; and he is astonished when a Wera (Vera), fully alive and not requiring to be rescued, walks into the room in this remote country as though coming in search of *him*.

There is an interesting—indeed, a crucial—cross-connection between Rilke and Valéry. Rilke's reading of the French poet seems to have been the crucible in which he fused the poetic ingredients of the *Sonnets to Orpheus*. First, he was moved by Valéry's poem "Orphée" to see the full symbolic possibilities of the figure of Orpheus. Second, in Valéry's prose dialogue "L'Ame et la Dance," he found the image of the dance as the archetype of all art. Third, from "Le Cimetière Marin" he learned of Valéry's aesthetic of *biological metamorphosis*.[3] In "The Bulgarian Poetess" there is no direct mention of Valéry as there is of Rilke, yet it is Valéry rather than Rilke who is recalled by many details in the imagery.

For example, Rilke visited Russia and met Tolstoy (whose house Bech, on his travels, found turned into the headquarters of the Russian Writers' Union). One of Rilke's early works, a poem inspired by Russian literature, is *The Book of Monkish Life*. Bech's visit to the Rila Monastery, however, links less naturally to that work than to Valéry's description of poetry as "une combinaison de l'ascèse et du jeu." It is while looking round the monastery, now almost deserted because the Bulgarian People's Republic disapproves of monks, that Bech learns how Vera has remained unmarried out of devotion to her work. Bech's informant also disapproves of the ascetic mode of life, calling Vera's choice *unhealthy*. Bech responds, "But she seems so healthy." (p. 61)

In the opening lines of the story Bech asks Vera whether her poems are difficult, and her reply is that they are hard to write. Like the dance, poetry is easy (*un jeu*) only through the discipline of a dedication as rigorous as that of a monk. It is his turning away from the discipline of hard work that has left Bech the victim of his "block." "A stimulus seemed needed" is Bech's excuse for travel. But travel does not stimulate literary production. Neither do drugs, as "Bech Takes Pot Luck" shows.

Valéry's doctrine of *biological metamorphosis* is, moreover, a constant theme in "The Bulgarian Poetess," and one which continues through the other Bech stories. This doctrine asserts that the whole of the natural world is to be seen as a tangible concretion of spiritual energy. The artist alone knows the "soul" of things, their true being. So the things of space and time that appear to be falling into the dissolution of death and oblivion are raised to eternal being by the artist's transforming power. Biological life becomes a new creation by passing through the spirit of the artist who imposes upon its natural chaos aesthetic form. In Rilke's *Sonnets to Orpheus* the symbol for art's transmutation of nature is a tree (the Tree of Life). In Sonnet I (First Part) he speaks of Orpheus creating by his singing a "tall tree in the ear." The dancer of Sonnet XVIII recreates this same tree by her body's motion. When Bech walks through the streets of Sofia he notices the tree that combines the characteristics of both Sonnets. It both moves and is full of sounds of singing.

Bech's second novel was entitled *Brother Pig*. The title, he explains at the Writer's Union meeting, comes from St. Bernard's name for the body. As Bech loses his power to tranform nature into art, he increasingly substitutes the biological for the poetic. In truth, he confuses the two realms. He goes from mistress to mistress, for "there always lurked the hope that around the corner of some impromptu acquiescence he would encounter, in a flurry of apologies and excitedly misaimed kisses, his long-lost mistress, Inspiration." (p. 180). But this forlorn hope that "one more wasting love would release his genius from the bondage of his sagging flesh was doomed to disappointment, because he never escapes from Brother Pig. Vera Glavanakova, who knows how physical love can serve the metamorphosis of art but who never offers him her body, brings him to a momentary renewal of understanding. At the Rila Monastery he sees a peasant woman accompanied by her small son who is being chased by a pig. He immediately thinks of Vera and himself.

His restored poetic vision is still active when he writes his parting message to Vera. The book which he selects for conveying his regrets that he and she must remain "on opposite sides of the world" is his third novel, *The Chosen*. He has chosen his world, and not even his love for her is strong enough to make him renounce it. This is not a matter, of course, of the geographical world in which Bulgaria and America are far apart, or of the political world in which an Iron Curtain divides East from West. He has chosen his venal world of unproductive fame in place of her world of ascetic devotion to the poet's calling. He, who eagerly confided to her that he too had written poetry, no longer writes poems—or even prose infused with poetic rigour. When he first heard her name, he assumed that she was a married woman because of the ending "—ova." Then he learned that the ending simply indicated the feminine gender. His imagination is so tied to the biological sphere that the word *ova* brings to mind physical fertility merely, overlooking the reality of artistic conception and the possibility that an unmarried poetess might bear soul-children.

Before Vera Glavanakova first enters the room at the Writers' Union, Bech has been looking at a bowl of fruit on the table before him. In the bowl is a pear, carrying on the side facing him a brown spot marring its golden skin. He identifies this spot with the entire falsity and futility of his present role. While talking to Vera, he finds to his surprise that he has taken the pear from the bowl and divided it precisely into two halves. He and she might have been a perfect "pair." But there is a corrupting flaw on his side. Deliberately, though unconsciously, he cuts himself off from this "golden" woman.

Bech comes nearest to realizing biological metamorphosis at the ballet, where he sees a performance of *Silver Slippers*. This ballet is based on a folk-tale about a princess who each night puts on silver slippers and dances through an oval mirror to keep tryst with a wizard. The wizard owns a magic stick with which the world may be ruled. The stick and the oval mirror are obvious sexual symbols. When the princess leaps through the mirror to her lover, Bech's heart leaps back to the "enchanted hour" he has spent with Vera before the performance.

But Bech's tryst with his princess has not been a sexual one. The enchanted hour had been spent talking about art. If sexuality unites man to woman biologically, there is also a union of souls in art. The dancer's art awakens Bech subconsciously to the nature of his love for Vera, a love not dependent upon her physical presence. When Vera spoke about her poems being hard to write, she pinched her fingers together, holding an "imaginary pen." The stick that can rule the world may be a pen rather than a penis. And, if mirrors are vaginas, they are also poets' souls reflecting the inspiration that comes from beyond our earth.[4] One Bulgarian author Bech meets is the translator of *Alice in Wonderland;* and the interpreter remarks that this book "truly takes us into another dimension." The same comment is made about Bech's *Travel Light.* The fact that Bech's Bulgarian hosts toss around this remark in cliché fashion does not alter the truth that it is indeed art's function to take us into another dimension. Not only on the stage can a girl pass magically *through the looking glass.* The metamorphosis wrought by art brings Bech's heart for once on the same side of the world with his soul-mate.

But the world of art is shattered by imperfect performance. The wizard in *Silver Slippers* was a poor dancer, and at one moment almost dropped the princess. Bech, a wizard who has lost his power, drops Vera altogether. She, on her side, shows herself to be always the flawless artist. Her parting gift to him is a book of her poems (printed in a script he cannot read), in which is written a message ending with the words "with much leave." Bech is sure she meant to write "with much love."[5] But it is not she who is the *slipper*. Her English may be weak. Her poetic instinct is sure. She knows that he has chosen to leave her.

"Bech Panics" picks up Bech's career at a later date when a crisis overtakes him. He is forty-six, and the month is March. Since his refusal to enter Vera Glavanakova's poetic world he has lived wholly in the biological one; and suddenly disgust with the universe of matter overwhelms him.

His unease begins in New York, where he is living with his third mistress since his return from Eastern Europe. She is a divorcée with three young children. He is upset that she can so easily combine love-making and mother-care. He feels "offended at his immersion in the ooze of familial promiscuity." Partly to avoid recurring emotional scenes that could be ended only by his submersion in marriage, he consents to take a speaking engagement at a girls' college in Virginia.

He arrives there by plane and car, physically upset, to find that spring-time has come to the South. Around the trim, green campus there walk elegantly demure young ladies who are apparently oblivious to the stench of horse manure that rises from the lawns. A writer's sensitivity evidently makes Bech associate "horse" with "whore's." The association, coupled with the "genteel appearance" of everything he sees around him, gives him a sense of the "profound duplicity" of the College environment. *All flesh is grass.* Bech is frightened by premonitions of his own death. During the next two days he is perpetually reminded of the "imbecile cycle" of Nature. The budding landscape, the proximity of so many virginal bodies ripening to sexual maturity, the discussions about literature that become diverted into anthropology, the disturbing presence of his own maleness that so easily raises blushes: all these convince him that life simply "vexes the void," is "a blot on nothingness," and that human consciousness is a casual by-product of the biological process. His desperation even drives him to religion. Alone in the woods, he flings himself to the ground and begs Someone, Something, for mercy. But, if there is any God to hear, He answers only in the silence of Nature.

An offer of help comes, instead, in human form. Ruth Eisenbraun, an intelligent professor of English from New York, first asks him to adjudicate poems written by her students, members of the college Lanier Club, and afterwards invites him to sleep with her. Bech is reduced to tears by her second proposal, which he joins to her first one. "Poetry and love, twin attempts to make the best of a bad job." (p. 129)

When Ruth first introduces herself, Bech jocularly asks her what she is doing here amid all this alien corn. Actually, he himself is the one to whom the lines about the biblical Ruth in Keats's "Ode to a Nightingale" properly apply. It is he who, knowing he is "far from home," stands "in tears." The lost home he grieves for is the realm of poetry. His cry for mercy to Someone, Something is torn from him because his disgust with the whole process of Nature has left him doubting the value of what once had been his driving concern: *the intolerable wrestle with words and meanings.* Earlier the same evening one of the girls has read from Lanier's "The Marshes of Glynn." *Behold I will build me a nest on the greatness of God,* Lanier affirms. The Southern poet's trust in a divine foundation for his poetry has the effect of driving Bech deeper into self-pity and disbelief. Yet, unknown to himself, he has already told the college girls exactly what he most needs to understand in order to climb out of his panic. This essential message comes from Paul Valéry.

Discussing the function of rhyme in poetry, Bech tells the girls how Valéry speaks of a poem's first line coming as the free gift of the gods. The second line we ourselves must make, "word by word, straining all our resources, so that it harmonizes with the supernatural first, so that it *rhymes.*" For Valéry, so Bech explains, without this transforming labour of art "our lives and thoughts and language" are simply a "familiar chaos."

Valéry has been named *the mystic without God.*[6] A poet does not have to be a theist in order to practise his art. But he does need to believe in a transcendent realm into which art transports him. Valéry's mysticism led him to posit a "supernatural" order beyond the brute givenness of Nature, an order intuited by the "soul" of the poet. Having long abandoned his ancestral faith, Bech has no belief in any divine Creator. Yet his scepticism concerning the existence of God has never affected his conviction of having a "divine" calling to be a writer. He has known what it means to receive "the gift of the gods." But, since inspiration has so long been denied him, he now is no longer upheld by the poet's religion. He repeats Valéry's phrases as shibboleths of a faith to which he pays only lip-service. Thus he panics as "familiar chaos" closes in upon his existence. He calls out blindly to Someone, Something to deliver him from the void into which he sees himself and his work being drawn relentlessly. The omnipresence of the biological world, of mindless Nature endlessly and meaninglessly perpetuating itself, convinces him that love and poetry alike are trivial diversions on the road to universal death.

Even in the extremity of his terror, Bech is not without some remnant of faith in Valéry's mystical credo. There is one memory of his stay in Virginia that brings him a little comfort. He had read a passage from *Brother Pig*, the scene in which his hero raped his step-daughter. Bech "has been amazed, as he read, by the coherence of the words, by their fearless onward march." (p. 117) Here was evidence that there is nothing in biological existence, however sordid or cruel, that cannot be transmuted through the magic of art so that chaos is overcome and the human spirit reaffirmed. Yet Bech lacks the courage to hold firmly to what he inwardly senses. When he returns from Virginia to New York, his mistress is aware that he is so spiritually shrunk "that there wasn't enough of him left for her to have any." (p. 132)

The last two stories in *Bech: A Book* show Bech the writer dwindling away into nothingness. In "Bech Swings?" a visit to London comes when a British anthology of his work, entitled *The Best of Bech*, is published. The visit proves a personal and professional disaster. His publisher, his short-term English mistress, and a fawning American interviewer exploit his weaknesses to advance their own ends. The germ of an idea for a new novel to be called *Think Big* is conceived one day, and dies the next. Nothing big can be born from the brain of this writer who has "spilled his seed upon the ground."

"Bech Enters Heaven" opens with a memory of a day in May 1936, when Bech at thirteen was taken by his mother into a huge auditorium. There he saw wonderingly, "the flower of the arts in America, its rabbis and chieftains, souls who while still breathing enjoyed their immortality." (p. 117. *Heaven*, presumably is the National Institute of Arts and Letters.) He knew that his mother had taken him into this heaven to show him her dream that he would earn the right to sit among the immortals. The scene then shifts to the present. In the same auditorium Bech now sits upon the dais, hedged in by poseurs and dotards. One of these is the decayed remnant of the famous playwright of the thirties who had provided the entrance tickets for Bech and his mother three decades ago. He confides to Bech, "Jesus Christ . . . the bastards always said, 'Let's wait until he writes another book, that last one was such a flop.' Finally I say to them, 'Look. The son of a bitch, he's *never* going to write another book,' so they say, 'O.K., let's let him the hell in.'" (p. 184) So Bech enters heaven and finds it to be hell. When he stands to hear his citation read, he is aware of rising no taller than a child.

Updike's cynicism about the publishing world seems unbounded in "Bech Swings?" and his contempt for the artistic establishment is searing in "Bech Enters Heaven." Yet it is Bech's personal tragedy that continues to be his main theme, and social satire is secondary. "Bech Swings?" revolves always around the discouraged writer who "could not perpetuate a romance or *roman* without seeing through it the sour parting and the mixed reviews." (p. 134) "Bech Enters Heaven" displays bitterness less in the ferocious portraits of the shabby "immortals" upon the dais than in the apparently casual thoughts of Bech. As he listens to his citation describing him as a singer of the continental distances, he wonders "why writers in official positions were always supposed to 'sing'; he couldn't remember the last time he had even hummed." (p. 186) Biological existence has come to dominate his vision so entirely that he does not remember that he is the writer who aspired to be the heir of the Titans of the twenties, and therefore of Rilke. And Rilke identified himself with Orpheus, the singer whose song is not silenced by the dismemberment of his body.

*Bech: A Book* is Updike's first attempt to deal specifically with the writer's calling. Yet this theme, and also the doctrine of *biological metamorphosis* as the key to artistic creation, has appeared previously in his work, though in a less developed form. Updike's novel *The Centaur* describes how the science teacher George Caldwell goes into one of the school lavatories and sees on the wall a four-letter word that has been altered to Book. Caldwell wonders whether his son Peter has been responsible for this transformation, which strikes his scientifically curious mind as a piece of new information. Every Fuck can be made into a Book.[7] In other words, biological existence can be transmuted into art.

"Rich in Russia," the first story in *Bech: A Book*, tells us that the name on Bech's mailbox in his apartment building has been "so often ballpointed by playful lobby-loiterers into a somewhat assonant verb," (p. 4) that Bech has been forced to leave the name plate space blank. The title which Updike has chosen for his collection of stories about Henry Bech the author, therefore, exactly corresponds to what George Caldwell saw in the school lavatory. The only difference is that the two words stand side by side instead of the latter being superimposed upon the former. Bech's tragedy is that, having allowed the focus of his life to shift to the "somewhat assonant verb," he leaves us *with nothing to read*. His name simply disappears from the world of the printed word, leaving a blank space where there might have been a BOOK.

Thus, when "Bech" banters with Updike about the latter having produced a "little *jeu* of a book," he is made to reveal his own principal flaw. According to Valéry, whose example Bech wished to follow, writing is both *jeu* and *ascèse*. Updike has undertaken the discipline of the writer's calling, and the result is a BOOK. Because he has not continued to school himself with a similar dedication, Bech will never write another book. His name plate will be empty in the hall of the true Immortals, as contrasted with the false Immortals who are honoured (and honour themselves) for not writing. The heaven of the false Immortals, as Updike indicated already in his statement of 1962 about the sickness of American literature, is heavenly only in that it is based upon an "unearthly" standard. It ignores reality, and therefore betrays art.

Updike does not content himself with writing a fable about an author's decline into artistic impotence, for he also suggests how literary sickness may be cured. Bech knows that a present-day renaissance in literature must start with the Titans of the twenties. Yet he does not profit from their example. His own "block" was paralleled in Rilke when the German poet was just his age. Like Bech, Rilke had sought inspiration in travel and in mistresses. But it was his reading of Valéry in 1921–22 that enabled him to break his long silence. The *Duino Elegies* and the *Sonnets to Orpheus* both appeared in 1923. This was a great productive period for the Titans. Eliot's *The Waste Land*, Joyce's *Ulysses*, and Valéry's *Charmes* were all published in 1922. Bech, then, need only look back to his exemplars to find out how they had been inspired *by books* to continue the writer's ceaseless wrestle with words and meanings.

Bech, however, neglects the "supernatural" inspiration through books. He turns to women, whom he views as "supernatural creatures" and makes into "idols." Alone among his women, Vera Glavanakova is a true goddess—*vera dea*.[8] She proves her divinity by pointing him to the asceticism of the writer's calling.

Bech's mother was his first inspiration, and she warned her son in his adolescence against being diverted from his path by his dawning admiration for girls. "You keep your nose in your books," said Hannah Bech, showing herself to be Hannah who has dedicated her "Samuel" to the Temple of Art. His mother and Vera coalesce in Bech's imagination, therefore, when at the Rila Monastery he sees Vera in the form of a peasant mother and himself as her small son being chased by a pig.

The pig pursues him to the end. As he rises to be received among the "immortals," he feels himself a small boy. And he despairs when, having imagined his mother to be in the audience, he remembers that she has been dead for four years. He realizes sourly that the woman he mistook for Hannah Bech may well be the mother of another writer being honoured that day, a "tip-toeing fellow" who displays a psychedelic pig painted on his stomach. (In "The Bulgarian Poetess," the pig chasing the small boy "moved, as pigs do, on tiptoe.")

Thus "Bech Enters Heaven," Updike's final word about Bech, echoes in its imagery "The Bulgarian Poetess," the first story that Updike wrote about him. During his Bulgarian visit Bech had stood inside a tiny church near the Rila Monastery. The walls of the narthex were painted to resemble Hell. At the other end of the building was the screened area representing "the next, the hidden world—Paradise." Looking through the screen, Bech had glimpsed a row of books, a chair, and a pair of oval spectacles.

Oval glasses; an oval mirror through which a dancing princess leaps; *Through the Looking Glass*, a book which takes us into another dimension; the other side of the world where his "golden woman" lives; and a Paradise of books: Bech has seen all these, but his "block" remains. The omnipresent sexual world must be transmuted into its poetic equivalent if the writer is to succeed in his quest for his long-lost mistress, Inspiration. The formula of metamorphosis is simple enough. Updike has put it succinctly in the title of *Bech: A Book*.

## Notes

1. "No Use Talking," *Assorted Prose* (New York: Knopf, 1965), p. 264.

2. See "The Art of Fiction XLIII: John Updike," *The Paris Review*, Winter 1968, p. 116.

3. See E. M. Butler, *Rainer Maria Rilke* (Cambridge: Cambridge University Press, 1941), pp. 340–58.

4. Updike identifies mirrors with vaginas in Canto IV of his long poem, "Midpoint." See *Midpoint and Other Poems* (New York: Knopf, 1969), p. 27. The image of the poetic soul as a mirror reflecting the "golden" sun—symbol of pure creative power and just judgement—is Valéry's. See Pierre-François Benoist, *Les Essais de Paul Valéry* (Paris: Editions de la Pensée Modernes, 1964), p. 132.

5. Updike ends his story with a succession of punning meanings. Vera's strict poetic sense extends to placing her message to the writer about to fly out of her life upon the *fly*leaf of her book of poems. For his part, Bech has no gift for her that he has the right to call his own. He steals a copy of *The Chosen* from the American legation. The copy is jacketless, while she stands perfectly dressed in a blonde coat. Her perfection shames him, causing him to say, "Don't look." He thinks he is referring to the message he has written inside his novel; but he really means that he does not want the judgement of her candid eyes upon either his work or his life.

6. See Jacques de Bourbon Busset, *Paul Valéry ou le Mystique sans Dieu* (Paris: Librairie Plon, 1964).

7. *The Centaur* (New York: Knopf, 1963), p. 247.

8. Updike has previously used the name Vera in *The Centaur*. There the character so named represents Venus; and the name is linked to the *Aeneid*, Book I, where Venus shows herself to her son Aeneas: *et vera incessu patuit dea*. Peter Caldwell is called upon to translate the relevant passage during a Latin lesson (*The Centaur*, p. 183). So here we have an example of Updike's "interlocking images." Vera Glavanakova represents both Wera Knoop—the type of the true artist—and the Goddess of Love—the truly divine female spirit that Bech has been seeking in his affairs with women.

# Updike's *Couples*:
# Eros Demythologized

**Robert Detweiler***

Much criticism of John Updike's fiction derives from the same middle-class repressions he writes about. We hear, for example, the Puritan critique—that Updike is not a good steward of his admittedly abundant talents, because he will not write "big" novels about "big" subjects. He does, it is granted, compose tightly controlled stories about mundane matters that capitalize on his technical prowess as a maker of metaphor—but this, we hear, only reveals a craftsman's pride that must be deflated by textual analysis exposing the imperfection of this or that phrase and image. Or it is said that Updike is too intellectual and self-conscious as a novelist, that he lacks the uninhibited style of many another artist who has not had the misfortune of being graduated *summa cum laude* from Harvard or working for *The New Yorker*. Or yet again, we learn that he is too flashy for his own good and indulges in gimmickry that gives away his essential superficiality. Being a novelist who does almost everything right, Updike can't seem to do anything right for most reviewers.

I thought that *Couples* would change this. It is a big novel about love and death, free-flowing and clever (but not intellectual), and socially significant enough to inspire a *Time* cover story on American morals.[1] Yet the reviews were largely negative. They sensationalized the sexual dimensions of Updike's fifth novel and concluded, for the most part, that Updike had substituted a collage of extra-marital scenes for credible metaphors of modern marriage.[2] My own experience of *Couples* was remarkably different. It was one of the few novels I had read in recent years to involve me in its "sense of life" (in Arthur Mizener's term), and I felt curiously at home with its setting and action. I was intrigued, of course, by the familiarity that it inspired and attempted to discover the reasons for it. Since some casting about in impressionistic directions gave me no satisfactory answers, I proceeded with a formal rhetorical analysis along the lines of Wayne Booth's vocabulary of perspective and Norman Friedman's classification of plots.[3] Gradually I realized that what I had responded to was not so much the literal story describing the promiscuous exercises of

*From *Twentieth Century Literature*, 17 (1971), 235–46, with permission of the journal.

the libido but rather the natural-physical model that underlies the narrative. An examination of narrator point of view, I found, reveals a variety and plurality of perspectives; these include the author's undramatized and occasionally editorializing omniscience, third person reflectors, interior monologues, dramatic dialogues, and camera-shot scenes. Furthermore, different characters assume and interchange and combine perspectives in a constantly shifting pattern unlike the singular and static vision of much traditional and conventional fiction. Perspective in *Couples* suggests as its basis the atomic motions and electromagnetic force fields of the Einsteinian universe rather than the more simply ordered time and space of an older world picture.

This relativistic perspective engenders a similarly complex plot. *Couples* functions (to use Friedman's distinctions) equally well through plots of fortune, characterization, and thought. The plot of fortune could be subcategorized as "pathetic," since the characters are more or less sympathetic individuals about whom our fears materialize and who seem caught not in a tragic but in a naturalistic situation. They suffer because they are confused by the complexity of marriage in a secular world. The plot of characterization could be labeled a degeneration, for one finds a steady change for the worse—at least in terms of traditional morality—in the behavior of most of the *personae*, resulting in various kinds of losses (spiritual, physical, vocational) that force them, in desperation, to choose new modes of living. The plot of thought works both as "education" and "disillusion," depending on how one reacts to the characters and wishes to understand the conclusion of the novel. If one accepts the moral irregularity of the characters without prejudging them, one could say that the couples of Tarbox indeed learn to see the world in a different way and are thus educated toward a new kind of wholeness and satisfaction. But if one views the adulterous liaisons as a departure from the old set of ideals, then the destruction of two marriages and the precarious survival of some others are evidence of a resulting disillusionment.

The point is that one can read *Couples* from many different angles of plotting—not because its author presumes that the reader will bring any such versatility *to* the novel but because the novel itself forces any fair reader to grant the legitimacy of its pluralism, as in fact we are learning to accept the plurality of thought and custom in our many-angled modern world.

Such a semi-technical examination of perspective and plot leads us to a formal observation on characterization that instructs us on the *weltanschauliche* modernity of *Couples*. The plurality and relativity of points of view and of plots cause us to realize that the novel has no single protagonist as such. It is true that the story focuses most steadily on Piet Hanema and Foxy Whitman, but eight other couples, along with Piet's wife and Foxy's husband, figure too strongly in the novel to be called merely supporting or background characters. Especially the second section, treating the double affair between the Smiths and the Applebys, suggests the strategy. The novel is about "couples," and together they present not really multiple protagonists but a composite protagonist. One reviewer complained that the characters seem interchangeable, but this must have been a good part of Updike's intention. To show the evolution (or dissolution) of a social body demands a certain amount of homogeneity among the respective subjects. To forfeit the convention of an individual protagonist in favor of a composite, organic concept is an artistic risk that succeeds because it too reminds us of the shape of contemporary life. This is the age of solid state physics, of corporations, of Gestalt psychology, and *Couples* projects the fictional equivalent of that orientation.

If this is a markedly secular novel based on scientific models in technique and execution, how does it relate to the past? Or to ask the question fictively, what is its mythic dimension? It is the mythic aspect of literature that we respond to mainly, it is said—to that aspect in which we recognize archetypal actions, persons, and ideas that help us locate ourselves in the present and plan our future. Can a contemporarily modelled story provide us such an orienting myth? Updike indeed offers such myth; it is a major part of the novel, but it functions in a unique manner, as what one might call a mythic progression. Piet Hanema is its key figure. He is a realistic mid-twentieth century adulterer, but Updike also extends him archetypally into both a Tristan and a Don Juan.

How do we recognize the two types? Updike has made it easy to anticipate Tristan. His short tale "Four Sides of One Story" (not a very good one) in *The Music School* collection is a reworking of the Tristan-Iseult legend, and another story in the same collection, "The Morning," stresses the Tristan theme: that "love begins in earnest when what we love is limited." But Updike also exhibited his interest in the two types in a lengthy and quite profound review in the August 24, 1963 issue of *The New Yorker.*[4] Here Updike gave a thorough critical summary of Denis de Rougemont's famous *Love in the Western World*, then used the Swiss author's later *Love Declared* to elucidate his own views on passion, marriage, death, and existential meaning. Granted that it is often tenuous to employ a novelist's occasional discursive writing to illuminate his fiction, in this instance it would be foolish not to do so, for the essay is a remarkable introduction to the mystery of Eros that is dramatized in *Couples;* it even previews some of the novel's imagery. For example, referring to the erotic longing that crystallizes our nostalgia for heaven, Updike writes in the review, "The images we hoard in wait for the woman who will seem to body them forth include the inhuman—a certain slant of sunshine, a delicate flavor of dust, a kind of rasping tune that is reborn in her voice." The triad of sensuous images, seemingly incidental illustrations in the essay, acts as the basis of a repetitive structure in *Couples.* The "slant of sunshine" becomes a phallic "shaft of sun" early in the novel (in Piet's memory of his youthful sexuality), and thereafter the sun is associated with the hot sensuality of the lusting men and wives of Tarbox. The sun, in fact, is the primary concrete image in the mystical diffusion of light that accompanies the Gnostic-tinged sexual atmosphere of the novel. The "delicate flavor of dust" translates into the construction dust that adheres to Piet, the building contractor, and this is also transferred to his mistresses and their houses—to the persons and locales of his nostalgic sojourn. The "rasping tune" sounds in Foxy's harsh voice, the voice of the woman who comes closest to settling his longing for assurance of identity in an infinite world.

Or again, in the review Updike stresses three other elements: the chastity mystique of courtly love as evidenced in the Tristan legend, the portentious and symbolic lion dream of Iseult, and the narcissistic trap of the pair who mistake a love of being in love for a love of each other. Early in *Couples* he mentions the black terror of the night (the other pole of the Gnostic light-dark imagery) and "the suspended skeletons of Virgo and Leo and Gemini." The three constellations represent the fateful forces of chastity, passion, and narcissism; Updike elliptically prefigures the tensions of the novel in that allusive trinity. And perhaps the indication that they are *dead* stars foreshadows the secular knowledge that pervades the novel's conclusion, that a technological realism has supplanted the power of destiny inhabiting nature and myth.

These examples may appear slight, but they show the author's careful craftsmanship that must be appreciated in its intricate detail before one can grasp the broad scope of his artistic success. The presence of the Tristan legend in the fundamental imagery leads one to expect it on the archetypal level, where it shares a relevance with the Don Juan legend. Since the two archetypes subsist simultaneously in *Couples*, it may seem misleading to speak of a "mythic progression," as I did earlier. De Rougemont describes Don Juan as the inversion of Tristan and treats both (in *Love Declared*) as viable types in the modern world. In his review Updike also grants that Tristan and Don Juan represent attitudes toward passion and marriage that abound today. In *Couples* Piet is the pivotal character who is now a Tristan, now a Don Juan, now both at once, while the other pairs and individuals supply added dimensions of the archetypal sub-structure. We must explore the many facets of the mythical patterns in order to see how Updike exhausts them and creates something new, how he works with myth to demythologize it and suggest a new reality that is indeed the latest step of a mythic progression. This analysis must proceed in three steps: the association of the fictive characters with the mythic personae, the establishment of the existential concepts residing in the fictive-mythic action, and the description of a just-discernable new ontic vision that the novel reveals.

In the indentification of fictive and mythic figures, Angela Hanema obviously plays both Iseult the Fair and Iseult of the White Hand. The heavenly connotation of her name, intimating that a higher force works through her; the whiteness that informs the descriptions of her; the combination of passion and inaccessibility in her temperament—all these define her double archetypal role. Of course, this is not an exact parallel to the triangle (or the quadrangle, including King Mark) of the Celtic legend, for according to that Piet and Angela should be lovers instead of husband and wife. Updike complicates the formula and has Foxy also act as mistress and pseudo-wife, as the two Iseults. The depiction of her in these terms is neatly done as an inversion of Angela's characterization. Like Angela, she is presented in terms of whiteness, but it is the color of her clothing and surroundings instead of her complexion; she also combines passion and unavailability, but her passion is marred by a sexual failure with Piet (she cannot reach orgasm with him) and her marriage instead of a personal aloofness constitutes the obstacle between her and her lover. The interchangeability that marks the characters on a literal level thus also extends to the symbolic level, although it is qualified there by a certain diversity-in-unity. The other characters, individuals and couples, reinforce the fictive and mythic parallels. Freddie Thorne's idealizing of Angela mixed with lust for her intensifies her Iseult role. Ken Whitman's dispassionate, objective relation with Foxy makes him a good King Mark. The voluptuous Janet Appleby, caught in a sexual tension between her husband and lover, is a secondary Iseult figure.

As if all this were not complex enough, Updike has the people of Tarbox act in a Don Juan drama as well. Piet is again the lead player. Whereas in his Tristan capacity he searches for the ideal woman who will allay his fear of death and his longing for the infinite, as Don Juan he seeks to conquer many women and thus violate the secret of the infinite hidden in Eros. Apart from Foxy and Angela he does in fact sleep with three other Tarbox wives. In the de Rougemont review, Updike says, "Don Juan loves Woman under the guise of many women, exhaustingly," and in the novel Foxy echoes the thought to Piet in a letter from the Caribbean: "When you desire to be the world's husband, what right do I have to make you my own?" Even Angela assigns the role to him when, after a rare lovemaking between them, she rejects his compliments with the remark, "I'm sure . . . we're all alike down there." As with the Tristan archetype, the other characters, individually and together, reinforce Piet's Don Juan vehicle. Eddie Constantine, piloting his airliner to Puerto Rico and sleeping with his many women there, is of the type. Freddie Thorne *talks* a Don Juan line, even though he does not (and perhaps cannot) relieve his multifarious lust through sexual action. The interchangeability of the characters that we observed in terms of scientific models and aesthetic strategy becomes promiscuity in the Don Juan context and shows how the couples together as composite protagonist seek to force meaning from existence via indiscriminate and cumulative sexuality.

The value of associating the characters of the novel with the Tristan and Don Juan legends emerges more clearly when we point out the existential dimensions beyond the mere correspondences. *Couples* exhibits many of the Gnostic elements that de Rougement identifies with the Tristan legend and the courtly love tradition and that Updike reports upon in his review. The light-dark imagery, the Mater Sophia, the twin narcissism, the search for self-identity in Eros all derive from such a Gnostic vocabulary. The light-dark imagery is one of the most constant and striking aspects of *Couples,* and one thinks immediately of analogies from Gnosticism and the later Manicheism (which, says de Rougement, directly influenced the courtly love tradition and the Tristan legend). In the Gnostic and Manichean systems, light stood for the spirit world and for goodness, while darkness represented the flesh and evil. Updike employs the traditional light-dark imagery but apparently wishes to challenge this antagonism, this dualism of spirit and flesh, for he often quite emphatically floods the adultery scenes with light instead of the conventional darkness. Angela as the inaccessible goal of passion is light, Foxy is "lit . . . from within" by adultery, the moments in which people are merely together are often described in terms of a special light. Only times of loneliness and death are dark. Updike allows his characters to believe what the courtly love tradition affirmed: passion reconciles spirit and flesh, good and evil, as a substitute for the Incarnation. Piet, quoting Freddie Thorne, articulates the compulsive togetherness of the couples: "He thinks we're a circle. A magic circle of heads to keep the night out. . . . He thinks we've made a church of each other."

The same kind of pattern appears with the Gnostic Mater Sophia, the Mother of Christ who becomes the Eternal Feminine and then, in the courtly love tradition, the subject of erotic worship. All of Piet's women are mothers; Angela and Foxy are endowed with an ethereal wisdom that Piet fears and respects. For example, "Piet still felt, with Angela, a superior power seeking through her to employ him." Sleeping with Foxy during her pregnancy brings Piet close to this wise maternal force. He is comforted (she is a substitute for his own dead mother) and sexually satisfied at the same time and receives thereby a double defense against loneliness and the thought of death.

De Rougement says that the illusory nature of romantic love is revealed in the knowledge that Tristan and Iseult do not genuinely love each other but only the idea of being in love. This twin narcissism, as he calls it, disguises the death wish. The lovers do not want a fulfilling love relationship but wish to suffer the pain of separation and longing. This concept clarifies a good deal of the liaisons in *Couples.* In one facet of his being Piet is a courtly lover. He is a "secret dandy;" he and Georgette, and later he and Foxy develop a ritual courtesy that replaces marriage. Foxy writes him, after their affair is found out, "Your virtues are obsolete. I can imagine you as somebody's squire." Piet and the others, it seems, indulge the narcissism that Tristan and Iseult mistake for love. It is apparent in the Hanema marriage; even though they are husband and wife, Angela's aloofness and Piet's blunt advances create artificial obstacles that are attempts to prolong the passion. They do not comprehend the basis of a sound union. Piet and Foxy have the hindrances that are a part of any affair. They are kept apart by a necessary secrecy and caution, and their passion thrives on the desire caused by separation. Both of them indulge, perversely, the narcissistic pleasures of the clandestine affair; it has an excitement lacking in the marriages of both. After the affairs come to light and Piet is alone, he finds that "what he felt, remembering Foxy, was a nostalgia for adultery itself—its adventure, the acrobatics its deceptions demand, the tension of its hidden strings, the new landscapes it makes us master." Even Freddie Thorne illustrates a gross caricature of the narcissistic pattern. He lusts for Angela and connives to sleep with her, but when he finally has the chance he is impotent. He is fascinated by the concept of passion but cannot share in an authentic love relationship. He exemplifies de Rougemont's statement that Iseult "rouses in the heart of a man who has fallen prey to the myth an avidity for possession so much more delightful than possession itself." When Angela falls asleep and Freddie masturbates in bed beside her he embodies the narcissistic absurdity that Eros can become.

Narcissim leads to another phenomenon, the sensation of self-identity found in Eros. As Updike puts it in the review, "a man in love, confronting his beloved, seems to be in the presence of *his own spirit,* his self translated into another mode of being, a Form of Light greeting him at the gate of salvation." This effect, so lyrically described, is the weakest of the Gnostic-Manichean elements in *Couples,* but it is frequently implied in the light imagery and occasionally by other means. Piet's lovemaking with Georgette early in the novel is tinged with this sense of self-identity. Later Updike accents the utter familiarity Piet experiences with Foxy, a feeling that gives him confidence in himself, and in many scenes he frames Piet's homecomings to her in angles and diffusions of light. Yet after the affair is uncovered, Piet confesses to Angela, "Being with you is Heaven," and later he begs, "Don't make me leave you. . . . You're what guards my soul. I'll be damned eternally."

Apart from his thorough use of the Tristan story, Updike also includes extensions of the Don Juan legend beyond the mere archetype in *Couples*; he works with concepts such as the attempted forcing of life's secrets through Eros, the Don Juanian obsession with quantity instead of Tristan's economy, the compulsion toward artistic variety that degenerates into sadism (in the formal sense of de Sade as an intensification of Don Juan), and the ultimate transformation of the passion-and-goodness combination into passion-and-evil. But since I have carried through the analysis of the Tristan ramifications in the novel, it should suffice to say that the Don Juan elaborations similarly exist there. We can proceed to the third major step, to an examination of the new ontic vision that the novel creates.

The vision is divided into three parts. One part is the creation of the extreme tension in the novel between love and death, Eros and Thanatos. Another part appears as a negative: the world strives to realize an incarnational event, yet the Incarnation is totally absent. A third part is the progression from the archetypes of Tristan and Don Juan to no archetype at all. This is the culminating demythologizing action of *Couples* that suggests more provocatively a new reality.

We have already seen how the Tristan and Don Juan legends relate to Eros and Thanatos and how the rationale is reflected in *Couples*. Tristan seeks to avoid death by losing himself in the passionate love of a woman, and yet that effort, precisely because it has the flight from death as its object and not the true encounter with another being, only betrays the continuing intensity of the death wish. Don Juan attempts to outdo and overcome death by the conquest of many women, and yet the variety and exhausting athleticism of his seductions are in themselves death-dealing. Piet acts out both of these roles, although he is a more thoroughgoing Tristan than a Don Juan, and embodies the different attitudes toward love and death. For example, when he makes love to Bea Guerin, "he experienced orgasm strangely, as a crisisless osmosis, an ebbing of light above the snow-shrouded roofs. Death no longer seemed dreadful." But certainly the stress upon death in the novel as a whole is as strong as the concentration upon sex. In fact, one is tempted to reply to the reviewers who have sensationalized its sexual aspects that *Couples* is really a death-ridden novel, and the sexuality assumes relevance only in its relationship to death. Piet tries to break his "nightmare," that magnificently written five page passage culminating in the catalogue of ways to die, by evoking sexual memories and at last reaches over to his sleeping wife for relief.[5] Scene after scene throughout the novel establishes the connection of sex and death: John F. Kennedy's assassination followed by a typically risqùe Tarbox party, Foxy's abortion of the baby conceived with Piet, John Ong's slow death by cancer accompanied by his wife's insistent sexual urges. It is most vulgarly and succinctly expressed by Freddie Thorne, who is aroused by thoughts of dying and tells Angela, "death is being screwed by God. It'll be delicious."

In the traditional teaching of the church, a fundamental relationship existed between love and death. God's love was actualized in the incarnation of Christ, and in the death of Christ the curse of death upon man was lifted. But this was Agape, a totally other-directed and self-giving love, rather than the narcissistic passion called Eros. By denying the full validity of the Incarnation in favor of a redemption through knowledge (Gnosis), Gnosticism weakened the power of Agape, strengthened the dualism of body and spirit, and prepared the way for the perverse combination of love and death exhibited in Eros and Thanatos. Updike remarks in his review, recapitulating a theme of *Love Declared*, that "Gnosticism is an attempt to make the transition from Eros to the Spirit without passing through the paradox of the Incarnation," and it seems that the people of Tarbox are attempting the same thing. Updike presents this surrogate for the Incarnation in terms of oral sex. Some reviewers have chided him for the predominance of fellatio and cunnilingus in *Couples* and have intimated that the scenes are immature creations of salaciousness. I do not think that the intention or effect are all that sophomoric. Rather, the acts represent an ingenious if startling resolution of the Gnostic and Manichean dualisms. For one, the mouth and tongue articulate knowledge, the Gnostic key to redemption: to have them participate in a sexual act as well is to join symbolically the flesh to the spiritual vehicle of salvation. For another, oral sex in *Couples* becomes a kind of sacrament, a travesty, perhaps (although not a parody), of the Eucharist. The last of these scenes between Piet and Foxy is described as follows: "Mouths, it came to Piet, are noble. They move in the brain's court. We set our genitals mating down below like peasants, but when the mouth condescends, mind and body marry. To eat another is sacred. . . . This on the Sunday morning, beneath the hanging clangor of bells." The echoes of courtly love in the imagery of that passage and the semi-pun in the last phrase push one's imagination toward the outlines of an erotic theology—the literal bodies of the lovers replacing the Eucharistic body of Christ—that might also substitute for an incarnational theology.[6]

Two parts of the new ontic vision, then, are the knowledge that Eros actually only increases the awareness of death and the discovery that suggestions of the Incarnation persist even when the Incarnation is suppressed. To discuss the third part I must return for a moment to the impressionistic approach I used earlier. I felt that the marathon love-making between Piet and Foxy toward the end of the novel in the Tarbox apartment was somehow a crucial, perhaps *the* crucial event of *Couples*, but I was at a loss to say why. Considering it now in the light of the two myths, I think that the scene is so important because it represents a final stage of demythologizing and at once the emergence of a new reality. First, their weekend of intense sex is a kind of catharsis. Through the emotional and physical exhaustion, Piet and Foxy purge themselves of the effects of suffering that their earlier passion and guilt have caused. Updike even glosses the passage with the comment that "we are all exiles who need to bathe in the irrational." But more than that, the strenuous three days destroy the power both of the Tristan and Don Juan complexes. Their sexuality loses its narcissistic and idealizing traits; they no longer love the idea of being in love but begin to love each other genuinely. But they also, in the intensity of their passion, move beyond a Don Juanian promiscuity. They gain an intimate knowledge of each other that draws them closer together rather than freeing them for new affairs, even though they are careful not to formally bind each other at this point.

What do they become, then, after they forfeit the instinctive orientation of the two archetypes? Updike implies at the end of the de Rougemont review that a myth is not necessary to articulate the contemporary situation. "Might it not simply be that sex has become involved in the Promethean protest forced upon Man by his paradoxial position in the Universe as a self-conscious animal? Our fundamental anxiety is that we do not exist—or will cease to exist. Only in being loved do we find external corroboration of the secretly high valuation each ego secretly assigns itself. This exalted arena, then, is above all others the one where men and women will insist upon their freedom to choose—to choose that other being in whose existence their own existence is confirmed and amplified." We have as yet, at least, no archetype for this existential man who asserts his identity by choosing to share himself with another person, and for this reason fiction such as *Couples* may be a cultural necessity. It shows us some possibilities for filling the void left by demythologizing. In fact, it may be that our relativist and pluralist age is too various to allow archetypes to emerge at all, and therefore such fiction is doubly important.

The issue that *Couples* embodies is the nature of love and marriage in relation to what the existentialists call "authentic living." The new vision suggests that freedom of choice is more basic to such authenticity than the institution of marriage. Updike himself, according to *Time,* had this bland comment on *Couples*: "There's a lot of dry talk around about love and sex being somehow the new ground of our morality. I thought I should show the ground and ask, is it entirely to be wished for?" One would like to ask in return, "what are the options?" but I suppose that Updike has already shown us in the novel. After the disintegration of the group of ten couples, four pairs continue to meet for bridge evenings, while a new social set forms in Tarbox that includes a Unitarian minister, former inhabitants of Greenwich Village, civic activists, and even experimenters with LSD. Although toward the end of the de Rougemont review Updike marks the advantages of Tristanism, its economizing of passion that allows the social structure to remain intact, even that seems to be dead in Tarbox, and Don Juanism likewise has no following there.

Are Piet and Foxy at last any different from the other couples? After all, they marry and settle down in Lexington, where Piet becomes a building inspector and "where gradually, among people like themselves, they have been accepted, as another couple." One would like a more forceful and decisive denouement than this, certainly; the passion of Tristan and the compulsive vigor of Don Juan promise more. But Updike is known for his ultra-low-key conclusions, and this one, on second thought, is artistically and morally apt. Piet and Foxy are different because their sexuality has broken the mold of common adultery and promiscuity. However sinfully and painfully, they have found their way to each other, to an abiding relationship that seems to me a configuration of Agape rather than of Eros. If we insist that Agape can abound only through the Incarnation, then perhaps we can also say that this is how they experience the Incarnation. It may not be a realization of the Christian *logos sarx egeneto*, but it is a decisive interaction of flesh and spirit that takes them through guilt and to a beginning recognition of grace. Put more practically in de Rougemont's own terms, they become "accustomed not to separate desire from love."[7]

Finally, Piet and Foxy as post-archetypal figures are distinctive because they are uniquely Protestant. Much of Updike's best fiction is pervasively Protestant—it is an aspect of his writing far too seldom discussed. Its essence is assuredly not the kind projected by the rumored plan for the new Congregational Church of Tarbox: "a parabolic poured-concrete tent-shaped peaked like a breaking wave." Rather, it consists of a coming-to-terms with the "fundamental anxiety . . . that we do not exist," what Paul Tillich in *The Protestant Era* calls "the human boundary situation."[8] We meet it in the intuition and knowledge that there is no security anywhere, not in the church, not in marriage, not in any world views or political structures, and yet in spite of all this the Protestant escapes despair by believing in a "Gestalt of grace," in a "sacred structure of reality."[9] This stance of faith is not identical with the autonomous secularism that otherwise informs the novel. The ontic vision that *Couples* strives toward is no less than the "New Being" that Tillich celebrates. The novel does not crystallize Christ as the historical-existential focus of the New Being; it does not even achieve a very strong image of the New Being among the variety of secular and relativist offerings. But in its protestant (in the fullest sense of the term) rejection of the old Eros myths and in its implied demand for a transforming incarnational event, it shows us that the love's body we need is indeed very like the form of the New Being. Piet and Foxy have found the love's body but not the New Being. Yet one would like to think that they are on the way.

## Notes

1. "View from the Catacombs," *Time* (April 26, 1968), 66–75.

2. Some representative reviews are William H. Gass "Cock-a-doodle-doo," *The New York Review of Books* (April 11, 1968), 3; Alfred Kazin, "Updike: Novelist of the New, Postpill America," *The Washington Post Book World* (April 7, 1968), 1, 3; and Granville Hicks, "God Has Gone, Sex is Left," *Saturday Review* (April 6, 1968), 21–22.

3. Wayne C. Booth, "Distance and Point of View: An Essay in Classification," *Essays in Criticism*, XI (January, 1961), 60–79; Norman Friedman, "Forms of the Plot," *Journal of General Education*, VIII (July, 1955), 241–253. Both of these are collected in Philip Stevick, ed., *The Theory of the Novel* (New York, 1967).

4. John Updike, "More Love in the Western World," *The New Yorker* (April 24, 1963), 90–94, 97–104. This review has been reprinted in Updike's *Assorted Prose* (New York, 1965), pp. 283–300.

5. John Updike, *Couples* (New York, 1968), 255–260.

6. Cf. Piet's stream-of-consciousness rambling (*Couples*, pp. 257–258) for a similar com-

bination of pun and erotic-incarnational theology: "Nothing sacred. Triune like cock and balls. . . . Patient parents thumbing home seeds in peat had planted a tree whose fruit he had fed to women. The voracious despair of women had swallowed God."

Updike himself has commented on the oral-genital sex in *Couples*. In response to an interviewer's question as to "why an act that is treated so neutrally in the later book is so significant in the earlier one [*Rabbit, Run*]," he had this to say:

> In *Rabbit, Run* what is demanded, in *Couples* is freely given. What else? It's a way of eating, eating the apple, of knowing. It's nostalgic for them, for Piet of Annabelle Vojt and for Foxy of the Jew. In De Rougemont's book on Tristram and Iseult he speaks of the sterility of the lovers and Piet and Foxy are sterile vis-a-vis each other. Lastly, I was struck, talking to a biochemist friend of mine, how he emphasized not only the chemical composition of enzymes but their structure; it matters, among my humans, not only what they're made of, but exactly how they attach to each other. So much for oral-genital contacts.

The interviewer's question and Updike's response are from C.T. Samuels, "The Art of Fiction: John Updike," *The Paris Review* (Winter, 1968), 102.

7. Denis de Rougemont, *Love in the Western World* (New York, 1966), p. 328.

8. Paul Tillich, *The Protestant Era* (Chicago, 1962), pp. 199ff.

9. Tillich, pp. 209ff.

# The Wide-Hipped Wife and the Painted Landscape: Pastoral Ideals in *Of the Farm*

That *The Centaur* (1963) did *not* say the "final word" and bid farewell to Olinger and the farm, as John Updike had intended it to, is made manifest in his writing a type of sequel to *The Centaur;* the sequel is the richly pastoral and anti-pastoral *Of the Farm* (1965). In contrast to the epic-idyllic surrealism of *The Centaur, Of the Farm* is relatively realistic, like the earlier Olinger stories of *The Same Door* and *Pigeon Feathers and Other Stories.* However, the novel predictably departs from the Howellsian tradition of realism through two technical devices characteristic of John Updike's fiction: 1) the employment of elaborately extended metaphors and symbols, and 2) the extensive employment of strikingly poetic lyricism. Both the metaphors and the lyricism are directly related to the overall pattern of pastoral and anti-pastoral elements which, as I have indicated, prominently runs through Updike's fiction.

*Of the Farm* begins with Updike's familiar symbolic actions of "turning off the highway" and "ushering in the land."[1] In terms of literary history, it is the familiar process of turning from the sophisticated Alexandrian court, and entering the idyllic pastures of Arcadia, Sicily, and Syracuse. Or, perhaps more pertinent to his novel, the process of leaving Duke Frederick's Court (New York), fleeing to Arden Forest (the farm), and finally returning to the court—wiser, more reconciled, and mellowed by the disillusioning but clarifying experiences in the rural setting. Like the characters in *As You Like It*, the characters in *Of the Farm* find the bucolic setting full of emotional violence, conflict, and potentially dangerous myths. In several ways *Of the Farm* becomes a parody of the peace and tranquility usually associated with the pastoral existence, in the way Arden Forest, for instance, becomes a parody of Arcady. In using certain linguistic and formal conventions of the pastoral mode (most notably the pastoral love lyric, since the novel is about loving), Updike comments on some fundamental premises of the agrarian myth. To the

*From Larry E. Taylor, *Pastoral and Anti-Pastoral Patterns in John Updike's Fiction* (Carbondale: Southern Illinois University Press, 1971), pp. 102–11. Preface by Harry T. Moore. Copyright © 1971 by Southern Illinois University Press. Reprinted by permission of Southern Illinois University Press.

extent that he uses those techniques partially to expose fallacies in that myth, he creates a work closely akin to the mock-pastoral. In that way, the novel echoes Hawthorne's technique in *The Blithedale Romance*, which is also a novel about sophisticated urbanites who spend a time on a farm.

But the book is much more than an anti-pastoral exposé. In a real way, the farm itself (as the title suggests) is the central subject and the main "character" in the novel. The farm, like the pastures and groves of the Theocritan *Idyls*, is an *idea* as surely as it is a tangible reality—in fact, *more surely* than it is a tangible reality. The farm stands for something different in the minds of each of the four characters in the book: for the old and dying mother, Mrs. Robinson, it is a paradise, a "people sanctuary"; for her middle-aged son Joey, it is a burden imposed by his mother upon him and his father; for Joey's new "broad-hipped" wife, it is an interesting piece of real estate; for Joey's precociously scientistic young stepson, it is a mildly interesting empirical phenomenon. But, in relation to Updike's epigraph for the novel, the significant point is not *what the farm stands for*, but rather, *that the farm stands*. The book's epigraph is from the existentialist philosopher, Jean Paul Sartre:

> Consequently, when, in all honesty, I've recognized that man is a being in whom existence precedes essence, that he is a free being who, in various circumstances, can want only his freedom, I have at the same time recognized that I can want only the freedom of others.

Possibly the best clarification of the ambiguous semantic sophistry involved in the terms *essence* and *existence* is William Barrett's lucidly direct explanation:

> The essence of a thing is *what* the thing is; existence refers rather to the sheer fact *that* the thing is. Thus when I say "I am a man," the "I am" denotes the fact that I exist, while the predicate "man" denotes *what kind* of existent I am, namely a man.[2]

Thus, on one level *Of the Farm* is a rather simple "existentialist" commentary saying, "Different realities exist for different people, depending on personal psychology and points of view"—a truism and cliché hardly worth saying. But the latter part of Sartre's epigraph involves the type of tension and conflict on which dramatic fiction can be based; that is, the struggle to recognize and desire "the freedom of others." I take it that such a desire involves love (or is love), and that *Of the Farm* is essentially a book about the relationship between loving and desiring freedom. Furthermore, the theme is a continuation of the treatment of love and freedom in *The Centaur* where Chiron's sacrificial act of love is directly associated with the attainment of Prometheus' freedom—that is, it ultimately becomes associated with Peter's freedom to become a second-rate abstract painter, if that is what he wants. "The farm" becomes a symbol of that freedom in *Of the Farm*. In the mother's mind, the farm is a kind of pastoral ideal, or paradise; in the son's mind, the farm is curiously associated with the "landscape" of his second wife's sexy body. Both visions employ a degree of imaginative idealizing peculiar to the pastoral manner. The conclusion of the novel shows the son and mother "striking terms" when the son admits, "I've always thought of it as *our* farm."[3] The statement is essentially an act of love and reconciliation which says, "I will give you the freedom to have your 'farm,' and I want to retain my freedom to have my 'farm.'" It is a reenactment of the compassionate father's act of love which had allowed Mrs. Robinson the freedom to have her farm in the first place.

Perhaps the most important fact about *Of the Farm* is that Updike chose the particular image of a farm to symbolize his existential statement about love and freedom. That is, in terms of imagery and language and symbols, characters in the novel become involved in a complex process of pastoral idealization. For example, the boy Richard's question, "What's the point of a farm nobody farms?"[4] indicates that the farm is not "real" in terms of, say, pragmatic agrarian economy. The question is comparable to "what's the point of the Arcadian ideal?" The answer implied throughout the novel is "The point is the Farm's symbolic value—its value *as an idea.*" In choosing to write about "a farm nobody farms," Updike connotatively appeals to all such farms, from Eden to Thoreau's hut at Walden Pond.

Symbolic of Mrs. Robinson's view of the farm is the framed print of a painting which she has hung on the wall to replace the photograph of her son's first wife. That first wife had fallen short of the mother's ideal, and her photograph is replaced by an extravagantly idealized painting of a farm. As in Theocritan *Idyls*, it is "a fabulous rural world" where the grass is "impossibly green." This "idyllic little landscape" suggests the mother's imaginative flight from reality, and her desire for the Arcadian ideal.

> In [the portrait's] place above the sofa, not quite filling the tell-tale rectangle of less discolored wallpaper, there had been substituted an idyllic little landscape, a much-reduced print of an oil, that had ornamented my room as a child, when we lived in my grandparents' house in the town. Instantly—and I wanted my mother to see me doing this, as a kind of rebuke—I went to examine the print closely. The pentagonal side of a barn was diagonally bisected by a purple shadow cast by nothing visible, and a leafless tree of uncertain species stood rooted in lush grass impossibly green. Beyond, I revisited, bending deeper into the picture, a marvellous sky of lateral stripes of pastel color where as a child I had imagined myself treading, upside-down, a terrain of crayons. The tiny black V of one flying bird was planted in this sky, between two furrows of color, so that I had imagined that if my fingers could get though the glass they could pluck it up, like a carrot sprout. This quaint picture, windowing a

fabulous rural world, had hung, after we had moved to the farmhouse, in the room at the head of the stairs, where I had slept as an adolescent and where, when I had gone away, my father had slept in turn.[5]

This painting is typical of the mother's vision of the world. She creates a pastoral mythology which her son has always seen as contradictory and unrealistic. For example, the son (who narrates the story in the first person) explains that his mother had "made a mythology of her life," a mythology which had a kind of mathematical consistency within its own limits, although it required "feats of warping and circumvention and paradoxical linkage" unintelligible to an outsider.[6] In speaking of the pictures in a nature book owned by his mother, Joey explains to his step-son, "I could never match the pictures up with the real things, exactly. The ideal versus the real."[7] As Mrs. Robinson's ideals and expectations are continually confronted by harsh reality, so her farm is becoming an island encroached upon by superhighways, housing developments, and shopping centers. As part of her ideal, she had wanted her son to be a poet; instead he became an advertising executive. She had never approved of his petite, self-contained, spiritual first wife; neither does she approve of his "wide-hipped" bikini-clad second wife. The mother's problem in loving is that she does not recognize that allowing the loved-one freedom is the first prerequisite. She insists on her private mythology—her painted pastoral landscape. The result is that she has maintained a possessive attitude toward her son which has played a part in the failure of his first marriage. Insofar as Updike shows her particular vision of the world as solipsistic and potentially destructive, the novel is anti-pastoral. But, insofar as he gives her humor, imagination, wit, and even beauty, the novel suggests that there is, after all, something of value in the idealizing pastoral attitude.

The most telling aspect of the novel is the imagery which indicates that Joey, while contemptuous of his mother's idealization and love of the farm, participates in a form of mythologizing very similar to his mother's. As his mother has centered her life around a personal myth about her land, Joey has centered his life around his sexy new wife. He has painfully decided to divorce his first wife, Joan, and lose his three children in order to marry Peggy. And Peggy's great appeal is her voluptuous sexuality—sexuality which he imagines throughout the novel as a *landscape*. In images every bit as ideally pastoral as Mrs. Robinson's "fabulous rural world" in the painting, Joey, as first-person narrator, says of his sexy wife, "she yields a variety of landscapes," and "my wife is a field." In a love lyric as lush and musical as the Theocritan *Idyls* themselves, he celebrates his wife's wide hips and her body:

> My wife is wide, wide-hipped and long-waisted, and, surveyed from above, gives an impression of terrain, of a wealth whose ownership imposes upon my own body a sweet strain of extension; entered, she yields a

> variety of landscapes, seeming now a snowy rolling perspective of bursting cotton bolls seen through the Negro arabesques of a fancywork wrought-iron balcony; now a taut vista of mesas dreaming in the midst of sere and painterly ochre; now a gray French castle complexly fitted to a steep green hill whose terraces imitate turrets; now something like Antarctica; and then a receding valleyland of blacks and purples where an unrippled river flows unseen between shadowy banks of grapes that are never eaten. Over all, like a sky, withdrawn and cool, hangs—hovers, stands, *is*—the sense of her consciousness, of her composure, of a noncommittal witnessing that preserves me from claustrophobia through any descent however deep.[8]

For Joey, freedom is associated with his sexy wife, and his sexy wife, in turn, is associated in his mind with the landscape. For his mother, freedom is associated with the landscape of her farm. Indeed, the mother and the son are both idealizing pastoralists. In a review of *Of the Farm* for *Commonweal*, Anthony Burgess comments on the above love lyric as a touch of "genuine pastoral"; he is perhaps the first of Updike's published critics to use the term in connection with Updike's fiction, and, to my knowledge, he is the only one.

> There is more of this [lyricism] in the novel, evoking the sexual landscape in the penultimate chapter of *Finnegans Wake*, but totally wideawake, a cunning rococo cadenza or perhaps something earlier and baroque—in the fantasy-making extravagance of the metaphysical poets. Sometimes the preciosity is unbearable—"sere and painterly ochre," for example—but on the whole the thing works. It is the sort of thing that brings poetry back to the novel—not the poetry of action or casual close description but the poetry of digression, the only kind really admissible.
> Touches like this give *Of the Farm* an intensity, as well as a relaxed quality of genuine "pastoral," very rare in contemporary letters.[9]

My only objection to these incisive comments by Burgess is to question his term "digression," which somehow suggests that such passages are fragmented tours de force, rather than integrated parts of a larger pattern—the pattern I have traced in this essay. Indeed, such lyricism becomes even more attractive and more praiseworthy, it seems to me, when seen in relation to the totality of John Updike's pastoral and antipastoral patterns.

Joey's imaginative equation of Peggy's wide-hipped body with the land is further reinforced in the novel. In the way that he sees her body as a landscape while he is making love to her, he conversely sees the landscape as her body while he is mowing the meadow. Complete with a stock pastoral catalogue of flowers, the following idyl shows the process by which Joey becomes sexually aroused as he rides the tractor over the hills and valleys of the meadow:

> Black-eyed susans, daisy fleabane, chicory, goldenrod, butter-and-eggs each flower of which was like a tiny dancer leaping, legs together, scudded

past the tractor wheels. Stretched scatterings of flowers moved in a piece, like the heavens, constellated by my wheels' revolution, on my right; and lay as drying fodder on my left. Midges existed in stationary clouds that, though agitated by my interruption, did not follow me, but resumed their self-encircling conversation. Crickets sprang crackling away from the wheels; butterflies loped through their tumbling universe and bobbed above the flattened grass as the hands of a mute concubine would examine, flutteringly, the corpse of her giant lover. The sun grew higher. The metal hood acquired a nimbus of heat waves that visually warped each stalk. The tractor body was flecked with foam and I, rocked back and forth on the iron seat shaped like a woman's hips, alone in nature, as hidden under the glaring sky as at midnight, excited by destruction, weightless, discovered in myself a swelling which I idly permitted to stand, thinking of Peggy. My wife is a field.[10]

Mindful that the story is told by a self-revelatory first-person narrator, we must remember that this is Joey Robinson's language, and *his* myth-making; in this lyricism he reveals that he has learned his mother's lessons in pastoralism perhaps better than he himself knows.

The pastoralism of Mrs. Robinson and her son is "genuine." And the novel as a whole would be an idyl, were it not for certain very unpastoral facts and realities brought out in the book; for example, how idyllic are the following details: divorce, three fatherless children, adultery, menstrual periods and soiled Tampax, screaming family fights with slappings and deliberately broken dishes, heart attacks, and an eleven-year-old child caught in the middle of it all? Certainly, there is nothing very extraordinary about these details; they are merely the more unpleasant "stuff of real life." But their very intrusion into Mrs. Robinson's farm is like the intrusion of violence, hypocrisy, and cloddish stupidity into Arden Forest—or, for that matter, like death and communal sin in *The Poorhouse Fair*, or like the ruthless killing in "Pigeon Feathers." Thus, Updike seems to be using the pastoral lyricism of this novel partly as a norm against which reality is measured. The idealized painting and the description of the "wide-hipped wife" serve to remind us and the characters how far we are from Arcady and Eden. In this way, at least, the novel is anti-pastoral.

The most important point made in *Of the Farm* is that all the characters learn something. They partially learn to see things as they are. In the opening paragraph, we see that honeysuckle and poison ivy grow from the same earth and tangle around each other. Similarly ambiguous, the possessiveness of Joey's mother has taught him how to receive Peggy's love; Peggy's earthy voluptuousness is a complement to Joey's poetic mythologizing; Joey's youth on the farm has taught him to love Peggy's earthiness. In short, the characters intuitively grasp what Sartre is talking about in the epigraph—that one must first long for and achieve his *own* freedom before he can love others; and, even then, the first step in loving others is to desire the freedom of the person loved. If "existence precedes essence," then attainment of self-freedom precedes the desire for the freedom of others.

*Of the Farm* is anti-pastoral without being satiric. At no point in the novel do we see the characters as ridiculous; at no point do we smile or laugh at them, as we sadly smile at Rabbit Angstrom, for example. Even the excessive ideals of the mother and the son have a kind of redemptive eloquence which reminds us more of human aspiration than human folly. In reading this novel, we see that the pastoral ideal has many variations, like a symphony composed around a central theme. For Joey Robinson to metaphorically make his wide-hipped wife into the land is merely an inversion of the process by which Mrs. Robinson makes the land her lover. Both involve the pastoral ideal. The process is ironic without being satiric; and the weekend at the farm is, likewise, parodic, without being satiric. The most caustic statement made by *Of the Farm* is that the pastoral attitude toward nature and the land is potentially dangerous. That is, Mrs. Robinson's pastoral idealizing has led to her possessiveness of her son, her inability to accept his spiritual first wife, and her attacks on the new wife Peggy. But Peggy, the very embodiment of earthiness and sexuality, is ironically *like the land;* thus the mother's rejection of Peggy (a conditioned reflex of her possessiveness) is a rejection of her (the mother's) most fundamental beliefs—her own mythology. Consequently, it is bound for failure. Therefore, the stage is set for either some kind of adjustment, or for pathos; and the adjustment occurs. In one of the few scenes of real reconciliation in Updike's fiction, characters adjust: the mother, the new wife, and the son Joey make concessions, and they are concessions which "desire the freedom of others." At the end of the novel, the mother says, "He's a good boy and I've always been tempted to overwork him." In response, "Peggy voluntarily grinned, grinned at me as in my dream or as she had the first time we met." And Joey, freed from his mother's dream of the ideal, concedes the validity of his mother's pastoral dream; that is, he too grants freedom: " '*Your* farm?' I said. 'I've always thought of it as our farm.' "[11] The reconciliation is made valid and is protected from sentimentality by the psychological terror and conflict which have preceded it during the weekend. The "farm" is recognized as existent, and that is sufficient. It no longer matters that Joey's "farm" is his wife, and that the mother's "farm" is the land.

The reconciliation and knowledge which terminates *Of the Farm* are by no means a definitive answer to human conflict. The wisdom attained is like the wisdom so often attained by characters in Shakespeare's plays—a matter of melancholy and faltering reconciliation rather than triumphant affirmation, and a matter of subtle concession rather than dramatic capitulation. Like so much of John Updike's fiction, the novel is concerned with reconciling opposites—farm and town, swain and sophisticate, male and female, spirit and body, past and present, heaven and earth. Here, as in *The Centaur*, the reconciliation occurs. In one sense, *The Centaur* is a pastoral elegy; in a similar sense, *Of the Farm* is a pastoral love lyric. As he had feared, John Updike exaggerated in his desire to make *The Centaur* a valediction to Olinger; if anything, perhaps that distinction belongs more to *Of the Farm* than to any other novel. With only minor exceptions, John Updike has not written anything so hopeful as *Of the Farm* since 1965. And in his most recent works, the "genuine" lyricism and pastoralism of *Of the Farm* have been reduced to painfully ironic norms by which spiritual distance and psychological loss are judged. In his stories collected in *The Music School*, in his novel *Couples*, and in *Bech: A Book* idyllic lyricism is present—but only as an ironic touchstone. To this date, Updike has written nothing so eloquent, so luxurious, and so sanely beneficent as *Of the Farm*.

## Notes

1. John Updike, *Of the Farm* (New York, 1965), p. 3.

2. William Barrett, *Irrational Man: A Study in Existential Philosophy* (New York, 1962), p. 102.

3. Updike, *Of the Farm*, p. 174.

4. Ibid., p. 4.

5. Ibid., p. 18.

6. Ibid., p. 31.

7. Ibid., p. 64.

8. Ibid., pp. 46–47.

9. Anthony Burgess, "Language, Myth, and Mr. Updike," *Commonweal*, 83 (February 1966), 559.

10. Updike, *Of the Farm*, pp. 58–59.

11. Ibid., p. 174

# Things Falling Apart: Structure and Theme in *Rabbit, Run*

Clinton S. Burhans, Jr.*

## I

Whatever else can be said of John Updike's writing since 1960, one judgment seems clear: *Rabbit, Run* continues to be his most popular and critically successful novel, the one work in which his artistic and intellectual voices sound their fullest and truest note. Certainly, the novel has attracted and continues to attract more critical attention than the rest of his writing together; moreover, in common with other challenging works, critical opinion of *Rabbit, Run* ranges over a wide spectrum. For some critics, Harry "Rabbit" Angstrom becomes an absurd saint rejecting a ridiculous world and an embodiment of positive values; for others, he functions as a deformed social growth and a devastating reflector of the soil that grew him.[1] The most interesting aspect of this critical divergence is less its extremes or their range than the possibility they offer of a dynamic tension at the heart of the novel: in this light, Rabbit Angstrom runs in tightening circles defined by the complex interactions between the potentialities and the influences indicated by these extremes. Structurally, the novel is built on such circles; and thematically, Updike explores the conditions, the relationships between Rabbit and his milieu, which explain them.

## II

*Rabbit, Run* begins with a wide geographical circle and ends in the disappearing point of a subjective one. Pulled back and forth between the poles of convention and revolt, of others' demand and his own desires, Rabbit Angstrom increasingly feels trapped in a net, caught in a life of incomprehensible complexity and meaningless triviality. Seeking escape, he runs, like his namesake, in circles, each one smaller than the last in a spiral twisting inwards. In each of these circles, he longs for something better, some straight road or straight line; but his longings are blunted or

From *Studies in the Novel*, 5 (1973), 336–51, by permission of the journal.

warped, and the sad spiral continues until he finally disappears in the infinite sterility of an empty solipsism.

In the beginning of the novel, the messiness of Rabbit's apartment symbolizes the increasing ugliness and frustration into which his life seems to be settling: "the clutter behind him in the room . . . clings to his back like a tightening net."[2] On a sudden impulse, he runs away, dreaming of driving south to the simplicity of a warm beach on the Gulf of Mexico. But "the more he drives the more the region resembles the country around Mt. Judge. . . . At the upper edge of his headlight beams the naked treetwigs make the same net. Indeed the net seems thicker now" (p. 32). Even his map seems another trap: "the names melt away and he sees the map whole, a net, all those red lines and blue lines and stars, a net he is somewhere caught in" (p. 34).

What Rabbit longs for is neatness and a straight road to a clear goal: "his image is of himself going right down the middle, right into the broad soft belly of the land . . . " (p. 30). He wants to go south, but the roads he takes keep bending him west until finally, confused and weary, he turns instinctively north towards home. Completing this first circle, the symbol of his condition and the structural pattern for the rest of the novel, he parks his car in front of the building where his old high-school coach lives. "He feels the faded night he left behind in this place as a net of telephone calls and hasty trips, trails of tears and strings of words, white worried threads shuttled through the night and now faded but still existent, an invisible net overlaying the steep streets and in whose center he lies secure in his locked windowed hutch" (p. 37).

Unable to return to the network of his life with his wife, Rabbit goes out with his former coach and meets Ruth in Brewer. After spending a night with her, he decides to move in; life with Ruth seems to him a way to remain in the calm and uninvolved center of the net. Driving back to Mt. Judge to get his clothes, he remembers that "yesterday morning the sky was ribbed with thin-stretched dawn clouds, and he was exhausted heading into the center of the net, where alone there seemed a chance of rest. Now the noon of another day has burned away the clouds, and the sky in the windshield is blank and cold, and he feels nothing ahead of him, Ruth's delicious nothing, the nothing she told him she did" (pp. 82–83). Here begins the second circle in the story of Rabbit Angstrom, the circle of movement between his home and family in Mt. Judge and his life with Ruth in Brewer. And his inability to break this circle and turn it into a straight movement dooms him to the final inward circle into a solipsistic nothingness with which the novel ends.

As his life with Ruth becomes increasingly complicated, lines of force reach out from Mt. Judge to circle him back in that direction. Reverend Eccles involves himself in the situation; and Rabbit, wondering how Eccles had heard about Ruth, concludes that "the world's such a web anyway, things just trickle through" (p. 108). Their conversations reveal that Rabbit's earlier attempt to find a straight road south symbolizes inarticulate but profound longings for an intangible road, for meaning and values to give purpose and direction to his twisted life. Playing golf with Eccles, Rabbit explains that he had left Janice because " 'there was this thing that wasn't there' " (p. 111). When the clergyman asks him what this "thing" is, Rabbit answers, " 'don't ask me. It's right up your alley. If you don't know nobody does' " (p. 112). But Eccles, who should know, does not; and Rabbit, who knows, has no way to articulate it. Upset and embarrassed, Eccles watches as Rabbit tees off:

> Very simply he brings the clubhead around his shoulder into it. The sound has a hollowness, a singleness he hasn't heard before. His arms force his head up and his ball is hung way out, lunarly pale against the beautiful black blue of storm clouds, his grandfather's color stretched dense across the east. It recedes along a line straight as a ruler-edge. Stricken: sphere, star, speck. It hesitates, and Rabbit thinks it will die but he's fooled, for the ball makes this hesitation the ground of a final leap: with a kind of visible sob takes a last bite of space before vanishing in falling. "That's *it*" he cries and, turning to Eccles with a smile of aggrandizement, repeats, "That's it" (pp. 112–13).

Notified by Eccles, Rabbit returns to Mt. Judge when Janice has her baby. At the hospital he talks with her and then assures Eccles that he will not return to Ruth, that he will stay with his wife and family. The two men "drive back to Mt. Judge along the familiar highway. At this hour it is empty even of trucks. Harry sits wordless staring through the windshield, rigid in body, rigid in spirit. The curving highway seems a wide straight road that has opened up in front of him. There is nothing he wants to do but go down it" (p. 172). He stays overnight at the clergyman's home and in the morning tells Mrs. Eccles that " 'last night driving home I got this feeling of a straight road ahead of me; before that it was like I was in the bushes and it didn't matter which way I went' " (p. 175). She seems attracted to him, but Rabbit thinks of the new straight road with Janice and refuses to respond.

Back at his own apartment, Rabbit finds that "the straight path is made smooth" (p. 182): his father-in-law has paid the rent and gives him a job selling used cars. At first, Rabbit finds meaning in caring for the apartment and for his son; he feels "the happiness in cleanness, order, and light" (p. 183). Soon, however, the same old constricting net of meaninglessness and despair settles over him again. After telling Mrs. Smith that he will not be able to work for her any longer, he takes Nelson to the playground, and here "he feels the truth: the thing that had left his life had left it irrevocably; no search would recover it. No flight would reach it. It was here, beneath the town, in these smells and these voices, forever behind him. The best he can do is submit to the system and give Nelson the chance to pass, as he did, unthinkingly, through it" (p. 188). But the system creaks; his mother is cold and disapproving not over his leaving Janice but over his abandoning Ruth (pp. 189–90), and his new job rests on lying and cheating (pp. 195–96).

Thoughts of death increasingly disturb him. In the hospital he had seen his old coach paralyzed and dying from strokes (pp. 177–79), Mrs. Smith has told him that she would soon be dead (pp. 186–87), and even Ruth's face in his memory seems dead (p. 192). Janice's imminent return begins to bother him; visiting her in the hospital, "the difficulty of pleasing someone" had begun "to hem him in" (p. 179). Now, thoughts of Tothero and Ruth "make on one side the vacuum of death and on the other side the threat of Janice coming home grows: that's what makes him feel tipped, lopsided" (p. 192). Even the wrinkles on his bed seem "black lines" making a "net" for him to lie on (p. 194).

After Janice and the baby come home, things go well for a few days, until Rabbit tries to make Janice serve his sexual desires. Caring nothing about her or her condition, he is infuriated by her discomfort and distaste; he is convinced that she "has gotten an unreal idea of what love is. She exaggerates its importance, has imagined it into something rare and precious she's entitled to half of when all he wants is to get rid of it so he can move on, on into sleep, down the straight path, for her sake" (p. 206). In the decay of all other values, only himself and his desires remain, and the straight road of meaning and purpose symbolized by the golf ball's flight has become only an alley of lust to the dead end of oblivion.

Thwarted, he deserts Janice again and returns to Brewer; and in his absence, she gets drunk and accidentally drowns the baby. Trying to understand why he had walked around Brewer all day instead of returning home in time to prevent the drowning, Rabbit thinks that "what kept him walking was the idea that somewhere he'd find an opening. For what made him mad at Janice wasn't so much that she was in the right for once and he was wrong and stupid but the closed feeling of it, the feeling of being closed in" (p. 225). Back in Mt. Judge for the funeral, he takes the only opening left to him; declaring himself not responsible for the baby's death, he runs from the cemetery into his last and smallest circle: a flight into himself.

Running from the net once again, he tries "to keep himself in a straight path" (p. 246). Around the mountain and into Brewer he runs once more to Ruth, but she calls him "Mr. Death" and tells him his love means nothing: divorce your wife, she demands, or forget me. "Guilt and responsibility slide together like two substantial shadows inside his chest" (p. 253):

> He decides to walk around the block, to clear his head and pick out his path. Funny, how what makes you move is so simple and the field you must move in is so crowded. Goodness lies inside, there is nothing outside, those things he was trying to balance have no weight. He feels his inside as

very real suddenly, a pure blank space in the middle of a dense net. I don't know, he kept telling Ruth; he doesn't know, what to do, where to go, what will happen, the thought that he doesn't know seems to make him infinitely small and impossible to capture. Its smallness fills him like a vastness. It's like when they heard you were great and put two men on you and no matter which way you turned you bumped into one of them and the only thing to do was pass. So you passed and the ball belonged to the others and your hands were empty and the men on you looked foolish because in effect there was nobody there (pp. 254–55).

With this, Rabbit runs again, circling into the sheltering "blank space" of his own insides. Unable to find a meaningful or lasting straight line through the net, he has run in ever-smaller circles and disappeared into this last nothingness, the pathetic emptiness of himself. Now, as he runs, there is truly no one there.[3]

### III

Structurally, then, the novel suggests that Rabbit Angstrom is less an absurd saint than a wasted victim; and thematically, it confirms and enforces this direction by exploring the milieu and the quality of life that Updike's fiction characteristically reflects: a foundation of malfunctioning institutions and a scaffolding of formal and informal relationships without real substance or meaning or value shoring up the ruins of a world in which no one can really love anyone else or redeem himself. The image of a triumphant athlete not dying young apparently germinated early in Updike's imagination and developed slowly towards its flowering in *Rabbit, Run*. In an early poem from *The Carpentered Hen*, "Ex-Basketball Player," Updike describes the once-great Flick Webb:

> Once Flick played for the high-school team, the Wizards.
> He was good: in fact, the best. In '46
> He bucketed three hundred ninety points,
> A county record still. The ball loved Flick.
> I saw him rack up thirty-eight or forty
> In one home game. His hands were like wild birds.
>
> He never learned a trade, he just sells gas,
> Checks oil, and changes flats. Once in a while,
> As a gag, he dribbles an inner tube,
> But most of us remember anyway.
> His hands are fine and nervous on the lug wrench.
> It makes no difference to the lug wrench, though.
>
> Off work, he hangs around Mae's luncheonette.
> Grease-gray and kind of coiled, he plays pinball.
> Smokes thin cigars, and nurses lemon phosphates.
> Flick seldom says a word to Mae, just nods

> Beyond her face toward bright applauding tiers
> Of Necco Wafers, Nibs, and Juju Beads.

Here, Updike simply presents a man alive only in his memories of a youthful glory. Apart from the stereotypic pathos of such a man, Flick Webb apparently has no particular significance for Updike.

In a short story, "Ace in the Hole," however, he complicates the problems of the bypassed athletic hero by extending it into personal and social relationships. A former basketball star and still holder of the county scoring record, Fred "Ace" Anderson has just been fired from another job. Driving home, he finds solace in snapping a match accurately into the gutter, like a basketball through a hoop, and by beating some boys in a race after stopping for a red light. He goes to his mother's to pick up his baby daughter, and his mother tells him to be glad he was fired—he was much too good for the job. At home, his wife, tired from working, is upset and wonders sarcastically what he plans to do now. Ace evades the issue by telling her that they must have a son to bring up as a basketball player and by making her dance with him. More and more, Ace feels "crowded" by his mother and by his wife and "tight," as he used to feel before a game. Then, the "tightness" vanished in the camaraderie of the locker room and in his feeling of greatness as a player; now, that feeling returns to him only in such trivial actions such as snapping matches and intersection drag racing and in the memories evoked by dancing: "he seemed to be great again, and all the other kids were around them, in a ring, clapping time."

Withdrawn and uninvolved with others, Flick Webb is apparently resigned to living in his memories of former glory. But Ace Anderson is more complex and significant, both in himself and in his relationships with others. More than just memories of past greatness, he wants something to recover that feeling in the present. His actions and reactions influence and are influenced by the many other people whose lives intersect with his; his mother, his wife, his daughter, the youths whom he understands and envies. Apart from the intrinsic pathos of his situation, then, Flick Webb has no meaning; but Ace Anderson, in his implied complexities and in the network of his relationships, offers a variety of human and sociological implication. An increasing imaginative grasp of these implications must have led Updike to see in Ace a point of view from which to study such a man and the culture which shaped him.

Essentially, therefore, the beginning of *Rabbit, Run* is "Ace in the Hole" with a few significant changes and much expanded; and as Ace Anderson develops into Harry "Rabbit" Angstrom, the novel extends and explores in detail the premises and the implications only sketched in the story of Ace and his milieu. Moreover, the single and simple point of view of the story becomes in the novel a brilliant and subtle counterpoint in which the point of view centers on Rabbit but shifts occasionally and briefly to other characters. In this way, Updike forces the reader to see things largely from Rabbit's position while at the same time keeping the reader sufficiently detached to be able to evaluate both Rabbit and his shaping milieu. And as the story of Rabbit Angstrom expands in detail the situation and character outlined in Ace Anderson, this complex point of view reveals the novel's thematic boundaries; an unflinching portrayal of a young man with the full human potentialities for good and evil, for success and failure, for love and lust, for life and death; and an equally unflinching probing of the milieu in which these potentialities find shape and direction.

This view of *Rabbit, Run* is sharpened by its epigraph—Pascal's *Pensée 507*; "The motions of Grace, the hardness of the heart; external circumstances." The terms of the epigraph balance on the semicolon; "the motions of Grace" and "the hardness of the heart" are two equal parts of a single term itself equal in grammatical value to "external circumstances." In other words, man's behavior and its related internal motivations are inseparable from and influenced by his external conditions. Whether he responds to "the motions of Grace" or to "hardness of the heart" will depend substantially on the nature of the milieu in which he grows and functions. In the epigraph, too, then, Updike seems to point thematically to the portrayal of a representative man's potentialities and through him to a study of the culture which shapes them.

The epigraph also marks out the primary materials of *Rabbit, Run:* the opposing possibilities in Rabbit Angstrom and the social forces and institutions which mold their issue. Rabbit is both inner and outer directed; Updike defines him as a warring complex of centrifugal and centripetal qualities. Around these poles and on Rabbit's increasingly frenetic movement between them the novel develops; and its ultimate significance lies in the gradual smothering of his centrifugal qualities in a centripetal selfishness which finally becomes total.

This increasing "hardness of the heart" on which the novel largely centers should not obscure Rabbit's potentialtities for "the motions of Grace," the centrifugal qualities which lead him outward to the world around him and to involvement with others. As a boy he had watched over his younger sister; now, they are both grown, but he cherishes the memories of her childhood dependence on and love for him (pp. 135, 24–25) and still feels protective towards her (pp. 152–53). For Janice, his wife, even after leaving her, he feels responsible: as soon as Eccles tells him she is having the baby, Rabbit replies that he should go to her and does (pp. 159,161). Back with his family, he considers his having left them incomprehensible, and he is horrified when Eccles asks if he intends to return to Ruth (p. 171).

Trying to understand his growing selfishness, Janice remembers that "he could be so wonderful when you didn't expect it . . . there was so much nice in him she couldn't explain to anybody . . . " (pp. 209–10).

Like Janice, Ruth finds in Rabbit at first a mildness and a concern for her as a person which sets him apart and above the other men she has known (pp. 123, 124). Eccles believes that " 'there's a great deal of goodness . . . ' " in Rabbit. " 'When I'm with him . . . I feel so cheerful I quite forget what the point of my seeing him is' " (pp. 137, 127). Eccles is convinced that "Harry Angstrom was worth saving and could be saved" (p. 140).

Given a goal or a purpose or a task which interests him, Rabbit can be a dedicated and diligent worker. Whether as a boy learning basketball or as a young adult working in Mrs. Smith's garden, " 'when he set his mind to something . . . there was no stopping him' " (pp. 136–37). He dislikes messiness (p. 138) and has almost a passion for neatness (p. 16); indeed, Eccles argues that Rabbit is " 'by nature a domestic creature' "(p. 131). Mrs. Smith tells him that " 'you kept me alive, Harry; it's the truth; you did. All winter I was fighting the grave and then in April I looked out the window and here was this tall young man burning my old stalks and I knew life hadn't left me. That's what you have, Harry: life. It's a strange gift and I don't know how we're supposed to use it but I know it's the only gift we get and it's a good one' " (pp. 186–87).

Clearly, Rabbit Angstrom cannot be written off as simply a bad man or even as just a weak one; he has too many centrifugal qualities which encouraging circumstances could give positive meaning and direction. But he also has other qualities, centripetal tendencies capable in different circumstances of turning him inward to selfishness, to "hardness of the heart." Like most Americans, to whom advertisers appeal most characteristically in terms of interchangeable youth and sex, Rabbit hates growing up. For him, to live is to be young, and he feels his youth eroding. The "kids keep coming," he thinks, "they keep crowding you up" (p. 7); and watching his son being fed, "he sees himself sitting in a high chair and a quick strange jealousy comes and passes" (p. 21). The streets he walks are alive for him with memories of his boyhood (p. 17), and even in Ruth's apartment, he is reminded of the warm, protective world of his childhood (p. 80). And in the end, when he runs away through the woods, he is terrified by them, and he recalls that "as a kid he often went up through the woods. But maybe as a kid he walked under a magic protection that has now been lifted; he can't believe the woods were this dark then" (p. 26).

Complementing this nostalgia for the cocoon of childhood is Rabbit's adolescent uncertainty about things outside himself. " 'All I know is what's inside me,' " he tells Eccles. " 'That's all I have' " (p. 91). When Eccles asks what is inside him, Rabbit replies, " 'Hell, it's nothing much . . . it's just that, well, it's all there is' " (p. 105). Later, after forcing Ruth to do something against her will, he thinks "he shouldn't have made her do it. He doesn't know why he did except it felt right at the time" (p. 160). To Rabbit, "everything seems unreal that is outside of his sensations" (p. 164).

In one of his first conversations with Eccles, Rabbit "doesn't want to tell him anything. The more he tells, the more he loses. He's safe inside his own skin, he doesn't want to come out" (p. 105). Ruth recognizes "that was the thing about him, he just lived in his skin and didn't give a thought to the consequences of anything" (p. 125). He "doesn't think much about what he gives other people" (p. 122). Indeed, he inflates this unconcern for others into a philosophy: " 'I'll tell you,' " he brags to Ruth. " 'When I ran from Janice I made an interesting discovery. . . . If you have the guts to be yourself . . . other people'll pay your price' " (p. 125).

These divergent tendencies in Rabbit necessarily must work themselves out and be shaped by the milieu in which he lives. But nowhere in his milieu is there anything to help him find either positive goals or clear directions. The traditionally central institutions of the family, the school, and the church continue to function, but they have become empty or meaningless or corrupt; and the values which characterize this society have become equivocal and often iniquitous. If we cannot fully explain or justify Rabbit by his world, neither can we understand him without it. In terms of Pascal's epigraph, Rabbit's opposing possibilities cannot be separated from their "external circumstances"; therefore, he becomes for Updike a sharp instrument with which to analyze and evaluate these circumstances and the civilization they reflect.

Whether others' or his own, middle-class family life as Rabbit knows it fails to give him a background of stable meaning, objective values, and mature guidance. Reminded of the Zims, his boyhood neighbors, he recalls that they had spent most of the time screaming at their little daughter and at each other (p. 20). His own parents have long been joined in a quietly savage and bitter struggle for supremacy, an endless combat in which Rabbit has been both foil and weapon for each against the other (pp. 136–39). When Rabbit deserts Janice, his father takes a strong moral stand and condemns him as irresponsible; but his mother defends him and helps him to rationalize away his father's moral stringency. A possessive mother (pp. 190–91), she has never liked Janice or accepted her as Rabbit's wife and has subtly but constantly disparaged her (pp. 16, 134–35). His mother is therefore a profound influence on Rabbit's growing dissatisfaction with Janice and on his leaving her. Caught in this prolonged Oedipal relationship, he is unable to grow either emotionally or intellectually.

If Rabbit's experience with and observation of family life have bent him towards self-centeredness and selfish indulgence, his school years encouraged this inward development. Lionized for his basketball prowess, he was shaped in high school primarily by athletics and the discovery of the opposite sex. The star of his team, he had set a league scoring record (p. 9). " 'I *was* great,' " he tells Ruth. " 'I mean, I'm not much good for anything now, but I really was good at that' " (p. 64). Indeed he was, but as a solitary star, not as a team player, the best among equals. He was the one who scored the goals; the rest of the team existed largely to feed him the ball. If basketball had joined him to others as part of a team (p. 147), it had also helped turn him inward to a subjective isolation, to "a calm flat world where nothing matters much. The last quarter of a basketball game used to carry him into this world; you ran not as the crowd thought for the sake of the score but for yourself, in a kind of idleness. There was you and sometimes the ball and then the hole, the high perfect hole with its pretty skirt of net. It was you, just you and that fringed ring . . ." (p. 35).

Moreover, as this imagery suggests, his mastery in basketball had become identified with his youthful sexual experience. Meeting him after the game, Mary Ann had come to him with a "touch of timidity. As if she wasn't sure but he was much bigger, a winner. He came to her as a winner and that was the feeling he missed since. In the same way she was the best of them all because she was the one he brought most to, so tired. Sometimes the shouting glare of the gym would darken behind his sweat-burned eyes into a shadowed anticipation . . . and once there the bright triumph of the past game flashed across her quiet skin. . . . So that the two kinds of triumph were united in his mind" (p. 166).

After his graduation and service in the Army, he finds that school has left him unprepared and that society has no opportunities to offer him to achieve on a more mature level the excellence he had known as a basketball star. Consequently, life becomes increasingly less satisfying to Rabbit: " 'I once played a game real well,' " he tells Eccles. " 'I really did. And after you're first-rate at something, no matter what, it kind of takes the kick out of being second-rate. And that little thing Janice and I had going, boy, it was really second-rate' " (p. 90). Small wonder, then, that Rabbit yearns for the sense of greatness lost in his irrecoverable youth, that he insists "on being the greatest thing that ever was" (p. 155). Nor should it be surprising that, beyond basketball now, he turns to the other kind of triumph linked to it in his experience—sex; or that in turning to sex as a selfish end in itself instead of as a means to giving love and pleasure to another he increasingly and desperately turns inward to a "hardness of the heart," not giving but taking, not sharing but dominating.

At best, family life and school experience blur Rabbit's values; at worst, they incline his growth inwards, from concern for others to his own impulses; from responsibility to indulgence. Nor, in spite of his vague but powerful religious feelings, are religion and the church healthier influences on his development. In Rabbit's milieu, disbelief is rampant; and the church, whether seeking involvement in the complexities and problems of daily living or withdrawing from them into doctrinal abstractions, has lost its relevance and waned in influence.

Though unformed and inarticulate, Rabbit's religious longings are real, but Eccles is surprised by them (p. 90), and Ruth laughs at them (pp.

77–78). Traditionally, his inchoate faith should be given shape and direction by the church, but like his family and his school, it, too, fails him. His own minister, the Lutheran Kruppenbach, argues forcibly that the church has no business whatever meddling in problems like Rabbit's, that the clergyman's only role is that of " 'an exemplar of faith. . . . There is nothing but Christ for us. All the rest, all this decency and busyness, is nothing. It is Devil's work' " (p. 143). Consequently, Reverend Kruppenbach exerts no influence whatever on Rabbit.

By contrast, the Episcopalian Reverend Eccles, Janice's pastor, involves himself deeply in the situation but succeeds only in making Reverend Kruppenbach's counsel seem valid. Eccles wants to help, partly because he is both a well-intentioned minister and a good man but largely because if religion can bring Rabbit back to responsibility, Eccles's own confused and faltering faith will thereby be revived and nourished. For Eccles does not know what he believes or why he is a minister; and in a moment of depressed candor, he tells his wife, " 'I don't believe in anything' " (p. 223). His wife is a professed atheist; her faith is Freudian psychology, and she believes that religion "should have gone extinct a hundred years ago" (pp. 101, 158). From Eccles, Rabbit gets companionship and golf, understanding and counsel, but his religious impulses are blunted by Eccles's doubts and confusion and lose any power they might have had to counter Rabbit's deepening centripetal turning.

Rabbit's religious feelings and the significance of their constant frustration are stressed throughout the novel by Updike, who, more than most contemporary writers, still finds in traditional religion a meaningful reading of human experience.[4] Like most people in Rabbit's milieu, with its declining religious practice and influence, he has no taste for theology (p. 197); but his religious feelings are the more powerful and revealing by contrast. Although he may argue at times that nothing exists except what is inside of him, "his feeling that there is an unseen world is instinctive, and more of his actions that anyone suspects constitute transactions with it" (p. 195). His longings for a transcendent reality rise fundamentally from common existential terrors: the fear of ultimate nothingness and the fear of death. Telling Ruth that he believes in God, he "wonders if he's lying. If he is, he is hung in the middle of nowhere, and the thought hollows him, makes his heart tremble" (p. 77). He envies churchgoers (p. 195), and on Sunday, "he hates all the people on the street in dirty everyday clothes, advertising their belief that the world arches over a pit, that death is final, that the wandering thread of his feelings leads nowhere. Correspondingly, he loves the ones dressed for church; the pressed business suits of portly men give substance and respectability to his furtive sensations of the invisible . . . " (pp. 77–78).

Overlooking the city of Brewer from Mt. Judge, Rabbit thinks, "his day has been bothered by God: Ruth mocking, Eccles blinking—why did they teach you such things if no one believed them? It seems plain, standing here, that if there is this floor there is a ceiling, that the true space in which we live is upward space" (p. 96). He is depressed and chilled by the secular morality of his former coach; Rabbit "wants to believe in the sky as the source of all things" (p. 233). Explaining his religious feelings to Eccles, he points out that " 'I don't know all this about theology, but I'll tell you. I *do* feel, I guess, that somewhere behind all this'—he gestures outward at the scenery; they are passing the housing development this side of the golf course, half-wood half-brick one-and-a-half-stories in little flat bulldozed yards with tricycles and spindly three-year-old trees, the un-grandest landscape in the world—'there's something that wants me to find it' " (p. 107).

Vague and diffuse these feelings and thoughts may be in Rabbit, but they are no less real for that, and they work their effects in him constantly. Looking out the window of Ruth's bedroom, he sees "the church across the way, gray, somber, confident. Lights behind its rose window are left burning and this circle of red and purple and gold seems in the city night a hole punched in reality to show the abstract brilliance burning underneath. He feels gratitude to the builders of this ornament, and lowers the shade on it guiltily" (p. 69). After his first night with Ruth, he lies in bed feeling depressed. "From deep in the pillow he stares at the horizontal strip of stained-glass window that shows under the window shade. Its childish brightness seems the one kind of comfort left to him" (p. 74). Going to church following his return to Janice, he feels "happy, lucky, blessed, forgiven, and wants to give thanks" (p. 195).

After the baby's death, Rabbit feels profoundly guilty: *"forgive me, forgive me,* he keeps saying silently to no one" (p. 231), and "he wonders why the universe doesn't just erase a thing so dirty and small as himself" (pp. 238–39). But from these feelings of guilt he is released, first by his mother (pp. 241–42) and then by Eccles's funeral service. Eccles's preaching seems to Rabbit a mechanical recital, but the meanings behind the words excite him. His "chest vibrates with excitement and strength; he is sure his girl has ascended to Heaven. . . . 'Casting every care on thee.' He has done that; he feels full of strength" (pp. 243–44). But this is only the strength of irresponsibility and a further measure of Rabbit's descent into solipsism. Earlier, he had recognized his own responsibility in the complex tissue of emotions and events leading to the baby's death: "it wasn't your fault," he had told Janice; "it was mine" (p. 231). Now, casting his cares on a convenient and distant God, he sees himself and everyone else as victims of things that just happen (p. 244); and reducing the whole situation to its simplified and superficial facts, he declares that he did not drown the baby. When everyone is stunned by this unfeeling and simplistic behavior, he is filled with hate and runs away; and passing the church whose window once had shown meaningfully for him, he looks up and finds it dark. "Afraid, really afraid, he remembers what once consoled him by seeming to make a hole where he looked through into underlying brightness, and lifts his eyes to the church window. It is, because of church poverty or the late summer nights or just carelessness, unlit, a dark circle in a stone facade" (p. 254).[5]

Family, school, church—all three, then, disintegrating and distorted, combine to fail in their central function: to civilize Rabbit, to give his centrifugal impulses meaning and purpose, the "motions of Grace," and thus keep his centripetal ones from "hardness of the heart." Instead, these basic institutions of his "external circumstances" warp and blunt and waste Rabbit's outward seeking and accelerate his inward turning, a movement which Updike outlines structurally as solipsism and details thematically as decay in the novel's almost clinical sexuality. On the literal level, the sexual scenes are the major terms of Rabbit's degeneration and dramatize its principal stages; on the symbolic level, these scenes form a pattern reflecting the decay of a self without context, the collapse into a neurotic sensuality in the absence of any clear meaning or value beyond it.

In the beginning, sex fills a double need for Rabbit. On the one hand, it is an expression of tenderness and gentleness, a profound centrifugal yearning to unite with and give comfort to another human being. Even with a prostitute he is hurt when he finds that her responses have been feigned, that he has actually given her nothing (p. 42). His early relations with Janice are an idyll of mutuality (pp. 15–16, 37–38), and it is the recapture of this idyll after its loss in the irritations and complexities of marriage that he seeks in Ruth (pp. 64, 65, 68). Love and its expression in sex begin for Rabbit as outgoing experience, as commitment to and involvement with someone beyond himself.

On the other hand, love and sex are also centripetal forces, pulling him inward to a sense of power and the pleasure of conquest. These were the forces which led him to identify his mastery and triumphs in basketball with his relations with his high-school sweetheart. And when he meets Ruth, he is glad to learn that she is younger than he: "you can't feel master, quite, of a woman who's older" (p. 51). Similarly, when he first meets Mrs. Eccles, "at once, absurdly, he feels in control of her . . . " (p. 98); and through their occasional meetings thereafter, her powerful sexual attraction for him develops in terms of this feeling of potential mastery.

As Rabbit is increasingly unable to find any clear meaning or direction to give form to his rebellion against the triviality and complexity of his life, he withdraws into a self lacking reference or value beyond itself. In this withdrawal, love and sex are inevitably warped into mere lust and domination, thereby becoming both fact and symbol of his degeneration. His relations with Ruth, which had begun less with the pleasure he could get than with the comfort he sought to give, become empty self-gratification without concern for her and end in his demeaning her to satisfy both a twisted lust and a compulsion to dominate and punish her.

Once, he had wanted "to comfort her completely"; now, he tells her that "tonight you turned against me. I need to see you on your knees" (p. 157).

Less than two weeks after Janice comes home from the hospital, Rabbit walks with Mrs. Eccles after church and returns to "his apartment clever and cold with lust" (p. 202). He tries every trick he knows to arouse Janice and when she rebels, he is angered and again deserts her. " 'Why can't you try to imagine how I *feel?*' " she asks him; and he replies " 'I can. I can but I don't want to, it's not the thing, the thing is how *I* feel. And I feel like getting out' " (p. 207). Once, he had given her love in a tender sharing; now, love is only lust and Janice a depersonalized "contact" (p. 206) whose being and feelings no longer matter. As with Ruth, this change measures Rabbit's withdrawal and degeneration; and the novel's detailed sexual scenes dramatize the stages of this regression with a clarity and an emotional impact which no suggestive exposition or partial action could even approximate.

## IV

Structure and theme work together brilliantly, then, to evoke in depth and in detail the disturbing central experience of *Rabbit, Run.* That experience is less social or individual criticism than it is an almost dispassionate inquiry, an effort, characteristic of Updike, to combine contemporary experience and observation with historical analysis and explanation. He demands not blame but understanding; he depicts neither hero nor villain, but rather, representative influences and effects in historical time and place, the points of function where individual and milieu interact in an age of disintegrating transition.

Rabbit Angstrom is thus no secular saint making a positive rejection of an absurd world. When he runs from the graveyard and then from Ruth, his flight is simply a desperately selfish denial of any human involvement with Janice or Ruth or in the situations he has helped to cause. But neither is his milieu a malignant society, blindly crushing the helpless individual. Rabbit and his society mirror each other; and caught in a time of muddled transition, neither can do anything to benefit the other. The novel develops from the dynamic tension between the two: the pathos of Rabbit Angstrom rises from the irredeemable waste of his alternative possibilities; and the significance of his story is the sobering point of view it provides on a civilization whose institutions and values are apparently disintegrating, a civilization losing the power to civilize.

In *Couples,* which *Rabbit, Run* clearly foreshadows and clarifies,[6] Updike writes of people on a meaningless sexual carrousel, "a magic circle of heads to keep the night out," people "suspended in this one of those dark ages that visits mankind between millennia, between the death and rebirth of gods, when there is nothing to steer by but sex and stoicism and the stars."[7] So it is too with Rabbit Angstrom: he runs because he can find nowhere to stand, either to move himself or his world, and the ultimate loss is frighteningly more than just his own.

## Notes

1. J. A. Ward, for example, sees Rabbit as an embodiment of positive values in "John Updike's Fiction," *Critique: Studies in Modern Fiction*, 5 (Spring-Summer 1962), 27–40; Graham H. Duncan feels that he symbolizes the meaning of life for Updike in opposition to the negative and death-centered values of other characters, in "The Thing Itself in *Rabbit, Run*," *English Record*, 13 (April 1963), 25–28, 36–37; David Galloway describes him as an absurd saint rejecting an oppressive world, in "The Absurd Man as Saint: The Novels of John Updike," *Modern Fiction Studies*, 10 (Summer 1964),111–27; Thaddeus Muradian views Rabbit as a symbol of the hope of self-discovery, in "The World of Updike," *English Journal*, 54 (Oct. 1965), 577–84; Alvin D. Alley and Hugh Agee argue that he is an existential hero running in an agonized search for identity in a distorted world in which his only hope is to endure, in "'Existential Heroes: Frank Alpine and Rabbit Angstrom," *Ball State University Forum*, 9 (Winter 1968), 3–5; and Elmer F. Suderman considers him weak and irresponsible but argues that he runs positively seeking a free and happy life, rejecting a meaningless and other-directed world, in "The Right Way and The Good Way in *Rabbit, Run*," *University Review*, 36 (Oct. 1969), 13–21. On the other hand, Robert Detweiler sees Rabbit as the sick reflection of a sick society, in "John Updike and the Indictment of Culture-Protestantism," *Four Spiritual Crises in Mid-Century American Fiction*, Univ. of Florida Monographs; Humanities; 14, Gainesville, Fla. (1963). 14–23; Sister M. Judith Tate regards him as a grotesque allegory of contemporary isolation, a twentieth-century sub-man, in "Of Rabbits and Centaurs," *Critic*, 22 (Feb.-March 1964), 44–47, 49–50; Paul A. Doyle depicts him as self-centered and irresponsible, uncovered by grace, in "Updike's Fiction: Motifs and Techniques," *Catholic World*, 199 (Sept. 1964), 356–62; Norris W. Yates views Rabbit as a deformed social growth, in "The Doubt and Faith of John Updike," *College English*, 26 (March 1965) 469–74; Gerry Brenner argues that Rabbit is a charming but narrow man whose domestic problems reflect Updike's lament for the loss of traditional values, in "*Rabbit, Run:* John Updike's Criticism of the 'Return to Nature,' " *Twentieth Century Literature*, 12 (April 1966), 3–14; and Joseph F. Brewer sees him as an antihero, rejecting the established order and its values but lacking any awareness of alternatives in "The Anti-Hero in Contemporary Literature," *Iowa English Yearbook*, 12 (1967), 55–60.

2. *Rabbit, Run* (New York: Fawcett World, Crest Books, 1962), p. 16. Subsequent page references will be made to this edition.

3. In the article cited above, Gerry Brenner finds a different structure in the novel, one based on the movement from an opening limitation through a central expansiveness to a final limitation.

4. Updike grew up in the Lutheran faith, though he now attends a Congregational church. He believes that "at the core of the core there is a right-angled clash to which, of all verbal combinations we can invent, the Apostles' Creed offers the most adequate correspondence and response" (*Assorted Prose* [New York: Fawcett World, Crest Books, 1966], p. 143).

5. John Killinger looks with historical perspective at the absence of religious absolutes in American life as reflected in American literature, particularly in many twentieth-century writers, including Updike, in "The Death of God in American Literature," *Southern Humanities Review*, 2(Spring 1968), 149–72.

6. For a similar but detailed—and, unlike most critical discussions of this novel, persuasively sympathetic—study of *Couples*, see Joyce Flint's "John Updike and *Couples:* The WASP's Dilemma," in *Research Studies*, 36(Dec. 1968), 340–47.

7. *Couples* (New York: Alfred A. Knopf, 1968), pp. 7, 372.

# *The Centaur*: Updike's Mock Epic

Suzanne Henning Uphaus*

There are two questions which inevitably confront the critic of *The Centaur*, and they relate, respectively, to the thematic and technical aspects of the novel. The first is that doubt which plagues Peter Caldwell, the narrator of the novel: have his father's sacrifices, his dedication to parenthood and denial of his spiritual needs, been worthwhile? This question operates on the thematic level, for it is concerned with the ostensible meaning of the novel. The second question operates on the aesthetic level, and is thus concerned with the mode of the novel's presentation: can we justify Updike's use of mythological framework in *The Centaur*?[1]

In approaching the first question we should turn to the end of *Rabbit, Run* where Rabbit perceives that the only kind of immortality which the twentieth century world can offer is "the vertical order or parenthood, a kind of thin tube upright in time in which our solitude is somewhat diluted"[2] (254). Updike's next novel, *The Centaur*, is concerned with that "vertical order of parenthood," and with the associations which the word "order" elicits. Can parenthood provide order out of chaos, and can it offer a substitute religious order, an alternative, natural priesthood? In *The Centaur* these questions culminate in Peter Caldwell's query *"Was it for this that my father gave up his life?"* (p. 201).

For Peter has become, in his own words, "an authentic second-rate abstract expressionist" (p. 81), and he is filled with doubts of his own worthiness.[3] Rabbit had been unwilling to accept a living death, that is, unwilling to succumb to this world and its demands, to relinquish that hope for religious truth to which he must sacrifice the needs of his family and his responsibilities as husband and father. In contrast George Caldwell sacrifices his spiritual search for religious truth at the end of *The Centaur* and chooses instead the role of parent and provider, a dedication to this world in which spiritual hopes must die. The Buick which George Caldwell walks toward is a hearse which carries Chiron, or that part of George Caldwell which was immortal and godly, to certain death in an environment which destroys the spirit. Thus George Caldwell accepts this

*From *The Journal of Narrative Technique*, 7 (1977), 24–36, with permission of the journal and the author.

natural world and the mortality in time which is inevitable within it. At the end of the novel Chiron dies, but George Caldwell lives on, a mere mortal.

Many critics have commented on the contrast between Caldwell and Rabbit—the sacrifices of George Caldwell may be a rejection of that irresponsibility which disturbed so many critics about Rabbit. There may even be an implied negation of Rabbit at the high school basketball game where there are spectators "in their middle twenties" who "continue to appear at high school athletic events, like dogs tormented by a site where they imagine they have buried something precious" (p. 175). While George Caldwell may be a rejection of Rabbit's *modus vivendi*, Peter Caldwell has many of Rabbit's characteristics.[4]

But there is one aspect of Peter Caldwell, and a major concern of the book as a whole, which is unique in Updike's fiction. Peter Caldwell is an artist, and it is as an artist that he constructs the book. It is at this point that we move from the events of the novel to the mind of the man interpreting the events of the novel. We move, in other words, from its meaning to its mode of presentation, and thus to my second question, concerning the use of classical mythology.

In this discussion of *The Centaur* I will demonstrate how the use of classical mythology, in conjunction (or perhaps disjunction) with realistic detail, reflects the ostensible meaning of the novel: the thematic loss of Christianity parallels the artistic loss of classical faith. I will demonstrate how this loss of faith in another world represents the confinement to this world: thematically, it means the decline of Christian faith into good works and, artistically, it represents the decline of myth into naturalism. The force of this world destroy the spiritual ideal in both father and son, leaving them confined to the physical world and especially to their bodies. The acceptance of the body, either its mortality or its sexuality, reflects this confinement.

In other words I will argue that Peter Caldwell's artistic dedication to this world, revealed by the mode of the novel, coincides with the theme of his father's dedication to this world. Finally I will show how an artist, confined to this world, lacking that duality which creates artistic tension, can only become what Peter Caldwell is by his own admission, a failure. For, in this novel, Updike is demonstrating the artist's need for a framework of belief, a metaphoric vision, whether Christian or classical, while he simultaneously shows the impossibility of resurrecting from the past a mythical framework, a scheme which answers to our spiritual needs.

Thus I have called *The Centaur* Updike's mock epic. The whole idea of a mock epic rests on the fundamental disjunction between classical allusions on a heroic scale and mundane events; on the contrast, if you will, between this world and the other. The heroic or mythic scale in *The Centaur* results from the veneration which the child attached to the father, making him almost a god, and from the inflated value he placed on the events of his adolescent life. As Updike has explained "there is a way in which to a child everything is myth size.[5] But everything is *not* myth size to the adult narrator, whose spiritual need for an ideal other world, for a belief beyond the mundane, opposes his increasingly strong sense of realism, his sense of the literal.

The mundane events which the increasingly realistic Peter becomes aware of contrast with the heroic scale of the mythology to produce that disjunction which we call mock epic. Updike admitted this disjunction and the humor it creates when he said of *The Centaur* that "it seems in memory my gayest and truest book; I pick it up, and read a few pages, in which Caldwell is insisting on flattering a moth-eaten bum, who is really the god Dionysus, and I begin laughing."[6] In some scenes, such as this one, the humor is mixed with regret for the loss of the mythic vision.

The sense of nostalgia is evoked because the mock-epic structure of the novel is a dramatization of that process which occurred in the mind of Peter Caldwell during the three days in 1947 which the novel describes. For want of a better word I will call that process a demythologizing, a loss of that metaphoric vision which makes art possible. In order to prove this we must accept the fact that the novel is written entirely from Peter Caldwell's point of view,[7] as Updike indirectly stated in his *Paris Review* interview when he called the mythology "a correlative of the enlarging effect of Peter's nostalgia."[8]

In the novel the adult Peter remembers himself as an adolescent attempting to maintain the heroic vision of the child, and finds that it cannot be sustained against the mundane, realistic events of those three days. For in the end the literal events of the novel are mundane in the most ordinary sense. Nobody dies, nobody gets hurt, grandfather gets his bread, George Caldwell doesn't lose his job, and the worst thing that happens is Peter Caldwell gets a cold. But these realistic external events, in their triviality, effect a change in perspective for the young Peter Caldwell. At the end of the novel Peter's perception is one in which the metaphoric or heroic vision dies, succumbing to the force of external reality, and giving rise to another artistic philosophy, naturalism.

So the death of Chiron also means the death of the heroic vision in the beholder, and the last glimpse which we have of Peter is one in which he resolves to "go to Nature disarmed of perspective" (p. 218).

Thus the technical emphasis in *The Centaur* is on Peter Caldwell's loss of the classical ideal, while the thematic emphasis is on George Caldwell's hopeless attempts to find meaning in Christian ideals. The Christian mythology in the novel is represented mainly by George's ineffectual and dying father-in-law, Pop Kramer. This old man's voice reminds Peter of "a giant calling from a distance" (p. 42), and the distance which he calls his blessing from is the difference in time and faith which separates the generations. Pop Kramer's faith allows him to read the newspapers and the Bible, to link the factual and the mythic without strain, in a way which the younger generations cannot. Pop Kramer feeds on bread alone, putting whole slices into his mouth at a time (p. 56) as if he were simultaneously feeding his body and the Christian faith for which bread is the symbol of nourishment. "Time stolen from food," the old man tells his grandson with a sense of unity between body and soul which the younger generation has lost, "is time stolen from yourself" (p. 54).

George Caldwell perceives his role as bringing the bread which will keep this faith alive. At the grocery store which they stop at before they finally return home, George buys bread for his father-in-law. Nonetheless he knows that death is imminent for the old man and that with his death will disappear the last vestiges of a strong Christian faith. George is constantly afraid that the old man has fallen downstairs (pp. 159, 213) even though he believes that "Pop Kramer deserves to live forever" (p. 47). But the two men operate by different time schemes, represented by the two clocks which hang in the living room. George's clock is the faster clock, "red and electric and plastic" (p. 49). George is a product of that modern mechanized society which accelerates time and destroys faith. The grandfather's clock is traditional, an heirloom from the past, "dark and wooden and ornamented and keywound . . . inherited from my grandfather's father" (p. 49).

The passing of Christian mythology into the past is reinforced by the account of Peter's maternal grandmother's death; the wine she drank on her deathbed is the sacramental counterpart to the bread her husband consumes. Remembering this scene, Peter writes: "Yes. We lived in God's sight . . . on a firm stage, resonant with metaphor" (p. 57). It is this firm stage of metaphoric vision, whether Christian or classical, which both father and son attempt to recapture in the novel.

George's father demonstrated to his son the failure of the Christian ideal to stand up to the ravages of time; at the moment of his death George's father lost the faith to which he, a minister, had dedicated his life. On his deathbed he asked his son and daughter "Do you think I'll be eternally forgotten?" (p. 73). The words have taught George Caldwell that "Things never fail to fail" (p. 149). This is the lesson of time, in which Christian faith is as unreliable as any other temporal phenomena. George strives to believe what he was taught as a child: "I was a minister's son. I was brought up to believe, and I shall believe it, that God made man as the last best thing in His Creation." But in the same breath he goes on to question time's power over man and his faith: "If that's the case, who are this time and tide that are so almighty superior to us?" (p. 52). He tells Reverend March that the only thing he sees as infinite about God's mercy is that it is at an infinite distance (p. 189).

Turning from the Christian faith that, for his generation, does not live, George Caldwell is left in his search for immortality with the hard-won belief that "Only goodness lives. But it does live" (p. 220). His sample obituary, imagined years later by the grown Peter Caldwell, describes

George as having a "more than human selflessness" (p. 133). Indeed, this novel is Updike's most affirmative statement of dedication to this world through good works. It is not just as a provider for his family that Caldwell demonstrates his selflessness. He picks up forlorn hitchhikers, he tells anxious students the answers to forthcoming tests, he, alone, applauds a swimmer who has performed poorly, and he gives an insinuating drunk his last handful of change.

Through these actions a pattern is created which Ms. Markle has called "the central thematic image" of the novel, in which "individuals give up immortality and freedom to create a community."[9] George Caldwell is not the liberal do-gooder who is ridiculed in so many of Updike's novels. Both Eccles' and Conner's spirits have given up searching for that religious transcendance which is real to George Caldwell. It is the sacrifice of his own search for spiritual satisfaction in order to sustain the joy of each of his family members a little longer which makes Caldwell's selflessness sincere. He gives up the other world for this, the mythic for the realistic.

As with all of Updike's protagonists, commitment to this world means an acceptance of the body and of the natural manifestations of the body. In Updike these natural needs are most often sexual, as they are with Peter. But for George Caldwell acceptance of the body means acceptance of the fact of eventual physical death.[10] (Sometimes, of course, Updike gives us the two together, as in Rabbit and Piet.) The natural world, and its temporality, is focussed, for George Caldwell, in his body and its mortality. To retain a spiritual identity he resists evidence of the body's mortality. While death may mean the release of the soul into immortality, the doubts of George's father at the moment of death throw an uncertainty on that assumption. Moreover, George must resist natural death in order to fulfill his responsibilities as a parent and family provider. And for George Caldwell, as well as the rest of us, the natural and instinctive resistance to death, man's attachment to this body, asserts itself continually. Yet constant pain accompanies the life of the body for George Caldwell, because he translates all injuries against his spirit into physical pain, as with the arrow at the beginning of the novel.

Doc Appleton recognizes George's problematical duality when he tells him that all his tension develops from the fact that "You believe in the soul. You believe your body is like a horse you get up on and ride for a while and then get off. You ride your body too hard. You show it no love. This is not natural!" (p. 101). Like all other Updike dentists and doctors, Doc Appleton concentrates on the body to the exclusion of the soul. He believes in nothing and belongs to no church (p. 99). According to him mankind has made two mistakes: "one was to stand up and the other was to start thinking. It strains the spine and the nerves" (p. 104). But this concentration on the body has brought him a domestic fate which presages the break-up of the family unit in *Couples*.

When Doc Appleton tells George his trouble is "you have never come to terms with your own body," the teacher answers "You're right . . . I hate the damn ugly thing" (p. 100). As the pressure of fears of death and losing his job increase, George "by searching through his body can uncover any color and shape of pain he wants" (p. 150), from toothache to ingrown toenail. Yet he finds it impossible to follow the doctor's advice to "Get rest and don't think" (p. 104).

The body manifests itself differently for young Peter, and in concentrating on his sexual needs Peter, both as adolescent and grown narrator, also relinquishes the spiritual vision of another world. For the young Peter all aspects of his body (even the psoriasis in which he secretly delights) have become adolescent obsessions. Dedman (whose name hints at the futility of this obsession), with his pornographic playing cards, is Peter's idol (p. 96). In a way which is reminiscent of Rabbit and foreshadows Reverend Marshfield, Peter mixes masturbation and prayer, and kneels before his girl friend Penny (p. 184). In this act of sexual worship the final futility of directing reverence to such an object, a futility which Rabbit has discovered before him, is indicated when he realizes that "where her legs meet there is nothing . . . This then is the secret the world holds at its center, this innocence, this absence . . . " (p. 184). This act initiates him into the house of Venus (Vera Hummel), and as he walks home with his father at the end of the novel Peter asks whether you can steer by the star Venus. His father responds "I don't know. I've never tried. It's an interesting question" (p. 212).

It seems that Peter *has* tried in the years between the event of the novel and the writing of it. The Negro mistress whom Peter, as narrator, addresses throughout the novel, represents to him a kind of sensuality which Peter admires but cannot wholly abandon himself to. He calls their relationship a "rather wistful half-Freudian half-Oriental sex mysticism" (p. 201). He says to her "I want to be a Negro for you . . . and forget everything but the crooning behind by ribs. But I cannot quite . . . I am my father's son" (p. 201). Total abandonment to sensual self-absorption is impossible for him: there is still that spirit in him, as there was in his father, and his grandfather before him, which longs for permanence, for understanding, for the inconceivable. The naturalism to which Peter has committed himself at the end of the novel is an affront to his duality, for it ignores the spiritual need for an ideal world, a mythic vision.

George Caldwell's dedication to this world through good works and through the acceptance of death means the departure of Chiron, that part of his duality which is spiritual and godlike; but Chiron also reflects his son's spiritual yearning to make his father god-like, to make of him a myth. One function which the mythological references in the novel serve is to vividly illustrate that duality, that division between man's body and soul, which is a constant concern for Updike. Peter's references to Chiron in the novel are to that aspect of George Caldwell which longs for permanence and immortality, and which gives the son a mythical framework which will give the world meaning.[11] The epigraph to the novel, taken from Karl Barth, describes George Caldwell's duality. The epigraph also reflects the tension between the metaphoric and the realistic visions: "Heaven is the creation inconceivable to man, earth the creation conceivable to him. He himself is the creature on the boundary between heaven and earth." Myths are those methods which man has created to make heaven conceivable to him, and empirical evidence or realism leading to scientific knowledge is the means by which the earth is conceivable to man.

Thus George Caldwell is the teacher of general science at Olinger High School and, as George Caldwell, he is concerned with earth, "the creation conceivable to man." Thus it is George Caldwell who presents the scientific-historical explanation for the origin of the universe (pp. 31–4), and his lesson begins, appropriately, with a blackboard dominated by zeros which remind George Caldwell of death. It is the death of the godly and the mythological, the death of Chiron, which those scientifically accurate zeros portend. On the other hand it is as Chiron, and not as George Caldwell, that the teacher presents to his students the mythical explanation for the origin of the universe, in which Eros, or Love "set the Universe in motion" (p. 78). Only when the empirical experiences of the earth become undeservedly threatening and destructive for George Caldwell, as when the students treat him unkindly just before the book opens, or as when he inadvertently sees Mrs. Herzog leaving Zimmerman's office, does he metamorphose into Chiron, the centaur also undeservedly wounded.

The last metamorphosis of George Caldwell into Chiron occurs in the most threateningly destructive circumstances in the novel; at the end of the novel Caldwell must go back to the hell from which he has been trying to escape for three days, and these last paragraphs portray his final farewell to Chiron, his soul's yearnings. These yearnings cannot be sustained in the atmosphere which George Caldwell, as provider for his family, must submit to. It was the tension between his search for the inconceivable and the reality of the conceivable which caused George Caldwell's pain; thus when Chiron dies, the pain disappears: "the gods took away his pain and his immortality." When Updike, or more correctly, Peter Caldwell writes at the end of The Centaur "Chiron accepted death" (p. 222) he is telling us that by the acceptance of bodily death, the recognition of mortality, George Caldwell commits himself to this world, accepts it on its own terms, and gives up the spiritual quest for personal immortality. At the end of the novel Chiron dies, but George Caldwell lives on to die only when his body dies.

The death of Chiron is artistically as well as thematically significant; by using classical mythology to interpret the events of those three days, the adult Peter at first infuses the events with the sense of importance with which youth views the world, and then demonstrates the collapse of that mythological vision with the death of Chiron. There is a constant tension in Peter's portrayal of his father between the tendency to see him as god-like, and the opposing tendency to see him as bumbling, ridiculous and in-effective. Peter is aware that on the one hand he deified his father: "to me my father seemed changeless" (p. 53). He writes:

> His face . . . to me seemed both tender and brutal, wise and unseeing; it was still dignified by the great distance that in the beginning had lifted it halfway to the sky. Once I had stood beside his knees . . . and felt him look level into the tops of the horsechestnut trees and believed that nothing could ever go wrong as long as he stood so (p. 53).

At the same time there is the adolescent Peter's increasing concern for his father's public image, his increasing tendency to look at his father objec-tively and dispassionately, that is, without metaphor. He wishes his father would appear and act more like a god. The real appearance, the unkempt man in an old hat and rumpled coat, detracts from the ideal image. The unselfish actions of the father make him the object of ridicule (p. 156) rather than an admired, even worshipped, ideal. For according to Peter none of those people for whom his father makes sacrifices are worthy; the hitchhiker is a "rotten bum" (p. 72), Diefendorf is "an obscene animal" (p. 80), and all his father's relationships with others, in which he tries to help them at his own expense, seem to Peter to be "mediocre, fruitless, cloying involvement" (p. 156).

These two opposing views create a novel which is mock-epic. The humor comes from the tension between the metaphoric and the factual visions, the heroic and the mundane. At the same time the end of the novel depicts the succumbing of the metaphoric to the factual vision. Not only does Chiron die and George Caldwell go on to work in a world which is hostile to the spiritual vision, but, at the same time, Peter Caldwell bids farewell to that metaphoric vision which, he will later realize, makes art possible. While *The Centaur* begins with Peter's profession of his father's similarity to the gods, it ends with his loss of it, and of the entire mythical framework which it sustained.

We have only to look at Peter's dreams on the four successive nights of the novel's time span to trace this gradual rejection of the old mythology under the influence of actual events. Peter's first dream is an encapsulation of the mythological process. In it Penny turns into a tree before Peter can seduce her. The slow proces of the live person becoming the changeless myth is detailed, and the metaphor excites Peter to mastur-bation. As in the novel, Peter uses past events in time to create the timeless myth: "The dream I had been dreaming returned to me. Penny and I had been beside a tree. The top buttons of her blouse were undone . . . as they had been weeks ago, before Christmas vacation, in the dark Buick on the school parking lot" (p. 42). The mythical dream is constantly interrupted by the reality of his parents calling him, but Peter manages to sustain the dream: "That was it, yes; and in the dream it didn't even seem strange. She became the tree. I was leaning my face against the tree trunk, certain it was her" [12] (p. 43).

Peter's dream on the next night is about the destruction by scientific reality of the essence of the past.

> "When I awoke, all I remembered was being in an endless chemical laboratory, like a multiplication with mirrors of the basins and test tubes and Bunsen burners in Room 107 and Olinger High. There was on a table a small Mason jar such as my grandmother used to put applesauce in. Its glass was clouded. I picked it up and put my ear to the lid and heard a tiny voice, as high in pitch as the voice that calls numbers in a hearing test, saying with microscopic distinctness, "I want to die. I want to die" [13] (p. 128).

The jar which Peter associates with the essence of the past has become cloudy, the mythological past is losing its grip on life in an environment which concentrates on the physical sciences, and is begging for death.

The third night Peter's dream is not all metaphoric (p. 201), and in describing the dream he simply summarizes the literal events of the last few hours before he went to bed. The harshness of nature and the threat of death in the snow have been the final blow to his faltering heroic vision. Back at home on the last night his dreams are of "a sluggish whirling world" which is a "shifting rootless flux of unidentifiable things" (p. 215). This whirling, shifting world has been reached by the loss of the "firm stage" (p. 57) of a metaphoric or mythological vision. Just as George Caldwell, at the first of the novel, condensed the scientific-historical explanation for the creation into three days, so has Peter condensed the loss of metaphoric vision, a kind of de-creation, into three days.

In the last direct glimpse we have of Peter Caldwell, Updike has given us an analogue of the writing of the novel, of the subject it portrays, and of the process of de-mythologizing which has taken place in Peter's mind throughout the novel.

> I turned my face away and looked toward the window. In time my father appeared in this window, an erect figure dark against the snow. His posture made no concession to the pull underfoot; upright he waded out through our yard and past the mailbox and up the hill until he was lost to my sight behind the trees of our orchard (p. 217).

The novel is, in fact, a portrait by the grown son of his father, whom he sees through the window of time: "In time, my father appeared in this window," the narrator writes. What he has seen through the window (and in the novel) is his father treading upon snow, achieving a personal victory over the dead of winter, the death in nature, making no concessions to the pull of gravity. For the son the father represents that spirit which makes no concessions to reality, or fact. Finally the father is lost to sight behind the trees. The trees, we know, are mythologically the bodies of immobilized women, encased in trees as the soul is in the body, as the soul's imaginings, or myths, are entombed in the natural and temporal world. A few paragraphs later Peter will portray Chiron searching for a message from the trees but finding none (p. 219); mythology fails the son, and the father perceived by the son, simultaneously.

Appropriately, it is only after his father is lost to his sight that Peter forms his new philosophy of art, hoping that through it he will reach the truth. He begins by recognizing the tension between the real and the mythical which is the basis of the mock-heroic, but now there is uncertainty in his mind concerning the heroic, or mythical, or metaphoric, significance of the scene he has pictured:

> I knew what this scene was—a patch of Pennsylvania in 1947—and yet I did not know, was in my softly fevered state mindlessly soaked in a rectangle of colored light. I burned to paint it, just like that, in its puzzle of glory; it came upon me that I must go to Nature disarmed of perspective and stretch myself like a large transparent canvas upon her in the hope that, my submission being perfect, the imprint of a beautiful and useful truth would be taken[14] (p. 218).

What Peter Caldwell knows is the empirical evidence, the historical factuality of the scene. What he does not know is its metaphoric meaning. Yet he decides that the way to represent that scene artistically is to "go to Nature disarmed of perspective," to try to capture meaning without metaphor and attempt to become the object, rather than interpret it. He will submit himself to earth, to Nature, abandoning the metaphoric perspectives which his father and his grandfather have used, in an attempt to reach "a beautiful and useful truth."

But truth has not been forthcoming in the intervening years. For Peter Caldwell the possibility of spiritual truth always came through his art. From the first he hoped that, in his art, he could fix time, and sustain a victory over natural death. "It was this firmness, I think, this potential fixing of a few passing seconds, that attracted me, at the age of five, to art" (p. 51). The natural mortality of the animal world drove him "into my book of Vermeer reproductions like a close-to-drowned man clinging to the beach" (p. 60). The main floor of the Alton Museum, permeated by reminders of death, filled the child with a dread which was only soothed by the second floor paintings which "radiated the innocence and hope, the hope of seizing something and holding it fast, that enters whenever a brush touches canvas" (p. 199). On the second floor the statue of the naked lady holding a scallop shell from which water forever fell, never to touch her lips, disturbed the child who was "troubled by her imagined thirst," and he imagined that by the moonlight that conceals even death in shadows she will drink. Her thirst would be satisfied, the fall of water would cease as she drank, and natural law, reality, would, for a moment be suspended by art.

But the grown narrator, committed to an art which has moved inevitably from naturalism to expressionism in the futile attempt to become "disarmed of perspective," is beginning to doubt whether such a purely personal art can suspend time, or reach eternal truths. Peter is no longer Prometheus. The metaphoric vacuum has led him to "earnestly bloated canvasses I conscientiously cover with great streaks" and he suspects that they are "straining to say . . . the unsayable thing, and I grow frightened" (p. 201). but the unconscious knows what the artist is just beginning to recognize, that we cannot live without heroes, that the metaphoric vacuum cannot persist in the mind of man. So Peter's atheism (p. 40) has given rise to dreams of new heroes, culled from recent history, who show disturbing signs of immortality: "last night I dreamt that Hitler, a white-haired crazy man with a protruding tongue, was found alive in Argentina" (p. 40).

The novel has been Peter Caldwell's attempt to resurrect the heroic metaphor of his childhood. He is nostalgically seeking a framework into which he can put the events of the past, a framework which will make history meaningful. This novel, then, deals directly with the artist's dependence on a framework of belief, a metaphoric vision, whether Christian or classical. We have the novel itself as proof of the necessity for such a vision. It is the work of art which Peter Caldwell has created from his recapturing of his lost heroic vision for the space of time during which the novel is written. And, although realistic detail counterpoints the heroic vision throughout the novel, the heroic metaphor *is* maintained sufficiently for him to create a work of art which is, though not heroic, mock-heroic.

The novel is mock-heroic because the adult cannot totally recapture the metaphoric vision of the past. In *The Centaur* Updike is demonstrating the dependence of the artist upon a mythical framework which will make art possible, as he simultaneously shows the impossibility of completely resurrecting that mythical framework from the past.

I am arguing then, that, not only does the myth act as a revelation of Peter's adolescent character, of the opposing tensions within his perception of the world around him, but it also acts as a force within the novel representing an option which has diminished within history. "Priest, teacher, artist": Peter writes, naming the occupations of the last three generations of his family. He calls it "the classic degeneration" (p. 201).

In the book that Peter has written, he not only tells a story but his method of telling that story gradually moves from a commitment to myth to a commitment to nature. In the book that Updike has written, Peter Caldwell is a character whose artistic sterility is broken by his intermittent recapturing of the heroic vision. Peter Caldwell is Updike's mock-hero, caught between the need for a mythical ideal and a twentieth century commitment to realism. Updike has described an artist as being "in some way a middleman between the ideal world and this, even though our sense of the ideal . . . is at present fairly dim."[15]

## Notes

1. The use of myth in the novel has been variously opposed and defended. In his article *"The Centaur;* Myth, History and Narrative," *Modern Fiction Studies,* 20 (Spring, 1974), 29–44, John Vickery has stated that "Critics in the main are still uncertain, therefore distressed, and thus ultimately dismissive concerning the presence of mythic materials in the narrative mix."

2. All page references included in the text are from the paperback Fawcett Crest editions of Updike's novels.

3. Doubts concerning the son's worthiness of the father seem, however, to be a fact of life in Updike's fiction. Peter feels he has, even as an adolescent, already let his father down: "I tried to walk in my father's footsteps but his strides were too great" (p. 211). But so does George feel he has disappointed his father: "how could his father's seed, exploding into an infinitude of possibilities, have been funneled into this, this paralyzed patch of thankless alien land, these few cryptic faces, those certain four walls of Room 204?" (p. 221).

4. For a fuller development of these similarities see Joyce B. Markle, *Fighters and Lovers: Theme in the Novels of John Updike* (New York: New York University Press, 1973), p. 81.

5. John Updike, *Picked-Up Pieces* (New York, Alfred A. Knopf. 1975), p. 499.

6. *Picked-Up Pieces,* p. 500. I suspect that some of Updike's delight in *The Centaur* is also in his success at teasing the critics with a profusion of allusions; I have tried, for instance, to simply count the references to arrows in the novel, without success. The appendix which Updike attaches to the end of the novel tells us that not all characters in the novel have stable classical referents, with a pun on the word "stable" of course. The fluctuating referents make the job of the critic who would try to tie down each reference doubly difficult.

7. In her article "Updike's American Comedies," *Modern Fiction Studies,* 21 (Fall, 1975), 459–472, Joyce Carol Oates also assumes, unlike earlier critics, that Peter Caldwell is the narrator of the entire novel.

8. Charles Thomas Samuels, "The Art of Fiction XLIII: John Updike," *The Paris Review,* No. 45 (1968), 103.

9. Markle, p. 72.

10. About George's sex life we have only the glimpse afforded by Cassie as her husband says goodbye: " 'If there's anything I hate,' my mother said, half to me, half to the ceiling, while my father bent forward and touched her cheek with one of his rare kisses, 'it's a man who hates sex' " (p. 56).

11. In his chapter on *The Centaur* Robert Detweiler makes the same distinction. See Robert Detweiler, *John Updike* (New York: Twayne, 1972), p. 91.

12. This is not to ignore the identification by the narrator of Penny as Pandora in the appendix to the novel.

13. Of course Pandora's box is a jar in Hesiod, and the sexual interpretation of this dream would develop from the possible pun on the word "die." The sexual interpretation and my own may co-exist, of course. The phrase " 'I want to die,' " is probably an echo from the epigraph to "The Wasteland," in which the mythical and particularly the Christian past is also recognized as exhausted in contemporary society.

14. See the article by Joyce Carol Oates mentioned above, in which she develops an argument which uses this paragraph as a starting point.

15. *Picked-up Pieces,* p. 499.

# John Updike and the Changing of the Gods

Back in the second decade of this century, Herman Hesse remarked that "Human life is reduced to real suffering, to hell, only when two ages, two cultures and religions overlap."[1] Hesse was thinking in particular of Nietzsche, that shrill prophet of the oncoming crisis in culture resulting from our civilization's transition from a Christian to a naturalistic view of life. But Hesse's remark applies with equal force to a great number of writers both before and after his own time. With the rise of the natural and social sciences, including quasi-sciences like Marxism and Freudian analysis, and with the concomitant erosion of Christianity as a stay against death, the search for beliefs to live by has visibly escalated from the merely urgent in Tennyson and Melville to the desperate in T. S. Eliot and Hemingway. In the figure of John Updike, Hesse's crisis of culture attains what we might call a culminating expression. Unwilling to exorcise the dilemma by making a game of it, in the mode of black humor widely prevalent among his contemporaries, Updike has confronted the problem of belief as directly as did Tolstoy and Tennyson a century earlier, but with the added authority of a mind keenly aware of twentieth-century science and theology. In the paper we shall follow Updike's shifting path across the spectrum of beliefs that undergirds his total literary canon. Moving out from an intensely imagined vision of death as its starting point, this search for a belief that might provide a stay against death comprises the "figure in the carpet" that Henry James spoke of, the master theme that, threading from book to book, gives design to Updike's work as a whole and marks him as one of the leading religious writers of his age.

## I. MOLOCH

"Our fundamental anxiety is that we do not exist—or will cease to exist." That statement from Updike's essay on Denis de Rougemont's writings (*Assorted Prose*, p. 233)[2] compresses within its narrow pith the

*From *Mosaic: A Journal for the Comparative Study of Literature and Ideas*, 12, No. 1 (Fall 1978), 157–75, published by the University of Manitoba Press, to whom acknowledgement is herewith made.

most recurrent nightmare in Updike's work, evoking as well some giant specters of our age—the near-madness of Eliot's Hollow Men, the nocturnal bouts with Nada in Hemingway's people, and much of the black humor literature of recent decades. The dread of Death stalks softly through all of Updike's books, scattering visions of extinction to characters like the narrator of "Lifeguard," who watches the sunbathers around him and muses, "Each of our bodies is a clock that loses time. Young as I am, I can hear in myself the protein acids ticking; I wake at odd hours and in the shuddering darkness and silence feel my death rushing toward me like an express train." (*Pigeon Feathers*, p. 148)

This mood has persisted. *The Poorhouse Fair*, Updike's first novel, dealt with aging people (its hero is 94 years old) dwelling precariously in death's imminent, towering shadow, "with Death at their sides, the third participant in every conversation, the other guest at every meal." (p. 57) *Rabbit, Run!*, his second novel, was written under the pressure of an intense personal crisis in its author's life, occasioned (Updike says) by "a sense of horror that beneath this skin of bright and exquisitely sculpted phenomena, death waits." *(TIME*, April 26, 1968, p. 74). Although he managed to survive this period of Kierkegaardian terror with sanity intact, the dread of death did not depart far from Updike's thoughts, for his third novel, *The Centaur*, is stuffed with mementoes of death, like so many grinning skulls reflecting the drunk's question, "Are you ready to die?" (p. 121) There are dead animals, dead gods, and dead languages (Greek and Latin). There is the sudden death of Charlie the hotel clerk, who had refused father's check with "Why not wait till morning? . . . I guess we'll all still be here." (p. 124) There is a lengthy, death-dreading wait for Caldwell's x-ray report, complete with prospective obituary, followed by a ride in the family car (a hearse) that stalls at the Jewish cemetery. Even dreams and memories tend to be death-haunted, as when Peter dreams about the Sybil's death-wish in *The Waste Land* ("I want to die, I want to die."—p. 128) or recalls the mummy room in the museum: "As a child this floor filled me with dread. So much death; who would dream there could be such a quantity of death?" (p. 199).[3]

In similar fashion, *Couples* (1968) notably places its erotic episodes against a background saturated with news of expiring flesh: the slow death of Pope John, the mysterious sinking of the submarine *Thresher*, the death of the Kennedy infant, the Diem assassinations, the murder of the President himself, the killing of Lee Oswald (which the Hanemas watch on television), two planes crashing in Turkey, a great Alaskan earthquake. The fictional world of *Couples* can hardly compete with such real life extinctions, but it does offer the slow dying of John Ong by cancer in counterpoint with the insomniac dread visited upon Piet Hanema ever since his parents died in a crash. The hero of *Bech: A Book* (1970) likewise fights the old metaphysical panic in this otherwise comic novel: "He felt dizzy, stunned. The essence of matter, he saw, is dread. Death hung behind everything, a real skeleton about to leap through a door. . . . His death gnawed inside him like a foul parasite while he talked to these charming daughters of fertile Virginia." (125–126)

Beyond this prospect of personal extinction lies that ultimate formulation of doom from the science of Physics, the theory of Entropy, which foresees the whole universe eventually burning out into a final icy darkness. This idea horrifies a good many Updike people, a typical instance being the tortured insomniac at the end of *Pigeon Feathers* who wakes his wife at last to share his terror: "I told her of the centuries coming when our names would be forgotten, of the millennia when our nation would be a myth and our continent an ocean, of the aeons when our earth would be vanished and the stars themselves diffused into a uniform and irreversible tepidity." (p. 177) Worst of all is the eternally "forgotten" state in the above passage, a final and total extinction of the self that has haunted George Caldwell in *The Centaur* ever since he witnessed his father's death, though Caldwell accepts both death and entropy cheerfully enough otherwise.

Throughout his books, then, Updike's original trauma about the protein acids ticking and death coming on like an express train lingers on. Updike might as well have been speaking of himself when he described Conrad Aiken's stories as projecting a world whose "horror is not Hitlerian but Einsteinian," concerned not with crime and war but with the "interstellar gulfs" and "central nihil" of "the cosmic vacuity." (*Assorted Prose*, 179) All of Updike's major work to date may be seen as some kind of response to this trauma; his people variously resist death through Christian faith (John Hook in *The Poorhouse Fair*), through the way of Eros (the Rabbit books, *Couples*), through Agape (George Caldwell), through art (Bech, Peter Caldwell), and through the metaphysical intuition that Updike himself calls "duality" (*A Month of Sundays* and elsewhere). A look at each of these responses in turn may reveal why *The Centaur*, which gathers them all in its purview, remains Updike's most satisfactory treatment of his grand obsession.

## II. FROM CHRIST TO EROS

To deal with the threat of non-existence, Updike has resorted largely to the oldest modes of immortality known to man—God and sex, more or less in that order, but sometimes meshed in a dubious combination. To judge from the bulk of Updike's writing, we might well surmise that Freddy Thorne, the high priest of *Couples*, speaks for his author when he says, "In the western world, there are only two comical things; the Christian church and naked women. . . . Everything else tells us we're dead., (p. 155)

Concerning these two "comical" (that is, life-affirming) things, piety dictates that God alone should grant the immortality counterposed against death and entropy, and Updike tried mightily to make it so in his lengthy stint as a Christian warrior. Born and raised a Lutheran *(Assorted Prose,* "A Boyhood"), at length he emerged from the usual adolescent doubt to seize—in his early twenties—upon Kierkegaard as a "giant brother . . . [beside whom] I could walk safely down . . . the street of my life." *(Horizon,* Autumn, 1972, p. 105) Kierkegaard was succeeded in turn by Karl Barth, whose blast against liberal Protestantism in his *Commentary on Romans* (1919) effectively launched modern Christianity's neo-orthodox movement. In *Assorted Prose,* Updike applauds Barth's "uncompromisingly supernaturalist exposition of the Apostle's Creed" and his thunderous rebuke "to all that is naturalistic, humanistic, demythologized, and merely ethical" in contemporary Christianity. ("Faith in Search of Understanding," p. 212, 216)[4] Updike's poem, "Seven Stanzas at Easter" (1963), likewise insists upon a clearly supernaturalist Christianity:

> Make no mistake: if He rose at all
> it was as his body;
> if the cells' dissolution did not reverse, the molecules
>     reknit, the amino acids rekindle,
> the Church will fall.

*(Verse,* p. 164)

These comments—Updike's own, not those of a dramatic character—seem assured in their orthodoxy, yet the doubt Updike expresses through his fictional characters seems far too corrosive to permit total exorcism. Back in his earliest novel, *The Poorhouse Fair,* where a head-on debate between a Christian and an atheist comprises the intellectual center of the work, it is ominously the atheist whose argument carries the weightiest evidence:

> The truth is, Mr. Hook, that if the universe was made, it was made by an idiot, and an idiot crueler than Nero. . . . Natural history is a study of horrible things. . . . Have you ever walked around the skeleton of a brontosaurus? Or watched microbes in a drop of water gobble each other up? . . . What was your second piece of evidence? Inner spokesman? . . . . We've sifted the body in a dozen directions, looking for a soul. Instead we've found what? A dog's bones, an ape's glands, a few quarts of sea water, a rat's nervous system, and a mind that is actually a set of electrical circuits. . . .
> (abridged from pp. 78–80)

Perhaps Updike's most harrowing—and most brilliantly written—plunge into the abyss of religious skepticism occurs in "Lifeguard" whose divinity—student narrator skewers the whole line-up of Christian theologies like so much shish-ke-bob:

For nine months of the year, I pace my pale hands and burning eyes through immense pages of Biblical text barnacled with fudging commentary, . . . through handbooks of liturgy and histories of dogma; through the bewildering duplicities of Tillich's divine politicking; through the suave table talk of Father D'Arcy, Etienne Gilson, Jacques Maritain, and other such moderns . . . ; through the terrifying attempts of Kierkegaard, Berdyaev, and Barth to scourge God into being. I sway appalled on the ladder of minus signs by which theologians would surmount the void. I tiptoe like a burglar into the house of naturalism to steal the silver. An acrobat, I swing from wisp to wisp. Newman's iridescent cobwebs crush in my hands. Pascal's blackboard mathematics are erased by a passing shoulder. The cave drawings, astoundingly vital by candlelight, of those aboriginal magicians, Paul and Augustine, in daylight fade into mere anthropology.

*(Pigeon Feathers*, pp. 146–147)

His faith reduced to such feeble embers, we need not marvel that our narrator, as mentioned earlier, cannot bear the thought of stars nor the nocturnal tick of the protein clock in his body announcing the onrush of death like an express train in the shuddering silence and darkness.

When God goes, half-gods arrive; and in our post-Freudian age, what other god can stand before Eros, "the Genesis of All Things," as the Centaur teaches (p. 78), and the one surviving deity who delivers a kind of immortality people may yet live by. Perhaps it is natural that when faith fails, God and sex become blurred, unified, so that latter-day theologians may see in the cathedral's rose window a huge vagina symbol, or take Eden's forbidden Tree of Life (later, the Cross) to have been, actually, a stiffened primal phallus. Some such subliminal transference seems to have worked itself out in Updike's fiction of the 1960's, whose tones have become steadily less Christian and more pagan, though without a clear victory on either side.

Updike's psychology of sex, as he himself has attested, owes a great deal to two books by Denis de Rougement, *Love in the Western World* and *Love Declared.*[5] Focusing on the myth of Tristan and Iseult (and its subsidiary, Don Juan), *Love in the Western World* announces its purpose to be an analysis of "the inescapable conflict in the West between passion and marriage." Updike's essay on de Rougemont explains that "perversity is the soul's very life. Therefore the enforced and approved bonds of marriage, restricting freedom, weaken love." (*Assorted Prose*, p. 233) In his Foreword (p. *lx*), Updike adds a confirming extract from Freud showing that "some obstacle is necessary to swell the tide of the libido to its height" so that mankind may enjoy copulation.

Whereas Freud found the necessary obstacle in the taboos of civilization, the obstacle in traditional literature, as the Tristan myth illustrates, is that of the Unattainable Lady; this is why romantic fiction invariably deals with the separation of lovers, and indeed goes to incredible lengths to raise obstacles to love's fulfillment. The secret reason for this, according to de Rougemont's formulation, is that "Tristan and Iseult do not love one another. . . . *What they love is love and being in love.*" (p. 41–2) The lady remains unattainable, then, precisely because the lover's soul, in its perversity, loves passion itself rather than the other's being: "Eros had treated a fellow-creature as but an illusory excuse and occasion for taking fire; and forthwith this creature had to be given up, for the intention was ever to burn more fiercely, to burn to death." (p. 68) And consequently, for our Western love myths—Heloise and Abelard, Paolo and Francesca, Romeo and Juliet, even Nabokov's Lolita—the Tristan story expresses *"the dark and unmentionable fact that passion is linked with death,* and involves the destruction of anyone yielding himself up to it with all his strength." (p. 21) Updike renders this connection between Eros, narcissism and death metaphorically in his Erotic Epigram III (*Verse*, p. 170), which reads:

> Hoping to fashion a mirror, the lover
> doth polish the face of his beloved
> until he produces a skull.

So Eros becomes another mask for death, after all, rather than death's adversary; and the servant of Eros becomes "Mr. Death," as Ruth calls Rabbit—that proud lover—at the end. Presumably, the very reason Rabbit insisted on having sex with Ruth without contraceptives was to loosen his seed against death, affirming his being in reproduction. (During his symbolic stint as a gardener, Rabbit likewise loves to plant seeds, seeing "God Himself folded into the tiny adamant structure."—p. 115) Yet the final effect of Rabbit's erotic adventures is to inflict death by water upon his new-born daughter, death by fire upon his girl friend (in *Rabbit Redux*), death by abortion upon his unborn descendant, and spiritual death upon both his wife and his concubine: "I'm dead to you, and this baby of yours is dead too. Now; get out." (*Rabbit, Run*, p. 253)

*Couples* is Updike's ultimate statement on the theme of Eros. Guided by Paul Tillich's headnote from *The Future of Religions* that our present world, like that of the Roman Empire, presents "a mood favorable for the resurgence of religion," we find in *Couples* just what that religion is like to be: a worship of Eros complete with its high priest and prophet (Freddy Thorne), its sacrificial victims (Angela and Ken), and its lay communicants (the couples)—all under the purview of the town church with its "pricking steeple and flashing cock." (p. 90) The ultimate sacrament of this Eros-worship is its near-blasphemous lovers' eucharist: the "Take, eat: this is my body" of oral-genital connection (Foxy swallows Piet's semen) and breast-feeding (he swallows her mother's milk). The association with the Christian communion service is made deliberate when Piet thinks, "To eat another is sacred," as he and Foxy service each other, oral-genital style on "Sunday morning, beneath the hanging clangor of bells." (p. 456)[6]

Piet—the name suggests both Piety and Peter, the rock on whom the church resides—sometimes is freed from his death-obsession in his copulations (with Bea Guerin, for example, "he experienced orgasm strangely. . . . Death no longer seemed dreadful"—p. 352), but of course this feeling is only momentary. In this book, Death is once again linked with Eros, in Foxy's abortion, for example, and even in the assassination of the President, who is seen as a martyr to Oswald's sexual problems. ("A martyr to what? To Marina Oswald's sexual rejection of her husband"—p. 470). More significant is the loss of personality, a kind of psychic death, that Eros exacts as its payment. Contrary to Freddy Thorne's sudden "vision" that "We're all put here to *humanize* each other" (p. 158), Eros obviously dehumanizes his worshippers in this novel, not only—again—in victimizing the (as Updike put it in his *TIME* interview, p. 67) "distressed and neglected children," but with respect to the lovers themselves: "Frank and Harold had become paralyzed by the habit of lust; she and Marcia, between blowups, were as guarded and considerate with one another as two defaced patients in an accident ward." (p. 169) Those critics and readers who complained of the lack of character development in *Couples*—the characters are mostly indistinguishable—have missed the point that it was meant that way. Such, as de Rougemont keeps saying, are the ways of Eros: *Love in the Western World* describes polygamy as "an indication that men are not yet in a stage to apprehend the presence of an actual person in a woman." (p. 315) And Karl Barth, in his "Eros and Agape" section of *Church Dogmatics* (p. 189), says "Erotic love is a denial of humanity."

Piet himself is at last a victim of this phenomenon. Although Updike stoutly insists that the book's "happy ending" is not a satire (Gado, "A Conversation with John Updike"), he does see a great loss of meaning in his hero's final state: "he becomes a satisfied person and in a sense dies. In other words a person who has what he wants, a satisfied person, a content person, ceases to be a person. . . . I feel that to be a person is to be in a situation of tension, is to be in a dialectical situation. A truly adjusted person is not a person at all—just an animal with clothes on." *(Paris Review* Interview, p. 101)[7]

So the case against Eros stands hard—an agent of death and loss and suffering deceitfully disguised. But this is only part of the story. The other part is the fact that, for better or worse, Eros is in reality a living god of this world to whom all flesh must render service. And in that service may actually reside some measure of joy and hope and meaning, for here we encounter a strange paradox: the Christian hedonism of John Updike. He that lusteth after a woman in his heart hath defiled her already, according to Jesus Christ, but Updike's religious people seem marvelously at ease in their compliance with the laws of Eros. "Lust stuns me like the sun," admits the divinity student watching the beach maidens in "Lifeguard," who then goes to to justify himself: "You are offended that a divinity student lusts? What prigs the unchurched are." Christ and Eros are not adversaries, he maintains, but collaborators, the asceticism of the Bible notwithstanding: "To desire a woman is to save her. . . . Every seduction is a conversion." *(Pigeon Feathers,* pp. 149–150)

De Rougemont finds support for this contention in the Don Juan myth, which sustains the idea that "the true expression of woman consists in her desire to be seduced." *(Love Declared,* p. 116) Freudian psychology similarly asserts that being sexually desired is indeed a woman's "salvation," absolutely crucial to the meaning of her life, whereas prolonged virginity means not virtue but simply a wasted life.

Far from judging the crowd harshly, then, the student-lifeguard sees a sanctity in the Sunday morning swimmers: "Protestantism's errant herd seem gathered by the water's edge in impassioned poses of devotion." They even drain, like communion wine, "our most platitudinous blessing, the moment, the single ever-present moment that we perpetually bring to our lips brimful." And the lifeguard's concluding dictate, "So: be joyful. Be Joyful," nicely anticipates George Caldwell's belief at the conclusion of *The Centaur*: "All joy belongs to the Lord." (p. 220) The joy Caldwell refers to is the drunken laughter emanating from a barroom, "a poisonous laughter that seemed to distill all cruelty and blasphemy in the world," but even this joy belongs to the Lord: "Wherever in the filth and confusion and misery, a soul felt joy, there the Lord came and claimed it as his own; into barrooms and brothels. . . . And all the rest, all that was not joy, fell away, precipitated, dross that had never been." (p. 220)

The lifeguard's changing investment of belief, shifting from God to sex—that is, from a supernatural to a naturalistic mainstay against death—portends, I believe, a significant movement in Updike's larger career. (The fact that "Lifeguard" was meant to be a novel but failed, as Updike told an interviewer, implies the unusual importance of its ideas.)[8] Certainly, his *Midpoint,* a collection of poems published in 1969 and narrated by Updike himself, would appear to verify a shift, though not a full break, away from Christianity towards hedonism in Updike's view of life.[9] While formally affirming his Christian faith in a couplet like "Praise Barth, who told how saving Faith can flow/From Terror's oscillating Yes and No," *(Midpoint,* p. 38) Updike altogether easily takes his own "Intelligent hedonistic advice" (p. 38, headnote) and joins "mankind's copulating swarm" (p. 8) in some of these verses.

That this drift toward hedonism stems from Updike's own philosophy rather than from some remove of aesthetic distance seems clearly evident in the book's title poem "Midpoint," which contains a confessional section most memorable for its author's boasts about his rich and varied sexual encounters. Subtitled "The Play of Memory," this part of "Midpoint" sheds a particularly interesting light on Updike's pornographic fiction, even though some of this sexual autobiography may be falsified by braggadocio or faulty memory. Here our poet boasts of having popped off

with a girl friend six times in one night "my prick toward morning a bat-
tered miracle of response" (even Johnson's Boswell, though proud of his
size, claimed a more modest five ejaculations); he crows how he brought
off another girl until "[her] head beat like a wing on the pillow"; he gloats
over getting another sweetheart from behind, just like a dog, until they
got snarled up in the mosquito netting down in the Caribbean; and he
celebrates the girl with the "shampooed groin" who nearly snapped his
neck during cunnilingus. Culminating the homage to Eros in this book is
the poem entitled "Fellatio" (which is brief enough to be quoted in its en-
tirety below), a lyric in the Imagistic tradition:

> It is beautiful to think
> that each of these clean secretaries
> at night, to please her lover, takes
> a fountain into her mouth
> and lets her insides, drenched in seed,
> flower into landscapes:
> meadows sprinkled with baby's breath,
> hoarse twiggy woods, birds dipping, a multitude
> of skies containing clouds, plowed earth stinking
> of its upturned humus, and small farms each
> with a silver silo.

Though obviously far more tender and lyrical and humane in its sexuality
than Philip Roth's *Portnoy*, "Fellatio" still registers rather more of a
pagan than a Christian mentality.

The "intelligent hedonism" of *Midpoint* and the "happy ending" of
*Couples* (Updike called it that in the *Paris Review* interview) would appear to reflect an increasing commitment to the pleasure principle in Updike's thinking, as supernaturalism wanes and naturalism waxes. But
Updike is nothing if he is not double-minded. *Rabbit Redux* (1971) gives
us a revulsion against naturalism as powerful as T. S. Eliot's, whereas
Eros is again the mad, cruel god, where all sexuality is joyless exploitation, and where drugs and the moon-landing (of 1969) prove empty
substitutes for spiritual meaning. Replacing the dying Christianity of the
times is a *spiritus mundi* fearfully similar to Yeats's sphinx in the desert,
with gaze blank and pitiless as the sun. In the literal desert of Las Vegas,
Rabbit's sister is now a prostitute; his wife becomes the discarded mistress
of a car salesman; his teenage girl friend is a heroin addict whose death by
fire is shrugged off by her black lover: "there's a ton of cunt in the world."

There is no subject, then, upon which Updike is so ambiguous in his
judgments as the subject of Eros, doubtless because sex is so ambiguous a
feature of actual life, almost evenly balanced between its pleasures and
pains, its warmth and its cruelty, its powers to create and destroy. Looking at *The Centaur*, we find both attitudes locked in a typically dialectical
configuration. On behalf of Love, Chiron (who is himself nearly seduced

by Venus—p. 24) tells of the Genesis of All Things, how Eros, hatched from the womb of Darkness, "set the Universe in motion" (p. 78) and presided over a Golden Age in antiquity. Caldwell, Chiron's successor, likewise accepts the primacy of Venus both in the planetary symbolism—"Venus is the brightest planet" (p. 32)—and in describing biological immortality: "those male sperm cells which enjoy success become the cornerstone of new life that continues beyond the father." (p. 37) On the other hand, *The Centaur* shows as plainly as ever the disruptive (if comic) effects of Eros at work, effects which only Caldwell is free from: Zimmerman's unruly lechery with Becky and Mrs. Herzog; the queer hitchhiker, whose coarse language ("What a fucking day. Freeze your sucking balls off"—p. 65) reminds us of Gregg in *The Poorhouse Fair;* the obscene graffitus which someone later converts into the word BOOK; Johnny Dedmon's pornographic playing cards; the equating of Peter's girl friend Penny, with Pandora, and her erotic regions with Pandora's Box—an equation largely borne out in Updike's other writings; and the fact that the Venus of our tale, Vera Hummel, is childless, the proprietress at best of a Bower of Bliss, not a garden of Adonis. Even the planetary symbolism is less than reassuring in its final recurrence:

> There was a star before us, one low in the sky and so
> brilliant its white light seemed warm.
> I asked my father, 'What's that star?'
> 'Venus'
> 'Is it always the first to come out?'
> 'No. sometime's it's the last to go. . . . '
> 'Can you steer by it?'
> 'I don't know. I've never tried. It's an interesting question.'
>                    (pp. 211–212)

Judging from those who have tried to steer by it in Updike's other books, Venus is not too reliable a guide. In fact, the "steer by " metaphor recurs in *Couples* in a context where Eros seems sovereign only because of men's despair: "he talked to her . . . about the fate of them all, suspended in this one of those dark ages that visits mankind between millennia, between the death and rebirth of the gods when there is nothing to steer by but sex and stoicism and the stars." (p. 372)

So the turn from Christ to Eros ends in paradox. On the one hand, in a time of failing belief Eros is at least one god that all men can believe in, one to whom bodies may be offered a living sacrifice and who may confer in return a provisional shelter against death and entropy and the protein acids ticking. On the other hand, the capture of civilization's inner citadel from its few rear-guard Christian defenders yields little joy to the army of neopagan victors, for the disappearance of Christianity in books like *Couples* and *Rabbit Redux* only displays the "central nihil" of the "cosmic vacuity" all the more intolerably. To find Updike's true refuge from death and its terrors we shall have to look to neither classical Eros nor orthodox Christian metaphysics but to a highly personal theology that sees Agape love and Erotic love as pointing toward "Duality," like two sides of a triangle or a Gothic arch whose base is Earth and whose tip pierces heaven.

## III. AGAPE/DUALITY

The Gospel of Mark (8:35) proclaims that he who would save his life will lose it, but he who loses his life for the gospel's sake, the same shall save it. What this means in Updike's system is best seen by comparing those companion novels, *Rabbit, Run* and *The Centaur*. In running to save his life, Rabbit flees from the face of death in its various guises, including expressly that continuous extinction of self which society calls obedience to duty: "If you're telling me I'm not mature, that's one thing I don't cry over since as far as I can make out it's the same thing as being dead." (p. 90)

This portrait finds its opposite epitome in George Caldwell, whose most important characteristic is contained in the statement, "Chiron accepted death." (p. 222) That Updike includes more than physical death in this statement is indicated in the book's closing litany: "*What is a hero?* A hero is a king sacrificed to Hera." (p. 221) Hera, the Matron goddess of the family Caldwell, a king sacrificed. Again, those critics who complained about the vagueness of Caldwell's destiny—did he die of cancer? commit suicide?—missed the point that he dies every day, in pain and humiliation and futility: a living sacrifice. As Updike put it in his *Paris Review* interview (p. 93–94), "The trauma or message that I acquired in Olinger had to do with suppressed pain, with the amount of sacrifice I suppose that middle-class life demands, and by that I guess I mean civilized life. The father, whatever his name, is sacrificing freedom of motion, and the mother is sacrificing in a way—oh, sexual richness, I guess; they're all stuck . . . [in the] irremediable grief in just living, in just going on." Thinking of the Greek mythology in this book, one of whose characters is named Penelope, we might consider how, of all the world's classics, *The Odyssey* may best reflect the perfect life of a man, spun out in various and continuous adventures. Measured against its pattern, Caldwell's "suppressed pain" in losing his "freedom of motion" assumes a touching and heroic magnitude, gauged by his envy of the wandering hitchhiker (Dionysus) and his wish for the stimulation of the city (a lifelong sacrifice to his wife's love of the farm).

So Chiron accepted death. But he who will lose life for the gospel's sake shall save it. This is where Updike's Christian bias reasserts itself most willfully, in the spectacle of "the Protestant kind of goodness going down with all the guns firing." (TIME essay, p. 74) The goodness Updike speaks of is what theologians call *agape*, that love which St. Paul placed at the top of his famous triad in I Corinthians 13; and though we see very little faith and not much hope in *The Centaur*, we do see an abundance of love in George Caldwell, love which in the Pauline phrases "suffreth long, and is kind . . . seeketh not her own, is not easily provoked, thinketh no evil." Moving through a world that otherwise seems a throwback to the pagan hedonism of pre-Christian antiquity, Caldwell anachronistically dispenses agape-love in all directions.[10]

Here perhaps a few words from Updike's religious mentor, Karl Barth, will focus Caldwell's role more clearly: "In *agape*-love a man gives himself to the other with no expectation of a return, in a pure venture, even at the risk of ingratitude." (*Church Dogmatics*, p. 188)[11] Or again: "In his love there takes place the encounter of I and Thou, the open perception of the other and self-disclosure to him, conversation with him, the offering and receiving of assistance, and all with joy." (p. 188) Caldwell's encounter with the queer hitchhiker appears consciously designed to bear out these Barthian precepts:

> 'I was living with a guy up in Albany,' the hitchhiker said reluctantly.
> 'What happened? He pull the old double-cross?'
> 'That's right, buddy,' he told my father. 'That's just what that fucking sucker did. . .'
> 'I've enjoyed talking to you,' my father called to him.
>
> (pp. 66–67; 72)

Earlier, in his science lecture, Caldwell had described death as the result of altruism on the part of the volvox, a primitive microorganism:

> '. . . the volvox, of these early citizens in the kingdom of life, interests us because he invented death. There is no reason intrinsic in the plasmic substance why life should ever end. Amoebas never die. . . . But the volvox, . . . by pioneering this new idea of *cooperation*, rolled life into the kingdom of certain—as opposed to accidental—death. For . . . while each cell is potentially immortal, by volunteering for a specialized function within an organized society of cells, it enters a compromised environment. The strain eventually wears it out and kills it. It dies sacrificially, for the good of the whole. These first cells . . . were the first altruists.'
> (p. 37)

From the beginning, then, "goodness" had created death, but it also transcends death, in Updike's thinking. In view of the traumatic dread of death evident throughout Updike's writings, his sense of the immortality of agape gathers paramount importance: "Only goodness lives. But it does live." (*The Centaur*, p. 220) This is his version of Karl Barth's assertion that "love, *agape*, never fails (I Cor. 13:8). . . . It is imperishable even in the midst of a world which perishes." (*Church Dogmatics*, p. 190)

For his "countless, nameless acts of charity and good will," as his obituary puts it, George Caldwell is spared the last despair of his dying father, the minister, over the prospect of being "eternally forgotten," (p.

73) committed without a trace to the geological eons. For George Caldwell, <u>the good is not interred but lives on after him</u>. The statement in  his obituary, "What endures, perhaps, most indelibly in the minds of his ex-students (of whom this present writer counts himself one) was his more-than-human selflessness," (p. 133) is borne out by ex-student Diefendorf's statement fourteen years later: "a great man, your Dad. Did you know that?" (p. 81) All the testimony of Caldwell's life is such as to bear out the theme, stated only ironically in *Couples*, that "we're all put here to humanize each other." In achieving this purpose, Caldwell also solves the mystery that Updike had left unclarified in his closing lines of *The Poorhouse Fair*: "[Hook's] encounter with Conner had commenced to trouble him. . . . A small word would perhaps set things right. . . . He stood motionless, half in moonlight, groping after the fitful shadow of the advice he must impart to Conner, as a bond between them and a testament to endure his dying in the world. What was it?" (p. 127) The small word was *agape*.

Love—as *agape*—is a mighty ethical force, but matters of even greater moment hang by this tale. Ultimately, love implies that the physical universe has a spiritual counterpart, that metaphysical dimension of reality whose existence has been so much in question, and whose power is the only final recourse against death and entropy. Updike's word that encompasses this metaphysical dimension is "duality," a word that threads back in Christian history through Pascal and Aquinas and Augustine and St. Paul to its source in Plato and ancient Oriental religions. Duality essentially means the division of reality into two dissociated spheres: earth and heaven, matter and spirit, flesh and soul, with ultimate reality being the spiritual. According to one Updike essay, the not entirely fanciful "Jesus on Honshu," Jesus Christ was a dualist. Embroidering upon a Japanese legend that Jesus actually escaped crucifixion by fleeing to the Orient and living in northern Honshu until his death at the age of 106. Updike writes that a certain "sage of Etchu [a province in Honshu] took him in and taught him many things. He taught the young Jesus that dual consciousness was not to be avoided but desired: only duality reflected the universe." (*Museums & Women*, p. 214–15)[12] In likewise calling Marcel Proust a dualist, Updike proceeds to define the term: "For all his biochemistry, Proust emphasizes the medieval duality of body/spirit: "the body imprisons the spirit in a fortress." (*Horizon*, Fall, 1972, p. 105)

In *A Month of Sundays*, Updike's most dualistic book, the author's Reverend-spokesman elaborately restates these Gnostic insights. "For what is the body but a swamp in which the spirit drowns?" inquires the narrator, who sees Christ's role as a prophet of dualism: "Before Him, reality was monochromatic. . . . After Him, truth is dual, alternating, riddled. . . . Christ stands in another light . . . ; by contrast our sunshine burns at His feet blacker than tar."[13] Like the Gnostics of old, the minister associates this doomed physical universe with Satanic power and sovereignty—"the universe *is* a dragon," "The Milky Way is a dragon" (pp. 137, 140)—and he sees his own function to be that of pointing the way of escape: "our task is to witness, to offer a way out of the crush of matter and time." (p. 70) Proving the existence of a transcendent world is love, "the spiritual twin of gravity," (p. 113) but as the minister admits, it is a troublesome term ("I have vowed to abjure the word "love' "). Though a Christian minister by profession, in act he is a Catharian heretic, seeking the higher world of love and transcendence through free sexuality. Of "free" and "love," he declares that "the words are the same underneath, and free love not a scandal but a tautology." (p. 190)

By setting off *The Centaur* against Updike's erotic novels—*Couples, A Month of Sundays*, and *Marry Me*—we may observe how the author designates Agape and Eros as the two alternative pathways that connect the dualistic realms of reality. The way of Agape is surer but much more difficult, of course—straight is the path and few there be who find it. None do find it after Caldwell, who was not the last Christian for Updike (for his lovers are all Christians too), but who was the last Christian capable of a life of *agape* love. The noble centaur's exit thus leaves Eros as the major vehicle of dual consciousness in our ongoing twilight era.

Here Denis de Rougemont's thought makes its greatest impact on Updike's writing, for de Rougemont's connection between Eros and Duality makes possible a molecular fusion between Updike's sexual and religious psychology. Beyond the pleasure principle, that is to say, the Unattainable Lady of Updike/de Rougemont, provides a stay against death by opening to her lover a secret corridor for periodic visitations into the next world. In *Love in the Western World*, de Rougemont fuses the sexual and metaphysical meanings of Tristan's Unattainable Lady thusly: "why should she not be the *Anima*, or, more precisely, man's *spiritual* element, that which the soul imprisoned in his body desires with a nostalgic love that death alone can satisfy?" (p. 90) In *Love Declared*, de Rougemont more clearly removes this Anima to an unattainable sphere by designating it as our "Angel," left behind in heaven upon our incarnation and reclaspable only after death. The great error of Passion, he says, lies in identifying one's lover with this missing part of the self, thereby denying her true person: "Is what we believe we see in her *herself* or the image of our Angel? Is what we see in her—and what we may deify at her expense—our projected *anima*?" (p. 223)

Just such a system of thought pervades Updike's latest novel, *Marry Me* (1976). Here the protagonist shatters two family units by pursuing his neighbor's wife, only to draw back from her when the other three parties to the affair—the cuckold and the two wives who are affected—agree that he may have her. His problem is that, like the minister in *A Month of Sundays*, he greatly prefers his lady to remain unattainable, so that passion may continue: "I look up, and there's this radiance I can never reach.

It gives you your incredible beauty, and if I marry you I'll destroy it. . . .
What we have, sweet Sally, is an ideal love. It's ideal because it can never
be realized. . . . Oh, we could make a mess and get married and patch up
a life together—it's done in the papers every day—but what we have now
we'd lose." (p. 46) Like de Rougemont's Tristan, Updike's Jerry loves not
his lady but the "idea" she represents, as he ruefully admits in the after-
math of his forsaking her: "As an actual wife or whatever, she stopped
being an *idea*, and for the first time, I *saw* her." (p. 284)

The "*idea*" in question is de Rougemont's "duality," the fallen world
of time and matter juxtaposed against the transcendent realm of spiritual
reality. For the Updike hero, the unattainable lady represents that part of
the self which continues to reside in that transcendent realm, having
never participated in the soul's earthly incarnation. By the grace of her
sexual favor, the Updike heroine affords her lover access, or even
"ascent," to that higher dimension of reality: " 'Heaven,' Jerry said one
night, entering her. . . . Afterward, he explained 'I had this very clear vision of the Bodily Ascension, of me going up and up into this incredibly
soft, warm, boundless sky: you.' " (p. 153)

As might be expected, the women in *Marry Me* bitterly resent this
metaphysical burden thrust upon them. Jerry's mistress protests that if he
won't marry her, "I must stop talking to you, because people will say I'm a
whore;" (p. 302) and his wife "disliked, religiously, the satisfaction he took
in being divided, confirming thereby the split between body and soul that
alone can save men from extinction." (p. 186) But to Updike's knights of
Eros, actual women do not matter. For Jerry, all that matters is that in his
unattainable lady he has glimpsed and touched his saving "Angel," as de
Rougemont called this Anima figure: "You're like a set of golden stairs I
can never finish climbing. I look down, and the earth is a little blue mist"
(p. 46); and again, "you're the only woman I want. You were given to me
in Heaven, and Heaven won't let me have you." (p. 56) So Jerry enacts Updike's premise via de Rougemont, concerning the Anima/Animal duality:
"people were animals, white animals twisting toward the light." (p. 47) At
the end of the book, Updike affirms de Rougemont's system one last time
by bringing into his text that classic movie archetype of the unattainable
lady, Marlene Dietrich, whose most famous film, *The Blue Angel*, bears a
title that happens to suit Updike's purpose to perfection.

In the end, then, the idea that poor Sally is asked to serve, at the risk
of being called a whore, is that of Jerry's immortality: "Whenever I'm
with her, no matter where, . . . I know I'm never going to die." (p. 144)
As his Anima or Angel figure, she is his one contact with the world beyond
time and matter; but she will remain so only so long as he does not marry
her. ("You're death," he tells his wife. "I'm married to my death"—p.
144.) The psychic force behind *Marry Me* thus remains the dread of death
made familiar to us in Updike's earlier books; but here the transition from
Moloch to Christ to Eros occupies, in elliptical fashion, barely a single

recapitulant sentence: "Jerry . . . suddenly dreaded death. Only religion helped. He read theology, Barth and Marcel and Berdyaev; he taught the children bedtime prayers." (p. 78) Perhaps it was some fine artistic reticence on Updike's part that moved him to remove from that list of Jerry's readings the theologian most important to this work, the theologian of Eros, Denis de Rougemont.

In *Couples*, Updike sometimes verges upon making a stilted morality play with de Rougemont's system, with Piet's name meaning "Hanema/Anima/Life" (according to the *Paris Review* interview) and with Piet's wife Angela taking the role of the Angel not possessable in this world. (Neither Piet nor Freddy—in that absurdly forced wife-swapping scene—achieves satisfactory sexual possession of her.) Piet even resists their divorce in terms straight out of de Rougemont's thinking: " 'Don't make me leave you,' he begged. 'You're what guards my soul. I'll be damned eternally.' " (p. 425) There is one significant difference between Updike and his mentor, however; in *Couples* the word *Anima* (Hanema) is not identified with the word *Angel*, but is the middle part of the psyche torn between its Angel and Animal propensities. (De Rougemont failed to note that Animal is another of the derivatives of the word *Anima*; in a later generation, Updike knows better.) So Piet Hanema gives up his Angela, and chooses instead an Animal, Elizabeth Fox, thereby becoming, in the "happy ending," himself an animal, according to Updike's *Paris Review* commentary ("A truly adjusted person is . . . just an animal with clothes on"—p. 101). In this fashion, the "splendid redheaded squire" of Eros, as Foxy calls him (p. 470), vanishes toward the "eternally forgotten" state while yet among the living, as the book's closing paragraph tells us: "Now, though it has not been many years, the town scarcely remembers Piet. . . ."

In *The Centaur*, duality works in the opposite direction, by means of the centaur symbol. Although he is, below the waist, a dung- and semen-spewing animal, his horse's body the very symbol of potent lust, Chiron nonetheless fends off Venus's attempted seduction:

> 'Have you ever wondered, nephew, if your heart belongs to the man or the horse?'
> He stiffened and said, 'From the waist up, I am told, I am fully human.'
>
> (p. 27)

Freed from Eros, Chiron-Caldwell may assert his above-the-waist identity, a mind and spirit capable of Christlike wisdom and selflessness. (In contrary fashion, Piet Hanema in *Couples* thinks oral-genital sex "sacred" because it resolves the duality that normally divides one's being, uniting the spiritual being above the waist with the animal below: "Mouths, it came to Piet, are noble. They move in the brain's court. We set our genitals mating down below like peasants, but when the mouth condescends, mind and body marry. To eat another is sacred."—p. 456)

Presumably the centaur's preposterously divided nature is the duality Updike had in mind when selecting the quotation from Karl Barth for his book's headnote: "He [Man] himself is the creature on the boundary between heaven and earth." But the *Church Dogmatics* from which the quote comes envision a larger duality, this death-bound universe being set off against the Resurrection of Christ and a New Creation. Not being a religious tract, *The Centaur* cannot speak in Barthian terms about the metaphysical meaning of duality, but there are intimations of it occasionally. One such instance is Peter's sensation of cosmic identity as he lies in bed drifting between consciousness and sleep: "As the sheets warmed, I enlarged to human size, and then, as the dissolution of drowsiness crept toward me, a sensation, both vivid and numb, of enormity entered my cells, and I seemed a giant who included in his fingernails all the galaxies that are. This sensation operated not only in space but in time." (p. 127) Something similar to this experience appears in one of Updike's poems, "Fever" (*Verse*, p. 163):

> I have brought back a good message from the land of 102°:
> God exists.
> I had seriously doubted it before;
> but the bedposts spoke of it with utmost confidence,
> the threads in my blanket took it for granted
> the tree outside the window dismissed all complaints,
> and I have not slept so justly for years.
> It is hard, now to convey
> how emblematically appearances sat
> upon the membranes of my consciousness.

Another poem, in *Midpoint* (p. 11), speaks of Updike's hope, "incapable of being dimmed," that beyond "the tide/That this strange universe employs/To strip itself of wreckage in the night" is a creative power offsetting entropy: "The motion that destroys/creates elsewhere."

These are, of course, mere intimations, but in a universe made more and more mysterious by our new knowledge of pulsars and quasars, black holes and white holes, sub-atomic particles and anti-matter, twisting spirals of coded genetic energy, and the like, intimations may be as effective as science in grasping for the nature of the whole thing. The stakes, in any case, are very high; as *Couples* says, in a different context, "All things double. Without duality, entropy. The universe God's mirror." (p. 58)

Such intimations aside, in the spiritual universe love is the one thing known to us with certitude, the one absolute, analogous to the speed of light in the physical cosmos. It is the one connecting link between the dualistic universes, according to Karl Barth's theology of the Incarnation; and even without the faith and hope of Barth's neo-orthodoxy, love remains a living remnant of St. Paul's triad, transcendent and efficacious. "Only goodness lives. But it does live." The ambiguity of Updike's erotic love, a life force harboring brutality, selfishness and a "mask of Death" quality, renders agape-love that much more efficacious by comparison. Parallels to Updike's theme of agape are obvious enough in several of the greatest writings of the West, including parts of the Bible and Plato's *Symposium*, but probably Updike's most immediate support for this theme is again de Rougemont, especially in the last few pages of *Love Declared*, where love is a positive antipode to the nihilism postulated by natural science: "If thought finds no answer to the fundamental question asked by the Void: *why not nothing?* it surrenders to the Void and is reduced to nothing. What can retain it on the brink of nothing is the direct intuition of love." (pp. 233–4) These last sentences from *Love Declared* comprise, I think, a perfect summary of the meaning of *The Centaur*:

> I might have doubted being, and becoming, and all our ideas about 'God': I have never doubted love itself. I might have doubted almost all the truths of Western morality and culture. . . . I have doubted most of the truths successively demonstrated by our sciences; and I do not cease to doubt our image of the world. . . . But I believe I have never doubted all this except . . . in the name of love. It is the indubitable grace. I have no other certain faith, no other hope, and I see no meaning save love.
> (p. 235)

It is this spirit that enables Caldwell-Chiron, in the book's last chapter, to accept death not only in the daily immolation of self for his work and family, but also with respect to his imminent final extinction: "His will, a perfect diamond under the pressure of absolute fear, uttered the final word. *Now*." (p. 222) Like the medieval Everyman, Caldwell has only Good Deeds as his companion going into the great darkness, but as Updike sees it, even among the burned out ruins of modern theology, this will suffice.

### IV. APOLLO

On his trip to the men's room (p. 185), George Caldwell spots a graffitus, now sanitized, that puzzles him: ". . . he absorbs the fact, totally new to him that every FUCK could be made into a BOOK. But who would do such a thing?"[14] Who indeed but the figure of the artist, forever bent to his sacred summons of transforming the gross crudities of the world into the delicate pressed flowers of perpetual memory? Through his ancient alchemy, FUCK becomes BOOK, life becomes art, flux becomes permanence: so that nothing of it may be eternally forgotten. The artist too, in our human scale, may confer immortality, and thereby share in it.

Updike's own aspirations as an artist appear most openly in "Archangel," a brief but consummate tally of his gifts and hopes and promises that seems to mirror his innermost craving. Like Wallace Stevens' Necessary Angel of Earth, Updike's Archangel works through the five senses, offering irresistible food and immaculate shelter and perfectly salvaged memories (including that of "the fair at the vanished poorhouse"). For the memories he reserves his greatest promise, in an archangelic prophecy worthy of Updike's favorite secular writer, Proust: "Such glimmers I shall widen to rivers; nothing will be lost, not the least grain of remembered dust, and the multiplication shall be a thousand fold." (*Pigeon Feathers*, p. 119) Here, at last, speaks a champion for the (otherwise) eternally forgotten.

In *The Centaur*, it is Peter Caldwell who must carry out the sacred mission: a Peter to his father's Christ; an apostle of art rendering the Master's example to the ages; a Fisher of Men like the artist in one of Updike's earlier sketches ("The Sea's Green Sameness"—1960): "I do not expect the waves to obey my wand, or support my weight. . . . All I expect is that once into my blindly spun web of words the thing itself will break: make an entry and an account of itself." (*Museums & Women*, p. 164) It doesn't matter that Peter, having denied his father over and over again, is the weakest of disciples; nor even does it matter that, as a third-rate painter requiring the props of a pad in the Village and a Negro mistress, he lacks the goods to do the job. All that matters is that he has caught the fiery vision and now burns to transmit its splendor, moved by the artist's eternal "hope that, my submission being perfect, the imprint of a beautiful and useful truth would be taken." (p. 218)

Critics like Leslie Fiedler and Norman Podhoretz have sometimes disparaged Updike's work, calling it poor, mindless, and irrelevant, but those of us who find *The Centaur* a brilliant, moving book will agree that in his portrayal of George Caldwell, Peter/Updike has netted a splendid catch indeed, worthy of its epic analogies.[15] In this apostle of agape-love, Updike has presented what still remains his surest answer to the problems of nihilism and the changing of the gods. As a side effect, he has also insured that his own name, while civilization lasts, is not likely to be forgotten.

## Notes

1. Herman Hesse, *Steppenwolf* (New York, 1963), p. 23.

2. I am incorporating all references to Updike's Fawcett Crest paperback editions within my main text; references to other editions of his work will be separately footnoted. In order to further economize on footnoting, I have also included certain references to TIME and HORIZON magazines within my main text.

3. The sovereignty of death is built into the structure of *The Centaur* by way of the geological sandwich, a metaphor also used by Melville (*Mardi*, chapter 132) to depict the earth's expiring fauna spread like meat over successive layers of the earth's crust. In *The Centaur*, Updike not only casts a geology teacher, George Caldwell, as the doomed meat about to be folded into the earth's sandwich, but he designed the book itself (so he stated in a television

interview) in the shape of a sandwich, with Caldwell's obituary precisely central (chapter 5) within the book's nine chapters.

4. In his Foreword to *Assorted Prose* (p. viii), Updike says that his essay on Karl Barth "was written in acknowledgement of a debt, for Barth's theology, at one point in my life, seemed alone to be supporting it (my life)."

5. Updike's debt to de Rougemont is acknowledged in his lengthy essay entitled "More Love in the Western World," *Assorted Prose*, pp. 220–234. In his Foreword to this book, Updike further states that his doubts about de Rougemont's theories have faded, while "his overriding thesis [that in the West marriage and passion are incompatible] seems increasingly beautiful and pertinent." (p. ix) The two books I shall be citing are *Love in the Western World*, first published in English in 1940 and republished under the title *Passion and Society*, translated by Montgomery Belgion (London, 1956), and *Love Declared: Essays on the Myths of Love*, translated by Richard Howard (New York, 1963).

6. See Robert Detweiler's essay, "Updike's *Couples*: Eros Demythologized," *Twentieth Century Literature* (October, 1971), pp. 235–247, for an illuminating discussion of the religious meaning of sex in *Couples*. Mr. Detweiler specifically points out the analogy between the Christian eucharist and the oral-genital connection in *Couples*.

7. The two interviews cited here are "A Conversation with John Updike," *The Idol*, ed. Frank Gado (Schenectady, New York, 1971) and "The Art of Fiction," *The Paris Review* (Spring, 1969), pp. 84–117.

8. *Paris Review* Interview, p. 96.

9. *Midpoint and Other Poems*, Alfred A. Knopf, Inc. (New York: 1969). This book is also available now in a Fawcett Crest paperback edition.

10. See David Myer's essay, "The Questing Fear: Christian Allegory in John Updike's *The Centaur*," *Twentieth Century Literature* (April, 1971), pp. 73–83, for a perceptive discussion of Chiron-Caldwell's role as a modern Christian in travail.

11. Karl Barth, *Church Dogmatics: A Selection*, translated by G.W. Bromiley (New York, 1962), p. 188. This is the text for my other quotations from Barth, also.

12. *Museums and Women, and Other Stories*, (New York, 1972), pp. 214–215.

13. *A Month of Sundays* (New York, 1975), pp. 46, 48.

14. This ingenious analysis of the word in the men's room was suggested to me by a magazine article I came across several years ago. Most regrettably, I have not been able to recall the name of the author or the magazine, and my substantial sleuth work in the library has failed to turn up the missing information. As I recall, it was a very short note, perhaps a page or less in length, and so may have escaped the usual bibliographical cataloguing.

15. I find it reassuring that in his note to page 106 of his novel *Ada*, Vladimir Nabokov shares my judgement: "*Chiron*: . . . an allusion to Updike's best novel." (*Ada*, Penguin edition, p. 467)

# Faith, Morality, and the Novels of John Updike

The novels of John Updike have spawned a criticism rather remarkable in its contentiousness. His books have evoked critical outrage, bewilderment, condescension, commendation, and an enthusiasm approaching the fulsome. The same novel might be hailed as a major fictional achievement and dismissed as a self-indulgence or a failure. And evaluations of Updike's importance in the realm of contemporary American literature reflect a similar truculent diversity. However, a careful review of the commentary on Updike's work reveals that much of it is structured by assumptions that have little relevance to the themes, methods, and intentions of his fiction. This is especially true of those studies which discuss the relation of Updike's Christianity to the form and texture of his novels. While Updike has repeatedly expressed his views on religious and theological questions, his critics continue to interpret his work according to theories, religio-ethical systems, and ontologies he categorically rejects and his fiction does not embody. Updike's faith is Christian, but it is one to which many of the assumptions about the Christian perspective do not apply—especially those which link Christian faith with an absolute and divinely ordered morality.

Updike's religious views are decidedly conservative. "Theologically, I favor Karl Barth," he has said,[1] and rarely does he discuss religious matters without invoking the name of the leading spokesman of Neo-Orthodox Protestantism. Barth's theology is complex and difficult to summarize, but his basic position has been outlined by Updike himself in his review of *Anselm: Fides Quaerens Intellectum*, where the novelist calls Barth "the most prominent, prolific, and (it seems to me) persuasive of twentieth century theologians":

> His theology has two faces—the No and the Yes. The No, which first resounded in 1919, when the original edition of Barth's impassioned commentary on Romans was published, is addressed to all that is naturalistic, humanistic, de-mythologized, and merely ethical in the Christianity that German Protestantism had inherited from the nineteenth century. The

*From *Twentieth Century Literature*, 24 (1978), 523–35, with permission of the journal.

liberal churches, as Barth saw them, were dedicated to "the god to whom in our pride and despair we have erected the tower of Babel; to the great personal or impersonal, mystical, philosophical, or naive Background and Patron Saint of our human righteousness. . . . this god is really an unrighteous god, and it is high time for us to declare ourselves thorough-going doubters, skeptics, scoffers, and atheists in regard to him." The real God, the God men do not invent, is *totaliter aliter*—Wholly Other. We cannot reach him; only He can reach us. This he has done as the Christ of Biblical revelation, and the Yes of Barth's theology is the re-affirmation, sometimes in radically original terms (for instance his virtually antino-mian doctrine of all-inclusive Grace), of the traditional Christian message.[2]

Theologians may challenge Updike's analysis, especially his emphasis on the "No" aspect of Barth's thought. But what is important is not whether Updike has precisely synopsized Barthian theology but that he has given *his* interpretation of it: if the theology sketched here is not Barth's, it is nevertheless Updike's. His recent discussion of the religious theme in *Couples* restates, in terms of the novel, his description of Barth's position:

I guess the noun "God" reappears in two totally different senses, the god in the first instance being the god worshipped within this nice white church, the more or less watered down Puritan god; and then god in the second sense means ultimate power. I've never really understood theologies which would absolve God of earthquakes and typhoons, of children starving. A god who is not God the Creator is not very real to me, so that, yes, it certainly *is* God who throws the lightning bolt and this God is above the nice god we can worship and emphathize with.[3]

Updike has often quoted approvingly Barth's remark that "one can-not speak of God by speaking of man in a loud voice." For both men the distinction between the divine and the human is absolute. God is Wholly Other. He is unreachable, unknowable. Thus the only religious—which is not to say theological—question is that of faith. But the existence of God, Barth and Updike jointly assert, cannot be proved. So the question becomes not, "Does God exist?" but rather, "Do I believe God exists?" To Updike, an affirmative answer to this question makes one a Christian: "I call myself a Christian by defining 'a Christian' as 'a person willing to pro-fess the Apostles' Creed.' "[4] And the Apostles' Creed is nothing more—and nothing less—than a statement of faith in the existence of God and the divinity of Christ. It requires only that one avow, "I believe."

Since Updike's Christianity is determined only by his profession of the Apostles' Creed, it contains no inherent moral system. Again his views are in accord with those of Karl Barth. In *The Word of God and the Word of Man*, which Updike recommends as "quite the best introduction to Barth's work,"[5] Barth's position on the moral and ethical questions of life is stated succinctly: "Man cannot begin to answer the ethical questions in

actual life. He can only recognize that he is wholly incapable of commanding an answer."[6] In another section of the book, Barth elaborates on this
view: "I think of the righteousness of our morality, of the good will which
we all, I trust, develop and exemplify in certain excellent principles and
virtues. The world is full of morality, but what have we really got with
it? . . . Is it not remarkable that the greatest atrocities of life . . . can
justify themselves purely on moral principles?"[7] Barth is not suggesting
that moral standards and precepts are in themselves harmful or un-
necessary. He is, rather, attacking moralism, or the self-righteousness of
humanistic morality, as well as the assumption that a rigorous adherence
to moral principles will solve human problems. The fact that "the greatest
atrocities of life . . . can justify themselves on purely moral principles"
indicates the fallibility of the best of ethical systems when applied to the
swirling confusion of human endeavor.

It should be noted that these remarks are from Barth's early work, a
part of the formulation of his theological "No"; later he does attempt to
establish in general terms an ethic consistent with biblical revelation.
Still, morality and ethics remain a human enterprise: "Ethics is the attempt to give a human answer to the question of dignity, correctness, and
excellence of human activity."[8] And implicit in his development of moral
guidelines is the belief that, ultimately, the Christian as well as the non-
Christian is engulfed by and "participates fully and very concretely in the
perversity and futility of all human efforts."[9] Updike agrees: "I believe
that all problems are basically insoluble and that faith is a leap out of total
despair."[10]

For Updike, then, religious questions are those arising from the relationship between man and God. Moral questions are those which concern
man's intercourse with his fellow man. The absolute qualitative difference between man and God, and consequently between ethics and
faith, is the sine qua non of his theology. And there is no question that for
Updike the problems of human morality are subordinate to that of faith.
The problem of faith, though difficult, is simple and absolute; those of
morality are relative, ambiguous, and "basically insoluble." Thus, insofar
as it treats moral problems, Updike's fiction must be ambiguous and
essentially static.

Updike has said that the central theme of each of his novels is "meant
to be a moral dilemma," and that his books are intended as "moral
debates with the reader."[11] But to develop a moral theme in such a way
that there is no resolution is to do something quite different from what the
novel has traditionally attempted. All novelists deal with moral questions.
Historically, however, the novelist has tried to resolve these problems, at
least tentatively; he has tried to view the problems of human life from a
moral perspective which indicates both their causes and possible solutions. Updike, however, believes that there are no solutions. And he
specifically rejects the notion that literature should inculcate moral prin-

ciples or precepts. On the other hand, many of his readers would agree with Wayne Booth's assertion that "an author has an obligation to be as clear about his moral position as possible."[12] The work itself, this theory holds, must create a moral universe which clearly establishes principles upon which the actions of its characters can be judged. But Updike is up to something else in his fiction. Since the theme of each novel is a moral dilemma, discriminations in the effects of human attitudes and behavior are essential to its development. Updike's focus on the complex implications of his characters' moral decisions is constant and sharp, so that the issues are always clear and the consequences of each decision fully developed. But while Updike's characters are quick to judge each other, their creator refuses either to bless or to condemn; and each novel clearly demonstrates that the specific moral problem it treats is irresolvable. The world Updike creates in his fiction is morally ambiguous. And it is so, in large part, because of the perpetual conflict between two antithetical forms of human morality.

Updike has suggested that the human conscience constantly suffers guilt for transgressing the laws of two different moralities. One is external, abstract, made up of biblical injunction, social and cultural mores, and all the precepts our civilization has established to enable men to live together in harmony. But "Another kind of morality is a sort of response to an inner imperative"; this subjective morality is less a system than a "feeling" or "sense" of the propriety of a given act. And while Updike believes that "Morality tries to keep us from pain," he admits that "I don't see either solution as being perfect."[13]

In Updike's novels the dilemma created by this dual morality is often embodied in the women between whom the protagonists must choose. In *Rabbit, Run* Rabbit Angstrom vacillates between his wife and his mistress. The external and codified morality, of which Jack Eccles is the chief instrument, demands that Rabbit return to Janice; but Rabbit's inner apprehension of what is "right" for him directs him to Ruth. Similarly, Joey Robinson's dilemma is represented by his two wives, and also by Peggy and his mother. Piet Hanema must choose between Angela and Foxy, the Harry Angstrom of *Rabbit Redux* between Janice and Jill. For Updike's latest hero, Tom Marshfield, the choice is between his wife Jane and first Alicia Crick, then Frankie Harlowe. But because of the inadequacy of either morality, these men are doomed to make the wrong choice—whatever it may be; because their dilemmas are "basically insoluble," they can neither protect themselves from pain nor prevent others from suffering on their account.

Many of Updike's readers find the moral ambiguity of his fictional world morally offensive. His refusal to establish a rigid and clearly discernible moral perspective from which his characters should be viewed often leads these readers to assert that Updike is unwilling or unable to deal with serious moral issues, that he has "nothing to say." The objective presentation of life's pervasive ambiguity also leads many of his sympathetic critics to misread him; they simply assume that Updike shares their own moral attitudes, or those associated with Christianity in general, and interpret his fiction accordingly. Thus one of Updike's most intelligent and sensitive academic critics can maintain that, in *Rabbit, Run*, Jack Eccles is a "liberal-redemptive presence," and that Rabbit Angstrom is "despicable."[14]

Much of the difficulty critics have with Updike's fiction stems from their unwillingness to acknowledge the validity of one or the other of the two moral imperatives Updike recognizes. To Updike, however, they are equally valid and equally imperfect. In his fiction they stand together as irreconcilable forces, distinct from and often irrelevant to the problem of faith. Thus they exist in ambiguity and tension, which are basic to the human condition as Updike understands it. It is this condition which is always the subject of his novels.[15]

Two of Updike's novels do not demonstrate this sharp distinction between morality and faith. In both *The Poorhouse Fair* and *The Centaur*, however, the attempt to yoke the ethical and the religious is unsuccessful. In addition, these two novels differ from Updike's others in that they are strongly autobiographical and have as their central characters members of Updike's family. His first novel was in part "some kind of memorial gesture" prompted by the death of his grandfather, who was "somewhat like John Hook in that book."[16] In *The Centaur* the autobiographical element is even more pronounced: Updike has admitted that "George Caldwell was assembled from certain vivid gestures and plights characteristic of Wesley Updike";[17] but more important is his description of the experience he wished to dramatize, that of "my father's immersion in the world of Christian morality, in trying to do the right thing and constantly sacrificing himself. . . ."[18] *The Poorhouse Fair* generally supports Hook's position on the relation of faith to moral probity, but it does so through authorial affection rather than through a dramatic rendering of the theme. And while Updike effectively captures the quality of his father's life in *The Centaur*, he has Caldwell come to a final perception of a humanistic immortality which Updike, both in fiction and in person, has unequivocally rejected.

For John Hook virtue is contingent upon faith. The traditional Christian society, to his mind, is both based upon and fosters a rather stern and masculine morality: ". . . Hook had a very clear inner apprehension of what virtue was: An austerity of the hunt, a manliness from which comes all life. . . . As the Indian once served the elusive deer he hunted, men once served invisible goals and grew hard in such service and pursuit, and lent their society an indispensable shadow" (p. 160). Without faith there can be no virtue, for there are no invisible goals to be pursued and served; there is nothing beyond man himself to structure his existence and order his values. Faith alone makes man responsible for his actions, and makes him accountable not to himself or to other men but to God. Thus, as Hook tells Conner at the conclusion of their debate on the existence of God, "There is no goodness, without belief. There is only busy-ness" (p. 116).

The debate between Hook and Conner is the philosophical center of the novel. With "controlled anger" the young prefect challenges the ex-schoolteacher: "Is it the wish to eliminate pain that strikes you as amusing?" (p. 108). Hook, his instincts for debate aroused, insists that pain and evil are not synonymous, that suffering often results from sin and at the same time affords an opportunity for virtuous action. For man is born with an innate understanding of God's wishes. And the existence of this God is demonstrated in two ways: "there is what of Creation I can see, and there are the inner spokesmen" (p. 112). Conner's sense of the injustice of an existence subject to fortuitous suffering is, Hook tells him, "the willful work of your own heart" (p. 111).

According to Hook, a lack of faith diminishes one's humanity, deprives one of "invisible goals," and reduces attempts at moral action to mere "busy-ness." Yet the novel as a whole does not embody this attitude. At its conclusion Hook's faith-structured morality is revealed to be as ineffectual as Conner's humanistic ethics in dealing with the basically insoluble problems of life: "He stood motionless, half in the moonlight, groping after the fitful shadow of the advice he must impart to Conner, as a bond between them and a testament to endure his dying in the world. What was it?" (p. 185).

In *The Centaur* there is no real moral dilemma. The narrative is structured in such a way that George Caldwell's positive attributes are underscored, and his suffering takes on a redemptive quality which renders it positive also. Caldwell's suffering is genuine, but it is rewarded with the perception that "in giving his life to others he entered a total freedom" (p. 296).

A man of "compulsive Christianity" (p. 71), George Caldwell believes that "God made Man as the last best thing in His creation," and that to the problems of human existence "Jesus Christ is the only answer" (p. 252). But the novel suggests that Caldwell's basic orientation is toward that part of Christianity which is "merely ethical," and that he is immersed "in the world of Christian morality" because he is afraid that there is nothing else. Caldwell's faith is troubled. He is obsessed with death, largely because he fears that it will bring with it the loss of faith. The realization that his minister father "lost his religion" (p. 249) on his deathbed leads Caldwell very near to despair. His own constant professions of faith are part of his performance before a distant and perhaps nonexistent audience, an existential shouting into the darkness as he passes the graveyard.

Several of Updike's critics have remarked upon the similarities between *The Centaur* and Updike's short story, "Pigeon Feathers." The characters are essentially the same in each, as is the concern with faith. In the story, however, the young protagonist David Kern absolutely rejects the conclusion about immortality to which Caldwell comes. Troubled by an adolescent awareness of death, David queries his minister about the nature of heavenly existence; but the answer he receives—"David, you might think of heaven this way: as the way the goodness Abraham Lincoln did lives after him" (p. 133)—leaves him in despair. The story ends with the renewal of David's faith in a living God and the reality of eternal life: "he was robed in this certainty: that the God who had lavished such craft on these worthless birds would not destroy His whole Creation by refusing to let David live forever" (p. 150).

The actual as opposed to the metaphoric or symbolic existence of God and eternal life is basic to Updike's theology. But this is not the final view of George Caldwell. Instead he shares that of the minister in "Pigeon Feathers." It is not the individual who survives into eternity. Rather, "Only goodness lives" (p. 297). So Caldwell's "total concern with the world at large" (p. 174) and his "cavernous capacity for caring" (p. 82) result from his deep-seated dread that there is nothing beyond this world and the human beings in it: The link between faith and morality is, in *The Centaur*, shown to be spurious. In the rest of Updike's novels it does not appear.

Actually, the severing of the ethical from the religious had taken place in Updike's fiction before the publication of *The Centaur*. His second novel, *Rabbit, Run*, clearly manifests the division. Its protagonist, Rabbit Angstrom, is the only character whose religious sense is in fact spiritual and not simply an adjunct of his existence in a nominally Christian society; yet he is at once better and worse, more and less moral, than the other characters. His faith in God is only that: it concerns no one other than himself and God, and has no influence on his human relationships.

This distinction between the religious and the moral mystifies the other characters in the novel (and, it should be pointed out, many of the novel's readers). At one point Jack Eccles angrily takes Rabbit to task for his apparent insensitivity to moral problems: "You don't care about right and wrong; you worship nothing but your own worst instincts" (p. 134). But this is true only in terms of Eccles' ethical humanism. Rabbit is as concerned with morality as any character in the novel. But he realizes that much of what people like Eccles call right is in fact wrong. Morally, the world of *Rabbit, Run* is one in which platitudes are piously pontificated and then winked at or invoked to excuse failure, mediocrity, or perversity. It is the confrontation with this world that forces Rabbit to turn inward for guidance. Still, he continues to live in the external world. So he is caught between the demands of two different but equally unsatisfactory moralities—the one requiring adherence to those modes of behavior enjoined by religio-social codes, the other demanding a complete and honest response to an "inner imperative." Conforming to the first, he violates the integrity of his subjective existence; but following the second, he creates social havoc and brings to those around him suffering and death.

Rabbit also faces a spiritual dilemma. In the novel's penultimate paragraph he articulates the attitude toward life and virtue upon which he has acted throughout the book: "Goodness lies inside, there is nothing outside . . ." (p. 208). But much of the novel concerns Rabbit's quest for God, the meaning of life, the "something that wants me to find it" (p. 127). And if there is "nothing outside" the self, then any quest must be of the self, must begin and end with the self. As such it is pointless. Rabbit's dilemma is acute: he has faith, but he "has no taste for the dark, tangled, visceral aspect of Christianity, the *going through* quality of it, the passage *into* death and suffering that redeems and inverts these things. . . . He lacks the mindful will to walk the straight line of a paradox" (p. 237). Nevertheless, Rabbit is clearly the spiritual superior of Jack Eccles, who, as Fritz Kruppenbach insists, doesn't know what his ministerial role is: "There is nothing but Christ for us. All the rest, all this decency and busyness, is nothing" (p. 171).

The moral dilemma Updike examines in *Rabbit, Run* is profound and at last overwhelming. This is also true of those in his later novels. Updike has described the vision of human existence which informs them:

> My books feed, I suppose, on some kind of perverse relish in the fact that there are insolvable problems. There is no reconciliation between the inner, intimate appetites and the external consolations of life. . . . There is no way to reconcile these individual wants to the very real need of any society to set strict limits and to confine its members. *Rabbit, Run* . . . I wrote just to say there is no solution. It is a novel about the bouncing, the oscillating back and forth between these two kinds of urgencies until, eventually, one just gets tired and wears out and dies, and that's the end of the problem.[19]

Updike's more recent novels continue the patterns established in *Rabbit, Run*. Like it, they deal with the problem of faith and the difficulty of moral decisions; and they too dramatize a moral dilemma through the complexities of sexual love. But the key to understanding Updike's treatment of this aspect of his sexual themes is found not in his second novel but in his third. In the first chapter of *The Centaur*, when Venus attempts to seduce Chiron, the centaur hesitates, listening for the rumble of Zeus's thunder. Suddenly Venus disappears, for "Love has its own ethics, which the deliberating will irrevocably offend"; Caldwell/ Chiron is left alone "with a painful, confused sense of having displeased, through ways he could not follow, the God who never rested from watching him" (pp. 30–31).

The "ethics" of love are of a piece with the "inner imperative" which Updike defends as a valid, if imperfect, form of morality. As such they will usually be in opposition to those ethical dicta by which society regulates the sexual impulse, and will demand behavior unsanctioned by that society—that is to say, adultery. However, while Rabbit Angstrom oscillated between these two ethics, the protagonists of Updike's later novels tend to hang suspended between them, to exist as best they can in an uneasy compromise with each. The inevitable result of this compromise is a constant sense of guilt and an overwhelming fear of decisive action.

This general inability to act is a primary brace in the psychological scaffolding Updike constructs around his lover/hero. Critics have made much of the "passivity" of his later protagonists, but the novels indicate that this is the result of something much more complex than moral indolence. These characters all become subject to so many conflicting moral demands, and are presented with so many insoluble problems, that they retreat into a sort of moral catatonia. In *Of the Farm* Joey Robinson sits silently as his dying mother and his new second wife savagely fight over him, each constructing her own "mythology," or moral universe, to account for the problems of four marriages. To Joey, Peggy's myth "painfully" fails to "harmonize with the simple, inexpressible way that things had been" (p. 134), while his mother's is "fabulous" (p. 135). But immediately he suggests another possibility: "Perhaps they both were right. . . . Truth, my work had taught me, is not something static. . . . Rather, truth is constantly being formed from the solidification of illusions" (p. 135). Where Mrs. Robinson and Peggy can argue with moral assurance, Joey is silenced by his perception of the ambiguity inherent in their lives and relationships. In much the same way priapic Piet Hanema, in *Couples*, is reduced to "passivity" by the conflicting demands of love and responsibility, so that all he can do is "let things happen, and pray" (p. 412). And in *Rabbit Redux* Harry Angstrom helplessly stands by as Jill proceeds to her inevitable destruction.

Updike has discussed the problems of moral action in terms which have particular relevance to his fiction: "I don't want to say that being passive, being inactive, being paralyzed, is wrong in an era when so much action is crass and murderous. I do feel that . . . there has been a perceptible loss of righteousness. But many evils are done in the name of righteousness, so perhaps one doesn't want it back."[20] Bereft of moral certitude, and realizing that any act is likely to be "crass and murderous" from some essentially legitimate perspective, Updike's protagonists simply refuse to act at all.

There is an additional reason for the inertia of these characters: each experiences what is clearly an existential and religious crisis. More specifically, each has reached the halfway point in his life—precisely that position between birth and death which Updike described in a long poem. "Midpoint" is a poetic recapitulation of Updike's past for the purpose of determining the proper course for his future. And three of his protagonists confront the same situation. Joey Robinson and Piet Hanema are thirty-five, Harry Angstrom thirty-six—each at the midpoint of his allotted threescore and ten; and each must attempt to make some sense of his life, to understand himself and his relation to God and to his fellow man, and to defend himself—with faith and love—against the ominous possibility of eternal death. The specter of mortality haunts these novels and their protagonists, who must leap again and again out of "total despair" to a faith assaulted on all sides by reason and doubt. And they must endure the distrust and recriminations of those characters who exist exclusively in the moral and merely human world. Invariably these characters are women.

Updike's remarks about the female characters in *Couples* apply to all the women in his later novels: "The women in that book are less sensitive perhaps to the oppressive quality of cosmic blackness, and it is the women who do almost all of the acting."[21] In *Of the Farm* only Joey Robinson has a genuine religious sense; in moments of crisis he instinctively expresses a faith in "the God who creates ironically" (p. 88). His mother is a nominal Christian, but as he observes, "her religiousity seems unaccompanied by belief" (p. 141); and Peggy is insouciant in her atheism. Piet Hanema's faith is essentially antinomian and eschatologically rooted, the object of which is "a Calvinist God Who lifts us up and casts us down in utter freedom, without recourse to our prayers or consultation with our wills" (p. 155). If Angela acknowledges a God, it is Freud; and Foxy, who respects Piet's faith, does not really share it, for hers is liberal and primarily a form of nostalgia. Janice Angstrom's God is Charlie Starvos, Jill's a dimly remembered LSD hallucination; but Harry at once has "No belief in an after life, no hope for it" (p. 104) and the conviction that "Yes. The Lord's last word. There is no other word, not really" (p. 125).

If Updike's protagonists are morally "paralysed," they are so in part because of their sensitivity to "the oppressive quality of cosmic blackness": obsessed by death, exhausted by their effort to believe, and convinced of the impossibility of sorting through the ramifications of each moral decision, they can merely wait, and hope, and suffer the guilt of the inactive even as they acknowledge that "all this decency and busyness, is nothing." Their women, unconcerned with the problems of death and faith, take control of love and life in the quotidian.

In Updike's recent novel, *A Month of Sundays*, the attitudes toward faith and morality which have been implicit in the earlier books are expressed vociferously by Reverend Thomas Marshfield in his "garbled and saddening audit" (p. 204). His theme is faith in the face of "lived life's muddle" (p. 182), his alliterative message "our earthly ills elude all earthly ease" (p. 182). His daily pages, written for "therapy," comprise a meditation on life and love, on sex and morality and faith.

Tom Marshfield's theology is "Barthian and rather hard" (p. 49). He believes in a God who "is not ourselves" (p. 111); and he labors to preserve this faith even though it has made his life "one long glad feast of inconvenience and unreason" (p. 21), and despite his awareness that in the multi-motived mess of human intercourse this faith "doesn't seem to apply" (p. 172). His wife Jane, whom he met, courted, and seduced while taking a seminary course in modern ethics from her father, is "liberal and ethical and soft" (p. 49). Jane, Tom repeats, is "good"; but she "doesn't believe in God, she believes in the Right Thing" (p. 154). To Tom, however, "Doing right is, to too great an extent, a matter of details, of tinkering. . . . Ethics is plumbing, necessary but dingy. Ethical passion the hobgoblin of trivial minds" (p. 192).

There is little question that Tom Marshfield's views on faith and morality are shared by his creator. Indeed, they pervade Updike's fiction. Unfortunately, they are rarely considered in the criticism of it. His secularly oriented readers focus on the social or psychological aspects of his novels, treating their religious themes as irrelevant or as "interesting only to the extent that they reveal the believer."[22] His Christian readers confuse Updike's God with the "good will and wordy humanism" (p. 209) he rejects. And the world of Updike's novels remains only superficially explored. Humanly, morally, this world is ambiguous and static; but spiritually it is a world which witnesses the dramatic confrontation of life with death, of faith with the void.

## Notes

1. Charles Thomas Samuels, "The Art of Fiction XLIII: John Updike," *Paris Review*, No. 12 (Winter 1968), p. 97.

2. John Updike, *Assorted Prose* (New York: Knopf, 1974), pp. 273–74.

3. Samuels, "The Art of Fiction XLIII," p. 101.

4. John Updike, "Introduction," in *Soundings in Satanism*, ed. F. J. Sheed (New York: Sheed & Ward, 1972), p. xi.

5. Updike, *Assorted Prose*, p. 273n.

6. Karl Barth, *The Word of God and The Word of Man*, trans. Douglas Horton (New York: Harper, 1957), p. 166.

7. *Ibid.*, pp. 17–18.

8. Karl Barth, *God Here and Now*, trans. Paul M. Van Buren (New York: Harper, 1964), p. 86.

9. Karl Barth, *Church Dogmatics: A Selection*, ed. and trans. G. W. Bromiley (New York: Harper, 1962), p. 50.

10. Jane Howard, "Can a Nice Novelist Finish First?" *Life*, 4 Nov. 1966, p. 80.

11. Eric Rhode, "Grabbing Dilemmas: John Updike Talks about God, Love, and the American Identity," *Vogue*, 1 Feb. 1971, p. 184.

12. Wayne Booth, *The Rhetoric of Fiction* (Chicago: Univ. of Chicago Press, 1961), p. 389.

13. John Updike, "Self-Comments on His Work and the Role of the Novelist Today," *Channel 13/WNET Program Guide*, Educational Broadcasting Corp. (Sept. 1966), p. 17.

14. Robert Detweiler, *John Updike* (New York: Twayne Publishers, 1972), pp. 158, 161.

15. The following editions of Updike's fiction are cited: *A Month of Sundays* (New York:

Knopf, 1975); *Couples* (New York: Knopf, 1968); *Of the Farm* (New York: Knopf, 1972); *Pigeon Feathers and Other Stories* (New York: Knopf, 1962); *The Centaur* (New York: Knopf, 1963); *The Poorhouse Fair* (New York: Knopf, 1972); *Rabbit Redux* (New York: Knopf, 1971); and *Rabbit, Run* (New York: Knopf, 1971; and *Rabbit Redux* (New York: Knopf, 1973).

16. Rhode, "Grabbing Dilemmas," p. 140.

17. Samuels, "The Art of Fiction XLIII," p. 91.

18. Rhode, "Grabbing Dilemmas," p. 185.

19. Frank Gado, ed., *First Person: Conversations on Writers and Writing* (Schenectady: Union College Press, 1973), p. 92.

20. Rhode, "Grabbing Dilemmas," p. 184.

21. *Ibid*.

22. George Stade, "The Resurrection of Reverend Marshfield," the *New York Times Book Review*, 23 Feb. 1975, p. 4.

# Reality, Imagination, and Art: The Significance of Updike's "Best" Story

George W. Hunt, S. J.*

John Updike remarked in a 1968 interview that "Nothing that happens to us [novelists] after the age of twenty is as free from self-consciousness, because by then we have the vocation to write. Writers' lives break into two halves. At the point you get your writerly vocation you diminish your receptivity to experience."[1] In a 1974 address he returned to this conviction and elaborated upon it by saying:

> A writer begins with his personal truth, with that obscure but vulnerable and, once lost, precious life that he lived before becoming a writer; but those first impressions discharged—a process of years—he finds himself, though empty, still posed in the role of a writer, with it may be an expectant audience of sorts and a certain habit of communion. It is then that he dies as a writer, by re-submitting his ego, as it were, to fresh drafts of experience and refined operations of his mind. *To remain interested*—of American novelists, only Henry James continued in old age to advance his art; most, indeed, wrote their best novels first, or virtually first. Energy ebbs as we live. . . . Almost alone the writer can reap profit from his loss.[2]

Updike's remarks resonate with a most personal ring, for a retrospective look at his writing career discloses, not only a life, but a career itself broken into "two halves." Updike has been a professional writer for two decades. His first decade's work, for the most part, records the strife, observation, and feeling of that pre-twenty year old wherein nostalgic recollections of boyhood are transmuted by an adult's imagination and youthful autobiography is altered into art. In his Foreword to *Olinger Stories* (1964) he characterized his early stories as "crystallizations of memory," a most apt description of most of the stories collected in *The Same Door* (1959) and *Pigeon Feathers* (1962). But it is also an appropriate designation for his novels, not only for the more obviously autobiographical *The Centaur* (1963) and *Of the Farm* (1965), but even for the futuristic *The Poorhouse Fair* (1959) and the contemporary *Rabbit, Run* (1960). As he later remarked, "I was full of a Pennsylvania thing

*From *Studies in Short Fiction*, 16 (1979), 219–29, with permission of the journal.

I wanted to say," and it is evident that the "Pennsylvania thing" of his youthful memory informs almost all the fiction of that 1955–65 decade.

Updike wrote that Foreword to *Olinger Stories* in 1964 with the intention of saying farewell to Pennsylvania and to his boyhood memories. Except for brief returns in *Rabbit Redux* (1971) and *Buchanan Dying* (1974), he has sustained that intention. After the novel, *Of the Farm* (1965), his favorite fictional locale moves from Pennsylvania to New England (often Tarbox) and his themes no longer reflect boyhood recollections but adult concerns. In the decade 1965–76 the tensions of marriage, the process of aging, and the varied losses of "faith"—religious, political, sexual—become his central themes. However, he himself observed that "the difference between Olinger and Tarbox is much more the difference between childhood and adulthood than the difference between two geographical locations. They are stages on my pilgrim's progress, not dots on a map."[8]

The years 1964–66, therefore, mark an important transitional stage in Updike's pilgrim's progress and so are of crucial significance for a complete understanding of his writing career. Unfortunately, this pivotal period has been the most neglected one in Updike criticism because most critical attention has been devoted to his novels to the neglect of his short stories.[4] After the publication of *Of the Farm* in 1965, however, there was a gap of three years before the publication of *Couples* in 1968, and so one must turn to the short stories, especially those collected in *The Music School* (1966), for the material that records this period of transition.

*The Music School* collection holds a distinctive place in the Updike corpus because it contains several stories that, in addition to more familiar Updike themes, specifically engage the issues of artistic self-consciousness and the act of composition itself. In the story, "The Bulgarian Poetess," published in March 1965, Updike created a spokesman who would explicitly engage these issues, Henry Bech. In 1970 he told an audience why he felt compelled to invent Henry Bech:

> Now, as for the Bech stories. . . . For a writer, life becomes overmuch a writer's life. Things happen to you that wouldn't happen to anybody else, and a way of using this to good advantage, of course, is to invent another writer. At first, he is very much an alter ego, but then, in the end, not so. At any rate I have used the writer in *Bech* as a subject in order to confess sterility in a truthful way. . . . In my book, I tried to—and I believe I did—package and dispose of a certain set of tensions and anxieties which I have as a practicing writer.[5]

But Bech's character is only the most obvious alter ego in *The Music School* collection. Most of the remaining stories reveal a narrator or character wrestling with similar "writerly" problems of sterility and creativity and the tensions that result. A cursory reading, though, might miss this artistic aspect. The primary and ostensible theme of almost every story is that of the mystery of sexuality and sexual relationships examined in the light of their sterility or vitality. Subordinate, but concomitant with it, is the secondary theme of the mysterious relationship between the imagined and the real, between artistic re-creation and Creation, between the sterile and vitalizing processes of the mind. Updike's later story, "Museums and Women," published in 1967, will explicitly conjoin these two "mysteries," but several stories in this collection do so with greater subtlety. The most obvious clue, however, that Updike is addressing these twin themes is found in the epigraph chosen for *The Music School*, a quotation from Wallace Stevens' poem, "To the One of Fictive Music":

> Now, of the music summoned by the birth
> That separates us from the wind and the sea,
> Yet leaves us in them, until earth becomes,
> By being so much of the things we are,
> Gross effigy and simalcrum, none
> Gives motion to perfection more serene
> Than yours, out of our imperfections wrought,
> Most rare or ever of more kindred air
> In the laborious weaving that you wear.[6]

These lines represent well Stevens' continuing poetic theme: that the apparent dichotomy that exists between the realm of reality, disorder, the actual (earth) and the realm of the imagination, order and the ideal (music) is bridged only through Art. The "One" addressed in the poem is the Muse of poetry who personifies man's power of imagination and memory. The "birth" referred to in the first line is that of human consciousness which separates us from nature (wind and sea) "yet so leaves us" in it that we see in nature a "gross effigy" of ourselves. But "the music summoned by the birth" of consciousness is Art which tries to unite man and nature, and none is more perfect and "rare" than poetry. Yet poetry is of a "kindred air" since as the bridge between, the more the poem retains of ourselves, the closer it brings us to nature.[7]

In a recent letter answering my inquiry about it, Updike wrote that "I chose the epigraph for *The Music School*, not only because it is a lovely stanza by a favorite poet (and fellow Readingite), but as a dedication to the unnamed woman, the one of fictive music, who is at the center of most of these love stories, from 'Leaves' on."[8]

Updike's choice of epigraph is most apt since most of the stories deal with the "Stevensian" theme of re-creating reality and the past via imagination and memory. As Updike's own letter explicates, the intractable "natural" reality that challenges this re-creative effort is that of Woman in the mystery of her sexuality. This is most apparent in "The Stare," "In Football Season," "The Morning," "Leaves," "Harv is Plowing Now," and "The Bulgarian Poetess." In each of these stories the sexual challenge is associated with the artistic challenge to *imagine* and so re-create the object of pursuit; implied in this effort, furthermore, is the narrator's desire for a new form of union, so that, in a Stevens-like way, the story not only recounts that effort but *becomes* the new form of union as well.

At first the brilliantly designed story "The Music School" seems excepted until we note that the adulterous narrator, now "unfaithful" to his wife and "faltering toward divorce," has been "unfaithful" to the novel he once planned to write and so now, "though unmusical," he waits in a music school attempting to sort out answers to both infidelities. In this and the other stories, composition and theme, frame and form are one in that each story's inner dynamic is heuristic in a composite way. We find the narrator, explicitly or not, seeking "connections" amid remembered or imagined events so that the resultant structure (i.e., where these connections intersect) both shapes and is shaped by this heuristic movement. Throughout, there is three-fold pursuit taking place as there is continually throughout the poetry of Wallace Stevens:[9] (1) pursuit of the elusive, disordered reality (Nature and Woman); (2) the conscious effort to draw upon the resources of the imagination through the medium of metaphor; and finally, (3) this heuristic movement outward becomes simultaneously a search for the self, the symbolic center of the pursuit. But the goal and instrument of these three quests are the same: recovery and re-creation.

The dense and difficult story, "Harv is Plowing Now," illustrates well this triple-layered attempt at recovery. In it the controlling metaphor is that of an archeological excavation. Just as the archeologist "unearths" both the precious and the dross, and a farmer like Harv plows the dead earth in order to revitalize it, so too the narrator-artist must mine his memory (memory of a Woman) in order to effect a re-creation by re-imagining, thus issuing in a "resurrection" of his very self at the story's end.

A more detailed investigation of these parallel heuristic movements in all the major stories found in *The Music School* would demand a book-length study itself. For our purposes it is sufficient to concentrate on one dense and difficult story, entitled "Leaves" which critics have overlooked, and offer it as a paradigm for such an investigation. Coincidently, Updike selected "Leaves" as his *best* story upon being asked to contribute to Rust Hills' anthology called *Writer's Choice*. His comments about it are worth noting and enlighten our argument thus far.

> ["Leaves"] is in a mode of mine, the abstract-personal, not a favorite with my critics. One of them, reviewing *The Music School*, expressed impatience with my lace-making, so-called. Well, if "Leaves" is lace, it is taut and symmetrical lace, with scarce a loose thread. It was written after long silence, swiftly, unerringly as a sleepwalker walks. No memory of any revision mars my backwards impression of it. The way the leaves become the pages, the way the bird becomes his description, the way the bright and multiform world of nature is felt rubbing against the dark world of the trapped ego—all strike me as beautiful, and of the order of artistic "happiness" that is given rather than attained. The last image, the final

knot of lace, is an assertion of transcendental faith scaled, it seems to me, nicely to the mundane.[10]

"Leaves" is a very brief story, only nine paragraphs long, but in its integration of imagery and subtlety of structure it represents well Updike's successful effort to engage the Reality-Art-Imagination relationships, and, as a prose-poem, it exemplifies the Stevens epigraph.[11]

The title "Leaves" itself suggests multiple meanings, each warranted in the story, for the word "leaves" can connote the product of Nature (as in grape leaves), and, as a verb, can indicate departure, loss, and time, and significantly, it can also suggest a book's "leaves," its pages, which are the outcome of art. The story is ostensibly a confession-meditation in that the narrator, now isolated in a forest retreat, is essaying to recover from the emotional disaster of imminent divorce by "sorting out the events" of his predicament. The story's framework is both heuristic and cruciform. The crux of X pattern is manifest in the sequence of reflections as the narrator pursues the "connections" among them.

The opening paragraph is reminiscent of the Stevens epigraph, for in it the narrator realizes that his previous self-absorption has blinded him from the paradoxical discovery that, on the one hand, although he and Nature are independent, his "curiosity" or attention now unites them and, on the other hand, although physically part of Nature, his spiritual consciousness—now ironically the source of his guilt—also separates him from it.

> The grape leaves outside my window are curiously beautiful. "Curiously" because it comes upon me as strange, after the long darkness of self-absorption and fear and shame in which I have been living, that things are beautiful, that independent of our catastrophes they continue to maintain the "effect," which is the hallmark and specialty of Nature. Nature: this morning it seems to me very clear that Nature may be defined as that which exists without guilt. Our bodies are in Nature; our shoes, their laces, the little plastic tips of the laces—everything around us and about us is in Nature, and yet something holds us away from it, like the upward push of water which keeps us from touching the sandy bottom . . . (p. 44).

This discernment about Nature and yet "that something that holds us back" from it, in turn, issues in another realization: man's limited power to make contact with and arrest Nature through language. Here the elusive natural object is a blue jay. The bird itself might "leave," but a book's "leaves" might capture it—another "curious" relationship for reflection.

> A blue jay lights on a twig outside my window. Momentarily sturdy, he stands astraddle, his dingy rump toward me, his head alertly frozen in silhouette. . . . See him? I do, and, snapping the chain of my thought, I have reached through glass and seized him and stamped him on this page. Now he is gone. And yet, there, a few lines above, he still is, "astraddle,"

rump "dingy," his head "alertly frozen." A curious trick, possibly useless, but mine (p. 44).

The third paragraph then merges these self-nature, art-nature contrasts and congruities and develops them by introducing the story's controlling images. These images will be re-"connected" and transformed in the story's final paragraph.

> The grape leaves where they are not in each other's shadow are golden. Flat leaves, they take the sun flatly, and turn the absolute light, sum of the spectrum and source of all life, into the crayon yellow with which children render it. Here and there, wilt transmutes this lent radiance into a glowing orange, and the green of the still tender leaves—for green persists long into autumn, if we look—strains from the sunlight a fine-veined chartreuse. The shadows these leaves cast upon each other, though vagrant and nervous in the wind that sends friendly scavenging rattles scurrying across the roof, are yet quite various and definite, containing innumerable barbaric suggestions of scimatars, flanged spears, prongs, and menacing helmets. The net effect, however, is innocent of menace. On the contrary, its intricate simultaneous suggestion of shelter and openness, warmth and breeze, invites me outward; my eyes venture into the leaves beyond. I am surrounded by leaves. The oak's are tenacious claws of purplish rust; the elm's, scant feathers of a feminine yellow; the sumac's, a savage, toothed blush. I am upheld in a serene and burning universe of leaves. Yet something plucks me back, returns me to that inner darkness where guilt is the sun (pp. 44–45).

Reality and imagination conjoin by contrast. The shadow-less "flat leaves" of Nature, by taking the sunlight "flatly," spontaneously transmute the sun's real shape and color the way a child's crayon would. A parallel transmutation takes place as well. The "shadows these leaves cast" take on a human coloration and suggest to the narrator's imagination a simultaneity of opposites, for they are at once barbaric and menacing, yet open and inviting. Invited outward, only his eyes can venture *into* the leaves; once there, he perceives, amid other ferocious shapes, that the elm leaves are "feminine yellow." Yet "something plucks him back," his realization of his ironic contrast with Nature. Whereas Nature's leaves, in receiving the sun flatly, had transmuted it, his guilt-consciousness which is *his* sun finally transmutes the "serene and burning universe of leaves" and returns him to the darkness of self-isolation.

The apprehension of his private predicament leads him to reflect upon its "connective" implications. Leaf-related imagery is introduced once more, but here its use dramatizes the ironic contrast between Nature and the human spirit. The implication is clear: despite the union of descriptive "images," *actual* union between spirit and Nature *seems* impossible; only a sharpening of one's awareness of our dialectical predicament seems possible.

> . . . And once the events are sorted out—the actions given motivations, the actors assigned psychologies, the miscalculations tabulated, the abnormalities named, the whole furious and careless growth pruned by explanation and rooted in history and returned, as it were, to Nature—what then? Is such a return spurious? Can our spirits really enter Time's haven of mortality and sink composedly among the mulching leaves? No: we stand at the intersection of two kingdoms, and there is no advance and no retreat, only a sharpening of the edge where we stand (p. 45).

The fifth paragraph, and hence "middle" section of this nine paragraph story, concerns the "sharpening edge" of memory, for the narrator remembers "most sharply" the black of his wife's V-shaped dress as she "leaves" to get her divorce.

> I remember most sharply the black of my wife's dress as she left our house to get her divorce. The dress was a soft black sheath, with a V neckline, and Helen always looked handsome in it; it flattered her pallor. This morning she looked especially handsome, her face utterly white with fatigue. Yet her body, that natural thing, ignored our catastrophe, and her shape and gestures were incongruously usual. She kissed me lightly in leaving. . . . And I, satisfied at last, divorced, studied my children with the eyes of one who had left them, examined my house as one does a set of snapshots from an irrevocable time, drove through the turning landscape as a man in asbestos cuts through a fire, met my wife-to-be-weeping yet smiling, stunned yet brave—and felt, unstoppably, to my horror, the inner darkness burst my skin and engulf us both and drown our love. The natural world, where our love had existed, ceased to exist. My heart shied back; it shies back still. I retreated. As I drove back, the leaves of the trees along the road stated their shapes to me. There is no more story to tell. By telephone I plucked my wife back; I clasped the back of her dress to me, and braced for the pain (pp. 45–46).

This paragraph recapitulates and broadens the color and fire imagery noted above, and the remembered "leaving" introduces a new "natural" association, for as his wife "leaves," her body "that natural thing," appears unconscious of the catastrophe of their divorce. Here Updike returns to a frequent association in his fiction—that between women and Nature. This association provides the central symbolic thread uniting the novel, *Of the Farm*, where the wife, Peggy, is allied throughout with "stupid Nature."[12] In *Rabbit Redux* Rabbit, not unlike the narrator here, reflects that he alone experiences guilt because "women and nature forget." A rather subtle explanation for this association is offered in the story, "The Bulgarian Poetess," from *The Music School* collection. There the novelist, Henry Bech, observes that sexual love is "a form of nostalgia. We fall in love . . . with women who remind us of our first landscapes" (p. 169). Bech is, of course, a fictional creation; however, two years before, in a review of De Rougemont's *Love Declared* Updike expressed remarkably similar sentiments by observing that a "woman loved, momentarily eases the pain of time by localizing nostalgia, the vague and irrecoverable objects of nostalgic longing are assimilated . . . the images we hoard in wait for the woman who will seem to body them forth include the inhuman—a certain slant of sunshine, a delicate flavor of dust. . . ."[13] In short, contemplation of the beloved Woman simultaneously returns the lover to remembered natural landscapes, "images" he hoards, and to his very self. This paragraph recounts this process artfully, for the narrator gradually realizes that his imminent divorce from "that natural thing" (his wife) has thus divorced him from "the natural world" (the leaves) and from his very self; only upon returning to his wife do the leaves again state "their shapes" to him.

This "middle" memory-interlude is brief and the next paragraph returns us to the present time and his painful dread of what the future might bring. He fears his wife's rejection, for, with that rejection, "the curious beauty of the leaves will be eclipsed again" (p. 46). Earlier, the blue jay had spurred on his imagination; his writing about him "had seized and stamped him on the page" and made him "mine." Now, however, a spider is sighted, hanging "like a white asterisk," and, unlike the earlier blue jay, it "feels a huge alien presence."

> I catch myself in the quaint and antique pose of the fabulist seeking to draw a lesson from a spider, and become self-conscious. I dismiss self-consciousness and do earnestly attend to this minute articulated star hung so pointedly before my face; and am unable to read the lesson. The spider and I inhabit contiguous but incompatible cosmoses. Across the gulf we feel only fear. The telephone remains silent. The spider reconsiders its spinning. The wind continues to stir the sunlight (p. 46).

Their "natural" alienation is his major realization: man's "self-consciousness" inevitably places him in tension with nature, and yet he continually seeks "fables" there. The depiction of the spider, seen as an "articulated star," seems a deliberate pun to imply this "fabulist" power in man, a power both re-active and creative. What, then, of art, of man's endeavor to bridge this gulf through language? This central question returns us to the story's central image of "leaves."

> In walking in and out of this cottage, I have tracked the floor with a few dead leaves, pressed flat like scraps of dark paper. And what are these pages but leaves? Why do I produce them but to thrust, by some subjective photosynthesis, my guilt into Nature, where there is no guilt? (p. 46).

At this point of apparent impasse, suddenly the narrator notices the vital green amid the shades of brown and that beyond the evergreens "there is a low, blue hill. . . . I *see* it, for the first time in months I see it. I see it as a child, fingers gripping and neck straining, glimpses the roof of a house over a cruelly high wall" (pp. 46–47). Just as in the third paragraph where a child's vision transmuted sunlight, here his child-like vision alters everything. This experience triggers a recent memory.

Under my window, the lawn is lank and green and mixed with leaves shed from a small elm, and I remember how, the first night I came to this cottage, thinking I was leaving my wife behind me, I went to bed alone and read, in the way one reads stray books in a borrowed house, a few pages of an old edition of *Leaves of Grass*. And my sleep was a loop, so that in awaking I seemed still in the book, and the light-struck sky quivering through the stripped branches of the young elm seemed another page of Whitman, and I was entirely open, and lost, like a woman in passion, and free, and in love, without a shadow in any corner of my being. It was a beautiful awakening, but by the next night I had returned to my house (p. 47).

The memory of this all-too-brief but "beautiful awakening"—its significant associations, the unexpected short-lived union of both Nature and Art in his imagination wherein the branches of the elm and the page-leaves of Whitman unite to make him feel "like a woman in passion"—all these not only once brought him awake but do so again in recollection. The story ends with appropriate images of illumination, for no longer is Nature wholly "barbaric" and alien; the remembered union of Art and Nature alters everything, and, just as the "flat leaves" transmuted the sunlight, imagination can so transmute guilt-less Nature that "sunlight falls flat at my feet like a penitent."

The precise barbaric shadows on the grape leaves have shifted. The angle of illumination has altered. I imagine warmth leaning against the door, and open the door to let it in; sunlight falls flat at my feet like a penitent (p. 47).

In both technique and theme we recognize similarities here between Updike and Wallace Stevens. Like so many of Stevens' poems, this story develops *through* an imaginative exploration of the potential implications of the central *metaphor*.[14] The plurisignificant metaphor becomes an instrument for discovery, therefore, the vehicle for grappling with the mysterious relationship between natural reality and man's imaginative consciousness. The poem, or the story here, not only records this process of discovery and the problems engaged, but *is* the process.

Furthermore, not only does this story proceed like a Stevens "meditation," but it deals specifically with the Stevens problematic, and, in a sense, reads like a commentary on the Stevens epigraph. In "Leaves," the "real" autumn leaves at the story's start are both inviting and repulsive, and make the narrator aware that he is "at the intersection of two kingdoms"; these real leaves then merge with a memory of his wife's "leaving" so that once again "real nature" (symbolized by the spider) seems alien for they "inhabit . . . incompatible cosmoses." These memories and thoughts then conjoin with his recollection of the imaginative *Leaves of Grass* which, in its turn, once had united with the elm tree "leaves" in his own imaginative "awakening," so that finally, memory of this previous union of "leaves" brings a "new angle of illumination" to the real autumn leaves which he now imagines falling "flat at my feet like a penitent." The story's structure, then, records the central theme in Stevens: that, despite the apparent dichotomy between the realms of imagination and reality, a reciprocal interpenetration is possible, and the "leaves" of an artist's book can capture it briefly—"it" being a merger of reality, memory, and imagination. Nature informs the artist's imagination, and in turn or reciprocally, his imagination *trans*forms Nature and the art-work is born.

## Notes

1. "The Art of Fiction XLIII: John Updike," *The Paris Review*, 12 (Winter 1968), 94.

2. John Updike, *Picked-Up Pieces* (New York: Knopf, 1975), pp. 38–39.

3. *The Paris Review*, pp. 90–91.

4. Robert Detweiler is the only critic who has given concentrated attention to *The Music School* collection as a unit. For a most perceptive reading, see Robert Detweiler, *John Updike* (New York: Twayne, 1973), pp. 111–129. For other less concentrated and more random readings, see Rachel Burchard, *John Updike: Yea Sayings* (Carbondale: Southern Illinois Press, 1971, pp. 152–59; Alice and Kenneth Hamilton, *The Elements of John Updike* (Grant Rapids: Eerdmans, 1970), *passim*.

5. Frank Gado, ed., "A Conversation with John Updike," *First Person* (Schenectady: Union College Press, 1973), p. 83.

6. These lines comprise the second stanza of "To the One of Fictive Music." Wallace Stevens, *The Collected Poems of Wallace Stevens* (New York: Knopf, 1967), p. 87.

7. This interpretation of the stanza agrees with those explications offered by the most reputable exegetes of Stevens. See Edward Kessler, *Images of Wallace Stevens* (New Brunswick: Rutgers, 1972), pp. 111–113; Eugene Paul Nasser, *Wallace Stevens: An Anatomy of Configuration* (Philadelphia: University of Pennsylvania, 1965), pp. 64–67; 127–27; Frank Doggett, *Stevens: Poetry of Thought* (Baltimore: John Hopkins, 1966), p. 192; also, *Letters of Wallace Stevens*, ed. Holly Stevens (New York: Knopf, 1966), pp. 251–252.

8. A private letter from Updike dated September 26, 1976.

9. An excellent analysis of this three-fold process in Stevens' poetry is found in J. Hillis Miller, *Poets of Reality* (Cambridge: Harvard University Press, 1965), pp. 217–284.

10. Rust Hills, ed., *Writer's Choice* (New York: McKay, 1974), pp. 391–392.

11. John Updike, *The Music School* (Greenwich: Fawcett, 1966), pp. 44–47. Hereafter, all page numbers within the text enclosed by parentheses will refer to this edition.

12. John Updike, *Of the Farm* (Greenwich: Fawcett, 1965), pp. 39: 47–48; *passim*. For a close analysis of this association in this novel, see Larry Taylor, *Pastoral and Anti-Pastoral Patterns in John Updike's Fiction* (Carbondale: Southern Illinois Press, 1971), pp. 102–111.

13. John Updike, "More Love in the Western World," *Assorted Prose* (Greenwich: Fawcett, 1965), pp. 220–221. Similar sentiments are expressed in *The Paris Review*, p. 102 and are found in Updike's *Couples* (New York: Knopf, 1968), p. 429.

14. Todd Lieber, "Robert Frost and Wallace Stevens: 'What to Make of a Diminished Thing,' " *American Literature*, 47 (March 1975), 66–70.

# The Novel as Lyric Elegy: The Mode of Updike's *The Centaur*

James M. Mellard*

Several critics have alluded to what is a most crucial matter in John Updike's *The Centaur*, the location of point of view in the novel,[1] but it remained for Edward P. Vargo, a decade after *The Centaur*'s publication, to put the issue bluntly: "the entire novel is presented to us as the experience of Peter, reliving three days in his life with his father, while he lies beside his black mistress in varying states of wakefulness or sleep . . . The entire novel is a fusion of the dreams and reveries and actual narration of Peter."[2] While I agree with the contention that Peter is the origin of the narration, I must disagree with Vargo's further argument that "the experience takes on the character of a rite for Peter." For Vargo to call the novel a "rite" or "ritual," not only contradicts the language of his second statement above, it also suggests that Peter plays a more public and ceremonial, even priestly, role than he does. The central issue may be nothing but a problem of definition. I suspect it is much more, however— being instead one of *modal* perception. In literary analysis, ritual is more properly associated with drama or the dramatic mode in fiction, but *The Centaur* is neither one nor the other. Rather, its art is essentially lyrical, the expressive symbol of Peter's elegaic feelings for his father. Peter's relation to the novel, therefore, is primarily that of the lyric poet to the poem in which every detail ultimately comes out of the creative center of the poet's emotions.

## I

Peter Caldwell gives the novel its lyrical, elegiac shape. It is he who accounts for the novel's point of view, its shifting formal modes, and, above all, for its metamorphic verbal styles. The role he plays as narrator is much like that of Hart Crane's poetic persona in *The Bridge*, embedded in the second section of the poem, the one entitled "The Harbor Dawn" in "Powhatan's Daughter." As in Crane's long poem, Updike's narrator does

*From *Texas Studies in Literature and Language*, 21 (1979), 112–27. Copyright © 1979. Reprinted by permission of the journal and the author.

not appear as a narrative persona until a portion of the story has been presented. In *The Bridge* one first sees both the "Proem" and "Ave Maria"; in *The Centaur* one sees the long chapter devoted to Caldwell-Chiron's receiving his arrow wound, visiting Hummel-Hephaestus to have it removed, and later resuming his classroom duties. When Peter does appear in his role as narrator it is precisely in the situation of Crane's persona, who is lying abed with his lover-mistress:

> And you beside me, blessed now while sirens
> Sing to us, stealthily weave us into day—
> Serenely now, before day claims our eyes
> Your cool arms murmurously about me lay.[3]

Peter enters *The Centaur* having just "dreamed," as he sleeps beside his lover, the account of a day in the life of his father given in Chapter I: "I wake now," he tells us, "often to silence, beside you, with a pang of fear, after dreams that leave a sour wash of atheism in my stomach . . . But in those days I always awoke to the sound of my parents talking, voices which even in agreement were contentious and full of life."[4]

Recurrently throughout the novel, Peter and his lover appear in the apparent relationship of storyteller to audience. In Chapter IV Peter asks, "Why is it, love, that faces we love look upon each remeeting so fresh, as if our hearts have in this instant again minted them?" (91–92). In Chapter VIII he says, "My love, listen. Or are you asleep? It doesn't matter" (198). Shortly after this, he says, "my story is coming to its close" (200), and, just a little later, he also says, 'The weariness I felt [after spending the night at the home of the Hummels] overtakes me in the telling" (209). But these brief notations identify Peter not so much in the role of a story *teller* as in the role of a lyric *persona* from whose experiences and emotions the novel grows. His role as mythic "poet," analogous, perhaps, to his vocation as an abstract expressionist painter, may give Peter an audience, but it is not an audience for which a "rite" could be performed such as Vargo perceives. As Peter realizes, an "external" audience "doesn't matter," for the lyrical expression, whatever form it takes, is mainly personal and private. The poet is his own audience.

The lyrical persona in fiction and poetry, often playing a metamorphic role, assumes many guises, many poses, many voices. In his role as a lyrical persona, Peter thus accounts for what Mizener calls the "mixture of genres," the different "modes of narration" in *The Centaur*.[5] But rather than "nominal and ineffective," as Mizener claims, Peter's role as lyrical persona simply exists *in* the various modes and voices and is effective in direct proportion to the extent to which Peter's own voice is disguised. The lyric poet's effectiveness comes in the achieved virtuosity of the poem. If a Crane can "speak," as L. S. Dembo says, through dream, meditation, and ecstasy in *The Bridge*, or a William Carlos Williams can "speak" through meditation, narrative, newspaper extracts, geological tables, and virtually every other form of human expression in *Paterson*, surely Updike's Peter Caldwell can speak through the objective omniscience of Chapter I, the first person of Chapters II, IV, and VIII, the formally decorous pastoral myth of Chapters III and IX, the newspaper obituary of Chapter V, the first-person stream of consciousness of Chapter VI, and the alternating third-person objectivity of Chapter VII. In *The Centaur*, as in the long yet essentially lyric poem (such as *The Waste Land, The Bridge*, and *Paterson*), the main principle of narrative is change, variation, discontinuity. But as there is always at the center of such poems a single figure (Tiresias, Crane, Noah F. Paterson) through whom the poet projects his voices, poses, guises, so at the center of *The Centaur* is the figure of Peter Caldwell.

The metamorphic and metamorphosing role of the persona in lyrical art also has considerable importance in other ways. Of primary significance in *The Centaur* is the way in which this persona determines the shape-shifting style. Speaking to his love about his life with his family, Peter says in one place, "We moved, somehow, on a firm stage, resonant with metaphor" (57). Peter's expressive, dreamlike, imaginative recreation of that world is itself "resonant with metaphor," and much of the texture of narrative comes from the metaphorical habit of language Updike gives Peter's narrative voices. The world of metaphor takes over entirely in those chapters, such as I, III, VI, and IX, in which Caldwell is Chiron and, as in VI, when Peter is Prometheus; in these chapters there is no projected distance between the figures in the narrative and the metaphorical world of myth. Yet even here the multiple perspectives of the novel's style permit the irony and humor of something very like the lowly pun. *Inside* this world the characters don't know that they are not simply "people," but are centaurs and gods and the like living in what, from *our* perspective, is a *locus amoenus*. Thus on a single page the centaur can say to Hummel-Hephaestus, "I got to *high-tail* it." And when the mechanic will not take any money for having removed the arrow from the centaur's ankle, George can think, "And this was the way with all these Olinger aristocrats. They wouldn't take any money but they did take an authoritative tone. They forced a favor on you and *that made them gods*." Finally, when Hummel tells George the days are bad, George can reply, "It's no *Golden Age*, that's for sure" (19). These words—"high-tail," "gods," "Golden Age"—become virtual puns, but only to us and to the one who dreams the dream. Because we share Peter's multiple perspective, we are the ones who have the binocular ability to encompass the mythic past and the nonmythic present. Such a vision is required to see the play on words.

But Peter's expression neither moves always in that world of total metaphor, which is one pole of the dialectic of language, nor in the world of total realism, the other pole of language, identified by Peter as that "patch of Pennsylvania in 1947" (218), the world emphasized by those critics like Mizener who value Updike's realism. There is, besides, a middle ground discernible in Peter's style. When the projected distance between the mythic and the realistic worlds increases, Peter's verbal technique shifts to the simile. As Peter uses them, the similes make connections between the other two polar realms by using "like" and "as" and "seems." When, for instance, George Caldwell speaks of Peter's skin condition to the hitchhiker, Peter, who is also rock-bound Prometheus, reports to us: "*In effect* my father had torn off my clothes and displayed my prickling scabs. In the glare of my anger his profile *seemed* that of a *blind raw rock*" (171). Similarly, Peter narrates about the hitchhiker, who is Hermes (or the winged Mercury): "through the dusty rear window I watched our guest, looking *like a messenger* with his undisclosed bundle, dwindle. The hitchhiker became a brown wisp at the mouth of the bridge, *flew upwards, vanished*" (72). Such simile—but with an occasional ascent into metaphor—plays a very large part in Peter's style when he relates details about himself. Of his skin problem, for example, he says: "Had the world been watching, it would have been startled, for my belly, *as if pecked by a great bird*, was dotted with red scabs the size of coins" (44). Of his bright red shirt (behind which stands the image of Prometheus' gift of fire to man), Peter remarks: "I would carry to my classmates on this bitter day *a gift of scarlet, a giant spark*, a two-pocketed emblem of heat" (46). In other places, both as first and third persons, he speaks similarly about that shirt: "I unbuttoned my pea jacket so the devil-may-care *flame* of my shirt showed" (92); "My shirt was eating my skin with *fire*" (134); "*On fire* . . . , he turns his red back on the crowd" (180).

Peter also speaks of other characters in terms of simile. Doc Appleton's mythic identity is Apollo, so Peter uses similes to draw into the texture of narrative two of Apollo's main roles, as the sun who brings light and as the slayer of the serpent, Python, at Delphi. When Doc Appleton (Apollo was also a healer) speaks his name, Peter says, "*like a ray of sunlight* the old man's kindness and competence pierced the morbid atmosphere of his house" (98). And when the doctor puts down his stethescope, Peter says, "it *writhed* and then subsided *like a slain rubber serpent*" (100). Minor Kretz, who runs the luncheonette where all the school kids hang out, is offered as a parallel to Minos, King of Crete, whose erotic interest is Pasiphae (Mrs. Passify in the novel). Of the man who runs the luncheonette and the woman who runs the post office next door, Peter says, "the symmetry [between the two establishments], carried right down to the worn spots of the two floors and the heating pipes running along the opposing walls, was so perfect that as a child I had imagined that Mrs. Passify and Minor Kretz were secretly married" (90). But Minor is also the minotaur (*borne* by Queen Pasiphae), so at one point Peter speaks of Minor's place as "a maze" (91); he says also, "Minor *charged* over to our booth. Anger flashed from his bald dome and *steamed* through

his *flared nostrils.* 'Here, hyaar,' he *snorted*" (139); and later he says,
"The luncheonette . . . is all but empty, like a stage . . . Within, Minor
is a cauldron of rage; his *hairy nostrils seem seething vents*" (153). Zimmerman, the school principal, doubles, in the mythic world, as Zeus. The
narrator or the other characters thus refer to him several times in figures
that suggest his role as an Olympian god. George Caldwell, for example,
moans, "I could feel Zimmerman sitting in there *like a big heavy rain-
cloud*" (157); and later the narrator says, "Zimmerman sees *as if through
a rift in clouds* that Caldwell's glimpse of Mrs. Herzog is at the bottom of
his fear and his mind exults" (186). At another time Peter thinks of Zimmerman's finger (like that of Michelangelo's God) as "dense with
existence" (182).

Finally, Peter's father also comes in for figurative treatment in those
chapters where realism dominates myth. The main referent for Peter's
images, of course, is the equine portion of the mythic centaur's body.
Thus, for example, once when Peter and his father are walking together,
we are told: "We seemed from our shadow to be a prancing one-headed
creature with four legs" (89). At another time, when George has felt Zimmerman as "a dark cloud" around him, we read: *"Lifting his head and
sniffling,* Caldwell experiences a vivid urge to walk on faster, *to canter
right past Hummel's, to romp neighing* through the front door and out the
back door of any house in Olinger that stood in his way, *to gallop* up the
brushy winter-burned flank of Shale Hill and on, on, over hills that grow
smoother and bluer with distance, on and on" (152). And near the end of
the novel, Peter sees his father walking toward home: "His shape before
me was made less human by the bag of groceries he was carrying and it
seemed, my legs having ceased to convey the sensations of walking, that
*his was the shape of the neck and head of a horse I was riding*" (212).

Figurative language such as this suggests one extra dimension Updike gives *The Centaur.* There is a very real sense in which Peter's search
through his memory and imagination, in the process of "dreaming" this
narrative, is for an original, innocent, prelapsarian world "resonant with
metaphor." He searches for a world in which identities exist between
reality and myth, existence and dream, earth and heaven, but the very
*need* to speak of Appleton, Minor Kretz, or his father in terms of
simile—of "as," "like," "seems"—reveals the distance the youth has fallen
away, has descended from his golden age. Consequently, Updike's epigraph for the book, from Karl Barth, creates an appropriate context for
the uses Peter makes of language, for Peter is that creature Barth
describes, "the creature on the boundary between heaven and earth,"
between the "creation inconceivable to man" and the "creation conceivable to him." The novel thus represents Peter's effort to recapture
through the lyricist's powers of language an image made resonant by his
father of the most felicitous time in his life.

## II

As a result of Peter's role in it and the attitude he brings, *The Centaur* belongs to that genre of lyrical expressions known as the elegiac. Larry E. Taylor has detailed many of the formal ways in which Updike has created a pastoral elegy. To begin with, Taylor suggests that the four interspersed short chapters—Chapters III, V, VIII, IX—help to generate the pastoral elegiac structure because each is a variation of a basic convention of the traditional form, both in its subject matter and in its language and imagery. "The language of these touchstone chapters," Taylor writes, "provides the lyricism and formality required to keep the novel from being ironic, satiric, and comic. Seen as a highly personal expression of both Updike's and Peter's sense of loss (Updike has left Shillington to become a writer for the *New Yorker,* and Peter is painting abstractions in a New York loft), *The Centaur* appeals to the impersonality of stock pastoral conventions as a vehicle for transforming life into art—the personal into the universal."[6] Drawing upon elements achieved by Milton in the *spirit* of the pastoral in an elegy such as *Lycidas,* Taylor outlines the parallels between the novel and the poem in subject matter.[7] But the limitations Taylor sets for himself will not allow him to get into the detailed analysis of those narrative and thematic patterns in the novel that relate directly to the more conventional elegiac elements. The most important such patterns are those associated with the elegy's concern with matters of eschatology, the "furthest things"—time, death, man's goal, or end, or *telos.*

One of the major concerns in *The Centaur* is with time. It is manifest in Peter's interest in the knowable historical past and the unknowable future. To know the past, Peter believes, is to know more about the present, so he is always fascinated by details of the lives of people he knows, whether details concern the more intimate relationships of a woman like Vera Hummel to various men or just the public triumph of one like Zimmerman on the Olinger track team. But even more than the past or the present Peter is concerned with and believes in the future. It is in the future that he believes his desires can be fulfilled. He knows, for example, that in the normal course of things, he will outlive Zimmerman, his father's viciously petty supervisor, so the future holds his dream: "Triumphantly, Peter feels descend upon him, his father's avenger, this advantage over the antagonist: he has more years to live. Ignorant and impotent here and now, in the dimension of the future he is mighty" (181). For Peter the future becomes his dimension, its airy spaces his natural element, as water is Deifendorf's: "The world of water was closed to me," he thinks, "so I had fallen in love with the air, which I was able to seize in great thrilling condensations within me that I labeled the Future: it was in this realm that I hoped to reward my father for his suffering" (83).

What, no doubt, Peter wishes to reward his father with is a reply to the question his father asks: it is a simple, but ultimate, question "what's the answer?" (168). Once he has inhabited his imagined future, however, Peter must admit that he is as impotent there as he was in the past to find "the answer." Neither his chosen form of artistic expression nor erotic attachment has given him answers to his eschatological questions. *Inside* his future he says:

> I glance around at the nest we have made, at the floorboards polished by our bare feet, at the *continents* of stain on the ceiling like an old and all-wrong *discoverer's map*, at the earnestly bloated canvases I conscientiously cover with great streaks *straining to say what even I am beginning to suspect is the unsayable thing*, and I grow frightened. I consider the Freudian half-Oriental sex-mysticism and I wonder, *Was it for this that my father gave up his life?* (201.

There are no empirical truths in eschatology, and while abstract expressionism and erotic mysticism may allow one to pursue his own personal answers, they will permit one only to say the thing to oneself, not to say the unsayable to another. The truths Peter may discover empirically and may relate concretely, rather than abstractly, lie in his experience. Experience itself can lead him to an appropriate art and a transcendent love, and the center of that experience is his relationship to his father.

Death is the furthest thing in man's experience, for it is the last final thing empirically he knows will happen to him. As most readers of *The Centaur* know, death is the primary concern of the novel, as it is the primary concern of most of Updike's work. The general theme is itself teleological, involving as it does man's end, his place in the universal scheme of things. This particular aspect of the eschatological, elegiac theme is exhaustively presented in the various cosmological systems the novel invokes. These systems are really "myths" of one sort or another. They appear in two groups, one broadly "scientific," the other broadly "humanistic." Among the scientific are the "myth" of biological evolution, the myths suggested by modern cosmological astronomy, and the mythic narrative of the oxygen cycle in nature; among the humanistic are the pastoral myths of the Greeks and the Christians.[8] Each of these myths represents an attempt by man to explain and/or to come to terms with the question of his own predestined end. In the elegiac *form* of the narrative we can see Peter review and discard the various "answers" until he discovers his own adequate answer in his myth of Art.

A *mythos* is a traditional story, and it is as a traditional *story* that George Caldwell tells to his class the history of biological evolution. He does it in terms of the "creation-clock" all of us have seen in one place or another. He begins with the estimated age of the universe, five billion years, speaks of various stars—the sun, Venus, Alpha Centauri, the Milky Way, the constellation Sagittarius—and of the hundred billion galaxies, each containing a hundred billion stars, numbers, in their unfathomableness, that remind Caldwell of death (34). Consequently, he says to his class, "Let's try to reduce five billion years to our size. Let's say the universe is three days old. Today is Thursday. . . . Last Monday at noon there was the greatest explosion there ever was. We're still riding on it" (34). This explosion, he tells his class, came five billion years ago from a "primeval egg," one cubic centimeter of which weighed two hundred and fifty tons. After a period of darkness and "the expanding flux of universal substance" (35), stars begin to shine, the Earth begins to form, and "for a whole day . . . , between Tuesday and Wednesday noon, the earth is barren. There is no life on it. Just ugly rocks, stale water, vomiting volcanoes, everything slithering and sliding and maybe freezing now and then as the sun like a dirty old light bulb flickered up there in the sky. By yesterday noon, a little life showed up. Nothing spectacular; just a little bit of slime. All yesterday afternoon, and most of the night, life remained microscopic" (35–36). With the advent of microscopic life, the evolutionary process accelerates rapidly. But Caldwell's concern, like every man's, lies in the relation of life to death. Thus, "the volvox of these early citizens in the kingdom of life, interests us because he invented death . . . by pioneering this new idea of *cooperation*, [the volvox] rolled life into the kingdom of certain—as opposed to accidental—death . . . It dies sacrificially, for the good of the whole, . . . the first altruists. The first do-gooders. If I had a hat on, I'd take it off to 'em" (37). The story of life goes very quickly now, from trilobites to the first vertebrate fishes, the first plants, the insects, the reptiles, and the mammals. Finally, at a point when Caldwell's "very blood loathed the story he had told, 'One minute ago, flint-chipping, fire-kindling, death-foreseeing, a tragic animal appeared . . . called Man' " (40).

In this now traditional story, man knows he is at the apex of a process that explains the fact of death. But knowledge can not reconcile this tragic animal to the death he foresees. Neither can the "humanistic values implicit in the physical sciences" Zimmerman speaks of in his report on Caldwell's lecture on the *mythos* of biological evolution. Caldwell's thought upon seeing the phrase is, "Maybe down deep in the atom there's a little man sitting in a rocking chair reading the evening paper" (87). Nor can the *mythos* of astronomy, the theory of the "big-bang" according to Hoyle. We discover astronomy's limitations when Peter imagines a universe falling through space as he watches snowflakes falling beneath a tall light:

> Directly under the light, the wavering fall of the particles is projected as an erratic oscillation, but away from the center, where the light rays strike obliquely, the projection parabolically magnifies the speed of the shadow as it hastens forward to meet its flake. The shadows stream out of infinity, slow, and, each darkly sharp in its last instant, vanish as their originals kiss the white plane . . . He turns scientist and dispassionately tries to locate in the cosmography his father has taught him an analogy

between the phenomenon he has observed and the "red shift" whereby the stars appear to be retreating at a speed proportional to their distance from us. Perhaps this is a kindred illusion, perhaps—he struggles to picture it—the stars are in fact falling gently through a cone of observation of which our earthly telescopes are the apex (191).

Peter can find a place from which to observe the relative motions of this snowflake galaxy, but that place in his imagined universe, "pinned, stretched, crucified like a butterfly upon a frame of unvarying geometrical truth," gives him a little security. Walking away from the light he seems "to arrive at a kind of edge where the speed of the shadows is infinite and a small universe both ends and does not end" (191). Thus the vision he has here of the universe as it is pictured by modern astronomy gives Peter little consolation. Only by returning his gaze to the concrete reality of the town can Peter overcome what he thinks of as the "sickly" nature of his "cosmic thoughts" (192).

The *mythos* of astronomy suggests to Peter a one-way process, of man and man's life disappearing into a nebulous "center," a cosmic black hole such as those only recently discovered by astronomers. Consequently, the *mythos* of the oxygen-cycle as it is seen in the formula,

$$C_6H_{12}O_6 + 6O_2 = 6CO_2 + 6H_2O + E,$$

may be somewhat more appeasing to one's imagination. The formula represents the creation of energy and thus, of life. As Caldwell explains to his class, " 'When this process stops'—he Xed through the equation—'*this* stops'—he double-Xed out the E—' and you become what they call dead. You become a worthless log of old chemicals" (142). But at least this process can be reversed. The equation can also be read backwards in order to represent the process of photosynthesis that occurs in plants: "that's the way the world goes round . . . Round and round, and where it stops, nobody knows" (143). The formula thus offers man an objective symbol for the *cyclic* process of death and renewal in nature. It *may* offer the illusion of death and renewal for man himself.

The *mythoi* of the Greeks and the Christians suggest that man as an individual can achieve the immortality once forsaken by that altruistic volvox. Moreover, these myths are more personal than the symbols for the organic process. They return human consciousness to the equations that science has formulated, and, at least potentially, they can express and contain the emotional impact of death. But for Peter, the Greek myths seem more germane than the Christian. Many critics read the novel as if it were a paean to the traditional church, yet Christianity in *The Centaur* offers little more than those myths of science. There really is not much to cling to in the doctrines expressed by its representative, the Reverend March. George comes to him troubled in mind and seeking "the answer" he has sought from others. "I can't make it add up," he says to March, "and I'd be grateful for your viewpoint." (188). George's own view, for example of the difference between Lutherans and Calvinists is, "the Lutherans say Jesus Christ is the only answer and the Calvinists say whatever happens to you, happens to you, is the answer" (188). The son of a minister, George also has a certain conception of Presbyterian doctrine: " . . . there are the elect and the non-elect, the ones that have it and the ones that don't, and the ones that don't have it are never going to get it. What I could never ram through my thick skull was why the ones that don't have it were created in the first place" (189). March's reply to these ideas is ministerial jargon about orthodoxy, Christocentrism, substantive Eucharistic transformation, and understanding the doctrine of predestination "as counterbalanced by the doctrine of God's infinite mercy" (189).

None of the Reverend March's answer is concrete enough for George to grasp. To George God's mercy itself is one of the furthest things, for it is "infinite at an infinite distance" from man as he lives his life. There is nothing either in the substance or the tone of what the Reverend says that will reconcile George to the death he lately has come to face. And there is nothing any more affirmative in the Christian cosmology the novel offers elsewhere, in a passage occurring just before the dialogue between Caldwell and the Reverend. The same snowstorm that gives Peter his cosmic thoughts enters into Updike's elaborate metaphor of Olinger as "yet one more Bethlehem. Behind a glowing window the infant God squalls. Out of zero all has come to birth. The panes, tinted by the straw of the crib within, hush its cries. The world goes on unhearing. The town of white roofs seems a colony of deserted temples; they feather together with distance and go gray, melt" (179). Whether it is only because the town does not listen or whether the infant is just one more rough beast, shuffling toward Bethlehem, such a vision can offer no consolation to one who has the thoughts besetting George Caldwell. Since they can not reconcile George, neither can they offer reconciliation to Peter Caldwell.

The Greek myths one sees in those interchapters offer much more to *The Centaur*. Their substance can be no more meaningful than the *mythoi* of evolution, astronomy, the oxygen cycle, or even Christianity. But the affective significance they bring to the novel gives them priority over all those others, for it is finally the emotional response to the fact of death that Peter's lyrical expression must contain. The Greek myths, more than the other *mythoi*, seem to express the archetypes that create the concrete patterns Updike favors and that Peter must eventually accept in his vision of Art. Carl Jung says that primitive man does not create his myths, he *experiences* them. In *The Centaur* it is the experiencing of Greek myth that we see, for these chapters (III, IX) more than any others are ones in which the world "resonant with metaphor" is achieved. Because Chiron *is* the centaur in these chapters, there is no distance between the mythic world man desires and the real world in which he resides. Consequently, when Chiron speaks to his students on "the Genesis of all things," there seems little in the story to make his blood sicken as Caldwell's does when he relates the *mythos* of evolution: "In the beginning," he says, "black-winged Night was courted by the wind, and laid a silver egg in the womb of Darkness. From this egg hatched Eros . . . And Love set the Universe in motion . . . Men lived without cares or labor . . . Death, to them, was no more terrible than sleep" (78).

Such a story, idyllic in both content and tone, can offer to Peter not only a symbolic narrative archetype that expresses in human terms the meaning of the oxygen cycle; it also offers a symbol to contain his feelings of love and goodwill toward his father. This archetype is connected to the themes of the pastoral elegy, but it also relates directly to the role of the scapegoat-dying god George Caldwell plays. It thus balances the waste-land against Arcadia, and in the formal pattern of the elegy, it joins Nature and human nature. Both father and son participate in the pattern because of their identifications with Nature itself. Each is related to the seasonal rhythm in some way: Peter's psoriasis, for instance, is a 'rhythmic curse that breathed in and out with [God's] seasons" (45); George's whole life—identified as it is with his birthdate near the winter solstice (just before Christmas, cf. 46)—and his role as the constellation Sagittarius seem interconnected with natural patterns. George himself, in relation to his son, becomes not just the "old man" Peter must replace or "trade in for" (71); he becomes "Old Man Winter's belly" (62, 147, 207, 209), that archetypal figure of the wasteland who holds life in bondage. But even as the Old Man or as Winter's belly, George can offer Peter hope. Although the "emasculate" Sky might leave "his progeny to parch upon a white waste," George can think: "Yet even in the dead of winter the sere twigs prepare their small dull buds. In the pit of the year a king was born. Not a leaf falls but leaves an amber root, a dainty hoof, a fleck of baggage to be unpacked in future time" (219). The hope George can leave Peter is finally to be found in Nature itself.

### III

The Greek myths allows Peter to discover the one *mythos* which is appropriate for him. That is *art* as an eschatology, as a way of expressing and containing those furthest things that trouble man. Peter's grandfather Caldwell had religion, his father had science, and Peter—the end of the classic decline from priest, to teacher, to artist—has Art. To Peter, Art, "however clumsy and quaint and mistaken," can radiate "the innocence and hope, the hope of seizing something and holding it fast, that enters whenever a brush touches canvas" (199). The paintings of Vermeer provide him with manifestations of that hope. They become, he says, "the Holy Ghost" of his adolescence: "that these paintings, which I had worshipped in reproduction, had a simple physical existence seemed a profound mystery to me: to come within touching distance of their surfaces, to see with my own eyes the truth of their color, the tracery of the cracks whereby time had inserted itself like a mystery within a mystery, would have been for me to enter a Real Presence so ultimate I would not be surprised to die in the encounter" (68). It becomes Peter's dream to be able to create in the profound way of a Vermeer. Eventually, Peter has a revelation as to how he too can create art's mystery within a mystery. He says, "I must go to Nature disarmed of perspective and stretch myself like a large transparent canvas upon her in the hope that, my submission being perfect, the imprint of a beautiful and useful truth would be taken" (218). It is a recognition that bears out Vargo's explanation of the connection of Updike's novel to Karl Barth's philosophy: "Man exists not on the boundary between God and creation, but on a boundary within creation itself: between the *visibilia et invisibilia*, the conceivable and inconceivable, the humanly attainable and the humanly transcendent" (454). The impact of *The Centaur* suggests that, in effect, Peter Caldwell has submitted himself to the attainable facts of his father's human life. The son may have been in his vocation only a second rate abstract expressionist painter, but in his avocation he has become a first rate representational artist, who, in the verbal contours of Greek pastoral elegiac myth, has sketched a beautiful and useful and transcendent truth.

Peter creates a beautiful and transcendent truth, but it is useful because it is also experiential. It is on this point that one must finally take issue with Vargo's fine essay on *The Centaur*. There are several problems one must point out. The first is simply that he stresses too much the form of the novel as rite or ritual. To the extent that it is formalized as a *thing done* the novel may constitute a ritual action, but in that case every work, every poem, becomes a rite since all can be defined as symbolic actions. Consequently, in this case, "rite" is clearly less useful a term than "myth," for myth suggests better than rite the verbal, the imaginary, dreamlike quality of the work and its locus in a mind. The critical superiority of myth becomes clear when Vargo states that "The chief function of ritual in this novel . . . is to serve as an action against death" (458). But the novel, instead, is no imagining of an action; it is an imagining of an imagining, an introjection, an emotional assimilation of the fact of death. The novel seems far less a rite than a cry, an utterance, an expression of love, grief, and consolation. A second problem is that even myth proves less useful as a means for understanding the novel when Vargo suggests the order by which meaning is attributed to it. Vargo writes, "By its transformation of a particular situation into a paradigm, myth makes rite dynamic and meaningful. Without it, ritual is an empty shell" (459). The movement of the novel, however, suggests that the basic, meaningful term is neither rite nor myth, but *experience*. Rite cannot give meaning to experience, nor can myth, but experience can infuse and give substance to rite and myth. To make myth primary is to discount the concrete fact of

George Caldwell in Peter's experience. For Peter, as, apparently, for Up-dike, existence precedes essence, the flesh precedes the world, and it is Peter's imagining of his father's life and death that makes possible the sacral univeral of which Vargo speaks and through which man can make contact with God. Art is finally the only answer to the eschatological questions Peter raises. Aesthetics becomes the eschatology. It is finally the Art of Peter's expression that transmutes experience and creates—as perhaps by definition, every new work of art must—a new myth for his time.

*The Centaur* is an elegy, not upon the death of a friend, a leader, or a god, but upon the death, real or imagined, of a man's father. As a lyrical expression of grief and love, this novel comes close to the spirit of a poem like e.e. cummings' "my father moved through dooms of love."[9] Like cummings' poem, Peter's is a celebration of a father's life, an act of atone-ment for the suffering that the father endures in his life. cummings' poem says his father has moved through conformity ("sames of am"), selfishness ("haves of give"), indifference ("dooms of feel"), and alienation ("theys of we"); Peter's says his father has moved through "Waste, rot, hollowness, noise, stench, death," "the many visages which this central thing wears" (188). But cummings' poem concludes with the kind of affirmation that seems possible to a man in the face of that furthest thing known as death:

> because my father lived his soul
> love is the whole and more than all

Peter's elegiac expression comes to a similar conclusion, and it comes directly out of his own and his father's experience. Knowing now he is not going to die momentarily from the cancer he had feared, George Caldwell feels at the end "that in giving his life to others he entered a total free-dom." As if this revelation also allows him to regain the innocent world of total, resonant metaphor, George is then cast as a mediator, as a meeting place wherein the forces of life can regenerate themselves: "Mt. Ide and Mt. Dikte from opposite blue distances rushed toward him like clapping waves and in the upright of his body Sky and Gaia mated again" (220). In his body, that grotesque medium formed from man and beast, the waste-land he might have bequeathed to his son is revivified. And the beautiful, useful, transcendent truth of Peter's art is revealed: "Only goodness lives. But it does live" (220). The most satisfying of the beauties of this truth, coming as it does from a celebration of a son's love for his father, is the fact that it is the *father's* father, George's father, who evokes it in the first place. The novel suggests not the Biblical notion that the *sins* of the fathers are visited upon the sons, but the more benevolent idea that it is the wisdom of the fathers that is passed along. The novel's form thus con-tradicts George Caldwell's repeated mutterings about his inheritance only of "a Bible and a deskful of debts." It clearly contradicts his feeling that he will pass on to Peter only a message of despair. The elegiac form Peter creates finally expresses more than a son's personal feeling; it expresses a reverence for life and a faith in the continuity of the human spirit. All this is what the novel as lyric elegy can achieve—does indeed fully achieve in *The Centaur.*

## Notes

1. Arthur Mizener, "The American Hero as High-School Boy: Peter Caldwell," in *The Sense of Life in the Modern Novel* (Boston: Houghton Mifflin, 1964), 265–266; Bryant Wyatt, "John Updike: The Psychological Novel in Search of Structure," *Twentieth Century Literature*, XIII (July 1967), 93–94; and David Myers, "The Questing Fear: Christian Allegory in John Updike's *The Centaur*," *Twentieth Century Literature*, XVII: 2 (April 1971), 73–82.

2. "The Necessity of Myth in Updike's *The Centaur*," *PLMA*, 83:3 (May 1973), 453. Vargo's essay is included in his fine study: *Rainstorms and Fire: Ritual in the Novels of John Updike* (Port Washington, N.Y.: Kennikat Press, 1973). Two other excellent recent studies of *The Centaur* are contained in Joyce B. Markle's *Fighters and Lovers: Theme in the Novels of John Updike* (New York: New York University Press, 1973), and John B. Vickery's *The Centaur*: Myth, History, and Narrative," *Modern Fiction Studies*, 20:1 (Spring 1974), 29–43.

3. Hart Crane, *The Bridge* (Garden City, N.Y.: Doubleday and Company, 1958), 11.

4. John Updike, *The Centaur* (Greenwich, Conn.: Fawcett Publications, Inc., 1964), 40. Further references to the novel will be cited by page numbers within parentheses in the text.

5. Mizener, 266, 262.

6. Larry E. Taylor, *Pastoral and Anti-Pastoral Patterns in John Updike's Fiction* (Carbondale, Ill.: Southern Illinos University Press, 1971), 90.

7. Here is Taylor's sketch of the parallels:

1. Chapter 1, only five pages long, shows the pastoral hero Chiron involved in his daily tasks of teaching the children of the gods in Arcadian groves. Idyllic in the strictest sense, the passage includes a conventional catalogue of flowers and herbs and celebrates the tranquility and beauty of the hero as he was in life. Roughly, it corresponds to lines 25–36 of *Lycidas.*
2. Chapter 5, four pages long, is a newspaper obituary, giving a coldly factual account of Caldwell's life. It suggests the conventional expression of communal grief. It is the elegiac announcement of death, roughly comparable to the flat shock value of the fact, "For Lycidas is dead, dead ere his prime," lines 10 and following of *Lycidas.*
3. Chapter 8 (the first four pages), is the expression of Peter's personal grief for the loss of the pastoral hero. Here Peter-Prometheus sings his lament to his Negro mistress. He questions the meaning of his father's death in a version of the elegiac interrogation of the universe, roughly analagous to lines 50–85 of *Lycidas.*
4. Chapter 9, four pages long, is a consolation and reconciliation, an account of the Centaur's acceptance of death, and his son's reconciliation to it. The short epilogue is an account of the Centaur's apotheosis as a star. Roughly, it corresponds to lines 165–93 of *Lycidas* (89–90).

8. Vargo speaks (456) of two other myths—one of "the City" and one of the Future (of which I have already spoken), but neither has quite the dynamic etiological quality these other "myths" possess; indeed, the Future is *the problem*, not the answer, as Peter realizes.

9. e. e. cummings, *e. e. cummings: A selection of Poems*, with an Introduction by Horace Gregory (New York: Harcourt, Brace & World, 1965), 119–121.

# The Poorhouse Fair:
# Updike's Thesis Statement

George J. Searles*

Along with many other current writers, John Updike sees in contemporary America a widespread loss of moral fortitude, a pervasive spiritual laxity that finds expression in cultural vulgarity and a clutchingly materialistic value system. His works consistently portray confused, unfulfilled characters bereft of the emotional psychological resources that sustained earlier generations; repeatedly, he juxtaposes unsettling images of the present with lyrical evocations of the American past. In *Couples* and the other "marriage" fictions, in the "Rabbit" novels, in *A Month of Sundays*, and certainly in the recent *The Coup*, social disintegration is clearly associated with the breakdown—or distortion—of traditional values. Perhaps nowhere is this cental motif more explicitly presented, however, than in his first novel. A much underrated book, *The Poorhouse Fair* is important both as an impressive novel in its own right and as a harbinger of Updike's subsequent works.

Mistakenly, several critics have claimed that *The Poorhouse Fair* is uncharacteristic of its author. Granville Hicks, for example, has compared it to Herbert Gold's first novel (*Birth of a Hero*) and to Bernard Malamud's (*The Natural*) in that context.[1] But if certain features of the work are indeed unique in Updike's corpus—e.g., the prominence of very elderly characters, and its futuristic, prognosticative nature—in its essential concerns the novel is fully consistent with the bulk of Updike's other work. *The Poorhouse Fair* squarely addresses the selfsame issues that have continued to interest Updike throughout his career: the past as a source of strength, the importance of religious faith, the primacy of the individual, and the essential emptiness that seems to be descending upon the American spirit.

In addition, the novel draws more on autobiography than may be initially apparent, and in so doing is similar to much of Updike's other material, especially the "Olinger" fictions. He has explained that "They were tearing the poorhouse down at Shillington and I went up to look at the shell. My grandfather, who is somewhat like John Hook . . . was

*This essay was written specifically for this volume and appears here for the first time by permission of the author.

231

recently dead, and so the idea of some kind of memorial gesture, embodying what seems to have been on my part a very strong sense of national decay, crystallised in this novel."[2] In its method, as well, the book is less anomalous than has been suggested. Although it is in the tradition of anti-utopian literature, and projects approximately fifteen years into the future,[3] it avoids the science-fiction overtones that so often permeate futuristic fiction, remaining steadfastly realistic. And its shifting narrative perspective anticipates similar handlings of point of view in later works such as *Rabbit, Run, The Centaur, Couples,* and *The Coup.*

Although 94-year-old John Hook is the nominal protagonist, *The Poorhouse Fair* is Updike's *Vanity Fair,* "a novel without a hero." It centers not really on the doings of any one character, but on a clash between two opposed views of life, two antithetical perspectives personified by Hook and Stephen Conner, the poorhouse prefect. In the envisioned future, international diplomacy has eliminated the threat of global war, while humanistic socialism has apparently solved all or most of America's domestic problems: life expectancy has been increased, poverty has been eliminated, racial conflict has been resolved, and population distribution and other ostensible advances have been achieved. Surely, however, Updike intends to convey here not a vision of utopian harmony, but of a world in which social "progress" has created instead a sterile, homogenized wasteland, a dehumanized environment productive only of bureaucratized ennui. Despite the social gains that have been made, other, obviously destructive developments have also taken place. The family, the basic social unit, has been abandoned, as has religion. Conner's vision is of "man living healthy and unafraid beneath blank skies"[4] similar to the "empty" sky described at the conclusion of *Couples.*[5] Having "lost all sense of omen" (p. 14), he becomes "infected with the repose . . . only suitable to inmates waiting out their days" (p. 66), because "the modern world afforded few opportunities for zeal anywhere" (p. 64). Updike provides a great many such indications that Conner's world is a devitalized void, stripped of all human meaning. When Hook laments that "This last decade has witnessed the end of the world" (p. 152) and anticipates Updike's BBC interview by saying "There is little store of virtue left" (p. 160), there can be no doubt that he is speaking for the author.[6]

Conner's well-intentioned but hollow (because godless) scientific humanism is juxtaposed with the simple religious faith of John Hook, *de facto* spokes-person both for the residents of the poorhouse and for an earlier, Christocentric value system. He realizes that Conner's dream of an earthly paradise is a delusion, for he believes (as Conner does not) that human life resists artificial regimentation, partaking of a divinely ordained disorder that rationalism is powerless to dispel, and which is linked to an innate need for difference, variation, and individuality. In short, Conner's world is deadeningly entropic, there being "no new cause for heterogeneity" (p. 65). Hook gently rebukes Conner for his compulsive orderliness, an almost neurotic need to structure and categorize, when he gibes, "I have sometimes thought, had you and your kind arranged the stars, you would have set them geometrically, or had them spell a thought-provoking sentence" (p. 114). He is more direct, however, in responding to Conner's avowed atheism. "There is no goodness, without belief," he admonishes the prefect, "There is nothing but busyness" (p. 116). Updike's strategy of contrasting two opposed characters—one an advocate of the spiritual, and the other an avatar of the pragmatic—is a device that appears elsewhere throughout his canon. These oppositions are always introduced for the same purpose: to suggest that the spiritual transcends the pragmatic, rendering it quite secondary in human affairs.

This is the very fact that Conner has so obviously failed to grasp. Obsessed with the practical, he is blind to the less immediately measurable aspects of life. Indeed, it is primarily this shortcoming that renders him inferior, in the eyes of the residents, to the former prefect. Although a flawed administrator and a semi-alcoholic, Mendelssohn had fulfilled the old people's need for ritual, leading them in hymns and prayers as a preparation for death. This detail is among the novel's many verbal ironies: Conner, supposedly a lover of music, cannot appreciate "Mendelssohn's" essential spirituality,[7] and never speaks to the residents of suffering or death, except with despairing distaste. The aged men and women of the poorhouse, however, feel otherwise. The symbolically named Amy Mortis ("friend of death") gives Conner's utopian rhapsodizing short shrift, advising him, "You expect us to give up the old ways, and make this place a little copy of the world outside, the way it's going. I don't say you don't mean well, but it won't do" (p. 43). Conner is morbidly "concerned about physical death . . . and has failed to consider the death of depersonalization, which is the real threat. The death the inmates fear . . . is spiritual death—loss of the vision of their significance."[8]

In his finicky infatuation with order and regularity, Conner imagines that affixing name tags to the residents' chairs will provide them with a "sense of ownership" (p. 19), but of course the response is one of offended dignity, for the aged inmates regard the arrangement as an attempt to control and legislate their movements. The feisty Billy Gregg, for example, likens the chair labeling to "branding f.ing cattle" (p. 11). This issue provides the novel with its opening vignette. Significantly, this introductory scene focuses on George Lucas, Gregg, and Hook, who are elsewhere described as the "man of flesh, the man of passion, and the man of thought" (p. 184), and thereby signify the three components of the Aristotelian anima.[9] The book's central opposition—that between the spiritual and the corporal—is thus symbolically encapsulated even in the first scene, as the trio voice their opposition to Conner. And the book's climactic moment, the "stoning" of Conner, is another effective symbolic rendering of this essential conflict. In a gesture of spontaneous, child-like self-assertion, some of the inmates fling stones at the astonished prefect, a seemingly gratuitous action actually motivated by their pent-up frustration at having been subjected to the demeaning impersonality and soulless rationalism of Conner's administration. Hook, who has not participated in the attack, explains it to the prefect by admonishing him that "Boredom is a ter-rible force" (p. 135), alluding, of course, to the inevitable dreariness that will result when the spirit is denied, a boredom from which Conner himself suffers.

In the stoning episode, Updike draws upon the legend of St. Stephen, the first Christian martyr (who was stoned to death), as Stephen Conner is symbolically "martyred" for his new "religion" of godless pragmatism. Updike has alluded to the St. Stephen connection,[10] and Conner himself earlier mentions that "he envied the first rationalists their martyrdoms" (p. 65). By inversion, the Christian inmates assume the role of St. Stephen's pagan antagonists, a reversal that is in keeping with the distorted world view of the society portrayed in the novel, and which recalls Huxley's anti-utopian *Brave New World*, in which the only truly "civilized" character is known as "The Savage." The stoning is additionally congruent in that it symbolizes the irrepressible spirit of individualistic self-assertion, an impulse that will survive even under the most repressive conditions.

Indeed, the fair itself serves much the same function, for by its very nature a fair is a festive, sportive occasion, generative of spontaneity and freedom of action. As in Charles G. Finney's neglected 1935 fantasy, *The Circus of Dr. Lao*, the carnival atmosphere provides a context in which fundamental truths about the human condition are revealed, just as certain works by Barth and Burroughs employ similar metaphors—the funhouse, the circus—that embody the counter-entropic spirit. It is hardly surprising, then, that Conner and his rather cold, almost android-like young assistant, Buddy, whose "mechanical generation had never learned how to laugh" (p. 122), do not understand the fair's importance. "What do these people want a holiday for, every day is a holiday for them" (p. 55), Buddy complains, totally blind to the event's significance.

Perhaps the most important feature of the fair, however, is that in its fundamental purpose—the peddling of the old folks' handicrafts—there is an inherent emphasis upon individuality and personal creativity and uniqueness. Amy Mortis's patchwork quilts, for example, or Tommy Franklin's ostensibly useless peach pit sculptures, are expressions of an innately human impulse: the projection of individual personality. These hand-crafted articles feed "a keen subversive need, at least in the cities, for objects that showed the trace of a hand, whether in an irregular seam, the crescent cuts of a chisel, or the dents of a forge hammer" (p. 145). An antique dealer who yearly visits the fair "had discovered that in this age there existed a hungry market for anything—trivets, samplers, whalebone swifts, buttonhooks, dragware, Staffordshire hens, bleeding knives, mechanical apple parers, ferrotypes, weathervanes—savouring of an old America" (p. 145). The handicrafts, like the old people themselves, are a link to the lost past.

In "The Happiest I've Been," an early Updike story, the young protagonist remarks that the principal tie between him and his best friend is that they both "lived with grandparents," and goes on to comment on the importance of this shared experience: "This improved both our backward and forward vistas . . . we had a sense of childhoods before 1900, when the farmer ruled the land and America faced west. We had gained a humane dimension that made us gentle and humorous."[11] This, of course, is why Updike centers his novel around the aged wards. Although initially they appear cranky and eccentric, in their embodiment of a strong-willed, intrinsically American sense of inviolable individuality, they personify the forgotten American heritage, a legacy of personal dignity and pride, which in the world of the novel has been entirely forfeited to material progress and bureaucratic efficiency. Although they are physically enfeebled, the old people clearly possess a strength of character that is lacking in the people who visit the fair from the outside:

> Heart had gone out of these people; health was the principal thing about the faces of the Americans that came crowding through the broken wall to the poorhouse fair. . . . History had passed on beyond them. They remembered its moment and came to the fair to be freshened in the recollection of an older America. . . . There was to be no war; we were to be allowed to decay of ourselves. And the population soared like diffident India's, and the economy swelled, and iron became increasingly dilute, and houses more niggardly built, and everywhere was sufferance, good sense, wealth, irreligion, and peace. The nation became one of pleasure-seekers; the people continued to live as cells of a body do in the coffin, for the conception "America" had died in their skulls. (pp. 158–159)

Hook (whose name might imply a sort of "connection" or "link"), with his extensive knowledge of classical and American history, is the personification of continuity. The novel's clear implication is that for America to survive, the old and the new must integrate, as in the context of the fair, where the elderly and the young, past and present, commingle. But the novel's mood is ultimately foreboding; even at the fair, the outsiders seek to exploit the oldtimers, and in any event the fair is but a once-a-year occurrence. Moreover, the novel ends with typical Updikean reservation, for Hook is unable to formulate the valedictory message that he feels he must somehow convey, before he dies, to Conner: "He stood motionless, half in moonlight, groping after the fitful shadow of the advice he must impart to Conner, as a bond between them and a testament to endure his dying in the world. What was it?" (p. 185)

Although *The Poorhouse Fair* falters in spots, particularly with regard to its somewhat inaccurate "historical" details, it remains a powerful and highly skillful rendering of a theme that is perhaps even more relevant now than when the book was written. Indeed, Updike's "most general predictions [have] come to pass: the collapse of public morale and the spiritual reduction of the whole country to a 'poorhouse.' "[12] As an articulation of Updike's belief in the importance of traditional American values as a stay against chaos, *The Poorhouse Fair* can be seen almost as a thesis statement, a staking out of territory that Updike has continued to explore throughout his prolific career. As such, this novel is the necessary starting point for any comprehensive study of his *oeuvre*.

## Notes

1. Granville Hicks, "Generations of the Fifties: Malamud, Gold, and Updike," in Nona Balakian and Charles Simmons, eds., *The Creative Present* (New York: Doubleday, 1963), p. 233.

2. Eric Rhode, "BBC Interview with John Updike," *The Listener*, 81 (June 19, 1969), 862. Like Hook, Updike's grandfather was a former schoolteacher and lived into his nineties.

3. This dating is not exact; on p. 84 of the novel, we learn that the St. Lawrence Seaway (which was completed in 1959) is "less than a year away from its crystal anniversary."

4. John Updike, *The Poorhouse Fair* (New York: Alfred A. Knopf, 1959), p. 65. Subsequent references are to this edition, and are cited paranthetically in the text.

5. John Updike, *Couples* (New York: Alfred A. Knopf, 1968), p. 457.

6. In that interview, Updike told Eric Rhode, "I do feel that . . . there has been a . . . loss of the sense of righteousness" (Rhode, p. 863), and has voiced similar sentiments elsewhere.

7. Devotional music was among the fortes of the eminent German composer Felix Mendelssohn. He was the first to perform Bach's *Passion According to St. Matthew*, for example, after Bach's death. Significantly, his philosopher grandfather, Moses Mendelssohn, was (with his associate, Lessing) a steadfast defender of religious tolerance.

8. Joyce B. Markle, *Fighters and Lovers: Theme in the Novels of John Updike* (New York: New York University Press, 1973), p. 15.

9. Alice and Kenneth Hamilton, *The Elements of John Updike* (Grand Rapids: William B. Eerdman's, 1970), p. 133.

10. Charles Thomas Samuels, "The Art of Fiction XLIII: John Updike," interview, *Paris Review* 12 (Winter, 1968), 104.

11. John Updike, "The Happiest I've Been," *The Same Door* (New York: Alfred A. Knopf, 1959), p. 223.

12. Anatole Broyard, "Twenty Eight Stories and Two Novels," review of *The Poorhouse Fair*, by John Updike, *The New York Times Book Review*, 17 April 1977, p. 12.

# *Rabbit Redux:* "Freedom is Made of Brambles"

Gordon E. Slethaug*

When *Rabbit Redux* was published in 1971, it appeared in a red, gray, and blue striped dust jacket, a design graphically illustrative of the book's concern for the American way of life, and the gray itself a nicely ironic touch, perhaps suggesting America's lack of purity and purpose. John Updike alludes directly to his intention for this book in a fictional interview with Henry Bech (the main character of *Bech: A Book*), first appearing in *The New York Times Book Review*. Asks Bech, here apparently the voice of Updike himself: "Didn't I detect . . . in . . . [your] later work, an almost blunt determination to, as it were, sing America?"[1]

Assisted by the provocative dust jacket and Updike's broad hint at a legitimate interpretation, critics have tended to focus on the question of America in the book, including such aspects as the American dream and its loss, Viet Nam, the history of American black-white relationships, and the first moon shot. Joyce B. Markle states that "Rabbit, indeed, is the dreamer of the American dream . . . ," and Wayne Falke says that " . . . it *is* America that *Rabbit Redux* is about."[2] Falke, however, notes the possible objection to this, yet another American novel treating the American dream: "It is surprising perhaps to find so talented a writer apparently dealing with the tiredest of clichés, . . . the fall from innocence, the failure of the American dream . . . , and . . . the connections which should link the individual to a society and to a cosmic scheme in oneness and harmony."[3]

Despite the critics' emphasis on America and the American dream in *Rabbit Redux*, they overlook Updike's treatment of the theme of freedom. The book depicts three months in the lives of the four characters—Janice, Jill, Skeeter, and Rabbit—who are all seeking some kind of freedom and whose mutually interlocking searches are seen primarily through the eyes of Harry (Rabbit) Angstrom.[4] His initial leap towards freedom in *Rabbit, Run* begins like a pebble dropped in the water, a tight circle concentrated around his own character, and then expands outward to include and involve his family, representatives of his cultural milieu, and finally the

*This essay was written specifically for this volume and appears here for the first time by permission of the author.

nation as a whole.[5] The book is primarily an exploration of the effects of personal freedom from established moral, social and legal conventions; it is secondarily a consideration of how that concept of freedom underlies national beliefs and values that are at least partially detrimental both to the United States and foreign countries.

Janice's quest for freedom is perhaps the book's most important, structurally. Her taking a lover, Charlie Stavros, and leaving Rabbit accounts for Rabbit's sustained depression and ennui within *Rabbit Redux*, as events and persons flow past him without his being able to absorb their implications or act on them. For Janice this leap to freedom is absolutely necessary for survival. Because she accidentally drowned her infant daughter, Becky, ten years before, she feels intense guilt and believes herself to have the touch of death. Rabbit has not helped her overcome this guilt, but rather reinforces it, by usually refusing to sleep with her on the pretext of not wishing to have another child. He has allowed her little satisfaction or feeling of human dignity: from him she receives no love or sexual satisfaction and is made to feel mentally inferior by his constant attempts to humiliate her.

Her affair with Charlie puts all of her dissatisfaction in perspective and makes her feel renewed, made over, and fulfilled—sexually, emotionally, and even mentally: "This love that has blown through her has been a miracle. . . ."[6] In Charlie's eyes, Janice is an angel, "a tiger," the wild mistress of his bed, confidante of his thoughts on sex, love, family life, politics, and even Rabbit; and Rabbit hears echoes in Janice's conversations of Charlie's speech. With Charlie, Janice ripens into a happy sensuous woman, capable of sexual vitality, affectionate love, and intellectual depth. For Rabbit, until Janice returns from her affair, she is boring and stupid, in short a "dumb bitch" (p. 64), an assessment which shows his fundamental inability to perceive the inherent strengths of those who should be closest to him.

Janice's is an intensely personal act of liberation, meant to free her from Rabbit's oppressive spirit and her own guilt, but her act goes far beyond what she envisions. She had no intention of leaving Rabit, but rather expected him to be outraged, fighting to keep his marriage intact and his wife in his own bed. When he fails to be outraged and merely recommends that Janice continue her affair, she does not know how to play this game. Even as she has broken the rules of marital fidelity, so Rabbit breaks faith with her expectations, partially because her affair so disconcerts and hurts him that he creates a shell around himself to keep him from feeling and suffering more. In leaving, she gives up her safe, comfortable world and later believes that she destroys her husband and dishonors her parents (p. 383); ironically she also sets up her lover for a heart attack. Janice comes to understand that once working agreements, rules, or social expectations—however arbitrary—have been violated, they can not be easily and meaningfully reinstated.

As in Janice's, Jill's quest for freedom is presented as necessary for her survival. A spoiled child of the very rich, she has been given much—sailboats, expensive schooling, her own white Porsche—but she is nevertheless emotionally deprived. Because her father, who doted on her and gave her lavish gifts as seals of his affection, dies, Jill is left with an enormous vacuum in her life: she has no one to love her. Too busy with her own affairs of the heart, her mother will not fill the void. Nor will Freddy, the one boy who Jill comes to love, because his only interest is tripping on drugs and seeing that Jill does too; he wants her to be as "free" or as "trapped" as he. She becomes free to be caged by someone else's ego-trip. So run Jill must—" 'Let freedom ring' ", she says (p. 128)—, away from the centre of pain, her mother's lack of love and the frightful consequences of drug addiction.

While her escape into freedom does not pose precisely the same destructive possibilities for her immediate family as Janice's does for Rabbit, she nonetheless finds that such an escape may personally be more harmful than beneficial. Her subconscious hope that Rabbit will take care of her, be a surrogate father (for example she once confusedly calls him "Daddy" [p. 256]), is dashed because he is so emotionally crippled and narcissistic that he is unable to reach out and love her in any capacity, whether as lover, sugar daddy, or father. She can not ease Rabbit's pain or break down the barriers he builds around himself; no matter what tricks or techniques she uses in love-making, and she tries them all, Rabbit is still self-contained, and Jill is left unloved, unprotected, and vulnerable.

As a girl on the run, a flower child, a hippie, she is easy prey for anyone, a Buchanan, a Rabbit, an Ollie, or a Skeeter. "Sold" to Rabbit (he pays Buchanan $20), she wins no love from him; Skeeter virtually rapes her, keeps her in bondage, and reduces her to a mere cipher, for to him she is just another cunt whose drug hallucinations will possibly give him evidence of his sought-after divinity; and Ollie apparently takes her for a few pieces of sheet music. Skeeter sarcastically remarks: " 'There's no dirt made that cunt won't swallow. With a smile on her face, right? Because she's *clean*' " (p. 122). This negative assessment of her and her own view of herself simply do not mesh, because she does not perceive herself clearly. It seems that at some point in her youth, perhaps her father's death, she has stopped facing reality: she conceives of herself as pure and untouched and nothing she does, however unclean, alters that view. So out of touch with reality is she that she does not recognize that freedom from her family in Stonington, Connecticut means bondage in Brewer, Pennsylvania.

Jill is truly the saddest case in the book, for although she tries to cleanse and empty herself, to share her love, that love is never properly received or reciprocated by an adult. Only Nelson in his childlike innocence sympathizes with and loves her, but even he can not prevent her self-destructive tendencies, continual debasement, and inevitable death. Pale, dressed in white, associated with the moon (pp. 202, 297, 380), she is too sensitive and delicate, too ethereal and other-worldly, too much a fairy child and out of touch with reality to live in Penn Villas. Consequently she is sacrificed, victimized by Skeeter, Rabbit, and the community. For her, only death can bring freedom, and ironically it is only her death which begins to straighten out Rabbit. Only when dead can her loss begin to bring the restoration and healing to him that she sought in life. And she does after all bring a message of love (and perhaps forgiveness) to Rabbit in his dreams.

Skeeter's bid for freedom has a significantly different quality than Janice's or Jill's. While Janice hopes to escape emotional deadness and Jill tries to flee both the emotional vacuum and drug addiction, Skeeter tries to run from his memories of Viet Nam, to keep free of the law, and to create confusion. Arrested and on parole for possessing and pushing drugs, he lives outside the accepted framework of law and order. Being a black, he argues, has put him outside conventional social frames of reference, for laws in these "Benighted States" exist basically to protect the property and rights of wealthy whites; the poor and the blue collar worker, black and white, are exploited to enhance the wealth of the already wealthy. The only time, in his recollection, that this caste system has not applied was in Viet Nam where white died for black and black for white, regardless of property or class. Skeeter tries to erase such positive recollections of Viet Nam, because they go contrary to his views on American discrimination.

Since he is invisible and has no identity within the context of American society, it is fitting that he has no known name: Rabbit knows him only as Skeeter and thinks his last name might be Farnsworth, but the police have still other names for him, with the real possibility that none of the names is right. To have no name might make one truly free and unfettered, but Skeeter knows that he is more slave than freeman because the laws that exist to protect the property-owning whites are aimed at him. (Given the red, gray, and blue dust jacket of the book, it is a nice bit of irony that Skeeter reads a book called "Slavery; the letters are red, white, and blue" [p. 242].) He sees himself as wrongfully discriminated against by those laws, consequently absolving him from any responsibility or guilt for the failure or success of that system. No matter what he does—peddle dope, shoot Jill full of drugs and let her die in the fire, participate in a riot, subvert the government through whatever means—he can not be blamed, for he is simply acting out the irresponsible role that society designates for him. If society has set him adrift in the first place, then he owes no allegiance to that society, and stands outside space and time, simultaneously free and slave.

Held by no law, he considers himself the black Christ, heralding a new age of peace which will arise Phoenix-like out of the ashes of the old order which is disintegrating daily. Whereas Rabbit has difficulty reconciling the real world with something that is truly extraordinary, miraculous and divine (" 'But all this fucking, everybody fucking, I don't know, it just makes me too sad. It's what makes everything so hard to run. . . . There must be something else' " [pp. 397–398]), Skeeter sees his new role as the logical extension of cosmic reality. His personal destiny is explained by a quasi-transcendental correspondence theory, positing that the individual's life reflects society's which in turn reflects the cosmic. So Skeeter's view of himself fits squarely his concept of creation, one that in a metaphysical way permits him to disregard all boundaries or limits, for in order for him/the cosmos to emerge from the centre of confusion, he/it must resist given laws and normal patterns of action in order to function in the role of the creator. Viet Nam is necessary for "It is where God is pushing through. . . . Chaos is his holy face" (p. 261). Skeeter must destroy the old, help it blow up, to assist in the creation of the new, the future great calm.

Destroy he does. His presence in the white neighborhood directly causes the burning of Rabbit's house; he can be held accountable for the death of Jill, insofar as he runs away from her in the burning house; and he is also responsible for helping to erode Rabbit's mental and emotional stability, although admittedly he has a positive influence on Rabbit insofar as he helps him put his bigoted ideas about America into better perspective. Even so, he can not be said to succeed in his function as destroyer of the old order and messiah of the new, for in the last moments of the book, he is seen as a small-time punk, a secondary link in dope peddling, watched by the police, and set afoot on a small highway leading away from Brewer. And as Rabbit is released from his passivity and virtual dependency on Jill and Skeeter, he begins the slow and painful process of repairing his life along the lines of the old order, not Skeeter's new messianic one. Skeeter's quest for freedom has interfered with the rights and lives of others, has done irreparable damage at least to Jill, and has not obtained the personal blessings he had planned.

Although Rabbit has himself made an active bid for freedom in *Rabbit, Run*, in *Rabbit Redux* he is acted upon, for the most part the passive recipient and nexus of the quests for freedom by Janice, Jill, and Skeeter. Together these two books and separate roles of Rabbit fully explore reasons for and effects of the quest for personal freedom and self-liberation without proper personal responsibility.

The issue of freedom in *Rabbit, Run* begins when Rabbit abandons Janice and Nelson in order to seek a life corresponding with some ill-defined vision of bliss. Disliking Janice's perpetual sloppiness and ennui and her addiction to television and alcohol, tired of a crying, bothersome child, fed up with a close, poorly furnished, dirty apartment, and mildly discontented with his job as a MagiPeel salesman, Rabbit lights out, at first heading "south, down, down the map into orange groves and smoking rivers and barefoot women",[7] then discovering that he has no purpose, direction, or final goal. His flight is purely instinctual, action without thought. The abortive journey and subsequent realization that he had neither a specific goal nor a road map function as appropriate metaphors for his own moral dilemma, his abandonment of familial and societal responsibilities without a specific alternative or direction.

As is the case with Janice, Jill, and Skeeter in *Rabbit Redux*, Rabbit's action can be seen as, in a sense, courageous and necessary. After all, his frustration over the domestic situation is fully understandable and provides adequate reasons for running away. Then too in leaving he seems to grow and mature, for he gains vitality, energy, and sensitivity through his sexual liaison with Ruth. Here, he is the embodiment of process and change, which Updike in his essay on "Cemeteries" calls the essence of life itself, as opposed to the static and fixed which is the condition of death (*PP*, p.62). One of the characters in *Rabbit, Run*, Mrs. Smith, affirms as much, telling Rabbit that he has life (p. 224). But for all the benefits he personally gains from his liberation and for all the merits of his spirit of liveliness, he causes pain, decay, and death in others and must be held accountable for his harmful actions. Not that he wants to hurt anyone, he just doesn't *think* about the consequences of his actions. It was thoughtless, insensitive, and physically dangerous of him to demand sexual intercourse of Janice immediately upon her return from the hospital after giving birth to Becky. Moreover, despite Rabbit's disavowal of guilt over Becky's accidental drowning, he must bear some measure of responsibility for it. After all, it was his second precipitous flight from Janice which provoked her to resume drinking and therefore accidentally to drown the child. And he was distinctly inconsiderate and even harmful in making love to Ruth without contraception, impregnating her, and then leaving her. In each case he exercises freedom and rejects responsibility. When Rabbit divorces himself from his past—wife, son, parents, job, church—he is not only himself lonely and vulnerable, but he also proceeds to make others lonely and vulnerable too. There is a sense in which, as a result of his personal *angst*, Rabbit creates a *strom*, a maelstrom or whirlpool which swamps and destroys the lives of others. Certainly the death of Becky is the most obvious case in point. But at the end of *Rabbit, Run* the net effect of Rabbit's running has not really been calculated for himself and for the others whom he touches. Ruth's indictment of him—" 'You're Mr. Death himself. You're not just nothing, you're worse than nothing' " (p. 304).—hasn't its full impact until *Rabbit Redux* when we see that Janice has to run partially because of the effects of Rabbit's quest for freedom ten years earlier.

When Rabbit is thirty-six years old, he shows those long-term, net effects of his act of personal liberation. And they are not altogether positive. What was meant to be a leap into personal sexual and moral freedom has unmercifully exposed him, rendering him vulnerable and helpless. A remark pertaining to Janice's act of liberated infidelity in *Rabbit Redux* applies equally well to Rabbit: "The possibility opens an abyss. She would not have known this. A gate she had always assumed gave onto a garden gave onto emptiness" (p. 66). Indeed once the initial instinctual flight is past, he is left immobile, inert, and worse than he was initially. Even as he once tried to flee southward and instead returned to the Brewer area, close to his home, so his flight to freedom and the arms of Ruth has ended with a return to Janice. This return—a triumph for her parents' philistine sense of social stability—proves disastrous for both Rabbit and Janice, especially for Rabbit. He returned to his marriage, but since he has previously broken the rules that undergirded the relationship, those original rules cannot be meaningfully reinstated. He hasn't realized what Thomas Wolfe did, that you can never go home again, never turn back the clock to a previous, more innocent life once you have violated the rules. So his return to Janice has something contrived, artificial, and unnatural about it. Overpowered by feelings of remorse and guilt over his infant daughter's death, he is unwilling to allow Janice to bear another child and in point of fact has for the most part grown frigid and sexually impotent: "Should he have let her have had another to replace the one that died? Maybe that was the mistake. It had all seemed like a pit to him then, her womb and the grave, sex and death, he had fled her cunt as a tiger's mouth" (p. 27). Still worse, by refusing Janice, "the murder and guilt [of Becky's death] have become all his" (p. 36).

While this frigidity is obviously real and partially accounts for Janice's affair with Charlie Stavros, it is also a metaphor for what Rabbit has become. He has become cold, static, inert, devoid of physical, moral, and spiritual energy. He has become a prisoner of forms without substance. His life has become circumscribed by routine duty, by meaningless daily recurrent activity. In the morning he goes to work at the printing house, symbolically out of the sun and lit only by pale, artificial, pink fluorescent lights. The very opening sentence of the work establishes the sense of unreality and lifelessness that clings to Rabbit: "Men emerge pale from the little printing plant at four sharp, ghosts for an instant, blinking, until the outdoor light overcomes the look of constant indoor light clinging to them" (p. 3). After leaving the plant in the evening, Rabbit returns to his tackily furnished suburban home with its unkempt flower beds and lawn, as sterile in its own way as the print shop. "Here, there is a prairie sadness, a barren sky raked by slender aerials. A sky poisoned by radio waves. A desolate smell from underground" (p. 60). He has ceased reading and now spends his leisure time watching television[8] and drinking beer, traits which he once so hated in Janice. He has given up physical exercise and sports, become "soft," "pale and sour" with a "thick waist and cautious stoop" (p. 4). His earlier sense of physical conditioning and prowess as well as his desire to perpetuate his basketball skills have disappeared. Gamesmanship, individual competition, and self-achievement no longer interest him. The reputed American values have gone sour. Instead, Rabbit is lethargic and physically decaying—the very embodiment of the inert atmosphere that marks the outset of the book: "The sky is cloudless yet colorless, hovering blanched humidity, in the way of these Pennsylvania summers, good for nothing but to make green things grow. Men don't even tan; filmed by sweat, they turn yellow" (pp. 3–4).

Rabbit's physical condition provides a fairly accurate barometer of his family and social ties and hints at his lack of moral integrity. In returning to Janice he has strengthened his dependency on Janice's parents, the Springers, with their financial assistance and baby-sitting. This dependency on the Springers is materialistic in nature and lacks any profound spiritual dimension: it is an example of mere observance of form, lacking in central meaning or significance. It is also well to remember that these are the same parents whom he despised in *Rabbit, Run* for their materialism, social aspirations and pretentions, and fundamental lack of understanding about the real nature of his personal crisis, Janice's part in Rabbit's running away, and the breakdown of the marriage itself.

Rabbit has more or less cut ties with his own parents, especially with his dying mother, a victim of Parkinson's disease. It is unfortunate that he so rejects his mother, for she is the one person who has always been honest with him, never ceasing to love and accept him. Rabbit in his thoughtless, self-preoccupied way only occasionally visits her, afraid of her plain speech and censure and disquieted by her ill health, despite his knowledge that a visit would be mentally and physically resuscitative for her. Rabbit is able to get along reasonably well with his father, because they work together at the print shop and because the comparatively weak Mr. Angstrom does not make the same emotional demands as Mrs. Angstrom. Rabbit and his sister, Mim, have little to do with one another since she moved to California and became a prostitute. Consequently, when Janice leaves Rabbit for her adulterous affair with Stavros—a mirror image of his own action in *Rabbit, Run*[9]—he has little family support system to rely upon. The Springer's are of no help; he won't seek advice from his Angstrom kin; and he has no friends. He has only his son, dependent on him but unable to help him sort out his emotions or values. He has successfully cut himself off from those who count and care.

More than that, his relations with his family illustrate the fundamental nature of Rabbit's problem: he refuses to accept any sort of responsibility, always choosing the easiest way, the path of least resistance, regardless of possible tragic consequences. He becomes an inverted male/father figure. Not only has he taken on Janice's former habits which he once so despised (television, beer, and lethargy) but he has also become the home-bound mother/housewife of the family, because it seems to involve the least amount of active involvement and participation in life. And of course he is just *in* the home, not running it. He even envisions living off his father's retirement pay after he loses his house and job. While he might usefully serve as a support for his father and mother, he still plays the role of a passive child. And instead of providing a model for and driving moral force behind the actions of his son, he takes little responsibility. For him, choosing freedom has meant finding the path of least resistance and involvement and ignoring any human claims upon him. Through this disavowal of responsibility, he is buffeted from one situation to another, a pawn of circumstances and people.

The physical decay and family breakdown relate directly to his own moral condition. When he left Janice, in *Rabbit, Run*, he abandoned all support systems—his wife, his parents, his friends, and his church; in trying to find a new, more meaningful life, he negated the old. And his return to Janice, a half-hearted attempt to revive those old systems of personal support, has failed, because he clearly does not believe in them. He has accepted the forms (marriage without love and commitment; the occasional uncomfortable and uncommunicative visit with a sick mother; a time or two at Sunday School for his son; the odd silent prayer on a bus) without investing them with meaning. Inside he is empty, simply going through the motions of being husband, son, and father.

So morally vacuous has he become that he virtually gives his blessing for Janice to move in with Stavros. As Janice says in her farewell note to Rabbit: " 'I was shocked by your idea that I keep a lover since I don't think this would be honest and it made me wonder if I mean anything to you at all' " (p. 84). The situation of his taking Jill home is about as morally compromising, although he takes her in partially because she has nowhere else to go. When Skeeter later moves in with him, Rabbit abandons discretion and parental concern, smoking up with Jill and Skeeter in front of Nelson. Furthermore, he refuses to take any affirmative action when he knows for certain that Skeeter is shooting Jill full of mescaline. When Nelson frantically asks him for help, he says feebly " 'I can't control what they want to do together. We can't live Jill's life for her.' " Nelson, understanding that not to interfere in this instance is intrinsically wrong, says: " 'We *could* if you wanted to. If you cared at all' " (p. 292). Rabbit has become too little a man of will and action and too much a voyeur, watching others but afraid to move or interfere himself. If he were to interfere, he fears he would resort to violence, destroying those around him. For instance when his mother asks him to pray for rebirth, all he can think of is murder: "He feels she is asking him to kill Janice, to kill Nelson. Freedom means murder. Rebirth means death" (p. 198). Although Rabbit says that freedom means murder, a hostile, aggressive action, for him it normally means something quite different. At the age of twenty-six in *Rabbit, Run*, freedom for Rabbit means running, instinctual action, or what Jill calls "action without thought" (p. 229). At the age of thirty-six in *Rabbit Redux*, Harry, as Rabbit is now fittingly called, is soft and sedentary, unable or unwilling to run; he is a relatively passive instrument upon which the other characters play. (The extraordinary amount of oral sex in the book and uncaring and indiscriminate sexuality reflects

Rabbit's combination of passivity and narcissism). Now he is free to drift, to absorb new experiences and impressions, and to allow things to happen to him without his having to commit himself to any one way of doing things. Jill can bring to him her youthful impressions of upper class life and her drug trips. Skeeter can share what it means historically and currently to live as a black man in America and what it is like to fight in Viet Nam. And both youths demonstrate for Rabbit what it is to be sexually uninhibited and promiscuous. From Janice he gains an impression of what it is like to have come to life sexually. From Nelson he learns the nature of real love and devotion and also how it is for a son to have to explain away a father's unconventional living practices. From the television and newspapers, he hears about the general crisis in America. All this he absorbs without having to decide on its value, without having to affirm or negate it, and without having to act on it. Rabbit is free to observe and drift. This condition obviously has advantages in allowing Rabbit to receive impressions about experiences that would not otherwise be his, but it has the disadvantage of rendering him inert and unable to respond when an occasion warrents action. Both action without thought (*Rabbit, Run*) and thought without action (*Rabbit Redux*) are equally unacceptable alternative forms of freedom in themselves.

Though Rabbit accepts his pair of horns, breaks the law in harboring fugitives and in smoking marijuana, violates a fundamental humanitarian impulse in allowing Jill to become addicted, and abnegates his fatherly responsibility by failing to guide Nelson's moral sensitivity through his dark night of the soul, he feels deep inside that all is not well: "Janice's desertion nags him from within, a sore spot in his stomach" (p. 114). Late in the book he admits " 'I'm a mess' " (p. 405) and confesses " 'I feel so guilty. . . . About everything' " (p. 406). While guilt may be paralytic, here it functions to foster his suffering and awaken an inner knowledge that he has betrayed others and himself. The guilt prepares him for the growing certainty that failure to act can be as immoral or criminal as a wrong action. Until this guilt has a chance to work, he continues to drift without direction or purpose, a ghost of a person who avoids bonds of affection and lacks a spiritual centre.

When the four quests for freedom—Janice's, Jill's, Skeeter's, and Rabbit's—coalesce, the questers find the illusion of freedom rapidly evaporating as they prey upon each other. Whereas they once considered themselves victims in need of freedom, now they become victimizers of one sort or another. This is clearly brought out in the way they treat each other. Once Janice makes her bid for freedom outside the home, she and Rabbit grow acrimonious, more and more hostile and vicious with each succeeding phone call. They denouce each other's sexual mores, threaten to make an issue of the legal possession of Nelson, and argue about the division of property in the projected divorce. After Janice goes on a spending spree with Rabbit's credit cards, he announces " 'So it's war' "

(p. 203). Jill's relations with Rabbit are little improvement, for shortly after she moves in, the two begin hurling insults at each other, trying to strike hidden nerve centres. Jill calls Rabbit a creep, goads him about his middle-class American chauvinism, jibes him about his impotency, and refuses to remain faithful to him, adding to his already heightened agitation. Rabbit accuses her of promiscuity—even to the extent of sexually initiating Nelson (p. 192)—,of revelling in her "great game of happy cunt" (p. 170), and of ducking any form of commitment or responsibility. He tells her she has "no juice" and is "all sucked out": " 'You've tried everything and you're not scared of nothing and you wonder why it's all so dead' " (p. 170). As a result of their painful tirades, they end up retreating more into themselves, or of fighting and trying to hurt each other mentally, physically and sexually. As Edward P. Vargo puts it, their mechanistic "angry sex . . . becomes a battlefield. . . . "[10] Skeeter and Rabbit follow a similar pattern, though the consequences are even graver for Rabbit. Defensive and hostile by nature, Skeeter can not resist treating Rabbit as an enemy, calling him Charlie or Chuck and equating him with the enemy he faced in Viet Nam. Rabbit is his enemy because he is a middle-class white male, a solid representative of everything Skeeter hates and finds oppressive about the American social and political system. Skeeter is also sure that Rabbit has an angle, some reason for taking him in. Accordingly, Skeeter baits him, testing the ground to discover Rabbit's social, psychological and sexual weaknesses. With Skeeter in the house Rabbit finds no peace; at times he fears that Skeeter might knife him or burn down the house (ironically he himself is partially the cause of that). But Skeeter is more dangerous than Rabbit perceives, for he assists in quietly eroding Rabbit's moral fibre and will to act. Skeeter rapes Jill and forces her to perform fellatio in front of Rabbit; and he masturbates while Rabbit sits beside him reading pro-black, anti-white propagandistic literature, by that means perhaps trying to entice Rabbit into a homosexual relationship and voiding Rabbit's nationalistic commitment. As Edward P. Vargo notes, Skeeter is responsible for "the downward progression . . . into orgy."[11] He treats all the occupants of the house as objects to be scorned and thrown away like Kleenex (p. 281) and so provides a negative influence on the susceptible Nelson. Skeeter would deprive Rabbit of all that he has left, the little affection from Jill, the respect and love of Nelson, and his own personal self-esteem. This hostility is enervating and debilitating for Rabbit to the extent that he virtually stops attacking Skeeter, though he believes him to be "a pit of scummed stench impossible to see the bottom of" (p. 208). In fact Skeeter does leave Rabbit free. After the fire "His house slips from him. He is free" (p. 332)—no house, no wife, no lover, no son, absolutely alone. He is stripped bare of possessions and encumbrances as well as legal and emotional ties; it is a type of death. The fact that, after he is freed of his property, Rabbit goes back to the room of his childhood, his womb, at first masturbating and then not even being able to arouse himself at all, indicates the truly disastrous effects of such freedom. He is emptied of affection and feeling.

Taken together the hostile confrontations—Janice-Rabbit, Jill-Rabbit, and Skeeter-Rabbit—suggest the degree to which these quests for freedom create armed camps, in fact, a real battlefield at Penn Villas, first inside the home and then inside each of the occupants, especially within Rabbit himself. This residence becomes a prison of conflict and despair, strongly suggestive of Dante's Inferno, where Rabbit will be trapped or pass to a new understanding of himself. But before he succumbs to or passes beyond the despair, he transfers his agitation and hostility to others outside the home. He accepts Skeeter's viewpoint that everybody's the enemy, everyone is Charlie (p. 259). This perception is best seen in the way in which he declares his neighbors to be his enemy—"They are at war" (p. 300)—and especially the way he treats his sister. Smarting from the pain of all that has happened, he verbally attacks Mim, talking to her in no conventional sibling fashion. As he asks her about her tricks, her life as a prostitute, in the hostile and crude language of confrontation, the very grossness of it suggests the total collapse of all his values.

The jarring and acrimonious relationships and Rabbit's moral collapse are heavily counterpointed and underscored by the societal disintegration of his time and place which he sees on television. He hears of a lady who is robbed and beaten in Brewer; of black riots in York; of the Students for a Democratic Society riot in Illinois over the issue of the American presence in Viet Nam; of Senator Kennedy's leaving the scene of death at Chappaquidick; of the trial of the Group of Eight in Chicago; of the traffic accident count for a holiday weekend; and of the kill figures from Viet Nam. Those unsettling televised events are also in some ways the effects of freedom, freedom to go as fast as possible on the highways, freedom to cheat, rob, and kill—on the personal or national level. Not that such freedom as driving and protesting are in themselves wrong, but they help to establish the feeling that the quest for personal freedom may lead to greater deprivation and death. Paradoxically freedom or revolution may also create annihilation or bondage; and in escaping an intolerable situation, the victim may ultimately become a victimizer, reversing the original intention. As Rabbit himself says ". . . I once took that inner light trip and all I did was bruise my surroundings. Revolution, or whatever, is just a way of saying a mess is fun. Well, it *is* fun, for a while, as long as somebody else has laid in the supplies. A mess is a luxury . . ." (p. 172). This statement puts into perspective the classic egotism of Rabbit's comment to Ruth in *Rabbit, Run*: " 'If you have the guts to be yourself . . . other people'll pay your price' " (p. 149).

Updike alludes to just this sort of moral issue—the right to pursue freedom and the possible unfortunate results—in an interview reprinted in *Picked-Up Pieces*:

> The question [in my novels] is usually, 'What is a good man?' or 'What is goodness?' and in all the books an issue is examined, Take Harry Angstrom in *Rabbit, Run*: there is a case to be made for running away from your wife. In the late Fifties beatniks were preaching transcontinental travelling as the answer to man's disquiet. And I was just trying to say: 'Yes, there is certainly that, but then there are all these other people who seem to get hurt.' That qualification is meant to frame a moral dilemma. (p. 502).

Later in the same interview Updike adds: ". . . my *work* says 'Yes, but.'" Yes, in *Rabbit, Run*, to our urgent inner whispers, but—the social fabric collapses disastrously" (p. 503).[12] As Updike indicates in *Rabbit Redux*, individually and collectively the results are mixed. Janice definitely grows as a result of her affair with Charlie, and Rabbit gains a new understanding of the world around him through the presence and conversation of Jill and Skeeter. But Jill dies; Skeeter is sought by the police and is on the run; Rabbit's house is burned; he thinks his son hates him; and he and Janice can barely make a tentative, halting, start at reconstituting their marriage. It is impossible to say that the characters are stronger as a result of their quests for freedom; and some suffer tragically. The strength may return, with some measure of psychological, mental, and spiritual restoration, but at the end of the book too much personal tragedy has ensued to auger for a wholly positive future. Perhaps, though, Rabbit's rebirth can only begin by being stripped bare and suffering greatly.

Through the presentation of this moral issue by means of the lives of these characters in this representative Eastern town, near as it is to Valley Forge and other important scenes of the American Revolution, Updike has created a sense of a significant moral issue for the American nation, past, present, and future. Indeed, the American nation virtually becomes a character, acting almost identically with the other four questers, holding the same faith in personal and corporate freedom and suffering from the results. Fittingly Rabbit is the one who champions the cause of unfettered, irresponsible freedom in America and in so doing also defines the problems of that position: " 'America is beyond power, it acts as in a dream, as a face of God. Wherever America is, there is freedom, and wherever America is not, madness rules with chains, darkness strangles millions. Beneath her patient bombings, paradise is possible' " (p. 47). Obviously, Rabbit overstates the case. Freedom is not limited to America, and the nation is not a Nietzschian *Übermensch* culture, beyond conventional moral and legal limitations. A position closer to the heart of the matter is one which acknowledges the obvious benefits of freedom—the democratic process and individual rights guaranteed by the Constitution and by convention—and still admits to the serious flaws in the system both in its inception and practice. As the character Bech substantiates of the author Updike:

> That, given the need for a contract, he preferred the American Constitu-

tion, with its 18th-century bow to the pursuit of individual happiness, to any of the totalisms presently running around rabid. That the decisions of any establishment, though properly suspect and frightfully hedged by self-interest and the myopia power brings, must be understood as choices among imperfect alternatives: power participates in the weight and guilt of the world and shrill impotence never has to cash in its chips. (*PP*, p. 12)

Seeing America in the same perspective as Rabbit ("yes, but") is consequently necessary. Whereas America was settled by those who hoped to escape religious oppression, grinding poverty, inhibiting customs or prison sentences in Europe, this settlement came only through the killing of the Indians, and expropriation of their land. Whereas George Washington and other patriots in such battlefields as Valley Forge fought to establish and preserve freedom in America, that very Revolution did an injustice to those who supported the rightful political and legal system: they were imprisoned, killed and their property confiscated, or driven back to the old world or to Canada. These founders of the nation never did have a completely egalitarian society in mind, but rather a privileged society with the Washingtons, Jeffersons, Adams, and their kind at the apex. Those very heroes actually held other men, black men, in bondage. Then, too, the Civil War, conceived in good part out of altruism with the intention of freeing the blacks, brought about a new kind of political system, a "dollarcracy" (p. 232) by which the blacks became economic slaves. According to Skeeter, " 'After the Civil War ended, there was space, only they let it fill up with the same old greedy muck, only worse, right? They turned that old dog-eat-dog thing into a divine law' " (p. 246). The modern era also has its ambivalent pursuit of freedom: the Americans fought in Viet Nam, napalming, maiming, and killing in order to achieve political freedom and preserve capitalism—free economic enterprise—whether or not the people wanted it. In conversation Rabbit and Charlie draw an exact parallel between Charlie's ambiguous "rescue" of Janice and "intervention" in Rabbit's marriage and the American presence in Viet Nam (p. 181). To some that rescue has positive consequences; to others it is an intervention, a gross violation of territorial integrity, significant interference and destruction of rules and working relationships.

This historical process in the United States is what so enrages Skeeter—that every attempt to establish freedom has negative side effects. He teaches Rabbit, Jill, and Nelson that the concept of freedom in America is based upon a lie, a lie which speaks of rights for all men but continues to enslave the blacks. He in turn wishes to free his people by destroying this system or letting it collapse, " '*every sect dashed into fragments, the national compact dissolved*' " (p. 244). Ironically, he suggests that in order for this new utopia to emerge, of which he will be the messianic leader, the present system must be completely destroyed and the whites decimated. Skeeter's blind resolution to the problem suggests that in the natural course of things, one's pursuit of freedom still leads to another's discomfort, hardship, servitude, or destruction.

The moon shot used as background for the story further adds to the ambiguities of freedom. Pop Angstrom rejoicing over the news of the American moon walk, shouts: "They're down! Eagle has landed! We're on the moon, boys and girls! Uncle Sam is on the moon!" Mom Angstrom haltingly and cynically retorts, "That's just. The place for him . . ." (p. 93). The central question of the book concerning freedom is projected into the future. Man is now freed from the laws of gravity (another law broken), enabling him to soar into space, conquer it, and perhaps eventually establish colonies. But is it not a likely possibility that, despite American "ownership" of the moon, wars might well be fought over the right to control it? Will not liberation and freedom from the earth lead to additional confrontations in other sectors? Or, even if no battle is fought, will Americans be any more responsible in filling the "space" than they were at any other time of great possibility and promise? Will it not be just another blank cheque, as Peggy Fosnacht calls herself, to be irresponsibly cashed in?

Since Updike implies that we are all Rabbits, instinctively and thoughtlessly leaping for freedom and in the process inadvertently creating problems, whether on a personal or national level, his drawing a parallel between Rabbit and Br'er Rabbit (pp. 122, 308) is especially important, for Br'er Rabbit had trouble with his own freedom. About the same time as Updike was writing *Rabbit Redux*, he penned a short poem, "Minority Report," later included in *Picked-Up Pieces*.[13] In this poem about America Updike asserts that "Br'er Rabbit demonstrated: freedom is made of brambles . . ." (p. 49), a view that is called "the old briar patch theory" in *Rabbit Redux* (p. 333). In the footnote to the poem he adds: "The reference is to his escape from Br'er Fox and other enemies; he said, Do anything you want to me, but don't, please *don't*, throw me into the briar patch. So they did. It was where he wanted to be. He had immigrated" (pp. 50–51). In the original Uncle Remus stories by Joel Chandler Harris, especially "How Mr. Rabbit Was Too Sharp for Mr. Fox," Br'er Rabbit was not satisfied with tilling his own bit of garden, so he went in search of greener pastures and new experiences in his brother's territory. But he intruded into places where he was not wanted and his "brother," the predatory fox, cunningly caught him and threatened to kill and eat him. But Br'er Rabbit made him believe that the bramble patch would be more horrible than anything Br'er Fox thought of, so he was thrown in there and the brambles protected him, despite the thorns he got in his paws. Although the bramble patch was not so secure and pleasant as his old burrow, it did provide him with a measure of security, and comes to signify the limitations and boundaries that must be imposed in order to demarcate where Br'er Rabbit can go and others can not. While brambles do not produce the finest grass and are restricting, they also provide a safe place with well-defined territorial rules that govern the context of life, protecting oneself and others.

Rabbit's sister, Mim, understands the concept of brambles all too well. She has run from the safety, security, and solid middle class values of Brewer for life as a prostitute in California. Yet she has rules, "survival rules, rules for living in the desert", necessitated "because off the straight path you don't live" (p. 359). Her cardinal rule is never to have intercourse with any given man more than three times, a rule designed to keep her at arm's length from others and not to get her affairs entangled with theirs. She is acting responsibly, though her freedom is secured by maintaining impersonality. As Rabbit and Janice are stripped of their old burrow, possessions, and way of life and begin to reconstruct their marriage, they will have to develop such mutually agreeable rules, rules that Rabbit has some inkling of early in the marital breakup: ". . . he sees now, in his wife's dark and judging eyes, that the rules were more complicated, that there were . . . rules beneath the surface rules that also mattered" (pp. 67–68). He needs the sort of code that Mim lives by, but he must not remain impersonal with Janice or he will lose her again: he must have a set of rules to govern his own bramble patch. He must come to acknowledge the restrictions on his freedom, the "ties of blood, of time and guilt, family ties" (p. 394) that keep Janice and him bound together. In reuniting, they together must begin to change the vacuum, the empty space they are in, to a genuine burrow (p. 406) with appropriate conventions and rules; they must discover that they can never be truly free. These rules will constitute a working relationship much like the basketball game that Rabbit enjoyed as a youth or the mathematics Nelson now studies. These games have "limits, with orderly movements and a promise of completion at the end" (p. 239). Rabbit must discover that he is no longer the single star of the game, but rather one of the play-makers, one of the team that works together for the common good, abiding by the self-imposed and self-maintained rules. He must discover what Nelson feels when he goes in the police car after the fire, that it is necessary and pleasurable "to be at last in the arms of order, of laws and limits" (p. 326). As America begins its third century as an independent nation, it too will have to discover similar rules that guarantee its peaceful coexistence with other countries. Americans, implies Updike, need to learn that unrestricted freedom can not exist, and that when one is most free, one may paradoxically become the most enslaved and enslaving. Freedom is only valid when hedged with rules and governed by responsibility; freedom is made of brambles.

Notes

1. Collected in John Updike, *Picked-Up Pieces* (New York: Alfred A. Knopf, 1975), p. 11. Hereafter this work will be cited within the text, identified as *PP*. Given the wish to

"sing America" the rhetorical tone is undoubtedly a conscious reminiscence of Whitman's "Song of Myself." But instead of lauding America, Updike shows his full awareness of America's inherent limitations by singing America's problems.

2. Joyce B. Markle, *Fighters and Lovers: Theme in the Novels of John Updike* (New York: New York University Press, 1973), p. 147; Wayne Falke, "*Rabbit Redux*: Time/Order/God," *Modern Fiction Studies* 20 (1974), 68.

3. Falke, "*Rabbit Redux*: Time/Order/God," 70.

4. Robert S. Gingher, "Has John Updike Anything to Say?" *Modern Fiction Studies*, 20 (1974), 102–03, hints at the freedom theme when he talks about the central passion-marriage theme. The passion-freedom-narcissism paradigm is opposed to the marriage-responsibility-mutual satisfaction paradigm.

5. Clinton S. Burhans, Jr., "Things Falling Apart: Structure and Theme in *Rabbit, Run*," *Studies in the Novel*, 5 (1973), 336 notes that thematically and structurally *Rabbit, Run* is built on circles. *Rabbit Redux* would seem to bear out the implications of his argument.

6. John Updike, *Rabbit Redux* (New York: Alfred A. Knopf, 1971), p. 388. Hereafter this work is cited in the text itself.

7. John Updike, *Rabbit, Run* (1960, rpt. New York: Alfred A. Knopf, 1970), p. 25. Hereafter this work is cited within the text.

8. The television comes to suggest a certain deadness in America. When turned on it brings to life violent, disconcerting, and silly programs, ranging from city riots to quiz shows and the Mouseketeers. When off, "the screen [is] green ashes, dead fire" (p. 68).

9. By this mirror image, Updike allows the reader to gauge the effects of both situations upon a human being.

10. Edward P. Vargo, *Rainstorms and Fire* (Port Washington, N.Y.: Kennikat Presss, 1973), p. 157.

11. Vargo, *Rainstorms and Fire*, p. 165.

12. In the original interview, "The Art of Fiction," published in *The Paris Review* 12, (Winter 1968), p. 100, Updike varies the wording slightly, saying "The social fabric collapses murderously," perhaps implying a much more violent collapse. In this same interview, p. 93, Updike hints at the theme of freedom which underlies *Rabbit, Run, Of the Farm, The Centaur* and *Pigeon Feathers*. He says ". . . there is . . . a central image of flight or escape or loss, the way we flee from the past, a sense of guilt . . . wherein the narrator becomes a Polynesian pushing off into a void." *Of the Farm*, of course, begins with the quotation from Sartre: "Consequently, when in all honesty, I've recognized that man is a being in whom existence precedes essence, that he is a free being who, in various circumstances, can want only his freedom, I have at the same time recognized that I can want only the freedom of others."

13. This poem intended for *The New Statesman* was written while Updike lived for nine months in London, England. As with *Rabbit Redux* the poem intimates not only Updike's concern for and criticism of America, but also his love of it.

# Fatherly Presences: John Updike's Place in a Protestant Tradition

Kathleen Verduin*

"Each home a temple," remarks the Rev. Thomas Marshfield in *A Month of Sundays* (1975): "What has our Protestant revolution promulgated but this?"[1] Subverted by his own antic prose, the minister's seriousness is always in question. But Marshfield's image of home as church invokes, as he is no doubt aware, a whole tradition of Protestant emphasis on family order and owes its very origin to seventeenth-century religious documents. For the English Puritan William Gouge, in his treatises *Of Domesticall Duties*, the family had also been "a little Church," indeed, "a little commonwealth, at least a lively representation thereof, whereby triall may be made of such as are fit for any place of authoritie, or of subjection in Church or commonwealth." In Gouge's view, a man who could not order his own family had no right to hold civil office or even to exercise control within the church; in the words of Gouge's contemporary John Bunyan, "A man that governs his family well hath one qualification belonging to a pastor or deacon in the house of God, for he that knoweth not how to rule his own family, how shall he take care of the church of God?"[2]

Although some three centuries removed from our time, such statements as these provide a necessary context not only for Updike's self-definition as a Protestant writer but also for the complicated ways in which religious orthodoxy and a pattern of responsible fatherhood are so firmly linked throughout his fiction. With Updike, as has often been said of his predecessor Nathaniel Hawthorne, religion is as much a matter of temperament as of doctrine; its consequences are psychological and sociological, it is a way of life as well as a matter of faith. His religious conservatism is therefore often inseparable from attitudes toward the family and most prominently toward the institution of fatherhood: so that however unexpected, given Updike's obsessively adulterous and divorce-bound characters, there is substantial evidence that in this author familial patterns established in the Protestantism of the seventeenth century continue to exert their power.

*This essay was written specifically for this volume and appears here for the first time by permission of the author.

# I

In its repudiation of celibacy and affirmation of marriage, seventeenth-century Protestantism transferred at least a degree of priestly authority to the father of the family, implying that if the household were to be "a little Church," he should be its minister. Presiding at family prayers, conducting catechetical instruction, Protestant paternal figures clearly achieved something like ministerial authority: and like the minister, the father too was obligated to act as moral exemplar and guardian of his family's piety. One senses, indeed, that it was incumbent upon a father to create for his children a microcosm in which all things were either permitted or forbidden, where the child's sense of security was dependent on these norms, and whose order and purity were assured by a concerned and vigilant father. Since religious orthodoxy in such households was necessarily contingent on filial reverence, the child who resisted his father's authority might be likely to resist God as well. But a father who was soberly and humbly mindful of his proper role might act almost as a type, a tangible and personal representation of benevolent authority and finally of God himself. Evident in all generations of the human race, the parallel between divine and human fatherhood becomes particularly meaningful for the conservative Protestant tradition. The Westminster Confession (1647), the pre-eminent standard of doctrine for the Puritans as well as for several other groups, teaches that children of God "are enabled to cry, Abba, Father; are pitied, protected, provided for, and chastened by him as a father; yet never cast off . . ." (Chapter XXI). The well-ordered family is thus easily enlarged into an emblem of the well-ordered universe, where God's fatherly control is manifest in just and unquestioned punishments, but also in blessing and benevolence.[3]

Updike's inheritance of such patterns is evident in many of his central characters: often lapsed, hardly beyond moral reproach, they nevertheless tend to be nostalgic for a time when Protestant Christianity was still a shaping power in American life. The childhood world of Olinger, setting of *The Centaur, Of the Farm,* and a number of Updike's early stories, is in a sense an emblem of such a time, and one notices that its name forms an anagram for "religion."[4] Yet this nostalgia is typically not merely for the innocence of childhood (and Updike's children are rarely very innocent) as much as for a child's sense of life watched over, upheld: "When one communes . . . down among the legs, as it were, of presiding fatherly presences . . . and the call to supper has a piercingly sweet eschatological ring" ("Packed Dirt, Churchgoing, A Dying Cat, A Traded Car," *Pigeon Feathers,* p. 247). Important too is the child's awareness of the permitted and the forbidden as clearly opposed alternatives. In the story "In Football Season," the narrator recalls nights in his adolescence when his father and two other men, sitting around a kitchen table, would count the proceeds from a high school football game. The simple scene, hazily nostalgic and still as a genre painting, radiates a peace that is near-ly holy in its silence and pictorial order.

> They were still counting; the silver stacks slipped and glinted among their fingers and the gold of beer stood in cylinders beside their hairy wrists. Their sleeves were rolled up and smoke like a fourth presence, wings spread, hung over their heads. They were still counting, so it was all right, I was not late. We lived ten miles away, and I could not go home until my father was ready. Some nights it took until midnight. . . . It was late, very late, but I was not blamed; it was permitted. Silently counting and expertly tamping the coins into little cylindrical wrappers of colored paper, the men ordered and consecrated this realm of night into which my days had never extended before. The hour or more behind me, which I had spent so wastefully, in walking when a trolley would have been swifter, and so wickedly, in blasphemy and lust, was past and forgiven me; it had been necessary; it was permitted.

"Now," the narrator adds regretfully, "I peek into windows and open doors and do not find that air of permission" *(Music School,* p. 8).

There is often latent in Updike's work this kind of filial reverence, a desire to be surrounded by benevolent fatherly presences. In the poem "The Angels," for instance, departed authors, painters, and musicians float benignly:

> They are above us all the time
> The good gentlemen, Mozart and Bach,
> Scarlatti and Handel and Brahms,
> lavishing measures of light down among us,
> telling us, over and over, there is a realm
> above this plane of silent compromise.
> (Midpoint, p. 56)

The last line of the poem sums up what certain fatherly figures in Updike seem to stand for: "a realm above this plane of silent compromise." Such fathers are models and exemplars, usually, of something religious, of a definition of man not merely as a creature comfortably natural, but as a theological being whose true home is in heaven, with God. This connection between fatherhood and religious belief is vivid when we examine Updike's acknowledged debt to the theology of Karl Barth: "Barth's theology, at one point in my life, seemed alone to be supporting it" ("Foreword," *Assorted Prose,* p. ix).[5] There are numerous references to Barth's neo-orthodoxy throughout Updike's work; but in what seems at first a casual remark Updike identifies in Barth qualities of personality rather than of creed. Reviewing Barth's *How I Changed My Mind,* Up-dike says, "Actually, in the three decades considered, Barth changed his mind rather little, holding fast to his central vision through all political and theological storms. The dominant impression these pages leave is of Barth's heroic subbornness" *(Picked-Up Pieces,* p. 126). In this passage

Updike presents Barth as an almost mythically paternal figure, fearless and tenacious in spite of all assaults. It is not surprising—given his several resemblances to his creator—that the minister Thomas Marshfield shares the author's reverence for Barth and describes the theologian in unabashedly patriarchal language. "I did not become a Barthian in blank recoil [from liberalism]," says Marshfield, "but in positive love of Barth's voice, of his wholly masculine, wholly informed, wholly unfrightened prose. . . . in Barth I heard, at the age of eighteen, the voice my father should have had" (*Month of Sundays*, pp. 24–5). Updike himself, in an interview, once described Barth's imagined voice as "fatherly, gravelly and omniscient."[6] It is clear that in Updike's vision Barth looms with an appeal that is not merely theological, but personal, as a paternal archetype in many ways a corrective to the moral and religious confusion of contemporary life.

As might be expected, given his reverence for paternal figures and his attraction for the patriarchal saintliness of Karl Barth, Updike has devoted a good deal of his fiction to the depicting of a recurrent father figure, called by various names but always recognizable, a comic, self-mocking, in a sense defeated, but highly compassionate and human individual. This father appears in various works, both short stories and novels, but is most lovingly portrayed in his incarnation as the teacher George Caldwell in *The Centaur* (1963). Despite his son Peter's frequent exasperation with him, Caldwell becomes essentially a model in the novel for the life of faith and Christian self-sacrifice; and his anticipated death implies ramifications which are cosmic, as might the death of God. "My father provided," says Peter; "he gathered things to himself and let them fall upon the world; my clothes, my food, my luxurious hopes had fallen to me from him, and for the first time his death seemed, even at its immense stellar remove of impossibility, a grave and dreadful threat" (pp. 92–3). While such a portrayal is to some extent a matter of autobiography (Caldwell being inspired by the author's own father), it is also clear that Updike places this fatherly character in a Protestant tradition. In an interview now collected in *Picked-Up Pieces*, Updike says frankly that the "main motive force" behind *The Centaur* "would be some wish to make a record of my father. For fifteen years, I'd watched a normal, good-doing Protestant man suffering in a kind of comic but real way. I think it left me rather angry" (p. 500).

The type of father figure exemplified by Caldwell and evidently derived from the author's own experience is hardly the domineering parent one might associate with the Protestant family tradition or with Karl Barth's forcefulness. Instead, he is persecuted and indulgent, self-punishing rather than vindictive. The following vignette is typical: "He kept a confiscated cap pistol in his desk, and upon getting an especially stupid answer, he would take it out and, wearing a preoccupied, regretful expression, shoot himself in the head" ("Flight," *Pigeon Feathers*, p. 57).

Updike's more recent character Ferguson, in the short story "The Egg Race," remembers that he "had never heard a paternal reprimand. His father had been encouraging and forgiving, purely. There had been some great unstated sorrow his father had been protecting him from, to the end" (*Problems*, p. 232). One might protest that the association of father on earth with Father in Heaven runs up against a denial here, since the Updike father is scarcely godlike or triumphant in the eyes of the world. Yet it is clear that for Updike this apparent contradiction of the father's link with divinity is in reality its essence: victim but conqueror, the father figure is a kind of saint whose existence affirms the paradoxes of Christianity. "It does not seem to me contradictory to posit a father who appears as both God and a victim of God," Updike writes in his essay on Kierkegaard. 'Such a paradox, after all, is fundamental to Christian theology" ("The Fork," *Picked-Up Pieces*, p. 116).

In spite of his idiosyncrasies, then, and in spite of his obvious origin in the facts of the author's own life, the Updike father is also an avatar of the idealized Protestant father created in the seventeenth century: his remembered presence acts at times as guardian and moral authority, and as an almost iconical representation of order and meaning in the universe. Like God himself, "A father enforces justice," Updike writes in a recent short story ("Son," *Problems*, p. 66). Yet regardless of his forbearing tenderness, the father also intimidates and unconsciously undermines his son's self-esteem: for in the presence of such a symbol of fatherhood many Updike protagonists know their own pretended fulfillment of the same role to be fraudulent. "My children, wounded and appalled in their competition, came to me to be comforted, and I was dismayed to see myself, a gutted shell, appearing to them as the embodiment and pledge of a safe universe" ("Packed Dirt," *Pigeon Feathers*, p. 262,). Reading Updike's fiction, then, one often becomes aware of a theme of patriarchal decline. Peter, the artist-son in *The Centaur*, sees his family's generations in terms of cultural loss: "Priest, teacher, artist: the classic degeneration" (p. 269).[7] Along with this sense of decline there is in Updike's work a concomitant suggestion of a recession of manhood in modern culture. In Updike's first novel *The Poorhouse Fair* (1959), the nonagenarian Hook judges and condemns the relativistic morality of the twentieth century in sexual terms. "Hook had a very clear inner appreciation of what virtue was: An austerity of the hunt, a manliness from which comes all life, so that it can be written that the woman takes her life from the man. As the Indian once served the elusive deer he hunted, men once served invisible goals and grew hard in such service and pursuit, and lent their society an indispensable temper. Impotent to provide this tempering salt, men would sink lower than women, as indeed they had. Women are the heroes of dead lands" (p. 160). In *A Month of Sundays* Marshfield laments that "the androgynous homogenizing liberals of the world are in charge, and our American empire obligingly subsides to demonstrate how right they are" (p. 203). An appreciation of traditional manliness, defined not in terms of sexual adventure but of work and responsible paternity, thus offers a perspective from which to judge modern society—and to assess one's own degree of delinquency from the ideal.

Most pertinent to the exemplary father's role, however, is his relationship to a problem increasingly important in Updike's fiction: the temptations to what Marshfield at one point in his narrative calls "those flanking menaces to the fortress of the household—adultery and divorce" (*Month of Sundays*, p. 43). These temptations, pervasive in the modern world and offering an exciting alternative to the respectable lives of many of Updike's male characters, make the Updike father's role as an admonitory model and internalized restraining presence all the more significant. In "The Egg Race," Ferguson, who has just divorced his wife, reflects that he could never have done so while his father lived. In an earlier story, "Solitaire," another narrator confronts the same temptation and desperately invokes the protection of his father's example. "He was the son of parents who had stayed together for his sake. That straight line, once snapped, could not be set straight again." (*Museums and Women*, pp. 182–3). "My father would have died before doing it to me," Richard Maple, in "Separating," confesses to the son he is about to leave (*Problems*, p. 129). Never, in Updike's fiction, does a divorced central character have a living father, and the distance between Updike's contemporary male protagonists and their remembered fathers is usually a significant gulf; as Joey Robinson finds in *Of the Farm*, his father's garments will always be too big (p. 49). In contrast to their often wayward sons, Updike's father figures, whether incarnate in characters like Caldwell or theologians like Karl Barth, tend to offer a standard of male sexuality subsumed and purified into what seems the nearly holy office of paternity. Not suppressed in celibacy, their masculinity nevertheless remains free from the taint of sensuality or self-indulgence: it has been turned inside out into a spiritual condition defined by self-denial.

For Updike's doubting Protestants, the proliferation of sexual departures from the confining security of marriage bears witness to the recession of fatherly control and points as well to the decline of other embodiments of patriarchal authority and restraint. In the fiction Updike has produced since the beginning of his career, the Protestant clergy has spoken with increasingly less authority, and a similar deterioration has often been extended to civil leadership. In *Rabbit Redux* (1971), a novel written out of the social upheaval of the late sixties, Rabbit is shocked at the way things are going: "The kinds of pictures kids used to have to pay an old cripple on Plum Street a dollar apiece for you can buy a whole magazine full of now for seventy-five cents right downtown. The Supreme Court, old men letting the roof cave in" (p. 106). In more recent stories, it is noted that the act of divorce is now officially guiltless: the narrator of "Here Come the Maples," the story of a Massachusetts couple about to be divorced, comments dryly that "the Puritan commonwealth in which they lived passed a no-fault amendment to its creaking, over-worked body of divorce laws."[8]

Adultery and divorce are further complicated in Updike not only insofar as they subvert responsible paternity and the social order, but because they often appear to threaten the cosmic order of which such paternity is the emblem: for in Updike the order and goodness of the universe often seem to be symbolized as they had been for the seventeenth century, by the stability of a family life built around the father's fidelity and proof against corrosive promiscuity. For many of Updike's self-doubting, younger fathers, adultery and divorce are therefore perceived as potential eruptions in the universe itself. Beset by an unexpected temptation, the young husband in "Packed Dirt" slips quickly into an overwhelming fear of personal extinction. "The universe that so easily permitted me to commit adultery became . . . a universe that would easily permit me to die" (p. 260). The narrator in "The Music School," in the collection by that name, considers a fictional hero who would "die of adultery. Die, I mean, of knowing it was possible: the possibility crushed him" (p. 187). If one is not struck down for so flagrant a crime as adultery, antithetical as it is to the maintenance of paternity and order, it seems to follow, for many of Updike's characters, that God's existence and the associated sense of order in the universe are called in question. One wonders, indeed, if for Piet Hanema in *Couples*, death-fearing and sensitive as he is to the decline of faith in modern culture, his compulsive adulteries are not a secret means to call God out of hiding—since in Piet's still-Calvinist world view sexual sins are apparently seen as most serious affronts to God. When Piet's liaison with Foxy surfaces, bringing about the loss of his family, he is surprisingly calm. His attempts to justify himself are half-hearted, perfunctory, for he is clearly relieved at his punishment: "even as he pleaded he knew it was no use, and took satisfaction in this knowledge, for he was loyal to the God Who mercifully excuses us from pleading, Who nails the joists of judgment down firm, and roofs the universe with order" (p. 399). Significantly, however, Piet's is a world in which the permitted and the forbidden are no longer quite so absolute; almost regretfully, he survives his own divorce and witnesses indeed the literal and symbolic destruction of his church.

Demonstrably filial in temperament, seriously threatened by the consequences of their own desires, many of Updike's male characters are like Piet in their growing estrangement from the modern world. The fathers—in nearly all their manifestations—have apparently receded or elected to keep silent; but rather than liberating their sons as might be expected, this leaves them shaky, unprotected, uncertain as to how to proceed: for Updike's typical protagonist is not able to adopt the perspective of the lonely but self-reliant existentialist, and looks to every quarter for the consolidation of some sort of authoritative, admonitory voice.[9]. It is because of such a filial, attentive consciousness, complicated by the withdrawal of paternal authority in a time of cultural transition, that many of Updike's characters are so unusually alert for signs. If one is not quite willing to rest on his own mental powers, if he is not able to live life without some kind of authoritative directive, the signs are necessary as personal and meaningful sources of direction. Recent Updike protagonists search for signs almost as a kind of divination. For what is the sign but a secret and divine message from some lofty authority outside the self, a directive beyond question which one need not dispute but is bound, humbly and filially, to obey? With the recession of fatherhood, the sign becomes crucial, not only as a source of guidance, but more significantly as a testimony that the universe is indeed meaningful, orderly, communicative, protective. Like their more orthodox forefathers, then, Updike's characters tend to look anxiously at nature and experience not as a blank and neutral surface, but as a fabric through which the divine imperative may at any moment be made manifest.

## II

From the earliest stories, Updike's characters long for a physical and tangible manifestation of the divine. The boy David, in "Pigeon Feathers," goes through motions easy to imagine in a seventeenth-century Puritan writer: "David prayed to be reassured. Though the experiment frightened him, he lifted his hands, high in the darkness above his face, and begged Christ to touch them. Not hard or long: the faintest, quickest grip would be final for a lifetime. His hands waited in the air, itself a substance, which seemed to move through is fingers; or was it the pressure of his pulse? He returned his hands to beneath the covers uncertain if they have been touched or not. For would not Christ's touch *be* infinitely gentle?" (p. 128). Like many things in the story, David's longing for palpable reassurance is paradigmatic, adumbrating the behavior of many of Updike's later and older characters. Even though the patriarchal voice of Karl Barth condemns theological searches for "proof that God exists in the manner of created things," Updike comments, "such, we must weakly confess, is the proof that we hoped for" ("Faith in Search of Understanding," *Assorted Prose*, p. 280). The doubting temperament that hungers for what the Puritans called "experimental knowledge"—the knowledge verified by the heart's subjective perceptions—will be alert to manifestation of the divine presence. Updike's work is therefore predictably emblematic. His own family, the author says, was "inclined to examine everything for God's fingerprints."[10] In Updike, what is ordinary may quickly turn into an epiphany and no phenomenon is therefore too small to merit attention. For the young minister in "Dentistry and Doubt," even his toothbrush "on good days presented itself as an acolyte of matinal devotion" (*Same Door*, pp. 43–4). In "Pigeon Feathers,"

David's quest for faith is at least momentarily resolved by the intricacy of birds' feathers: "God who had lavished such craft on these worthless birds would not destroy His whole creation by refusing to let David live forever" (p. 150). In this sacramental view, the outward and sensible sign acts as a manifestation of the divine if properly understood: "Just as a piece of turf torn from a meadow becomes a *gloria* when drawn by Dürer" ("The Blessed Man of Boston, My Grandmother's Thimble, and Fanning Island," *Pigeon Feathers*, p. 245). Updike's characters are accordingly sensitive to the appearances of things and the possible meaning of those appearances; and their eagerness for symbol and emblem is, I think, directly related to problems more central in their lives.[11] As has been charged against Hawthorne's male characters, Updike's protagonists too seem passive and indecisive, as though waiting to be told what to do—as indeed, in a certain sense, they are. For decisions, in Updike's men, are rarely made rationally; instead, their choices often come as a result of some event, some fleeting impression which may be taken as a sign.

Yet signs may deceive, or at best be disturbingly ambiguous; aware of the modern habit of doubt, Updike will sometimes subvert the images his characters take as messages from God by recalling the mind's will to impose meaning on natural experience. "Hope bases vast premises on foolish accidents, and reads a word where in fact only a scribble exists" (*Pigeon Feathers*, p. 120). The father's voice inaudible, civil and religious authority increasingly in retreat, Updike's characters in their poignant hope for guidance are typically too intelligent—or too self-doubting— quite to believe what they see. Particularly over the last ten years, therefore, Updike's novels portray the deepening uncertainty of the modern vestigially Protestant American. For Marshfield, the fallen minister whose hopeful and questing visits to his senile father invariably end in disappointment, illicit sexuality turns paradoxically into a surrogate for lost faith rather than its antithesis: "sex as the exterior sign of interior grace, as the last sanctuary for violence, conquest, and rapture, in a world as docilely crammed as an elevator ascending after lunchtime" (*Month of Sundays*, p. 218). To Marshfield, the gracious bestowal of herself by "Ms. Prynne" becomes a kind of sign, indeed one that seems to verify his personal sense of election (p. 215) and his earlier proposal of adultery as a modern sacrament (p. 47). But Ms. Prynne, as the apparent reincarnation of Hester in the *Scarlet Letter*, is both prototype and culmination of those women in Marshfield's parish who have undermined his religious mission; consistently presented as maternal, of the earth, she may symbolically oppose fatherhood and its associations with divinity: "O you are the matrix of us all; grain by grain you bring us down, and rightly scoff at the thunder of skyey bluffers such as me" (p. 180). Though Marshfield's praise, even in its hyperbole, is surely sincere, its language is nevertheless suspect, particularly in the light of Updike's recurrent associations between the female and the natural as opposed to the paternal and heavenly. In lovemaking, Ms. Prynne resembles "the trunk of a solid but warm tree" (p. 227) and lies beneath. She embodies, magnificently, the alternative consolation of the flesh, and from a religious point of view is therefore as ambiguous as anything in Hawthorne.[12] For other characters in Updike, such as Jerry Conant in *Marry Me*, the blessing must come from "above," a "fatherly smile, enveloping, forgiving" (p. 53).

As is usual with Updike's characters, Jerry's time is "the twilight of the old morality, and there's just enough to torment us," as he tells his mistress sadly, "and not enough to hold us in" (p. 53). Yet *Marry Me* (1976), similar though it is to some of Updike's earlier novels, presents the representative Updike character in what is nevertheless another phase. Jerry's personal history, as summarized briefly by the narrative voice, is typical; like Piet Hanema, Tom Marshfield, and a number of characters from Updike's short stories, Jerry has been so paralyzed by his sense of mortality that "Only religion helped. He read theology, Barth and Marcel and Berdyaev; he taught the children bedtime prayers" (p. 78). Alone even in this attenuated sort of faith, he is hypersensitive to the religious indifference around him; the postponement of his child's baptism torments him, "as a face of his own extinction" (p. 78); he lacerates his wife Ruth in times of stress for not being "a decent even half-assed Christian kind of a mother" (p. 106) and hates his mistress Sally's husband Richard "Because he's an atheist like everyone else and you're all trying to put me in a coffin" (p. 173).

The familiar triangle—husband, wife, mistress—of *Marry Me* presents us with the recurring problem of much of Updike's fiction: a Protestant man is confronted with the choice of abdicating his definition of himself as a theological and therefore immortal being by way of a divorce, which represents to him a capitulation to a natural realm where God and his own death have no relevance. Far from being a childhood universe in which the permitted and the forbidden are strictly defined alternatives, Jerry's is one where the act of divorce, and all it means to him, seems inexorable in that no paternal hand, either personal, divine, or civic, is interposed to hold him back. Jerry's own father is not even mentioned in the novel—a situation highly unusual in Updike's longer fiction—and the world in which he lives is patently free from restraints and confinements. "The courts don't really care who commits adultery any more," Jerry remarks (p. 67). Near the beginning of the novel there is a cameo appearance by a man named A. D. Wigglesworth: the "A. D.," we are teased, is of course for "Anno Domini" (p. 64), and the surname seems an obvious allusion to the Puritan poet Michael Wigglesworth, author of the memorable poem *The Day of Doom*. Jerry and Sally encounter Wigglesworth, an old friend of theirs, at an airport during one of their assignations, and fear discovery: Wigglesworth, will bring about their doom by seeing, guessing, and telling of their affair. Instead, however,

Wigglesworth—clearly, I think, a representative of New England's Puritan legacy—politely withdraws, even wishing Jerry and Sally good luck. The novelist notes, "And in his farewell, in the way he bowed from his rigid height, there was something genuinely gracious, almost a blessing" (pp. 65–6).

In resistance to this ambience of approval, Jerry protects himself from the looming act of divorce by various half-hearted protests. But more significant to Jerry's inner struggle is the importance with which he, like many of Updike's characters, invests the act of seeing. An artist, a creator of animated cartoons, Jerry is concerned with appearances, with the blurred differences between reality and illusion. Related to his drawing is his love of photography, especially the strange process whereby the negative is transmuted into the positive, contributing finally to the picture, the new way of seeing. Not surprisingly, then, Jerry is highly sensitive to the appearances of various surfaces of his own life. When Richard, Sally's husband, discovers the affair, the world *looks* different to Jerry: "Richard's knowing had swept through things and left them bare; the trees were stripped, the house was polished and sterile like a shop window, the hills dangled as skeletons of stones" (p. 258).

But appearances may be shifting: for if looked at long enough the fabric of the world manifests only a semblance of imperatives. When Jerry decides not to marry Sally, even "the ominous nature his childhood had known seemed reborn; the air had the taste of humiliation and disgrace, which is also, strangely, the taste of eternal life" (p. 273). Yet this decision is easily reversed, and with no accompanying retaliation. As Sally contemplates running away to meet Jerry in Washington, the ocean is "a smooth plane reflecting the command, Don't go" (p. 20). Yet she does go, and gets away with it. Despite the principal characters' anxious scanning of nature and the human world for paternal restraint or prohibitive sign, the world of the novel is not a source of emblem but a thoroughly neutral surface, reflecting human states of mind but never commanding them. And those few characters, invisible but known by reputation, who inhabit a sort of middle distance in the novel, and who might conceivably resemble God the Father in their age, their benignity, and their ownership of the surrounding forest—all remain graciously, tactfully unseen, seemingly detached from the conflicts central to the novel (cf. pp. 159, 261 ff.).

This moral silence in the cosmos becomes conspicuous in *Marry Me* in that Jerry, like other Updike protagonists, is noticeably passive and reluctant to make choices. Sally observes privately that Jerry believes in choices, mistakes, damnation, whereas she and Richard, unbelievers, merely assume that "things happened" (p. 45). Their frustrating failure to find passage on an airplane yields her the insight that Jerry seems "relieved to have one more possibility closed, one more excuse for inaction provided"; by contrast, "Richard would somehow have managed" (p. 58). "Men don't like to make decisions," Jerry explains to Ruth; "they want God or women to make them" (p. 287).[13] Rejecting both psychiatry and humanistic ethics as aids to responsible choice, Jerry is thus alert throughout the novel for signs and seemingly unable to act without directives from outside. He admits that he is waiting for God to do something (p. 171), and his discourse is marked by a hopeful dependence on the word "clearly"; for "in this life we must seize on anything that is clearly right or wrong, so much is neither" (p. 201). Unfortunately, nothing is clear; seeming "signs" can be recalled, and no decision is irreversible. Ruth does not die when her car crashes, but lives, and what might have been an "act of God" is neutralized; fears of her pregnancy (potentially another sign, in Jerry's mind) are proved false. There is to be no revelation, Jerry sees. Jerry is left, then, in a universe in which his proposed divorce—an act he has invested with almost apocalyptical significance— seems less and less meaningful. Neither God nor nature speaks; all father figures are absent or silent. Jerry's recourse to Barthian theology, the "wholly masculine voice" so powerful before, proves ineffectual; when Jerry says that to abandon his family would be a sin, that "to do it I'd give up all claim on immortality" (p. 55), he invokes a once-authentic religious insight that is now petrified into formula, memorized and recited. It is hardly surprising, then, that *Marry Me* ends not with a conclusion, but with alternative resolutions, held out by the author as if for the reader's choice: in one, reconciliation with Ruth, in another, marriage to Sally. It is as though the author were too fearful of the consequences of his own moral choice to act with any boldness; like Jerry himself, he hangs back from a final decision.

With Jerry Conant, Updike brings his typical protagonist to a recognizably modern predicament. Standing alone in a universe to which religion alone had seemed to give meaning, fatherless amid institutions that no longer speak with an authoritative voice, the central figures in his novels lack, as Benjamin De Mott observed of the author a few years ago, a principle with which to go forward.[14] Most of the characters of Updike's fiction of the last few years continue to be concerned with the collapse of the family; in a process parallel to the author's personal life, his characters are either anticipating, undergoing, or—as is now the case—looking back on a divorce. There has been no preventive sign: the natural father is gone, and the heavenly father has not retaliated. Indeed, as one of Updike's recent reviews noted almost casually, even the irreproachably paternal Karl Barth has been revealed as an adulterer.[15] But such personal freedom as these circumstances encourage confers, in Updike's work, an occasionally exhilarating but ultimately dubious reward. The divorced father in "Domestic Life in America" perceives that he has "forfeited his right to moral indignation with his children."[16] No longer the presiding figure in a little church, the Updike son has given up his place among his forefathers, nullified his heritage, and lost an important element in his own identity.

What remains meaningful now, in the most recent collection, *Problems* (1979), is most often a retrospective contemplation of divorce, meticulous anatomizing of personal guilt, and a cumulative and meditative sense of loss. Surveying nineteenth-century church furniture up for auction, a confused and wandering character with the hopeful name "Credo" looks at a massive wooden deacon's bench and muses, "It would strain seventeen laymen to lift and move it; there must have been giants in those days. Giants of faith" ("Believers," p. 18). The latest stories find Updike still exploring, as he did first in *The Centaur*, the mysteries of fatherhood, of sonship, and of their fragile relation—but from the sober, slightly hesitant perspective of one who has stepped away from the buttress of an authoritative tradition and knows he must now speak not in confident echo of the old ways, but with his own voice merely.[17] For the Protestant reader in the last quarter of the twentieth century, Updike's great gift is that his fiction has gone straight to the core of what has always been the Protestant's central dilemma, as perhaps, after all, it is everyone's: whether to follow the insistent voice of the self, or to sustain the loved and admonitory example of the ancestors. "You're not the man your father was," an old high school friend accuses the divorced and self-contemptuous Ferguson in "The Egg Race." But in Ferguson's honest reply we must admire an unsparing self-knowledge that has won through to its own dignity. "I know," he says. "I'm sorry."

## Notes

1. *A Month of Sundays* (New York: Alfred A. Knopf, 1975), p. 43. All quotations from Updike's works, except for miscellaneous periodical pieces, refer to the Knopf editions.

2. *Of Domesticall Duties* (London, 1622), p. 18; the quotation from Bunyan is found in Christopher Hill, *Society and Puritanism in Pre-Revolutionary England* (New York: Schocken Books, 1964), p. 454.

3. Levin L. Schücking's *The Puritan Family: A Social Study from the Literary Sources*, trans. Brian Battershaw (1929; rpt. New York: Schocken Books, 1970), is a classic study of family life under English Puritanism; also highly valuable is Hill, pp. 443–81. For discussions of family life and the paternal role as established by American Puritanism and other conservative Protestant groups, see Philip Greven, *The Protestant Temperament: Patterns of Child-Rearing, Religious Experience, and the Self in Early America* (New York: Alfred A. Knopf, 1977); Emory Elliott, *Power and the Pulpit in Puritan New England* (Princeton: Princeton Univ. Press, 1975); William J. Scheick, "Anonymity and Art in *The Life and Death of that Reverend Man of God, Mr. Richard Mather*," *American Literature*, 42 (1971), 457–67, and *The Writings of Jonathan Edwards: Theme, Motif and Style* (College Station: Texas A & M Univ. Press, 1975); John Demos, *A Little Commonwealth: Family Life in Plymouth Colony* (New York: Oxford Univ. Press, 1970); and two still useful studies, Edmund S. Morgan's *The Puritan Family: Religion and Domestic Relations in Seventeenth Century New England*, rev. ed. (1944; rpt. New York: Harper and Row-Torchbooks, 1966) and Sanford Fleming,

*Children and Puritanism: The Place of Children in the Life and Thought of the New England Churches, 1620–1847* (1933; rpt. New York: Arno Press, n. d.) Ann Douglas, in *The Feminization of American Culture* (New York: Alfred A. Knopf, 1977), has traced the decline of patriarchal authority in America during the late eighteenth and early nineteenth centuries; the image of the Puritan father as caricatured by nineteenth-century fiction is discussed by Michael Davitt Bell in *Hawthorne and the Historical Romance of New England* (Princeton: Princeton Univ. Press, 1971).

4. I am indebted to Professor William F. Donnelly for this suggestion.

5. See Updike's reviews of Barth's books in *Assorted Prose* and *Picked-Up Pieces*, as well as his praise of Barth in the poem "Die Neuen Heiligen," *Telephone Poles*, p. 69.

6. The Dick Cavett Show, PBS, 14 Dec. 1978. Barth himself awarded human paternity a supreme place by acknowledging its source in God the Father: "It is therefore not that there is first of all human fatherhood and then a so-called divine Fatherhood, but just the reverse: true and proper fatherhood resides in God, and from this Fatherhood of God what we know as fatherhood among men is derived. The divine Fatherhood is the primal source of all natural fatherhood. As is said in Ephesians, every fatherhood in heaven and earth is of Him." *Dogmatics in Outline* (New York: Harper and Row: Torchbooks, 1959), p. 43. For further discussion of sexual concepts in Barth's theology, see "The Triumph of Patriarchalism in the Theology of Karl Barth," in *Women and Religion: A Feminist Sourcebook of Christian Thought*, by Elizabeth Clark and Herbert Richardson (New York: Harper and Row, 1977).

7. Although set not in America but on the African continent, Updike's 1978 novel *The Coup* translates the fatherly role into mythic terms as the novel's central character, Felix Hakim Ellelloû, regrets his own deposition of his nation's king: "Under the old king, there was a kind of life possible, which we borrowed from him, his vitality and his unexamined assumption that he was right . . ." (p. 63). A self-styled "fatherless son" (p. 207), Ellelloû considers the tyrannical old king "the closest approximation to a father the barren world had allowed him" and clasps the old man's severed head in a paradoxical admission of love (p. 216).

8. *New Yorker*, 11 Oct. 1976, p. 38.

9. My debt to Julian Jaynes, *The Origin of Consciousness in the Breakdown of the Bicameral Mind* (Boston: Houghton Mifflin, 1976), will be apparent to his readers here and throughout this study.

10. Jane Howard, "Can A Nice Novelist Finish First?" *Life*, 4 Nov. 1966, p. 74.

11. In *Buchanan Dying*, the nineteenth-century president James Buchanan asks a minister named Paxton to explain "what an experience of religion is." In line with the modern liberal ministry of Updike's fiction, Paxton discredits "ecstatic and convulsive" manifestations, proposing instead that "in the normal tenderness of father to child, of man to wife, of poets, if you will, toward natural splendor, we experience intimations of divinity—indeed, all our experience warrants the epithet 'religious' . . ." (pp. 162–8). The dialogue is paradigmatic of the Updike figure's anxious quest for verification of faith, as well as his alienation from official religious spokesmen of the day.

12. In many of Updike's novels the central male character seems to be antagonized by a woman, often his wife, who holds a non-theological, naturalistic view of life which accepts the soul as inseparable from the body and doomed to die with it. Marshfield's wife Jane, cheerfully capable and adaptable though she is, alienates her husband by the matter-of-fact frontality with which she treats sex: "It's meant to be natural" (*Month of Sundays*, p. 53). "Have me without remorse," Foxy writes Piet. "Remorse is boring to women" (*Couples*, p. 264). In Updike's fictional treatment of St. Augustine, Augustine suffers secret distress in intercourse: "*Concupiscentia*. Its innocence disturbed him, the simplicity of her invitation to descend with her into nature, into Nature, and to be immersed. Surely such wallowing within Creation was a deflection of higher purposes" ("Augustine's Concubine," *Problems*, p. 137). The primal mythological patterns of Mother Earth and Father Sky is invoked in *The Centaur* in the mating of Uranus and Gaia (p. 294). On sexual polarities in Updike's fiction, see Larry

E. Taylor, *Pastoral and Anti-Pastoral Patterns in John Updike's Fiction*, Modern Critiques Series, gen. ed. Harry T. Moore (Carbondale: Southern Illinois University Press, 1971), p. 56; Edward T. Vargo, *Rainstorms and Fire: Ritual in the Novels of John Updike*, National University Publications (Port Washington, NY: Kennikat Press, 1973), p. 90.

13. Updike's comments on *Couples* are relevant here: "In *Couples* Piet is quite a modern man in that he really can't act for himself because he's overwhelmed by the moral implications of any act—leaving his wife, staying with her. While the women in that book are less sensitive perhaps to this oppressive quality, of cosmic blackness, and it is the women who do most of the acting. . . . I suspect that the vitality of women now, the way many of us lean on them, is not an eternal phenomenon but a historical one, and fairly recent" (*Picked-Up Pieces*, pp. 502–03).

14. "Mod Masses, Empty Pews," rev. of *A Month of Sundays*, *Saturday Review*, 8 March 1975, p. 20.

15. John Updike, "To the Tram Halt Together," *The New Yorker*, 12 March 1979, pp. 135–44.

16. *The New Yorker*, 13 Dec. 1976, p. 44.

17. See, especially, "Son," "The Gun Shop," "The Egg Race," and "Guilt-Gems," all collected in *Problems*.

# Stylus Dei or the Open-Endedness of Debate?: Success and Failure in *A Month of Sundays*

Gary Waller*

Nowhere do the peculiar strength and weakness, the fascination and irritation, of John Updike become more apparent than in *A Month of Sundays*. Side-by-side with his celebrated (though, strangely, rarely analyzed) stylistic subtlety can be seen a tendency to rhetorical and self-indulgence; at times, his intense intellectual seriousness edges nervously into dogmatism; his keen eye for the ways we search for significance with, and within, each other topples over into farce or sentimentality, his delight in opening up and participating in moral discussion into self-indulgent debating tricks. In short, readers and critics can find ample material to reinforce their existing views, whether positive or negative, of Updike. But what *A Month of Sundays* does not do is to show him developing a different or more complex vision in response to the disturbing world of the 1970s. Lovers of Updike will indulge themselves with recognizing familiar insights and tricks; hostile readers will be bored and shrug him off.

Looking back at the sixties and seventies, we can see Updike within, but standing slightly aside from, the excitement and richness that has characterized contemporary American fiction. The strength of fiction in the past two decades (even if we do not take too seriously Jerome Klinkowitz' assertion that the 1967–8 publishing season marks a watershed[1]) has been perhaps unrivalled, in both its frantic experimentation and disparate visions, in any literary form since the Jacobean drama. It is our extraordinary and disturbing age, perhaps, expressing itself, as if our socio-cultural and psychic cataclysms are erupting unpredictably yet inevitably through our artists and writers. Sixty years ago, D. H. Lawrence wrote that "America, being so much worse, falser, further gone than England, is nearer to freedom. America has dryrotted to a point where the final seed of the new is almost left ready to sprout."[2] Mailer, Malamud, Barth, Roth, Oates, Bellow, Sukenick, Nabokov, Barthelme, Federman, Pynchon—the list goes on and on, along with a frustration of

---

*This essay was written specifically for this volume and appears here for the first time by permission of the author.

possessing so much insight into ourselves and yet standing so helplessly before the anguish of our age. John Fowles, in *The Magus*, reminds us that the great work of art is acted—and then continues to act.[3] The great question that plagues Shakespeare, and Tolstoy, and plagues all of us today, is "yes—but how?"

It is here that Updike enters the debate. As I say, he stands slightly aside from our most interesting and innovative fictionists because he believes, with a mixture of humility and absurdity, that the answer is clear. With Bellow's Mr. Sammler, he agrees that our burden is that "We know. We know. We know,"[4] yet he would add we are unable to translate that knowledge into meaningful action because we are, all, as a community and as individuals, radically fallen. His fiction, as George W. Hunt puts it, has always been characterized by "reflection about the consequences of the Fall"[5] and *A Month of Sundays* merely makes it more explicit. Commentators have for a decade and more dutifully pointed to the deep-rooted Barthian theology of Updike's work. They have quoted his innumerable interviews, essays, and stray remarks on his "favoring" or "clinging to" Barth and by annotating his works by reference to the Swiss neo-Calvinist theologian, whose "formulas," asserts Updike, "fit" the human lot. "Pain and plague and destruction are everywhere," and while ultimately the reality of evil is ontologically illusory, nonetheless evil is a contingent reality, "a nothingness which combines with and undermines our humanity and our attempts to act on our understanding of ourselves."[7]

Morris Dickstein, in his intense and stimulating study of the sixties, writes of how in *Couples* Updike downplayed the theological *parti pris*, but most critics would surely point to Updike's neo-orthodoxy as an obvious and important element in all his writing,[8] although I will suggest, one that requires serious demystifying and deconstructing. *A Month of Sundays* is one of the theologically more explicit of Updike's works; such critics as Fr. Hunt, Robert Detweiler and Bernard A. Schopen have pointed to the theological dimension of the novel, have faithfully quoted Updike's statements that the theme of each of his novels is "meant to be a moral dilemma," and that his books are intended to bear witness to a God who is wholly other: "we cannot reach him; only He can reach us" through Grace,[9] Updike asserts. *A Month of Sundays* provides continual signposts to Updike's intention: the novel is a set of letters, some explicitly didactic and doctrinal, directed to the reader, who like Updike, is the uneasy inhabitor of the fallen, modern world. The fundamental question he poses is " 'What is the good man?' or 'What is goodness?' "[10] We may find the question difficult, problematic, Updike suggests but ultimately the answer is given by God.

Now, what strikes readers—and not merely the imperceptive reader anxious to fill up an hour or two in an airport lounge—is more likely to be not the presence of a theological level to the work but rather the curious juxtaposition of the discussions of evil, grace, the totally Other God with a flippancy of tone and a detailed preoccupation, variously witty, clinical, and obsessive, with some of the most intimate areas of human sexuality. Updike, whatever else one says about him, has no superior as a writer of high-level serious pornography, uninhibited yet tasteful, analytical yet emotionally evocative, just as he has few equals in the succinct depiction of men and women caught in ludicrous sexual situations. Tom Marshfield, crawling across his lawn "the flirtatious brushing of Japanese yew needles on his exposed buttocks . . . the ideal bare-bummed burglar" (14) spying on his organist and his curate is one of the most outrageously funny scenes in recent fiction. We laugh at the Freudian slips of Marshfield, his wordgames, puns, his childish self-indulgence—in short at Updike's brilliant display of verbal pyrotechnics and titillation, the witty shock of juxtapositions like "indentured cunt," the marvelously outrageous combination of sexual and theological fireworks such as the following:

> My acquaintance with the girls of Ned's generation was (at this point) purely scholastic, but I read often enough in the fidasustentative newsletters and quarterlies that pour through a minister's letter slot like urine from a cow's vulva that they (these girls), deprived of shame and given the pill, had created a generation of impotent lads the like of which had not been seen since nannies stopped slicing off masturbators' thumbs. Impotent, I must say, I was (then) never: as ready to stand and ejaculate as to stand and spout the Apostles' Creed. (59–60)

Amusing, disconcerting, outrageously disarming—but when we are overwhelmed by 200 pages of such stuff, it is easy to see why some readers find the work a "disappointing self-indulgence by a very gifted writer,"[11] excessive and over-written. Yet Updike clearly means us to take his novel very seriously, to enter into an intense moral debate—otherwise we might simply enjoy (or not, as the case may be) his work in the way that Ronald Sukenick suggests we enjoy the "Bossa Nova" style of Federman, Baumbach, Wurlitzer and other Surfictionists. Their fiction, he says (speaking specifically of Wurlitzer) has "the interesting effect of passing through your mind the way ice cream passes over your tongue—you get the taste and that's it. The experience exists in and for itself. It is opaque the way that abstract painting is opaque in that it cannot be explained as representing some other kind of experience."[12] Updike clearly strives for a different kind of effect. How do we assess his success? Most especially, can we account for the dramatic critical disagreement about his work, and this novel in particular?

I suggest that Updike's work raises for us two questions about the nature of interpretation that have rapidly become central parts of the contemporary critical paradigm. In the past twenty years, the dominant Anglo-American critical fashion since the 1930s, the New Criticism, has been challenged, invaded and is gradually being replaced by a new model for understanding the interactions of mind and text, between the text and its surrounding socio-cultural world, and between the text in its world and the reader in his or hers. There is not the space to go into details but the new paradigm has focussed most acutely on two issues especially relevant to our reading of Updike—the interaction between the author and his text (a relationship New Criticism tried to brand as the "intentional fallacy") and the interaction of the text with its readers (likewise castigated by New Critics as the "affective fallacy").[13] I shall look at each issue in turn as it affects *A Month of Sundays*.

With most of Updike's fiction, we are aware of close, though not inevitably direct, relationships between the intellectual structure of the work and Updike's own beliefs. In his most serious fiction, his narrators, whether in or outside the fiction, are unusually transparent: we become aware of a pressure upon us as we read of what we may describe as the book's overriding vision—or, if our model of interpretation is a phenomenological one like those of Poulet or Bachelard—as the writer's personality: "when I am absorbed in reading," Poulet argues, "a second self takes over, a self which thinks and feels for me. . . . This *I* who thinks in me when I read the book, is the *I* of the one who writes the book."[14] Poulet's case is probably overstated—his model, for instance, renders the reader passive, a state which fits only a limited number of our literary experiences—but it certainly seems to fit the intention of Updike's work. The repertoire of his text is intended not merely to engage, as he would have it, the reader in a debate; he wants, as far as is possible and tactful, to set the terms of that debate, and to outline the positions in it. In *A Month of Sundays* he brings the theological framework, which is usually less explicit, into the open: his narrator is a witty, self-obsessed, sexually adventurous clergyman and his natural habit of mind is precisely that which has permeated Updike's earlier work—Barthian theology, the dilemmas of the contemporary Christian, and the interconnections between sexuality, fallenness, and redemption. We are titillated by witty references to the Barthian concepts of God as totally Other—"*Noli me tangere*. God as Supreme Disease" (5) as Marshfield flippantly puts it—or to the world as a desert in which, despite our sinfulness and poverty of spirit we are nonetheless in the palm of God's hand and can be "born in the soul of *entwerden*, the opposite of becoming" (166, 226). The theological center of the novel is a debate between Marshfield and his liberal, Tillichian curate Ned Bork about the "terrible absolute unknowable" otherness of God (90). The same theological debate is what Tom's marriage founders upon. Tom is "Barthian and rather hard" in his theology (49); his wife Jane, whom he courted while taking a philosophy course from her liberal father is, by contrast, like Tillich or Bultmann, "liberal and ethical and soft." She believes not in her husband's "hard" God, but in "the Right Thing" (154). Her concept of God, in Barth's words, merely "gives us the chance . . . to take flight to Christianity as to an eternally green island in the gray sea of the everyday." "It is high time," he expostulates, that we "confess freely and gladly: this God . . . is an idol. He is dead." Man needs more than goodness; he needs grace. It is because, argues Barth, of "*God himself* and *God Alone*" who "lends our life its possibility that it becomes so impossible" for us to live by what the Barthian Marshfield terms the mere "plumbing" (192) of ethics.[15]

In their commentaries, Schopen, Hunt and others have outlined the coincidence of Updike's own theology with Marshfield's. What readers notice however, more obviously, is the breathless audacity with which Updike combines (to some tastes, thus undermining his serious intent) his theology with his obsessive fascination with sexuality. Here again, Marshfield seems uncannily close to the "personality", to use Poulet's term, which Updike projects in his work from *Couples* (1968) on. Updike perceives the traditional interconnection of theology and sexuality in American history as central to our self-understanding. Man, one of his characters in *Couples* remarks, "is the sexiest of the animals and the only one that foresees death."[15] Joyce Carol Oates remarks perceptively that Updike's special insight is that the attempt to spiritualize the flesh is all that may remain for many of us today of religious experience. In *Couples* he wrote of how adultery had become for his hero "a way of giving yourself adventures. Of getting out in the world and seeking knowledge,";[17] in *A Month of Sundays* adultery is presented, with ample biblical parallels and Barthian precepts, as the enactment of "our inherent condition . . . not a choice to be avoided; it is a circumstance to be embraced." God's Word, Marshfield argues, "is ever a scandal" and it is our unavoidable adulteries which remind us most forcefully of our sinfulness, of our freedom, our possibility of redemption. "The sacrament of marriage," he concludes, "exists but as a precondition for the sacrament of adultery" (44–47).

Now, how seriously are we meant to take these views? How close are Marshfield's views to Updike's? Is he merely using the equation of adultery and redemption for its shock value? Is he endeavouring to bring us into a debate? One of Updike's problems is the high degree of indulgence he seems to show towards his central character. In particular, the combination in Marshfield of flippant blasphemy and theological absolutism tends to dominate the book and too frequently may come across primarily as a means of avoiding, not promoting, a serious debate about the issues he is raising. Marshfield won't allow us to see sexuality as anything but wry, ironic, amusing—and we are very unsure whether Updike ever creates any distance between himself and his character. We laugh at the fertility of Marshfield's ingenious analogies between sexual and spiritual health—his inability to achieve an erection an hilarious comment on his wavering Barthianism, for instance—but it is very doubtful whether Updike perceives his character as we may too easily experience him. It is all too easy to see Marshfield as immature and tiresome: the incessant puns cloy after a while, and we sense an immaturity in Marshfield's perception of women, sexuality, and human relations generally. We can argue that he seems to search for sexual adventure largely from immaturity, and seems to regard his sexual partners only as proof of his own virility, sinfulness or self-consciousness. Indeed, even without taking up a rigorous feminist position, a reader might all too easily see his idealization of women as adolescent, patronizing, egocentric, coy, trivializing, and his self-congratulatory analysis of the current "gale of female discontent" (135) brutally superficial. Even more significant, it's difficult to find evidence that Updike is able to see his character in such a harsh light. By the novel's end, Updike wants to suggest, Marshfield has come to a deeper realization that the desert in which we dwell, growing, poisonous, an emblem of the human heart, is nonetheless "in the palm of God's hand" (165). For the first time, his confessional epistles are given a response from the stern figure of Ms. Prynne, the motel manageress. It is she who takes Marshfield and his fellow wayward clergymen to a local dinosaur-bone quarry to emphasize the lessons of the individual's mortality, the ludicious pretentions of humanity and the care of God. At the end, Marshfield's apparent spiritual development is rewarded first by Ms. Prynne's explicit remark, on his twentieth day's epistle, "yes—at last, a sermon that could be preached" (212), and finally, on day thirty-one, at Marshfield's "minutes last point," in John Donne's words, [18] his renewed faith, we are meant to assume, is rewarded by the arrival in his bed of the mysterious Ms. Prynne, his reward for perceiving the connection between sexuality and sinfulness a jolly romp in self-indulgent fun.

This climax, long prayed-for by Marshfield, is amusing, outrageous, but perhaps a little gratuitous for a reader; Updike clearly does mean us to be amusingly outraged, but a lot more besides. The gift of Ms. Prynne to Marshfield is Updike's culminating allegory, which attempts to give the novel a historical as well as a theological dimension. Ms. Prynne's name obviously recalls *The Scarlet Letter*, and Updike's novel can perhaps be seen as a late twentieth-century meditation on the same mysterious conjunction of sexuality and theology which Hawthorne was exploring. The Puritan dualism of body and soul, flesh and spirit, which so fascinated Hawthorne has been updated by Updike, just as his Ms. Prynne is an updating of Hester Prynne. Just as Hawthorne saw Hester's adultery as an ambiguous symbol of the American condition, embodying the temptation and freedom of the wilderness and yet being, paradoxically, the means to self-discovery and even redemption, so Updike is intent on what he believes to be the essential "American mystery" of sexuality, "having to do with *knowing*, with acceptance of body by soul, with recovery of some baggage lost in the Atlantic crossing, with some viral thrill at the indignity of incarnation, with some monstrous and gorgeous otherness the female and male genitals meet in one another" (135). In part because of our age's greater frankness, not least in literature, Updike can deal more explicitly with the sexual dimension of his subject. Where Hawthorne's age afforded him the romance as the most appropriate literary mode, Updike is the inheritor of the sexually explicit, confessional novel of Henry Miller or Norman Mailer. He can be equally explicit both theologically and sexually.

Thus, the intention of the novel is to bring us to recognize that Marshfield comes closest to an acceptance of his nature in relation to the Otherness of God in his culminating relationship with Ms. Prynne. In their coupling the soul and body, Puritan theology and frank sexuality, are reunited. Our craving for spiritual reality is expressed most authentically in not escaping our sinfulness but acknowledging, through our sinful condition, our utter dependence on God. "Sin" says Barth, voicing the central commonplace of Calvinist anthropology, "is that by which man as we known him is defined."[19] The sermon in *Rabbit, Run*, which functions as the intellectual node of that work much in the way that Marshfield's four sermons do in *A Month of Sundays*, expounds this theme:

> There exists a sense in which *all* Christians must have conversations with the Devil, must learn his ways, must hear his voice . . . suffering, deprivation, barrenness, hardship, lack are all an indispensable part of the eduction, the initiation, as it were, of any of those who would follow Jesus Christ . . . Harry [the hero of *Rabbit Run*] has no taste for the dark, tangled, visceral aspect of Christianity, the *going through* quality of it, the passage *into* death and suffering that redeems and inverts those things.[20]

Like Piet Hanema in *Couples*, Marshfield has learnt that through the acceptance of his radical sinfulness, that redemption is possible, and that it is in man's sexual nature that, paradoxically, both sin and redemption are found most intensely.

At least, such is the scheme of Updike's novel—and at this point, my examination of the relationship between author and text merges into a consideration of the second central concern of current criticism, the relationship between the text and its reader. A reader inevitably brings his own horizons of expectation and preconception to any reading, and the skillful author knows that it is through the repertoire of his text, by the manipulation of generic or social norms, literary and extra-textual allusions, the recodification of the familiar, and by elements of surprise and deviation, that the reader's response can be guided. The writer's strategies will never determine, but will always attempt to manipulate, his or her reader's responses. If, like Updike, an author wishes to challenge and grasp the reader's attention by a distinctive viewpoint, then his textual strategies, to use Wolfgang Iser's terms, "can be devised in such a way that the range of virtual possibilities" of meaning "wil be eclipsed during the processing of the text." On the other hand, the tactful writer is aware that it is the reader, not the author, who unfolds the grid of possible meanings, connections, and implications, and that the reader must be implicated and involved in the act of reading, preoccupied with the self-consciousness of the work constituting itself within the reader. We become aware of the opening of an inner world, "a layer of the reader's personality . . . brought to light which had hitherto remained hidden."[21] But in the process of constituting its own reader, the text needs to seek for reciprocity and interaction, to allow for a necessary indeterminacy within its repertoire which may stimulate our participation, not merely our passivity, before it. The more didactic or propagandist a work, the more the connections, not the indeterminacies, are stressed. Here is Updike's problem in *A Month of Sundays*. Typically, he presents his subject matter, the essential truth of the Christian, and specifically the Barthian, understanding of the modern world, as if it were a given object.[22] At the key theological points of the novel, his strategies attempt to limit the reader's participation to a minimal level. And yet, in the sexual dimension of the novel, Updike is happy to let the reader's own experience contribute eagerly to the making of meaning. The result is the curious dislocation in the work's effects I originally commented upon.

Let me go into some detail. The aspect of his novel in which Updike can rely on the interest and participation of his reader—regardless of an individual reader's approval or disapproval—is his witty, outrageous, and intimate sexual revelations. Updike is at his most relaxed, genially trusting the reader's acceptance and participation in the unfolding of events, scene, and character, when he evokes so vividly the detail and texture of contemporary American life. Updike's great gift has always been his feel for the interaction of American idiom and day-to-day experiences—bars, restaurants, suburban life, sexual intimacy. In *A Month of Sundays*, his skills are unquestioned, as he evokes the "frilled pistachio uniforms" (5) of the motel waitresses, with worlds of social and emotional suggestion encapsulated in "pistachio"; or the delicacy and intimacy of sexual revelation where Updike demonstrates his status as one of our most sensitive and revealing erotic writers. He is at his most endearing when, in Joyce Carol Oates' words, he evokes "the lyric possibilities of tragic events that, failing to justify themselves as tragedy, turn unaccountably into comedies."[23] Few contemporary writers can evoke with such telling power the ambiguous mixture of comedy and tragedy that lies inextricably attached to our most intimate experiences. Like Oates herself, Updike wants to use the smallest details of domestic life or seemingly innocent traits of personality to open up the significance or what Oates terms the "transparency" of America.[24] Both writers share an uncanny ability to immerse their readers and evoke their participation in a search for meaning—writing not only about the search, but evoking, as we read, what it is like to feel that search as an infinitely detailed and surprising experience.

But there is an important difference: Updike wishes to convey, finally, a pre-existent interpretation of that search. His strategies are therefore designed to disarm rather than involve the reader. "The didactic text," Iser comments, "anticipates the norms of its intended public" and "adapts itself to its readers in order to adapt the readers to its own purpose."[25] To achieve his end, Updike is prepared to involve the reader as a participant in solving typographical puzzles, deciphering puns and word-play, fulfilling the role of the Ideal Reader Marshfield gradually identifies with Ms. Prynne—and enjoying the metafictional dimension built into his novel: the arbitrariness of writing (19), the ambivalent relationship of fiction to the world (33, 91), life itself as a fiction (117), in which the reader, it is acknowledged, is a necessary participant (202, 220). But elsewhere, in the crucial ideological nodes of the sermons of Days 6, 13, 20, and 27 and in the allegorical climax of the seduction of Ms. Prynne, Updike tries to achieve a more determinative control. Any *roman à these*—indeed, any effective propaganda or publicity, Iser argues[26]—works with such a technique of the apparently open but ultimately determined decision and is successful insofar as the reader's grasp of the thesis arises, apparently, from his own acts of ideation. But Updike does not or cannot grasp the delicacy with which this process must be carried out. His key allegorizations—the omega-shaped motel, the world as desert—are often too insistent and crude, limiting rather than opening up meaning, relying too often on a reader's pre-existent agreement than on the reader's participation in a debate. The reader, therefore, is given the simple choice of acceptance or rejection of an imposed meaning. If we are sympathetic to Updike's theology, we tend to admire Marshfield's insight and growing maturity; if we are ambivalent or repelled by it, we may throw the book over in disgust. So Thomas R. Edwards speaks of the novel as aggressive, preachy, coy and overwritten; Fr. Hunt, on the other hand, of how Marshfield perceives, experientially, how he "will recall Meister Eckhardt's description of God as 'the simple ground, the quiet desert' and . . . become ready to accept creation (as not empty) once again."[27] Inevitably, all readers bring a forestructure of expectation and questioning to a reading; where *A Month of Sundays* falters is in, finally, allowing only those readers who render themselves passive before Updike's theological *parti pris* to be satisfied by the key ideological nodes of the work. We can all explicate the sermons and grasp the intended climax of the work, but the participation of the reader is restricted to a yes or no judgment—and that judgement determines our assessment of the novel. The first sermon, on adultery, is sufficiently titillating to allow us to not take too seriously Updike's insistence on adultery as a sacrament; the outrageousness of the suggestion carries our emotional interest without necessarily asking for intellectual assent. The second sermon, on God as totally Other, is a more detached epistle: we can accede to its argument or can read it as defining Marshfield's character further. The third sermon, on the world as a desert, is patently allegorical, and again may be read as characterising the hero. But when we evaluate the end of the novel, if we have not acceded to Updike's argument, then we may well judge Marshfield to be immature and imperceptive—and his creator as self-indulgent and tactless. As Iser puts it, such a decision inevitably "remains entirely the province of the reader . . . for the intention of such a text can only be fulfilled if the decision is ideated by the reader—Otherwise . . . the purpose of the novel would . . . be defeated."[28] With the given repertoire of the text, and especially with Updike's explicit theologizing, it is all too possible to read the novel as "merely a self-indulgent display" or a coy, condescending failure.[29]

Updike himself has had some interesting comments on his dilemma as a writer. He argues on the one hand that he wishes to engage in a moral debate with the reader. The essence of a debate, however, is that the reader should be able to locate his own norms or preconceptions within the framework of the debate. But in *A Month of Sundays*—the burning of the church in *Couples* is a similarly problematic episode—the reader is given only two possibilities within the text, so that his or her participation is limited. We are either Barthians, with Marshfield, or liberal Tillichians, with Ned Bork. We may, of course, take up any other position—but to do so is to refuse the terms in which Updike has set up his debate. Essentially it is to put down his novel and wish he had written (or we were reading) a different one.

By contrast, and closer to the truth, is another remark of Updike's that he writes in hope that his words will be invaded by the *ding am sich*, that "into my blindly spun web of words the thing itself will break."[30] Behind such a remark is, in fact, not the open-ended insistence on debate, but rather the strict Augustinian belief in the writer as the *stylus dei*, and so the hope that words will be invaded by, or finally be transcended by, the Divine Word. Interestingly, one of Updike's two epigraphs is a quotation from Psalm 45, one of the supreme embodiments of the poet as the vehicle of the Divine, "my tongue is the pen of a ready writer." It is when Updike is most conscious of his allegiance to such a doctrine that his writing reduces the possibilities of the reader's participation in the process of meaning and, so, in any debate. Updike is at his strongest and most persuasive when he is able to trust his reader, allowing his text to guide or modify the reader's activity, but never overwhelming it. *Of the Farm*, *The Centaur*, parts of *Rabbit, Run* and *The Coup*, and above all, many of Updike's short stories (where requirements of space pressure him into a greater tact towards his reader) show a willingness to let readers locate their own presuppositions within their experience of the text. It is then more easy to acknowledge that even if one is finally led to reject Updike's reading of human experience and contemporary reality, one can nevertheless find it serious, provocative and disturbing. With *A Month of Sundays*, the less one can locate the experience of the work within one's initial horizons of expectation, the more likely we are to reject Updike's vision, and so the novel, as dogmatic, patronizing and worthless.

The contradiction between Updike's insistence on dialogue and on his belief in the prophetic writer waiting on the inspiration of the Spirit is, nonetheless, a most interesting one. When we deconstruct any author's pronouncements on his work, we inevitably discover tensions, irresolutions, repressions and discontinuity. Such discoveries become all the more exciting when we are wrestling with a contemporary writer. Living in the same era, we dwell to an extent that the writer need not acknowledge in the same emotional and mythical neighbourhood. We are both attempting to make sense of our ongoing lives and are therefore, inevitably, in a dialogue with more than the writer's book between us. It becomes the role of the reader and critic to struggle with the text and to locate its meanings within the complex world of common experience shared by writer and readers alike. *A Month of Sundays* helps us focus on this struggle with great acuteness. Aware of our anxieties and uncertainties we can read Updike's novel and see them clarified, analysed and explored for us—and, as well, we can see his attempt to dogmatize, to circumvent the debate he would otherwise wish to open with us, as an unfortunate but understandable inability to trust us—and, perhaps, to trust contemporary life with its perplexities and ambiguities. It is clear that Updike finds complexity a problematic, even perhaps a paralysing experience—and we should accept that. What we should not accept is the temptation to project his paralysis upon us. After all, it is finally only by dialogue and debate that we will be able to understand our place in history; and only by entering into others' experiences and allowing others to find means of entering ours, will dialogue (or debate) be able to proceed. *A Month of Sundays* is, finally, unwilling to accept such open-endedness as part of the condition of being human in our time.

## Notes

All quotations from *A Month of Sundays* are from the New York: Alfred Knopf, 1975 edition.

1. Jerome Klinkowitz, "Preface" to his *Literary Disruptions* (Urbana: University of Illinois Press, 1975).

2. D. H. Lawrence, *Collected Letters*, I, ed. Harry T. Moore (New York: Viking Press, 1962), pp. 481–482.

3. John Fowles, *The Magus: A Revised Version* (New York: Dell, 1978), p. 402.

4. Saul Bellow, *Mr. Sammler's Planet* (1970; rpt. Harmondsworth: Penguin, 1977), p. 286.

5. George W. Hunt, S. J., "Updike's Pilgrims in a World of Nothingness," *Thought*, 53(1978), 384.

6. Charles T. Samuels, "The Art of Fiction XLIII: John Updike," *Paris Review*,

12(Winter 1968), 97; *Time*, 26 April 1968, p. 68; John Updike, *Picked-Up Pieces* (New York: Alfred Knopf, 1975), p. 90.

7. Updike, *Picked-Up Pieces*, p. 87; Hunt, "Updike's Pilgrims," 387; G. F. Waller, "Updike's *Couples*: A Barthian Parable," *Research Studies*, 40(1972), 10–21.

8. Morris Dickstein, *Gates of Eden* (New York: Basic Books, 1977), p. 94.

9. Hunt, "Updike's Pilgrims," and "Updike's Omega-Shaped Shelter: Structure and Psyche in *A Month of Sundays*," *Critique*, 19, no. 3 (1978), 47–60; Robert Detweiler, *Story, Sign, and Self* (Philadelphia: Fortress Press, 1978), pp. 155–158; Bernard A. Schopen, "Faith, Morality, and the Novels of John Updike," *Twentieth Century Literature*, 24 (1977), 523–535; Eric Rhode, "Grabbing Dilemmas: John Updike Talks about God, Love, and the American Identity," *Vogue*, 1 Feb. 1971, p. 184.

10. Updike, *Picked-Up Pieces*, p. 502.

11. Thomas R. Edwards, "Busy Minister," *New York Review of Books*, 3 April 1975, p. 19.

12. Ronald Sukenick, "The New Tradition in Fiction," in *Surfiction*, ed. Raymond Federman (Chicago: Swallow Press, 1975), pp. 44–45.

13. See e.g. David Bleich, "The Subjective Paradigm in Science, Psychology and Criticism," *New Literary History*, 7 (1976), 313–334; Wolfgang Iser, *The Act of Reading* (Baltimore: Johns Hopkins University Press, 1977); Hans Robert Jauss, *Lituraturgeschichte als Provokation* (Frankfurt a.M., 1970); Richard E. Palmer, "Phenomenology as Foundation for a Post-Modern Philosophy of Literary Interpretation," *Cultural Hermeneutics*, I (1973), 207–232; Ralph Cohen (ed.), *New Directions in Literary History* (Baltimore: Johns Hopkins University Press).

14. Georges Poulet, "Phenomenology of Reading," in H. Adams (ed.) *Critical Theory Since Plato* (New York: Harcourt, 1971), p. 1215.

15. Karl Barth, *The Word of God and the Word of Man*, trans. Sidney A. Weston (Boston: Pilgrim Press, 1928), pp. 19, 22, 262.

16. John Updike, *Couples* (New York, 1968), p. 242.

17. Joyce Carol Oates, "Updike's American Comedies," *Modern Fiction Studies*, 21 (1975), 459, 465; Updike, *Couples*, p. 429.

18. John Donne, Holy Sonnet 3, *The Divine Poems*, ed. Helen Gardner (Oxford: Clarendon Press, 1952), p. 7.

19. Karl Barth, *The Epistle to the Romans*, trans. Edwyn C. Hoskyns (London: Oxford University Press, 1933), p. 167.

20. John Updike, *Rabbit, Run* (1960; rpt. Harmondsworth: Penguin, 1964), p. 192.

21. Iser, *Act of Reading*, pp. 126–127, 154, 157.

22. Iser, p. 190.

23. Oates, "Updike's American Comedies," 459.

24. Alfred Kazin, *Bright Book of Life: American Novelists and Story-tellers from Hemingway to Mailer* (Boston and Toronto: Little, Brown, 1973), p. 199.

25. Iser, p. 191.

26. Iser, p. 191.

27. Edwards, "Busy Minister," p. 18; Hunt, "Updike's Pilgrims," p. 393.

28. Iser, pp. 190–191.

29. Edwards, "Busy Minister," p. 19.

30. John Updike, *Museums and Women* (New York: Alfred Knopf, 1973), p. 141.

# *The Coup*: Illusions and
# Insubstantial Impressions

Joyce Markle*

> "The truth of a dream is the renewal we
> feel when we wake up."
> —Updike in *The Coup*

John Updike's *The Coup* is a puzzling novel—puzzling at the surface level, more puzzling when one looks deeper. Certainly, for the long-time Updike reader, it is ostensibly what critics like to call "a departure" from his previous technique and style. It is set in an exotic African land, represents speakers speaking more than half a dozen languages (mostly African dialects), has seemingly to do with politics rather than personal relationships, and is filled with startling, ludicrous, and sometimes inexplicable events including two violent deaths (one euphemistically called an execution). Certainly the clear view of blood spurting from a decapitated body is unexpected from a writer whose closest previous approach to violence is an occasional angry slap, the shooting of pigeons, or accidental deaths by drowning or fire. More unexpected is that a writer as much in love with the language as Updike ("overwriting" being one of the most frequent charges levelled against him) would risk the interference of foreign languages imaginatively interposing between the spoken and written ('translated') dialogue. And perhaps the greatest risk is that Updike—who builds his rhetoric from the familiar shapes and surfaces around him—would set a full-length novel in a foreign land where he has only travelled briefly.

What this essay attempts to do is not to wave the critic's magic wand and make these puzzlements vanish, but, more humbly, to explore and examine in detail some questions, contradictions, apparent inconsistencies, and other difficulties *The Coup* presents in order to put them, at least, into some kind of analytical perspective.

It is always safest to begin on familiar ground; consequently, the first thing to notice about *The Coup* is its basic similarity, despite the surface differences, to Updike's previous novels in terms, especially, of its

*This essay was written specifically for this volume and appears here for the first time by permission of the author.

character-types and the dialectic between them. Ellelloû and Ezana are an easily recognizeable reincarnation of Hook and Conner from *The Poorhouse Fair*, Rabbit and Eccles from *Rabbit, Run*, or even Piet and Freddy (or, on another level, Piet and Ken) from *Couples*: the philosophical but impractical old-school believer versus the atheistic, practical, modern man of facts and plans. Thus Ezana is described as "all facts and figures, a proponent of loans from the World Bank and grants from UNESCO, of schemes for dams and irrigation, of capital investments cleverly pried from the rivalry between the two superpowers" (p. 65).[1] Ezana wears a digital LED watch, a symbol of himself, which can display all kinds of numbers when the right button is pressed. However, the face of such a watch is normally blank and this blankness is compared to the empty sky, recalling a similar image in *The Poorhouse Fair* when Conner symbolically sees only a blank sky and thus cannot explain distant thunder (as he is unable to see and understand many other things).

The portrayal of Ellelloû as sensitive and visionary but frequently unsympathetic recalls the Rabbit of *Rabbit, Run*. Both are self-centered, demanding, and occasionally malicious, exacting from people around them a high price for their gift of faith. When irritated with their mistresses, both men demand oral sex in exchange for forgiveness. Rabbit, however, seems to have a deeply-rooted faith even though he neglects the externals of religion, whereas Ellelloû scrupulously observes his Moslem rituals but raises questions in the reader's mind regarding the depth of his actual belief. Nevertheless, both Rabbit and Ellelloû are characterized by an instinctive sense that belief in man's cosmic significance is essential to human life. The numberless stars in the night sky may hint that we are "less than dust in the scheme of things," Ellelloû warns Sheba, but "we must pray that it not be so" (p. 162).

Joey's mother-fixation in *Of The Farm* seems in *The Coup* to be actualized into the Oedipal dream of sex and marriage. Ellelloû's first wife, Kadongolimi, is an earth-mother figure, a wise older woman (by four years) whose "superiority" has never disappeared from their relationship, Ellelloû observes, and to whom he would "always be a child who had just left his mother's hip" (p. 107). Like Joey's mother who feels life and spirit in her land, Kadongolimi believes in the old African gods who "gave life to every shadow, every leaf. Everywhere we looked, there was spirit" (p. 107). The Oedipal ingredients in *Of The Farm* serve to highlight Joey's psychology and give shape to his struggles to become a man. In *The Coup* these nuances run parallel to the Fisher-King myth and help suggest that Ellelloû, like Oedipus, is causing the blight on the land.

Piet, of *Couples*, is chronologically the first of Updike's protagonists to give up the struggle for spiritual significance and settle for the comfortable, easy way out (with Foxy)—a decision which foreshadows Ellelloû's acceptance of a pensioned life in exile on the French Riviera with the most attractive of his wives. Both protagonists are promiscuous (although not being a Moslem, Piet cannot marry his various lovers) and both seem to see their life as what Ellelloû calls a "continuum of women."

Skeeter's spicy but wrathful dialogue in *Rabbit Redux* can be heard again in the mouths of Ellelloû's stateside Black friends like Oscar X and Barry Little, and Janice's nasty, tough style after the separation seems a slightly milder forerunner of Candy's acid sarcasm. Such women (Ruth in *Rabbit, Run* is another) provide a kind of Homage to Mercutio—another possible, if cynical, view of the same reality.

Tom Marshfield in *Month of Sundays* gave Updike his first practice at the extended memoir and Marshfield's half-patronizing, half-romantic tone of voice seems from time to time to be audible in *The Coup*, for instance when Ellelloû envisions Mrs. Gibbs during sex (the "helpless feeling," the "twist at the end") or imaginatively addresses her: "Dear lady, why are you one of this quintet gathered, in the haze of my mind's eye, to make alliance against Colonel Ellelloû. . . . I 'zero in' on your face, dear Mrs. Gibbs, you mother of fatherless sons, you trekker through endless supermarket aisles . . ." (p. 222).

Thus for a reader familiar with the Updike canon, there is much here to recognize. But there is much more to puzzle-over—primarily, the appearance of what seem to be massive problems of plausibility at the surface level of plot and dialogue. On nearly every page the reader is confronted by things that strain his credulity beyond the powers of the willing suspension of disbelief we cheerfully grant any novelist. At the outset, for instance, belying Updike's acknowledgements of his geographic and historical sources (and our gossipy knowledge of his visit to Africa), the Kush that Ellelloû describes appears to be a physical impossibility. Ellelloû says that there are only one hundred and seven miles of paved road (p. 15) yet his Mercedes drives all day towards the northwest border (on one tank of gas?), stops for the night at the Russian installation, continues the next day through, essentially, desert and somehow follows Ellelloû after he joins a party of primitive nomadic well-diggers. It rejoins him at the border outpost where U.S. envoy Donald Gibbs has piled up the aid boxes, even though Ellelloû himself implies there are no roads and only a single tire track in the sand of the adjoining country, leading up to the boxes. Later, the Mercedes somehow drives to the Balak mountains, where "not even the National Geographic has been."

Barry Amis, an American Black scholar who has spent several years in Africa, confirms our impression that the country described in *The Coup* is a pastiche of inaccuracies:

> The area he describes is one which might include parts of present-day Mali, Niger, and Upper Volta. In this area one does not find Indian shops (which are a feature of East Africa) nor does one find *souks* (which are a feature of North Africa). Juju is not a feature of the lives of the overwhelmingly Moslem population and the Tuaregs do not have slaves.

Young women do not walk around "utterly naked" in front of their parents and others, and driving a Mercedes through the Bad Quarter is an automotive impossibility.[2]

Even if we grant a novelist the right to create his setting independent of geo-political facts, the narrative itself presents bizarre episodes such as Ellelloû drinking his wife's urine or having a sour mouth from holding a burning coal (to make good his disguise as a dervish, he explains). He adopts an illiterate and "rank"-smelling whore who cooked for and "serviced" the itinerant well-diggers and slept in ditches, and he takes her back to the capital of Istiqlal. Shortly thereafter, he inexplicably gives her a sophisticated and abstract analysis of the role of the previous king, the imprisoned Edumu, which includes passages such as the following:

The private vices of Edumu would have been trivial had his political orientation been correct, that is, had he offered in any way to overthrow the ancient patterns of adventurism and enlightened self-interest which were tolerable when moderated by the personal interplay of the small tribal unit but which are sheerly brutalizing when that interplay is outgrown. His conservativism, which I would rather describe as a feckless impotence, was masked by. . . . the smiling obscurantism of the hopeless cynic. (p. 62)

Kutunda (still illiterate and odorous, one presumes) appears to follow this speech keenly and replies thoughtfully that if the king dies a natural death, it will not be advantageous because "it would deprive the government of whatever appearance of incentive might be gained by his execution as a sky-criminal." Within what appears to be only a few weeks (time-lapse is everywhere vague in the novel) we hear Kutunda, now a high government advisor, describing her conversations with Ezana: "We talk of the refugee camps, of re-education, of irrigation, of eliciting capital investments from the superpowers and multi-national corporations, with low interest rates and twenty-year moratoriums" (p. 92). She is also, we learn, taking typing lessons. Again a short time later, after expressing confusion about different parts of the world having different times of day ("Michaelis has tried to explain it a thousand times, he says the world is round like an orange and spins and the sun is another orange—"), she reports on the new library she's arranging: "Klipspringer absolutely promises there won't be any CIA people among the Braille instructors, he hates the CIA more than we do, he says they've gone and pre-empted the policy-making powers of Congress . . ." (p. 122).

The most spectacular of the suspiciously unrealistic elements is, of course, the city which has been built in the desert near the center of Kush in an area called the Ippi Rift. A tiny miniature of a modern American metropolis, it has apparently grown up around an oil-refining rig. It has "MacDonald's," [sic] drugstores, Army-Navy Surplus stores, supermarkets, ice cream stands (in the shape of sundaes), Five-and-Tens, auto dealers, a "downtown," and a small suburban area. The city and the refinery have somehow been built with Ellelloû's knowledge. Although only two or tree blocks square and essentially brand-new, it is apparently responsible for a whole truckload of crushed auto bodies glimpsed early in the narrative. Yet, how many abandoned cars could there be? How likely is it the tiny town would have a giant crusher? What about more basic questions: How do goods arrive? From where? Where did the inhabitants and skilled labor come from? Where did the building equipment, materials, and other construction facilities come from? Additionally, it is a strange city. We see no local townspeople speaking English (Arabic and Berber are mentioned[3]), yet the only jukebox songs are American. The recordings are twenty years old (significantly, the songs mentioned are from the time when Ellelloû was in the states); yet clothing fashions and slangy talk seem very up to date.

The reader is soon forced to realize that he is confronted with a choice: either Updike has suddenly abandoned his talent (and his sanity) or *The Coup* is not a straight narrative told by a reliable narrator. There have been indications in Updike's recent works that he is moving gradually away from the realistic school of Lawrence and Hemingway and closer to the fantasy world of Nabokov. He even occasionally employs some of the self-satirical techniques Barth included in the term "literature of exhaustion." *The Centaur* was a very early attempt to depart from straight realism and was largely experimental. But more recently we have the episode of Bech in heaven, the highly subjective and questionable memoirs of Tom Marshfield, and the two alternate endings in *Marry Me.* Marshfield contradicts himself and seems to make errors of inconsistency (for example, what he tells us are pajama bottoms in one chapter, strangely acquire a zipper in the next chapter), strains our credulity (Would even an emotionally stressed minister run around naked peeping into windows?), and makes jokes about his own prose and typing errors. His final seduction of Ms. Prynne has the ring of a punchline, and he teases us with names from Hawthorne throughout. In the next novel, *Marry Me*, it is possible to read the second ending as the dream of what might have been; however, it is given a narrative realism equivalent to the first ending, and both seem to exist with equal status in the realm of the possible—as Humbert-Humbert seems to envision three different versions of Quilty's death in *Lolita*.

Once we begin to look for them, clues that the narrator is not playing straight with us abound in *The Coup*. Joyce Carol Oates points out in her review that the basic plot is parallel to Nabokov's *Pale Fire*: the narrator's story of his removal from power in his native country. Oates further notes that Colonel "Sirin," called by Ellelloû his "opposite number," is a pseudonym for Nabokov.

As a long-time student of Updike's imagery patterns and diction, I prefer to look there. One of the most frequently-used images in *The Coup*, is that of crystal—Nabokov's symbol for the multi-faceted nature of reality, reflected, as it is, in human minds. On p. 28 Ellelloû describes the former king's eyes as "loci on a plane of crazed crystal" and then describes "reflections" cast by deeds and the sky "shining like the flat of a sword." The king's laugh is a crackling of his "crystal plane" and when Ellelloû prepares to decapitate the king, "the path the scimitar must descend through air appeared a long flaw in crystal" (p. 85). Ellelloû tells us on p. 66 that he tolerates Ezana because "it was etched on the crystal plane of things possible" that Ezana would never succeed him.

The second most common image in *The Coup* is that of dreams and dreaming. Ellelloû describes his sojourn in the U.S. as "a dream from which I will someday wake refreshed" (p. 167) and repeats later "America will fade for me as even the most intense dreams fade" (p. 216). But it is not only his life in America which is compared to a dream; his experience in Kush is also called a dream. He tells Kadongolimi that he feels Ezana "all about me, obstructing my dreams" and his experience with Sheba in the desert is intermixed with dreams about America: "When I awoke Sheba's head was heavy on my sandy belly or my Ec textbook was open in my lap . . ." (p. 148).

In a key description, Ellelloû combines the images of crystal and dream and tells us, "Crystals of dreaming erected within me and the nation of Kush as it exists is the residue of those crystals" (p. 176). On one level this can be read simply as Ellelloû making plans which eventually were actualized. But on another level, could it be Ellelloû telling us that the Kush we are reading about is a dream, a fantasy? Certainly, at the first level, the statement is false: the Kush we see in no way reflects Ellelloû's plans and values; it is being shaped by the Ezanas of the world. Ellelloû says, Kush, *as it exists*—a very provocative phrase. That the whole story is a fantasy is implied by a passage from the Koran which Ellelloû quotes; the world, it says, is "a vapor, a dream." It continues: "The mountains, for all their firmness, will pass away like clouds" (p. 267). Earlier Ellelloû had said the same thing in his own words when he described life as "woven of illusions and insubstantial impressions" (p. 83).

A clearer signal for the reader who isn't sifting sentences quite so closely is the considerable amount of what I would call parallel story-making—internal narratives of one kind and another which are partly or wholly fantasy. Kutunda's stories are the best example. When Ellelloû first meets her she tells him, in a long story, that she must follow Wadal, the well-digger, because frustrated at his own impotence he had once urinated on her and rendered her unfit for marriage. The story sounds believable (though barely) until near the end of the book when she tells the same story again, substituting Ellelloû for Wadal. To entertain Ellelloû one night when he is unable to make love, she tells him a wild story about Ezana being Roul the desert devil and about a city in the Ippi

Rift where water is kept in a giant transparent sack underground. The story contains strange monsters and magical events (camels turning into dolphins, etc.) but concealed in it is not only a basically correct view of Ezana as Ellelloû's political enemy, but also a description of the city we later see which is, indeed, located over a giant underground water supply.

Ellelloû shows his own creative talents when he reveals to the citizens of Kush that the previous king, thought dead, is alive and will be executed. Developments, Ellelloû says, were staged through a "successive lifting of veils of rumor." The first rumor is that the king had been living in exile. The next rumor is that the king had returned as a rebel. This is replaced by the third rumor which hints that the king has been arrested. The fourth version states that the food shortages have been caused, not by drought, but by anti-government activity. The fifth rumor explains that traitors are being captured and contraband food (the US aid boxes) is being seized and destroyed through the actions of Michaelis Ezana and "female patriot" Kutunda Traore. The king is forced, by torture, to confess to these crimes and an announcement is then promulgated explaining that the king will be executed. Of course the king had been held a secret prisoner ever since the original revolution.

Similarly, when it is time to dispose of Ellelloû, Ezana and Dorfu release a series of bulletins: Ellelloû is away on a fact-finding mission; Ellelloû is feared abducted by "leftward leaning terrorists;" Ellelloû, long missing, is presumed dead; Ellelloû has been "sorrowfully" replaced by an acting president.

Earlier, when Edumu's head is seized after the execution by unknown men on horseback, Ezana suggests that the Americans can be held responsible. "We will have no trouble producing evidence of culpability," he tells Ellelloû.

Ezana:      . . . . the footprints they left on the dust showed a tread pattern peculiar to American sneakers.

Ellelloû:   They were on horseback.

Ezana:      Several dismounted in the flurry. Abundant clues fell from their pockets. Jacknives, dental floss.

Ellelloû:   Overabundant.

Ezana:      We can send irrefutable wirephotos.
                              (p. 101)

We can create reality, Ezana is saying, to be anything we want it to be.

Here, as in writers like Nabokov, Robbe-Grillet, Borges, and others, art can even substitute for reality. Ellelloû disguises himself as an orange-seller in order to walk among the people. However, due to the drought, there are no oranges; so Ellelloû offers the image of oranges put into a song. He imagines in exact detail the look and feel of the skin and the sharp oils when the skin is torn. Then he conjures up the pulp and juice:

> when the hide is scattered like thick rose petals,
> the fruit is found partitioned in quarter-moons,
> each in its papery baby skin dulcet as dust;
>
> parted from its many brothers too greedily
> each segment will weep bright tears of juice
> foreshadowing the explosion in the consumer's mouth
>                                        (p.89)

The orange-seller's song suggests itself as a miniature of the entire novel, of course—the song does not merely describe an orange; it exists *in place of it*.

IS there an actual Kush, however, as there is an actual orange? Certainly, if so, its characteristics are unknown or at least uncertain. At the opening of the story Ellelloû says that boxite, manganese, sulphur, and laeterite are the only known minerals—yet we later discover there there are apparently large oil deposits. He says that in the north there are only remnants of ancient mining settlements—yet we are later told that the modern metropolis of "Ellelloû" exists there, and the memoirs are being written from a time present when Ellelloû has already visited there and knows about the oil. The "one hundred and seven miles of paved road" does not, as previously noted, correspond with events and settings either.[4]

If the Kush being described is real, what are we to make of an obscene rock and roll song which Ellelloû apparently hears on a radio or record-player near Kutunda's apartment one morning

> Chuff, chuff,
> do it to me baby,
> do it, do it.
> Momma don't mind what Daddy say,
> we're gonna rock the night away.
> Do it, do it,
> do it to me, baby,
> chuff, chuff, sho' enough,
> ohhhhh.
>                   (p. 94)

This "alien" music, as he then terms it, later strangely reappears as Sheba's presumably native song accompanied by her *anzad* on their desert trek:

> Do it to me baby,
> do it if you can.
> If I can't have a drink of water,
> I'd as soon suck off a man.
>                   (p. 144)

and—

> Do it to me baby,
> do it, do it.
> Take that cold knife from its sheath,
> stick it in me underneath,
> backwards, frontwards,
> down my throat,
> this trip has gone on
> too long
>                    (p. 159–60)

Even his tendency to dream about America during this trip would never put in the mouth of his dearly-beloved Sheba the hated music of the decadent, commercial United States.

But if the three appearances of the song are suspicious by being too nightmarish and strange, the ending of the book is suspicious by being too neat and predictable. Deposed and imprisoned, Ellelloû is visited in prison at "the end of the wet season" by the current president, just as at the beginning of the story he, Ellelloû, had visited Edumu at the same time of year. Ellelloû's dignified requests for freedom parallel Edumu's earlier dialogue, and we are reminded of Kutunda's second telling of the story of her pollution by urine: the same events but a reshuffling of actors.

If, then, *The Coup* is Ellelloû's fantasy as *Lolita* is Humbert Humbert's or *Pale Fire* is Kinbote's,[5] if the clues we seem to find are to be heeded, if the "transparent stairs" which are an image of Ellelloû's plans (p. 125) are an echo of the "false azure" of a windowpane—then a considerable number of things make sense which are otherwise incomprehensible.

Firstly, it would be clear why the time scheme in the novel is often vague or why events sometimes seem not to fit comfortably into the amount of time they are theoretically given. How long before Ellelloû in his Mercedes reaches the well-diggers? He only says "the days of the journey merge in my memory." How long was he with the well-diggers? Days? Weeks? Months? We are never told how long Kutunda lives in the capital as Ellelloû's mistress before she becomes interested in government, or how long before she joins with Ezana and metamorphosizes into the political personage we see at the end. It is presented as a very brief time. There are only two weeks from the king's execution to the next month of Dhu'l-Hijja when Ellelloû and Sheba depart, yet a great deal seems to happen. How long do Ellelloû and Sheba sojourn through the desert with the caravan? Ellelloû only says that the moons waxed and waned and "Dhu'l-Hijja became Muharram, Muharram became Safar, or else I had lost count." Two lunar months then? Longer? After his removal from power, Ellelloû works as a short-order cook for three months and a parking lot attendant for two more weeks before returning to confront Ezana,

Dorfu, and Kutunda. Is the entire time span of the story one year then? Wet season to wet season approximately? Or two? Or more? In most fantasies, time is irrelevant; only the flow of images and emotions matters. The detailed logistics of linear time would be merely an incumbrance.

It is partly the problem of time which makes the incident of the talking head implausible from a realistic point of view (but perfectly understandable as an emotional fantasy). If we count only the amounts of time directly mentioned by Ellelloû, about three lunar months, or a little more, pass between the seizure of the head and Ellelloû's discovery of the ingeniously wired "oracle" which the Russians have made of it. What has presumably happened during this twelve (or perhaps fifteen) week period? The head has been embalmed in some way and intricately wired to create normal facial movements. An entire computerized system has been created to co-ordinate the recorded speech with lip movements (although Ellelloû notes that these get out of synchronization at the end). The "oracle" has been advertised and the cave in which it is located (which is in high desert) has been embellished with other tourist attractions. Motels, lodges, and food concessions (dispensing "croissants and caviar, terriyaki and chili, kebab and hot dogs") have been built. Travel agents have added trips to the cave to their normal tour packages. Busloads of tourists from countries all over the world have come to see the head—so many that candy wrappers, ticket stubs, bits of popcorn, and other rubbish cover the area. And finally in nearby caves there is a plethora of spray-paint graffiti representing several countries (mostly America) and, amazingly, several time periods: *Stop War* from the sixties; *Helter Skelter* from the seventies; and, just in case we didn't catch on, *Class of '55*—even though the head was set up in about 1972.[6]

What is apparently important to Ellelloû's fantasy is the commercial corruption along with the malicious and devious attack on his power. He needs to emphasize the ludicrous nature of the event and is unconcerned with details like how tourists arriving in buses would obtain cans of spray paint.

The commonest kind of implausible occurrence in the novel is dialogue which is either inconsistent for the character, inconsistent within itself, or both. On some of these occasions it would seem that the emotional requirements of Ellellou's fantasy over-ride the realistic requirements, for instance when Sheba his mentally retarded but apparently most-loved fourth wife fears for her life in the desert. Supposedly well below normal intelligence, exhausted, dehydrated, and high on drugs, she is still, in his mind's eye, able to say quite lyrically:

> My President, I think, has no cause to fear. He does not love his life, and such men travel enchanted . . . But I have not lived two decades, and am a woman, and my life is of the earth . . . such peace as I have must come

in the chewing of kola nuts and khat, and in the music which lifts one's soul a little free of sadness.

(p. 224)

Ezana, who is self-consciously modern and pro-American and who reads contemporary American novels for pleasure, appears not to know the common term *peanutbutter-and-jelly sandwich*, or even to be familiar with the concept, when he says, "Apparently, spread on so-called 'crackers' and unappetizingly mixed with fruit-imitative chemical 'jellies' between slices of their deplorable rubbery bread, this paste formed a staple of the benighted masses' diet" (p. 97). Here Ellelloû is apparently less concerned with the fact that Ezana is something of an "American-o-phile" and more interested in enjoying some anti-American satire.

Although Ellelloû appears to be serious about his religious, political and social ideals, and although he harbors deep corrosive hostilities, he repeatedly shows a love of comedy—sometimes highly seasoned into satire, as above, other times dispensed with a lighter touch. This might account for games with language such as the dialogue from his third wife, Sittina (the daughter of a Tutsi chief, we are told). Sometimes she speaks very formal euphemized English which has the right sound for a woman who spent only a few college years outside of Africa: "I have an appointment to go out but if my lord . . . has come in search of his . . . rights, I will stay. It once . . . we . . . I am attempting to apologize for something I am not certain I caused. Until the Revolution, we were together enough. Is that not so? Did I become an enemy of the people, that I had to be rebuffed?" (p. 74). Yet during the same scene, at an admittedly less delicate moment, she can say, "Face it, Africa is crazy about trading. Where else can you buy in the marketplace honest-to-god fingernail clippings? I mean, if you stand back and look at it, it's wild" (p. 71).

Even minor characters who appear only briefly often produce decidedly comic moments. Speaking Berber (the original galley says), Ellelloû asks a "tall black Hassouna" counterman in a drugstore if there is a soda fountain. The drugstore man replies:

Such frills went out of modern use years ago when the minimum wage for soda jerks went skyhigh. You are living in the past, it seems. A machine that vends cans of soft drinks purrs in the rear of the store. . . .

(p. 255)

What the Berber equivalent for *soda-jerks*, *skyhigh*, or *purrs* might be, the reader is left to puzzle-out for himself, if he cares to. Moreover, where would this counterman—an African native working in a new drugstore in a new city—acquire his off-hand knowledge about when soda fountains went out of style and what the minimum wage for "soda jerks" is? But the humor of the situation is enjoyable and it becomes more overt when the counterman ends with a joke of his own: "Take care, my friend, not to drop the pull-tab, once removed, back into the can. Several customers of mine have choked to death in that manner. We call it the Death of the Last Drop."

Sometimes, however, the reader's laughter must be maintained amidst a writhing tangle of style levels and mixed character-portrayal. The leader of the caravan which Ellelloû and Sheba join for their long trek through the desert, is described as "a hirsute, jittery brute of the Kelulli tribe" named Sidi Mukhtar who runs his caravan with an iron hand and would, Ellelloû suspects, kill or sell them if it profitted him. On the day they leave the caravan, we listen to Sidi Mukhtar, who apparently knows several languages but speaks something that emerges as stage-Indian dialect:

> The Shahanshah has much wish to modernize. In his hurry he buy typewriters from West Germans and paper from Swedes and then discover only one type spool fit typewriter, only one type eraser not smudge paper.
>
> (p. 195)

When Ellelloû reveals his identity, however, the desert nomad switches, almost mid-sentence, to a sophisticated man of the world: "*Je sais*. Otherwise I kill. We see Benzi following us before mountains become too bad. Super car, gives ride free of sway." Then, still not quite abandoning his Tonto-talk, Sidi Mukhtar suddenly becomes a grad student in the liberal arts. Ellelloû asks why Sidi Mukhtar would have killed him and is told:

> To sell Madame to the Yeminis. Good posh black girls with correct long neck and hollow back, very hard to come by. Only shoddy slaves come on market now. Mostly drug addicts from bourgeois European families, decadent riff-raff looking for security. German ministers' daughters, wispy French boys in the footsteps of Rimbaud. [Last line in original galleys.][7]

Ellelloû says, about this incredible speech, only that he "distrusted the note of socialist snobbery."

Ellelloû the narrator is apparently a serious and philosophical man with very little understanding of what might be called "crowd rhetoric." On at least two occasions he describes a speech made to a crowd in language no speaker (except possibly Ellelloû himself?) would use in a public situation. It is difficult to say whether it is naiveté on Ellelloû's part or, again, his enjoyment of satire which is responsible for such ludicrous moments.

When the talking head begins its speech to the crowd of assembled tourists, the rhetoric sounds normal enough. "Patriotic citizens of Kush, there is great evil among you. A greatly evil man whose name is known to you all, and whose face is known to few." But within a few sentences, the language has become comically abstract and intellectual:

He has projected upon the artificial nation of Kush his own furious though ambivalent will; the citizens of this poor nation are prisoners of his imagination and the barren landscape . . . mirrors his exhausted spirit. . . . Just as nostalgia leaks into his reverie, while he dozes above the drawing board of the People's Revolution so vividly blue-printed by our heroic Soviet allies, so traces of decadent, doomed capitalist consumerism creep into the life-fabric of the noble, beautiful, and intrinsically pure Kushite peasants and workers.

(p. 228)

Through the veils of his fantasy, Ellelloû admits that he feels "the hand of a hack writer" in this speech. What we feel is the dark underside of Ellelloû's own view of the situation which he cannot openly admit to himself.

When Ellelloû discovers the modern city in the Ippi Rift which, ironically, bears his name, he attempts to incite the people to destroy the oil refinery which supports the metropolis. An oil company P.R. man calms the crowd with a speech increasingly outrageous and finally overtly satirical:

Your hopes of real happiness, that is to say, a relative absence of tension and deprivation, lie not with absolutists and charismatics but with an orderly balance of capitalist incentives and socialist mediations.

(p. 265)

He goes on to discuss the "neurotic sublimations of the Christian West" and the "African humanism" of their forefathers and urges them not to "yield your priceless personhood to destructive gestures by alleged saviors." The speech ends, "There is no God, though you are free to worship as you wish, as you are free to indulge in bizarre sexual practices with another consenting adult." The scene then rises to its comic climax as the P.R. man shouts, "Open the gates, we're not afraid of these good folks" and after Ellelloû's rebuttal fails, the oil company offers everybody one free beer, reminding them "Remember, don't put the pull-tab back into the can." As they surge forward, Ellelloû, trampled under the feet of the crowd, cries, "This is treason." Lost temporarily in the comedy of the scene is the fact that a tiny cloud appears at the moment of Ellelloû's loss of power and the overdue rains finally come.

Apart from the occasionally disconcerting mixture of serious thematic threads with low and high comedy, scenes such as those described above can be entertaining, and Joyce Carol Oates even speculated that *The Coup* was "immensely enjoyable to write." Yet the reader's delight in these scenes is somewhat inhibited by inconsistencies and incoherencies that go much deeper than can easily be explained by a whimsical or otherwise unreliable narrator. There are disturbing problems of logic in the events of the plot itself.

Early in the narrative, Ellelloû describes how Kutunda, newly rescued from the ditches, convinces him to execute Edumu. She tells a wild yarn complete with suggestions for torture and methods for excising demons. "Fingers make favorite burrows for the bad spirits; a reasonable precaution would be to slice off the old king's hands." "Tear out his eyes and stuff them up his rectum so they can spy out where his demon lives" (p. 64). Ellelloû, furthermore, already senses that she is a political antagonist. Why does he allow her senseless tale to move him? The suspicion that he himself wants the execution doesn't really explain the use of her speech as motivation.

The central episode of the theft of the head is similarly fraught with logical problems. The head's theft and its subsequent use as an oracle are both extremely effective in discrediting Ellelloû and bringing about his final fall from power. It makes no sense, however, that the Soviets would perpetrate such a deed since Ellelloû is strongly pro-Soviet and anti-American; moreover, his removal from power would elevate pro-American forces to the top government positions. When Ezana tells Ellelloû about the head he first uncharacteristically blames it on the Americans, his allies; next it appears he is trying to tempt Ellelloû to personally go and investigate although Ellelloû and the reader both sense a trap. However, such shennanigans aren't at all Ezana's style and we later learn from his own thoughts that he knew nothing about the theft and didn't approve of it.

Even after Ellelloû hears the vicious speech the head makes and sees for himself that the Soviets have engineered it, he responds with only a mild censure and seems to believe their lame explanation that they only wanted to lure him there to reveal the existence of the secret modern city in the Ippi Rift. The explanation cannot be true nor would anyone likely be fooled by it. Yet not only is Ellelloû apparently satisfied, but he maintains his pro-Soviet allegiance even to the time of the writing of his memoirs. Surely not even his rabid anti-Americanism can explain such wrong-headed loyalty. And not even the requirements of a subjective fantasy would likely inspire Ellelloû to recount such a political blunder on the part of the Russians, his supposed friends.

What does account for Ellelloû's burning hatred of all things American? All of his reveries about his time in the U.S. are not only fairly pleasant but often romantic. He remembers late-night political discussions over beer, the excitement of associating with the Black Muslims, the seasons changing in picturesque Wisconsin, and his love affair with Candy. The occasional satirical descriptions of a drugstore or middle-class livingroom often feels like after-thoughts by the still politics-conscious exiled Ellelloû. Nowhere do we find in these fantasies justification for his hatred of *toubabs*, as he likes to call Americans. He says that the Black Muslims taught him hatred "the source of all strengths" but the memories themselves do not seem colored by hatred nor do they contain evidence of what caused it. Are we really to believe that the B- he got in African History from Professor Craven prompted all this rancor?

This kind of logical inconsistency leads us to our final question: Who is "Ellelloû"? In a fantasy, such as *Lolita* or *Pale Fire* or Camus' *The Fall*, attention ultimately focusses on the narrator—on the quality of his madness, if he is mad, or of his eccentricities if he is merely eccentric. Certainly, for starters, we cannot trust the "autobiography" he supplies about being the child of the "rape of a Salu woman by a Nubian trader"— indeed Ezana's later reference to that father as a "whirlwind" recalls Kutunda's boast that her great grandmother was a leopard. Was Ellelloû a death-defying hero in the French Indo-China Wars, as he tells us? We are given no details of the years he spent there, nor any incidental, off-hand references to the Indo-China penninsula, nor any references to military life (although incidental American images and references are everywhere).

This kind of factual uncertainty about the narrator may not be unheard of in extended fantasy narratives but, more seriously, even after reading Ellelloû's thoughts for hundreds of pages, we don't really know or understand his feelings, either. Even a second or third reading—usually necessary when a novel reveals itself to be non-realistic—does not give us an understanding of Ellelloû's emotions or point of view in most scenes. How does he feel about Edumu, for example, when he talks to him in prison? As the cat to the mouse? As an Oedipal son to his 'father'? As a loving son to his symbolic father? As a sorrowful monarch upset at what he knows he must eventually do? Or as a madman to his next victim? When he tells Edumu the outrageously untrue story that Kushites hate capitalists so much that during the revolution he had to prevent them from killing all the traders—does he *believe* what he is saying or is he only being argumentative?

Does Ellelloû care about human life at all, or only about the right alignment of the human spirit? He burns the tons of US aid food which would have fed thousands of starving people, implying that a righteous death is better than a contaminated life; but he thinks later, "Lives, millions of lives, hung on Ellelloû's will and dragged it down. The famine weighed upon him sickeningly" (p. 100). He complains to Edumu that "The people starve. . . . The hair of the children turns red. Their eyes and bellies bulge. . . . When they grow too weak to whimper, their silence is the worst" (p. 24) and he is shocked into silence by the king's religious reply, "It anticipates the silence of Paradise." But, on the other hand, he tries to destroy the oil refinery whose profits could buy food. Critic Barry Amis was deeply disturbed by the handling of this aspect of the narrative: "Updike's handling of Ellelloû seems to make a mockery of the all-too-real human tragedy that occurred in the Sahel."

We see in Ellelloû evidence of sensitivity, intelligence, and the kinds of sympathetic characteristics which have won our support for other of Updike's protagonists in spite of their often annoying faults. Ellelloû's view of an American drugstore is both delightfully nasty and philosophically provocative:

> Boxes contained little jars, little jars contained capsules, capsules contained powders and fluids that contained relief. . . . In another area there were intricate instruments, sealed upon cardboard, with transparent bubbles, for the plucking and curling and indeed torturing of female hair . . . and farther on, rows of Mars Bars and Good 'n' Plenties and Milky Ways laid to bed in box after box proximate to a rack of toothbrushes, dental floss, and abrasive ointments phallically packaged and chemically fortified to resist the very decay that these celestial candies . . . were manufactured to generate.
>
> (p. 115)

His ritualistic trek through the desert (it turns out he could have driven in the Mercedes on a "well-marked" road with "all tourist services") is a symbolic honing of his spiritual mettle. Instinctively, we feel he is right to resist Capitalistic commercialism which will, as Klipspringer envisions it, decorate the Braille institute with "a little *souk*like string of shops, boutiques, and travel agencies, nothing noisy, along the ground-level mall."

On the other hand, we also see in Ellelloû evidence of madness and deep-seated malice. He admits that he considers hatred the source of all strengths. Although he conceals it at first, he was secretly responsible for the assassination of General Soba, part of the original revolutionary triumverate—an act which elevated him to the presidency. He arranges for brutal tortures of Edumu (although he claims he "squeamishly" absented himself) and he threatens to torture Candy if she attempts to leave him. He orders his soldiers to rape, beat, and kill the tourists (mostly retirees) at the cave of the talking head and describes himself as grief-stricken when he later discovers that his soldiers let them go unharmed. He sees Sittina's children only in terms of the extra money they will bring in on his pension and all in all he seems to fit Candy's angry description when she calls him "the most narcissistic, chauvinistic, megalomaniacal, catatonic schizoid creep this creepy continent ever conjured up" (p. 136). Critic Barry Amis feels that Ellelloû "appears to be fashioned after not quite equal portions of Idi Amin, Stepin Fetchit, and Malcolm X."

The ambivalence of Ellelloû's character is represented allegorically in the novel by his love of disguises—what Kutunda calls at the end his "masks." He can be an orange-seller, a beggar, a dervish, a Sufi, a "claims adjuster," a street-singer, a short-order cook, or a parking lot attendant. It is said that almost no one knows what he looks like and this certainly applies to the reader. IS there an Ellelloû? Perhaps we are getting a clue within the novel when Professor Craven speculates: "I sometimes wonder if your experiences, as you describe them, do not partake of the fabulous."

He doubts Ellelloû's account of his own identity, doubts even his African heritage, and concludes, "That would explain why, in your examination, you showed so little feel for the heart of the matter"—a sentiment shared by Barry Amis and quoted earlier in this essay.

Whose fantasy is it, then? Certainly not *President* Ellelloû's—for he's part of it. Like the minor characters noted earlier, Ellelloû's own language bounces dizzily from stiff, formal African-sounding diction to nonchalant and even crude Americanisms. He refers to a woman's menstrual period as her "uncleanness" but calls Kutunda his "doxy." Seemingly unaware of the word for *cracker* (although he went to college in Wisconsin), he describes "those salty biscuits called HiHo" yet pops up with terms like "GoGo Dives," "freaky sunglasses," and "illegally parked in a loading zone." In a single statement he can say, "Only one man, a white man in a *button-down* shirt and *seersucker* suit showed himself [reminding Ellelloû of] dozens of small businessmen, toothpicks between their lips [who] stroll, *eye* the competition and *glad-hand* one another. This *toubab* had . . ." (p. 47–48). Then when picturing this *toubab*'s wife during sex, he imagines her body "primed like a jammed bazooka."

After only a short time in the States, Ellelloû's American English seems strangely advanced when he argues politics in a student watering hole:

> It seems to me the truth of a mythology should not be judged evidentially piece by piece but by its gestalt result. This Mr. Yacub, with his big head and his resemblance to Frankenstein seems more than we need from the standpoint of plausibility; but then so do Hitler and Joan of Arc and Jesus.
>
> (p. 153)

Clearly the important thing about this scene is what it communicates about the importance of organized belief—of myth—to human life. Ellelloû's language powers are simply adjusted accordingly.

But by whom? Again, if President of Kush, Colonel Hakim Félix Ellelloû, is partly or wholly fantasized, who is the fantasizer? Although it is presented as first person memoirs, the novel contains a considerable amount of material that "Ellelloû" could not have known and even material written from the personal internal view of Michaelis Ezana.

At the outset we notice that the narrator sometimes refers to Ellelloû as *I* and sometimes as *he*. He explains this on p. 17 and says that the third person refers to the one "who acts" and the first person refers to an *I* "who experiences." This latter, he continues, "is passive and guiltless and astonished." Perhaps so, but the switches from first person to third person and back, in the narrative, do not always seem to follow this explanation. He pictures Angelica Gibbs, the wife of the envoy, arriving at Kush International Airport, for instance, in the first person—even though he isn't even there—and says "This was Angelica Gibbs whom I had widowed." But isn't it "Ellelloû the President" who caused Gibbs' death? So why is the use of *I* appropriate? This would be a small enough point were not the changes in person so frequent, intrusive, and confusing.

The narrative begins with the (supposedly) factual history and geography of Kush, all in the third person, and not until Colonel Hakim Félix Ellelloû is named as "SCRME's chairman and the Commander in Chief of the Armed Forces, Minister of National Defense, and President of Kush" does the narrator add "that is to day, myself" suggesting, perhaps, an emotionally-involved story-teller who has just imaginatively joined his own fantasy.

This story-teller wants and needs to tell us things which happened in Ellelloû's absence and does not hesitate to do so. Near the beginning when the doomed Edumu makes a final speech to the crowd (quoted word for word) in a language Ellelloû doesn't know, the narrator remembers to say that Colonel Wambutti, "who spoke Wanj," gave Ellelloû "the gist" of the king's speech. But late in the story, when Ezana escapes from prison (Ellelloû is far away on his fact-finding mission where he loses the presidency), the narrator enthusiastically follows his flight, step by step, and even tells us his thoughts as he makes his way through the complex corridors of the Palace of Administration. We see his trembling in fear, his meditations about what motivated the early colonizers of Africa, and amazingly, even his decision that the Russians were probably responsible for the theft of the head, an act he finds disgusting.

What is especially peculiar about this last overheard thought is that earlier we see Ellelloû telling Kadongolimi that Ezana arranged the theft to discredit him. But if this is Ellelloû's fantasy, why would he fantasize such a statement to his wife when, it turns out, he knows it to be false? To show that he gained the information later? When? And this introduces an aspect of linear time into a fantasy which frequently ignores it.

We are, then, being strongly coaxed by this novel to suspect another narrator, or at least to suspect the existence of a Felix Ellelloû who is not revealed directly to us and who does not necessarily resemble President Ellelloû. (He even jestingly recalls in the novel that his name was invented.) What might this narrator be like?

First, it seems possible that he might not be an African. As shown above, his African scenes contain frequent errors of fact—geographic and other—and seems often strangely devoid of concrete detail. (He even creates an American city in Africa.) On the other hand, his American scenes are much more vivid, detailed, and accurate. His knowledge of Africa seems approximately equivalent to that of an observant tourist. To quote Barry Amis again: "There is nothing in the novel that is authentically African. The customs are not African, the language is not African, and the characters certainly are not African . . . they are not characters that any African would recognize."

His not being African might account for the language shifts noted above and the fact that the foreign words which appear seem sprinkled-in largely for decoration and not because they represent an object for which there is no good English word. Professor Craven suggests that Felix could be an American Black from Detroit "who affects a French accent and the prissy African manner." This would certainly explain Ellelloû's frequent spontaneous use of peculiarly American images such as rocks that look like "Reddi-Whip" and camel's eyelashes that are "disneyesque." It might even explain where he gets such a detailed knowledge of oil refineries. He knows, on sight, which structures are "storage tanks" and which are "fractionating towers" and how "hydrocarbon refining" works. And he tells the crowd to shoot "the exposed conduit removing the volatile gasoline vapors from the top of the fractionating tower, below the condenser ball." One is not likely to learn such things in Indo-China nor in "Franchise, Wisconsin" on the picturesque shores of "Lake Timmebago."

Certainly the narrator is someone who is fascinated with language, enjoys manipulating it in every possible way, and will sacrifice every other narrative consideration to such manipulations. Thus an Ellelloû who is walking in horror through the tiny city which bears his name and thinking, apparently, in French (he calls the Five and Ten a *Cinq and Dix*), describes a window display as "gimmicky, plasticky, ball-and-jacky, tacky, distinctly dusty" (p. 253).

It is even possible that our invisible narrator is not Black. Certainly, beyond the convincing reproductions of the speech of Oscar X and Barry Little, the narrator shows relatively little of what might be called "black awareness" and sometimes says things shockingly at odds with such awareness. At the beginning of chapter two he says, "In Kush we never cease dreaming of intercourse between dark and fair skin, between thick lips and thin lips." Barry Amis draws on his experiences both as an American Black and as a lecturer in Africa when he says, "Whether or not such a fantasy has any basis in American society, it certainly has none in the African region Updike purports to depict." Moreover, Amis reacted angrily to the portrayal, terming it the "bigotted attitude of some white Americans."

We do know the narrator believes deeply in the importance of myth as a way of dealing with reality. It gives us, he believes, "a handle on the reality that would otherwise overwhelm us" and it enables us "to live, to keep going" (p. 153). He sees the importance of believers and myth-makers and instinctively mistrusts modern men with strictly practical, problem-solving mentalities. Who then do we have? The most obvious answer, of course, is Updike himself; and here is the novel's deepest and most unyielding problem. The picture of the narrator which gradually evolves leads us back to Updike-the-writer in a way that *Lolita* or *Pale Fire* do not lead us back to Nabokov-the-writer or *The Fall* does not lead us back to Camus. The narrators of other fantasy novels, whoever they ultimately reveal themselves to be, have coherent, if sometimes insane, personalities and become tangible independent fictional characters even through the veils which obscure their presence. If such a narrator is not to be created, then a fantasy or absurdist novel can be written strictly from the outside, such as Borges often does—throwing out his delightfully preposterous incidents or allegorical fables with an impenetrable shrug. But in *The Coup* the narrator's voice is all-important, yet it never defines itself in a meaningful way.

These problems aside, the meaning of Updike's fable comes through loud and clear. "It takes," says Ellelloû, "a mountain of myth to make even a grain of difference." Like Updike's protagonists who have gone before, Ellelloû, the president, and Ellelloû, the narrator (whoever he may be) are believers in the myth of man's spiritual elegance, his specialness in creation, which he is in danger of burying in scientific definitions and commercial manipulations. Fables are the spiritual backbone of homo-erectus and when they are discarded, then he can no longer stand above and apart from the rest of creation. Yet, Kutunda tells Ellelloû that "the time of fables is over for Africa" (p. 302) and Ellelloû is expelled. He is, it turns out, that "last elephant to give up its ivory"—the last man to give up his dreams and the beliefs which shaped them.

But like all of Updike's stories, the ending is ironic and double-edged. Ellelloû is the Fisher King—sterile and impotent—waiting for the renewal of himself and his land; yet he is also Oedipus and when he is banished, fertility returns and the desert gets its rain. Ellelloû believes it is the sterile rain of Eliot's poem, but he is mad and so who is to say? This is a fable about the inability to integrate old beliefs and new pragmatism. This is a fable about the end of fables.

## Notes

1. John Updike, *The Coup* (1978; rpt. New York: Fawcett Crest, 1980). I am using the paperback edition since that is the edition available to most people. All subsequent page numbers from the novel refer to this edition.

2. From a paper presented at the Modern Language Association Convention in San Francisco, December 1979. It is this extremely interesting and informative essay which I refer to several times below. Mr. Amis's experiences in Africa during the course of several Fulbrights and his excellent credentials as a literary critic made him an invaluable resource for discussing *The Coup*.

3. Updike apparently removed the phrase "in his halting, rusty Berber" from editions after the original galley proofs were distributed to reviewers. However no other substitutions were made to indicate any other language.

4. The narrator does hedge here by claiming that he is copying his facts from "an old Statesman's Yearbook" and so "some of them may be obsolete."

5. Several critics suggested that the entire story, including Zembla and Kinbote, are the creations of the mysterious Professor Botkin.

6. Another kind of clue that the graffiti cannot be real is the one which reads "Happy Loves Candy," a reference to Ellelloû and his American wife which no actual person could have written.

7. This is another of those places where Updike made more than a small change after the galleys had been printed. He removed the sentence "German ministers' daughters, wispy French boys in the footsteps of Rimbaud." But why? Certainly if it was an attempt to make the dialogue more appropriate, then most of the novel would need similar revisions. Did he feel that the comedy got out of hand, one wonders? Similarly, he removed a sentence from the scene of the sergeant determining Ellelloû's identity in front of the aid boxes. In the galley the word "misspelled" was misspelled (the first "s" omitted) in what might have been a tiny joke. Updike did not merely correct the spelling, however, he removed the whole jest which read: "As the sergeant considered, I considered the medal he still held to his chest, *Lenin staring upward with the prophetic fury of a scholar who has just found his own name mispelled in a footnote.*" Too anti-Soviet?

# INDEX